MISSISSIPPI WRITERS
Reflections of Childhood and Youth

MISSISSIPPI WRITERS

*Reflections of Childhood
and Youth*

Volume III: POETRY

Edited by
DOROTHY ABBOTT

UNIVERSITY PRESS OF MISSISSIPPI
Jackson and London

Center for the Study of Southern Culture Series

Copyright © 1988 by the
University Press of Mississippi
All rights reserved
Manufactured in the United States of America

Library of Congress Cataloging-in-Publication Data
(Revised for vol. 3)
Main entry under title:

Mississippi writers.

(Center for the Study of Southern Culture series)
Contents: v. 1. Fiction—v. 2. Nonfiction—
v. 3 Poetry.
1. American literature—Mississippi. 2. American
literature—20th century. 3. Children—Literary
collections. 4. Youth—Literary collections.
5. Mississippi—Literary collections. [1. American
literature—Collections. 2. Mississippi—Literary
collections.] 1. Abbott, Dorothy, 1944–
II. Series.
PS558.M7M55 1985   813′.008′09762   84-5131

ISBN 0-87805-232-1 (pbk. : v. 1)
ISBN 0-87805-231-3 (hard : v. 1)

CONTENTS

Contents

ACKNOWLEDGMENTS

THE EDITOR is grateful for the assistance given by consulting editors Samuel Prestridge, Janice B. Snook, Jerry W. Ward, Sterling Plumpp, Gwen Porter, Ann J. Abadie, Barbara Watkins, and by JoAnne Prichard, my editor at the University Press. The editor also wishes to thank the following authors and publishers or magazines for permission to reprint the designated selections. Rights in all cases are reserved by the owner of the copyright.

JAMES A. AUTRY "Communication," "The Snakes," "Grave Digger," "Genealogy," "All Day Singing with Dinner on the Grounds," "Baptism," and "Death in the Family" copyright © 1983 by James A. Autry. Reprinted by permission of Yoknapatawpha Press from *Nights under a Tin Roof*.

ANGELA BALL "Surgery" copyright © 1988 by Angela Ball. Printed by permission of the author.

RANDOLPH BATES "Dolphin Island" (first appeared in *Prairie Schooner*) copyright © 1987 by University of Nebraska Press. Reprinted by permision of the publisher.

CHARLES GREENLEAF BELL "The Tower" (first appeared in *Southwest Review*) copyright © 1955; renewed 1966 by Charles G. Bell. "The Break" (first appeared in *Chicago Review*) copyright © 1954; renewed 1966 by Charles G. Bell. "The Circus," "Gar," and "Moundbuilders" copyright © 1956; renewed 1966 by Charles G. Bell. Reprinted by permission of Indiana University Press and the author from *Delta Return*.

KATHERINE BELLAMANN "At Moon Lake" and "The Bayou" copyright © 1958 by the Estate of Katherine Bellamann. Reprinted by permission of the Estate of Katherine Bellamann from *A Poet Passed This Way*.

LERONE BENNETT, JR. "Blues and Bitterness" copyright © 1973 by Lerone Bennett, Jr. Reprinted by permission of the author.

D. C. BERRY "On Reading Poems to a Class at South High" (first appeared in *Poet Lore*) copyright © 1971 by D. C. Berry. "Shaving Daddy" (first appeared in *Poetry*) copyright © 1985 by D. C. Berry. "Annette" (first appeared in *Shenandoah*) copyright © 1972 by D. C. Berry. "Climbing the Family Tree" (first appeared in *Texas Review*) copyright © 1983 by D. C. Berry. "Grandma's Pet Wild Rabbit" (first appeared in *Colorado North Review*) copyright © 1982 by D. C. Berry. Reprinted by permission of the author.

MAXWELL BODENHEIM "Rattle-Snake Mountain Fable" and "Daniel Boone" copyright © 1946 by Maxwell Bodenheim. Reprinted by permission of the Beechurst Press, Bernard Ackerman, Inc. from *Selected Poems of Maxwell Bodenheim, 1914–1944*.

THEODORE BOZEMAN "Pocket the Blues" and "TV Child" copyright © 1988 by Theodore Bozeman. Printed by permission of the author.

CHARLIE R. BRAXTON "Say Hey Homeboy," "Childhood Remembrances," and "Jazzy St. Walk: An improvisational poem" copyright © 1988 by Charlie R. Braxton. Reprinted by permission of the author. "Working the Nightshift" (first appeared in *Black Nation*) copyright © 1986 by Charlie R. Braxton. Reprinted by permission of the author.

BESMILR BRIGHAM "The Will's Love" (first appeared in *Symptom*) copyright © 1966 by besmilr brigham. Reprinted by permission of Hill & Wang, Inc., from *31 New American Poets* and Thomas Y. Crowell Co., Inc., from *I Hear My Sisters Saying*. "The Sevier County Runaway" (first appeared in *Pen: An International Quarterly*) copyright © 1972 by besmilr brigham. Reprinted by permission of the author. "To the Unwritten Poems of Young Joy" and "The Figures' Math: eight and four" (both first appeared in *Southern Review*) copyright © 1972 by *Southern Review*. Reprinted by permission of the publisher. "Morning of Love" copyright © 1988 by besmilr brigham. Printed by permission of the author.

VIRGIA BROCKS-SHEDD "Southern Roads/City Pavement" (first appeared in *Jackson Advocate*) copyright © 1982 by Virgia Brocks-Shedd. Reprinted by permission of the author.

JONATHAN HENDERSON BROOKS "Still I Am Marveling," copyright © 1948 by Kaleidograph Press. Reprinted by permission of Josie Brooks from *The Resurrection and Other Poems*.

ISABELLA M. BROWN "Prayer" (first appeared in *New Negro Poets U.S.A.* edited by Langston Hughes) copyright © 1964 by Isabella M. Brown. Reprinted by permission of the author.

WILLIAM BURT "Hank and Peg" and "Mamaw and Frank" copyright © 1988 by William Burt. Printed by permission of the author.

JACK BUTLER "Preserves" (first appeared in *Cedar Rock*), "Ember-whistle," "A Myth of Snakes (first appeared in *Texas Quarterly*), "Stuck Tractor" and "The Buzzard" (first appeared in *New Yorker*), "The Kid Who Wanted to Be a Spaceman" (first appeared in *New Orleans Review*) and "The Edges, the Fractions, the Pieces" copyright © 1984 by Jack Butler. Reprinted by permission of August House from *The Kid Who Wanted to Be a Spaceman*.

ROBERT CANZONERI "To a Campus Tree in Spring, Seen Out a Second Story Window," "Cleaning Up," "The Day the Cold Came" (first appeared in *Red Clay Reader III*), and "Mississippi" (first appeared in *Mississippi Poetry Journal*) copyright © 1968 by Ohio State University Press. Reprinted by permission of the publisher from *Watch Us Pass*. "Bird Dog Man" (first appeared in *Antioch Review*) copyright © 1973. Reprinted by permission of the author.

ANNE CARSLEY "Demesne," "Catalogue," "Festival," "The Natchez Trace," and "Menu" (first appeared in *Wordcraft*) copyright © 1980 by Anne Carsley. Reprinted by permission of the author.

HODDING CARTER "Flood Song," "Slave Story," "Ashes of Sackcloth," and "In Depression Time" copyright © 1964 by Hodding Carter. Reprinted by permission of Betty W. Carter from *The Ballad of Catfoot Grimes*.

TURNER CASSITY "Cane Mill," "The Lumber Baron," and "A Song to Be Vindicated" (both first appeared in *Poetry*) copyright © 1966 by Turner Cassity. Reprinted by permission of Wesleyan University Press from *Watchboy, What of the Night?* "WW II in the City of Homes" (first appeared in *White Trash* published by New South) copyright © 1984 by Turner Cassity. Reprinted by permission of the author. "Hedy Lamarr and a Chocolate Bar" (first appeared in *Sewanee Review*) copyright © 1986 by Turner Cassity. Reprinted by permission of the publisher. "Summer of 1942" copyright © 1988 by Turner Cassity. Printed by permission of the author.

CECILE BROWN CLEMENT "Lillie Learned to Read" (first appeared in *Mississippi Poetry Journal*) copyright © 1983 by Cecile Brown Clement. Reprinted by permission of the author.

WILLIE COOK "Not the Starlights," "Wake," and "55 Confession," copyright © 1988 by Willie Cook. Printed by permission of the author.

CAROL COX "Listening to James 'Son' Thomas Sing Delta Blues" (first appeared in *Southern Exposure*) copyright © 1979 by Carol Cox. Reprinted by permission of Hanging Loose Press from *Woodworking and Places Near By*. "Silver Pins" copyright © 1982 by Carol Cox. Reprinted by permission of Hanging Loose Press from *The Water in the Pearl*. "In the Fifties" copyright © 1987 by Carol Cox. Printed by permission of the author. "In the Room of the Civil Rights Exhibit at the Old Capitol" (first appeared in *New Virginia Review*) copyright © 1986 by Carol Cox. Reprinted by permission of the publisher.

HUBERT CREEKMORE "To the Very Late Mourners of the Old South" and "Encounter with a Dog" copyright © 1940 by Hubert Creekmore; renewed 1968 by Estate of Hubert Creekmore. Reprinted by permission of John Schaffner Associates, Inc.

JOHN CREWS "Caught Caught Caught" (first appeared in *Carolina Quarterly*) copyright © 1981 by John Crews. "Sabbath Coin" (first appeared in *Texas Review*) copyright © 1983 by John Crews. Reprinted by permission of the author.

JACK CROCKER "Bear Hunt" copyright © 1988 by W. J. Crocker. Printed by permission of the author.

HENRY DALTON "Hill Born" copyright © 1954 by Henry Dalton. Reprinted by permission of the author from *Hill Born*. "Spring Songs" copyright © 1977 by Henry Dalton. Reprinted by permission of the author from *Process of Becoming*.

ROSALIE BURKES DANIELS "Ballad of the Sandrock" and "Biloxi Beach Drama" copyright © 1988 by Rosalie Burkes Daniels. Printed by permission of the author.

JEAN DAVIDSON "Constellations" copyright © 1988 by Jean Davidson. Printed by permission of the author.

L. C. DORSEY "Silent Communication" copyright © 1988 by L. C. Dorsey. Printed by permission of the author.

SYBIL PITTMAN ESTESS "The Country Idiot" copyright © 1988 by Sybil Pittman Estess. Printed by permission of the author.

WINIFRED HAMRICK FARRAR "Remember Corn Fields?" copyright © 1968 by Winifred Hamrick Farrar. Reprinted by permission of the author from *Cry Life*.

WILLIAM FAULKNER "Mississippi Hills: My Epitaph" and section I from *A Green Bough* copyright © 1933 by William Faulkner. Reprinted by permission of Jill Faulkner Summers.

JACK FENWICK "Reverend Cole's Epistle" copyright © 1988 by Jack Fenwick. Printed by permission of the author.

WILLIAM FERRIS "For Amanda Gordon" (first appeared in *Afro-American Folk Art and Crafts*) copyright © 1983. Reprinted by permission of the author.

CHARLES HENRI FORD "One day, one day," "The Overturned Lake" (first appeared in *Poetry*), "Somewhat Monday," "Reptilia," and "The Dead Spring" copyright © 1972 by Charles Henri Ford. Reprinted by permission of the author from *Flag of Ecstasy* published by Black Sparrow Press.

JOHN P. FREEMAN "A Barn in the Morning Light" and "The Sycamore" copyright © 1988 by John P. Freeman. Printed by permission of the author.

RICHARD FREIS "The Beach Hotel" (first appeared in Poetry) copyright © 1977 by Poetry. Reprinted by permission of the publisher. "Tornado Warning" (first appeared in *Southern Review*) copyright © 1979 by *Southern Review*. Reprinted by permission of the publisher.

ELLEN GILCHRIST "Sharecropper," and "There Will Be Seven Fat Years (first appeared in *Shenandoah*) copyright © 1979 by Ellen Gilchrist. Reprinted by permission of the author from *The Land Surveyor's Daughter*. "Where Deer Creek Runs Through Cary" copyright © 1986 by Ellen Gilchrist. Reprinted by permission of the author from *Riding Out the Tropical Depression* published by Faust Publishing. "The Best Meal I Ever Had Anywhere" copyright © 1988 by Ellen Gilchrist. Printed by permission of the author.

SID GRAVES "H. Desoto: Notes from a Diary" copyright © 1987 by Sid F. Graves, Jr. Printed by permission of the author.

DOUGLAS GRAY "Mosquito Man" and "The Reluctance of Spring in Ohio" copyright © 1988 by Douglas Gray. Printed by permission of the author.

ROBERT HAMBLIN "Requital" (first appeared in *Cape Rock*) copyright © 1978 by Robert W. Hamblin. Reprinted by permission of the author from *Perpendicular Rain*.

RABIUL HASAN "Night Blooms" (first appeared in *Daring Poetry Quarterly*) copyright © 1986 by Rabiul Hasan. Reprinted by permission of the author.

BROOKS HAXTON "Recess" (first appeared in *Tendril*), "Justice" (first appeared in *American Poetry Review*), "I Live to See Strom Thurmond Head the Judiciary Committee," "The Conversion Shift" (both first appeared in *Tendril*), "Breakfast ex Animo," (first appeared in *Poetry*) and "Pond" copyright © 1986 by Brooks Haxton. Reprinted by permission of Alfred A. Knopf, Inc. from *Dominion*. "Landscape with Figures" copyright © 1988 by Brooks Haxton. Printed by permission of the author.

KENNETH HOLDITCH "Red Clay" (first appeared in *Newark Review*) copyright © 1987 by W. Kenneth Holditch. Reprinted by permission of the author.

JOYCE HOLLINGSWORTH-BARKLEY "Old Mag," "Eva," and "White High Tops" copyright © 1984 by Joyce Hollingsworth-Barkley. Reprinted by permission of the author.

M. CARL HOLMAN "Picnic: The Liberated" and "Mr. Z" copyright © 1980 by M. Carl Holman. Reprinted by permission of the author.

REBECCA HOOD-ADAMS "Cotton Choppers" and Diphtheria" (both first appeared in *Delta Scene*) copyright © 1979 by Rebecca Hood-Adams. Reprinted by permission of the author.

T. R. HUMMER "Hanging Fire," "Night Burning" (first appeared in *Western Humanities Review*), "The Shell," "A Crazy Girl Brings the Rural Carrier a Dime," and "The Rural Carrier Admires Neil Varner's Brand New Convertible" copyright © 1980 by T. R. Hummer. Reprinted by permission of Louisiana State University Press from *The Angelic Order*. "The Beating" (first appeared in *Quarterly West*) and "Sorrow" (first appeared in *Texas Reveiw*) copyright © 1984 by T. R. Hummer. Reprinted by permission of University of Illinois Press from *The Passion of the Right-Angled Man*.

ANGELA JACKSON "Make/n My Music" (first appeared in *NOMMO*) copyright © 1972 by Angela Jackson. Reprinted by permission of the author. "Greenville," (first appeared in *Black Collegian*) "Early Evenings," "Home Trainin" and "The Charmed Circle (first appeared in *The Greenville Club* published by BkMk Press) copyright © 1977 by Angela Jackson. Reprinted by permission of the author. "George, After All, Means Farmer" (first appeared in *Callaloo*) copyright © 1979 by Angela Jackson. Reprinted by permission of the publisher. "mary mariah," "What I Said As a Child," (first appeared in *First World*) and "Why I Must Make Language" copyright © 1987 by Angela Jackson. Reprinted by permission of the author. "Dr. Watts Meets the Man with the White Liver" (first appeared in *Contact/II*) copyright © 1985 by Contact II Publications. Reprinted by permission of the publisher.

AUROLYN JACOBS "I want to name my children after poems," "it ain't hard being a woman just time consuming," and "Wilma" copyright © 1988 by Aurolyn Jacobs. Printed by permission of the author.

JOAN JOHNSON "Elegy for the Girl Who Died in the Dump at Ford's Gulch" (first appeared in *Poem*) copyright © 1980 by *Poem*. Reprinted by permission of the publisher.

LARRY JOHNSON "Near Eastabuchie, Mississippi" (first appeared in *Texas Quarterly*) copyright © 1974 by Larry Johnson. Reprinted by permission of the author. "Once" copyright © 1988 by Larry Johnson. Printed by permission of the author.

EMORY D. JONES "Whitey Remembers" copyright © 1988 by Emory D. Jones. Printed by permission of the author.

MARGARET KENT "Living with Animals" (first appeared in *Greensboro Review*) and "Watching the Island" (first appeared in *Poetry*) copyright © 1980 by Margaret Kent. Reprinted by permission of the author.

ETHERIDGE KNIGHT "A Poem for Myself (or Blues for a Mississippi Black Boy)," "The Bones of My Father," "Ilu, the Talking Drum," "Once on a Night in the Delta: A Report from Hell," and "The Idea of Ancestry" copyright © 1986 by Etheridge Knight. Reprinted by permission of the University of Pittsburgh Press from *The Essential Etheridge Knight*.

SINCLAIR O. LEWIS "Anyone Who Rejects Me Gotta Be Crazy" copyright © 1988 by Sinclair O. Lewis. Printed by permission of the author.

R. G. LOWREY "Remembrance of Things Past" copyright © 1956 by R. G. Lowrey; renewed 1982 by Mildred W. Lowrey. Reprinted by permission of Mildred W. Lowrey from *Stones and the Sea*.

BIRTHALENE MILLER "remembering who you are" copyright © 1987 by Birthalene Miller. Printed by permission of the author.

WILLIAM MILLS "Politics," "Unemployment," and "Cock" copyright © 1974 by William Mills. Reprinted by permission of Louisiana State University Press from *Watch for the Fox*. "Silhouette" copyright © 1984 by William Mills. Reprinted by permission of Louisiana State University Press from *The Meaning of Coyotes*. "Our Fathers at Corinth" copyright © 1979 by William Mills. Reprinted by permission of Louisiana State University Press from *Stained Glass*.

KAREN L. MITCHELL "The Eating Hill (first appeared in *Thirteenth Moon*) copyright © 1982 by Karen L. Mitchell. Reprinted by permission of the author. "Black Patent Leather

Shoes" copyright © 1987 by Karen L. Mitchell. Printed by permission of the author. "Birmingham, Alabama: 1963" (first appeared in *Open Places*) copyright © 1979 by Karen L. Mitchell. Reprinted by permission of the author.

CHARLES MOORMAN "September Song" (first appeared in *Texas Review*) copyright © 1980 by Sam Houston State University. Reprinted by permission of the author.

SANDRA NAPIER-DYESS "The Gravel Pit" copyright © 1987 by Sandra Napier-Dyess. Printed by permission of the author.

JOHN NIXON, JR. "I Remember 1929" (first appeared in *Georgia Review*) copyright © 1958 by University of Georgia Press. Reprinted by permission of the publisher. "Miss Maggie and the Voices" (first appeared in *New Southern Poets: Selected Poems from "Southern Poetry Review"* edited by Guy Owen and Mary C. Williams) copyright © 1974 by University of North Carolina Press. Reprinted by permission of the publisher. "Ornamental Knowledge" (first appeared in *Mississippi Poetry Journal*) copyright © 1957 by Mississippi Poetry Society, Inc. "A Niche for the Architect" (first appeared in *New Yorker*) copyright © 1958 by New Yorker Magazine, Inc.

LEWIS NORDAN "He Fishes with His Father's Ghost" (first appeared in *Southern Humanities Review*) copyright © 1980 by Lewis Nordan. Reprinted by permission of the author.

STEPHEN OWEN "Confessions from Childhood" (first appeared in *Teaching English in the Two-Year College*) copyright © 1980 by Stephen Owen. Reprinted by permission of the author.

PATSY CLARK PACE "Saigon Sky" and "Distant Kin" (first appeared in *Lyric Mississippi*) copyright © 1982 by Patsy Clark Pace. Reprinted by permission of the author.

LINDA PEAVY "Some Keep the Sabbath" (first appeared in *Southern Exposure*), "Poem for a Sister Three Decades Dead" (first appeared in *Poets On: Surviving*), and "The Telling Tree" (first appeared in *Texas Review*) copyright © 1983 by Linda Peavy. Reprinted by permission of the author. "Dark Quartet" copyright © 1988 by Linda Peavy. Printed by permission of the author.

WILLIAM ALEXANDER PERCY "Home" and "Overtones" (both first appeared in *In April Once*) copyright © 1930 by Yale University Press from *Selected Poems;* renewed 1987 by Leroy P. Percy, Executor Estate of William Alexander Percy. Reprinted by permission of the Estate of William Alexander Percy.

ERIN CLAYTON PITNER "Apples in October" (first appeared in *Voices International*) copyright © 1980 by Voices International, Inc. Reprinted by permission of the publisher. "To a Child on her Sixth Birthday" and "Wind Child" copyright © 1988 by Erin Clayton Pitner. Printed by permission of the author.

STERLING D. PLUMPP "Blues" (first appeared in *Black Nation*) copyright © 1986 by Sterling D. Plumpp. Reprinted by permission of the publisher. "Clinton" (first appeared in a slightly different version in *Savage* and in *Clinton* published by Broadside Press) copyright © 1976 by Sterling D. Plumpp; renewed 1982 by Thunder's Mouth Press. Reprinted by permission of the publisher from *The Mojo Hands Call, I Must Go.* "I Hear the Shuffle of the People's Feet" (first appeared in *Obsidian*) copyright © 1982 by Thunder's Mouth Press. Reprinted by permission of the publisher from *The Mojo Hands Call, I Must Go.*

NOEL POLK "I Make Love to a Fat Woman, ca. 1960" copyright © 1987 by Noel Polk. Printed by permission of the author. "I Sonned a Father" (first appeared in *Southern Review*) copyright © 1983 by Noel Polk. Reprinted by permission of the publisher.

MARGARET PORTER "Sugarman" (first appeared in *Sunbury 9*) and "Reunion" copyright © 1986 by Margaret Porter. Reprinted by permission of the author.

SAMUEL PRESTRIDGE "How to Tell a Story," "The Lord God, He Made All That Stuff," "Speaking," "The Outlaw Bonnie Parker Advises My Uncle on the Advantages of a Higher Education," "Scenario in which My Grandma Feeds a Famous Indian," "Song of the Old Men's Noses," and "What We Got Is Idiom" copyright © 1988 by Samuel Prestridge. Printed by permission of the author.

SUSAN PROSPERE "Farm Life" and "Silver Thaw" (both appeared in *New Yorker*) copyright © 1981 and 1982 by *New Yorker*. Reprinted by permission of the publisher. "Sub Rosa," "Star of Wonder," and "Passion" (all first appeared in *Antaeus*) copyright © 1984 and 1985 by Susan Prospere. Reprinted by permission of the publisher.

LAVINE ROGERS "Saturday Night" copyright © 1988 by LaVine Rogers. Printed by permission of the author.

PAUL RUFFIN "Cleaning the Well" and "The Rolling Store" copyright © 1980 by Paul Ruffin. Reprinted by permission of Spoon River Poetry Press from *Lighting the Furnace Pilot*. "Frozen Over," "Jody Walker: The First Voice" (both first appeared in *Mid-American Review*), and "Batting Rocks" copyright © 1987 by Paul Ruffin. Reprinted by permission of the author.

VELMA SANDERS "Ghosts" (first appeared in *Mississippi Poetry Journal*) copyright © 1970 by Velma Sanders. Reprinted by permission of Elsie S. Harville.

ROBERT SARGENT "Aspects of a Southern Story" copyright © 1983 by Robert Sargent. Reprinted by permission of the author from *Aspects of a Southern Story* published by the Word Works.

BRENDA E. SARTORIS "Hawks Descending" (first appeared in *Cotton Boll/Atlanta Review*) copyright © 1986 by Brenda E. Sartoris. "Skeletal Remains: Museum of Natural History" (first appeared in *Texas Review*) copyright © 1982 by Brenda E. Sartoris. Reprinted by permission of the author.

JESSIE SCHELL "Delta Summer" (first appeared in *Dragonfly*), "To the Children Selling Lightning Bugs" (first appeared in *Greensboro Review*), "The Blessing" (first appeared in *Southern Poetry Review*), and "Zora" copyright © 1976 by Jessie Schell. Reprinted by permission of the author.

JAMES SEAY "Grabbling in Yokna Bottom" and "One Last Cheer for Punk Kincaid" copyright © 1968 and 1970 by James Seay. Reprinted by permission of Wesleyan University Press from *Let Not Your Hart*. "On the Way" and "It All Comes Together Outside the Restroom in Hogansville" copyright © 1974 by James Seay. Reprinted by permission of Wesleyan University Press from *Water Tables*. "Said There Was Somebody Talking to Him through the Air Conditioner" copyright © 1985 by James Seay. Reprinted by permission of the author.

EDGAR SIMMONS "Impressions," "Early Passion in a Puritan World," "World of Child Drummers," "Sons of Sad Dreams," and "At the Seed and Feed" (first appeared in *New York Times*) copyright © 1968 by Louisiana State University Press; renewed 1987 by Estate of Edgar Simmons. Reprinted by permission of Jes Simmons from *Driving to Biloxi*.

JES SIMMONS "Letters," "Old McGehee," and "Indian Mound • Winter • The Search" copyright © 1987 by Jes Simmons. Printed by permission of the author.

SUE SPIGNER "Grandfather" and "Revival" copyright © 1988 by Sue Spigner. Printed by permission of the author.

FRANK STANFORD "The Picture Show Next Door to the Stamp Store in Downtown Memphis" and "The Burial Ship" copyright © 1979 by Estate of Frank Stanford. Reprinted by permission of Ginny Crouch Stanford from *The Singing Knives* and *You*.

JOHN STONE "Piano Lessons" copyright © 1979 by John Stone. Reprinted by permission of the author from *The Smell of Matches*. "Double-Header," "Losing a Voice in Summer," and "The Truck" copyright © 1975 and 1980 by John Stone. Reprinted by permission of Louisiana State University Press from *In All This Rain*. "Trying to Remember Even a Small Dream Much Less the Big Gaudy Ones in Color with Popcorn and High Ticket Prices" and "A Word from the Teacher" copyright © 1985 by John Stone. Reprinted by permission of Louisiana State University Press from *Renaming the Streets*.

WILLIAM SULLIVAN "Beneath the Surface" (first appeared in *Cotton Boll/Atlanta Review*) copyright © 1986 by William Sullivan. Reprinted by permission of the author.

GLENN ROBERT SWETMAN "Uncle Bob" (first appeared in *Pteranodon*) copyright © 1980 by Glenn Robert Swetman. Reprinted by permission of the author. "A Little Sonnet on a Contemporary Subject" copyright © 1980 by Glenn Robert Swetman. Reprinted by permission of the author from *Concerning Carpenters and Childhood Saints*.

D. L. TARTT "An Easter Egg Hunt" copyright © 1988 by D. L. Tartt. Printed by permission of the author.

JULIUS THOMPSON "Natchez" copyright © 1988 by Julius Thompson. Printed by permission of the author.

HENRY TIM (CHAMBERS) "If God So Loved His Children All That Much, Why Couldn't

Uncle Ed?" copyright © 1988 by Henry Tim Chambers. Printed by permission of the author.

GLENNRAY TUTOR "There's a Boy" (first appeared in *Texas Review*) and "Flying Saucers and a Gila Monster" (first appeared in *Old Hickory Review*) copyright © 1981 and 1980 by Glennray Tutor. Reprinted by permission of the author. "On a Day of Good June Fishing Weather a Dog Would Like to Be a Boy" copyright © 1987 by Glennray Tutor. Printed by permission of the author.

DOROTHY TWISS "Bossier City Saturday Night" copyright © 1988 by Dorothy Twiss. Printed by permission of the author.

OVID VICKERS "Lola Forest" (first appeared in *Printed Matter*), "The First Amendment" (first appeared in *Texas Review*), and "Miss Pearl Parkerson (first appeared in *Southeastern Miscellany*) copyright © 1979, 1981, 1983 by Ovid Vickers. Reprinted by permission of the author.

MARGARET WALKER "For My People" (first appeared in *Poetry*), "Delta," "Molly Means," "Kissie Lee," and "Big John Henry" copyright © 1942 by Yale University Press. Reprinted by permission of the author from *For My People* published by Yale University Press. "The Ballad of the Free," "Jackson, Mississippi," "For Andy Goodman—Michael Schwerner—and James Chaney," and "Ballad of The Hoppy-Toad" copyright © 1970 by Margaret Walker Alexander. Reprinted by permission of the author from *Prophets for a New Day* published by Broadside Press. "A Poem for Farish Street" copyright © 1985 by Margaret Walker. Reprinted by permission of the author from *For Farish Street Green*.

JERRY W. WARD, JR. "Your Voice" (first appeared in *Pound*) Copyright © 1978 by Jerry W. Ward, Jr. "*From Meditations on Richard Wright: Black Boy*," (first appeared in *Blind Alleys*) copyright © 1982 by Jerry W. Ward, Jr. "Don't Be Fourteen (in Mississippi)" (first appeared in *Black Scholar*) copyright © 1980 by Jerry W. Ward, Jr. "Trueblood" (first appeared in *Black Box* 5) copyright © 1975 by Jerry W. Ward, Jr. Reprinted by permission of the author. "The Impossible All These Years" (first appeared in *The Otherwise Room*) copyright © 1981 by Jerry W. Ward, Jr. "Fusion," "Something in the Gulf," "Unentitled," and "Jazz to Jackson to John" copyright © 1988 by Jerry W. Ward, Jr. Printed by permission of the author.

NAGUEYALTI WARREN "Mississippi Woods," "Prayer," "Southern Memories," and "Nature Poem" copyright © 1988 by Nagueyalti Warren. Printed by permission of the author.

NAYO-BARBARA WATKINS "A Frame of Mind," "A Picture of My Mother," "Mama's Children," "Do You Know Me?," "When Wells Run Dry—For Muddy Waters and Associates," and "Missions and Magnolias" copyright © 1988 by Nayo-Barbara Watkins. Printed by permission of the author.

EUDORA WELTY "A Flock of Guinea Hens Seen From a Car" (first appeared in *New Yorker*) copyright © 1957 by Eudora Welty. Reprinted by permission of Russell & Volkening, Inc.

JOHN MILTON WESLEY "Son Child," "Fannie Lou," and "Disturbing the Peace" copyright © 1988 by John Milton Wesley. Printed by permission of the author.

JAMES WHITEHEAD "The Young Deputy," "Two Voices," and "A Local Man Goes to the Killing Ground" (all first appeared in *Domains* published by Louisiana State University Press). "He Remembers Something from the War," "He Loves the Trailer Park and Suffers Telling Why," "His Slightly Longer Story Song," "The Travelling Picker's Prayer and Dream," and "Pay Attention, Son" (all first appeared in *Local Men* published by University of Illinois Press). Copyright © 1966, 1979, 1987 by James Whitehead. Reprinted by permission of University of Illinois Press from *Local Men and Domains*. "A Natural Theology" copyright © 1985 by James Whitehead. Reprinted by permission of the author from *Actual Size*.

BENJAMIN WILLIAMS "And Not Just in Sorrow" copyright © 1988 by Benjamin Williams. Printed by permission of the author.

JOHN A. WILLIAMS "Before Electricity 1926" copyright © 1988 by John A. Williams. Printed by permission of the author.

OTIS WILLIAMS "The Blues Man," "B. B. & Bobby at the Howard Theatre," "About the Blues," "My Old Home Church: Bell Flower Missionary Baptist," "Dixie Hum-

mingbirds," "Fannie Lou Hamer," and "South African Suite" copyright © 1982 by Otis Williams. Reprinted by permission of the author from *The Blues Is Darker Than Blue*.
TENNESSEE WILLIAMS "Impressions Through a Pennsy Window" and "Descent" copyright © 1977 by Tennessee Williams. Reprinted by permission of New Directions Publishing Corp. from *Androgyne, Mon Amour*. "Nonno's Poem" copyright © 1962 by Tennessee Williams. Reprinted by permission of New Directions Publishing Corp. from *The Night of the Iguana*.
AUSTIN WILSON "Bus Trip" copyright © 1988 by Austin Wilson. Printed by permission of the author. "Sonnets for My Son" (first appeared in *Poem*) copyright © 1975 by Austin Wilson. Reprinted by permission of the author.
RICHARD WRIGHT "I Have Seen Black Hands" (first appeared in *New Masses*) copyright © 1934 by Richard Wright. "Between the World and Me" (first appeared in *Partisan Review*) copyright © 1935 by Richard Wright. "Haiku" (first appeared in *Studies in Black Literature* and *New Letters*) copyright © 1970 and 1971 by Estate of Richard Wright. Reprinted by permission of Ellen Wright and John Hawkins and Assc.
GAYLE GRAHAM YATES "Daughterlove" copyright © 1988 by Gayle Graham Yates. Printed by permission of the author.
AL YOUNG "Birthday Poem" and "A Little More Traveling Music" (both first appeared in *Dancing*) copyright © 1969 by Al Young. Reprinted by permission of Louisiana State University Press from *The Blues Don't Change*. "The Problem of Identity," "Pachuta, Mississippi/ A Memoir," and "For Poets" (all first appeared in *The Song Turning Back Into Itself*) copyright © 1971 by Al Young. Reprinted by permission of Louisiana State University Press from *The Blues Don't Change*. "Teaching" and "Aunt" (both first appeared in *Geography of the Near Past*) copyright © 1976 by Al Young. Reprinted by permission of Louisiana State University Press from *The Blues Don't Change*. "A Sunday Sonnet for My Mother's Mother" and "The Blues Don't Change" (first appeared in *The Blues Don't Change*) copyright © 1982 by Al Young. Reprinted by permission of Louisiana State University Press from *The Blues Don't Change*.
STARK YOUNG "Written at My Mother's Grave" copyright © 1906 by Stark Young. Reprinted from *The Blind Man at the Window and Other Poems*.
AHMOS ZU-BOLTON II "the seeker," (first appeared in *A Niggered Amen*) copyright © 1975 by Ahmos Zu-Bolton II. "The Basketball Star" (first appeared in *The Last Cookie*) copyright © 1973 by Ahmos Zu-Bolton II. "Sister Blues" (first appeared in *Black World*) copyright © 1974 by Ahmos Zu-Bolton II. "Struggle-Road Dance" (first appeared in *First World*) copyright © 1976 by Ahmos Zu-Bolton II. Reprinted by permission of the author.

INTRODUCTION

ROSELLEN BROWN

No one has ever made plain just what the Southern school is or which writers belong to it. . . . At least, however, we are all known to be anguished . . . as a result of our isolation from the rest of the country. . . . The anguish that most of us have observed for some time now has been caused not by the fact that the South is alienated from the rest of the country, but by the fact that it is not alienated enough, that every day we are getting more and more like the rest of the country, that we are being forced out not only of our many sins, but of our few virtues.

> Flannery O'Connor:
> "The Fiction Writer and
> His Country"

EVER SINCE the Romantic poets cast aside anonymous conventional forms and put themselves at the center of their poems, we have thought we could hear the speaker behind his words, or hers. Is it fair to assume that, similarly, we should be able to read an anthology like this—a collection of 112 disparate voices—and assemble a face behind them? Could we draw a portrait of the place from the clues, the obsessions, the affections, the familiar sights?

Snakes. Singing in church. The flat fields, the levee. Talk and more talk. Blues and more blues. An overflowing blackberry bucket. The sweltering heat, the stripped trees in January. Dinner spread out on the table: fried chicken, biscuits, something cold to drink. . . .

I don't know if such a thing might be true of every state—I've lived in enough to doubt it—but Mississippi has given its children a very distinctive personality. (Anyone who's read the first two volumes in this series needs no convincing.) To look for that personality in hundreds of poems is to assemble broken fragments word by word, image by image, a mosaic to be put back together in these pages. The separations between many of the pieces are sharp and jagged, they can draw blood; at other points they are almost non-existent. Seen from a sufficient distance the bits cohere and the face becomes unmistakable. And it is an astonishingly accurate portrait that any sociologist would recognize.

To be perfectly fair, there is probably not enough sports here—especially football—to be true to the southern experience. There may be a few more snakes than most people have to deal with (though in the matter of murderous crawling things, one encounter might just be enough to guarantee a lifetime preoccupation.) And there is surprisingly little explicit mention of the Civil War: clearly the time has passed for that, at least among poets, who would probably find such ancient grievance embarrassing, and hardly expressive of their complex feelings about southern history. In an era when poets tended to represent the agrarian aristocracy, that history was still a burden, the old order only freshly overturned. But to look at the biographies of the majority of the poets in this collection, from the least well known to the luminaries like Richard Wright and Tennessee Williams, is to be reassured that the gift and the need to make poetry is these days spread pretty evenly throughout the population.

With those few exceptions, the absence of football heroes, the silence of gatling guns on the hillsides, almost everything else we associate with Mississippi is brought us by this democracy of speakers. And like a single face, this one is both fixed and changing. All these poets are old enough to remember Mississippi when it was almost entirely rural. Many of them come from towns with the kinds of names that promise they have no hope and no intention of becoming metropolises: Ecru and Paden, Typlant and Eastabuchie. Now, in 1988, Mississippi is still rural—few of those towns have disappeared—but the balance of population has shifted. No one is terribly far, now, from the blandishments of the malls, of the larger cities, of TV and anonymity: some may not be able to afford them but the shopping centers are nothing like town on a Saturday, the old white men sitting around the courthouse, black folks come shopping in a wagon or a wobbly pick-up. More and more rural lives resemble suburban lives, and those not so different from Ohio or Florida or New Hampshire lives.

When I took my daughter back to see the house we were living in when she was born twenty years ago—it was a frail bungalow in Tougaloo, an unincorporated town, with a cornfield out back and wildflowers blowing across the front lawn in changing ranks of size and color—she was disappointed. No more cornfield now, a new paved road alongside; no more pigs, I dare say, to escape from their pen next door and come noisily rooting under our house, whose brick stilts are no longer visible. No frail-shouldered house, either, but a shored-up structure that just might keep the wind out. And the town is part of Jackson now, as it moves inexorably northward. Much of the charm is gone, but the life looks a lot easier for whoever lives there—there is no sense romanticizing poverty. But there are losses, and they tend to be losses of the things poets hold dearest: particularity, attention to the individual, small gestures, simplicity. (In "Grave Digger," James Autry's Otis Cox digs graves as an act of love: "Machine digging/ don't seem right if you know/ the dead person.")

Another change for the better, another loss of the tension that makes literature, not to be romanticized or regretted: with the leveling of regional differences has come a good deal of leveling of the cruelest differences between black and white lives. But if we look at the poetry, something interesting emerges. In the elegiac feeling for the life that's gone as times have changed, at certain moments black and white lives don't seem as harshly divided as they seem the same:

Snakes. Singing in church. The flat fields, the levee. Talk and more talk. Blues and more blues. An overflowing blackberry bucket. The sweltering heat, the stripped trees in January. Dinner spread out on the table: fried chicken, biscuits, something cold to drink. . . .

Look at those James Autry poems, for example, those wonderful clusters of nostalgic detail that read like novels that only lack a story:

Now we dial the phone
but Aunt Callie still yells into it
and ends every sentence with a question mark
as if she can't believe that all her words
can get through those little wires

They yelled about babies born and people cured
about fires and broken bones and cows loose and dogs lost
the words always short and spaced
for the distance they had to travel.

("Communication")

You are
in these hills
who you were and who you will become
and not just who you are . . .
Her daddy was no count and her daddy's daddy
   was no count . . .
        Might's well send that chile
        to the penitentiary soons he's born
        gonna end up there anyway . . .
But that lineage could also forgive
with benign expectation
or transgressions to come
     'Course, what do you expect
     his granddaddy was a Wilkins
or

     The Whitsells are a little crazy
     but they generally don't beat up nobody
       outside the family.

                              ("Genealogy")

You can read Autry's poems and not be sure, much of the time, if he's talking about white folks or black. Just as southerners have always told northerners there are certain shared experiences that override color and bind the races together, Autry's characters, himself and his remembered relatives, have in common with their black neighbors the intimacy of country life, hard work in the hot sun, tiny churches like family (for better and worse, everyone's secrets known), and real family in every direction. Or read Richard Wright's mournful "Haiku"—quick jabs of memory, an isolated voice remembering Mississippi winter—and all but two of the miniature poems could be anyone's, any sensitive boy's, alone under the winter sky.

Another binding force between the races shows itself in the guilty acknowledgements that hang like grim weather over the poems of so many white writers of the last generation: race is almost as much a presence in their poems as it is in those of the black poets. Dangerous and fruitful, this is the tension that informed these childhoods: helplessness, anger, remorse, confusion. In Vermont, say, or Montana, weather is the primary antagonist. In California there isn't even weather. In Mississippi, history, conscience and the cruelties of their own local realities are like shadows across the landscape. The current generation and those to come, black and white, will have fewer such shadows—though they will never be without them—to color their work.

I think there is another reason the face of this state—this state of mind as well as of geography—emerges as clearly as it does in these poems. Many of these writers see themselves called to poetry the way ministers are called to the pulpit. Not surprisingly, most of the black poets accept their didactic role without apology. Margaret Walker, for example, writes in two modes: Whitmanesque celebration as static and monumental as a mural on the side of a public building—

> For my people everywhere singing their slave songs repeatedly:
>   their dirges and their ditties and their blues and jubilees, praying
>   their prayers nightly to an unknown god, bending their knees
>   humbly to an unseen power
>
> ("For My People")

and ballad-like narrative, story upon lively story crying out to be sung alongside "Frankie and Johnnie" and "Barbry Allen."

> Old Molly Means was a hag and a witch;
> Chile of the devil, the dark, and sitch. . . .
>   O Molly, Molly, Molly Means
>   There goes the ghost of Molly Means.
>
> ("Molly Means")

Sterling Plumpp's "I Hear the Shuffle of the People's Feet" is another massive dirge, a public call to solidarity and strength.

Angela Jackson, Jerry Ward, Nayo-Barbara Watkins, Otis Williams—just about every black writer here—give us jazz riffs or bits of the blues, energetic, irresistibly rhythmic, layered with irony and sadness, defiance, pride. Etheridge Knight's "Ilu, Talking Drum" provides an epic history that pre-dates the presence of his ancestors in this country. Only a few of the black poets here speak intimately, self to self, without a sense of mission, and even they (like Karen Mitchell, whose "The Eating Hill" might seem a bit of personal memoir about her grandmother) describe their work in terms of its usefulness: "'The Eating Hill' is a look at the land and how our people become one."

Among the white poets, a good many pay tribute to that same pain, from their own point of view: Brooks Haxton's "Justice,"

Carol Cox's "In the Room of the Civil Rights Exhibit at the Old Capitol," besmilr brigham's "The Sevier County Runaway." This is the moment when a reader wonders whether poets are in fact accurate representatives of the community psyche, or whether they vibrate too sensitively, register affronts to others too intensely, to tell us what ordinary civilians are thinking. In any event, as spokesmen for whatever portion of Mississippians are haunted by racial injustice, these poets attest to their own passionate concern.

But interestingly, even those who seem to be writing the purely personal lyric poem, descendants of those romantics who thought their own psyches worthy of advertisement, also seem to me to be turned out toward their audience as often as they are turned in toward themselves. For every poem about family intimacy—Susan Prospere's, Jessie Schell's, Angela Ball's, for example—or every poem of personal obsession—Frank Stanford's possessed, astonishing "The Burial Ship"—there seem to be many explications of an artifact called "southern life." James Seay, Samuel Prestridge, T.R. Hummer, James Whitehead: there is a long file of poets giving lessons in local life, "the way we do it here." Many tell illustrative stories, not as ballads like Margaret Walker's but in order to people the stage with colorful characters at home. See, for example T.R. Hummer's "The Beating" or his poems about the rural carrier. Ellen Gilchrist's could walk right out of her stories:

> Baby Doll was there,
> two hundred pounds of woman
> with the pin that said REMEMBER,
> then a real pearl, HARBOR.
> ("Where Deer Creek Runs Through Cary")

Any of these characteristics—this slight inclination in the direction of the reader, away from the self singing to its own reflection—can, of course, be attributed to the editor's predilections. But I can vouch, from a familiarity with the ample number of books these poets have produced, for the representative nature of the selection: Mississippi poets are in love with their paradoxical land, and they have a double sense of what the world-at-large thinks of that love: that it is perverse, because Mississippi's bloody history has kept it half-unreal in the headlines, exaggeratedly evil; and because they believe, themselves, that it *is* exotic, extreme, blessed, cursed. Many have had to leave home to be able to see it and speak without vendetta or confusion. (Margaret Kent writes of "the sad overloading/ of the heart's circuits, this dark house/ condemned by love . . ." ("Living With Animals")

But even after they have left, home remains a subject that fills the eye, whose voices engage the ear, whose contradictions pique the conscience. Since writers usually stand just outside the charmed circle of those who "belong," comfortably and unselfconsciously; since writers tend to be alienated from self or family, home or country (or why would they need to write?), it comes as no surprise that a place as complex and difficult as Mississippi should have produced the disproportionate number of writers we always hear about. Having begun with Flannery O'Connor, I think it seems right to end with her and her devious, just slightly defensive chauvinism: "We have gone into the modern world with an inburnt knowledge of human limitations and with a sense of mystery which could not have developed in our first state of innocence—as it has not sufficiently developed in the rest of the country."

These poets, devoted to the documentation and evocation of that mystery, have made a composite face for us—truly, to show it to us—whose expression is mercurial, dark and light, benign and malign by turns. Al Young salutes it as deeply and off-handedly as poets are meant to do in his "Birthday Poem":

How I got from then to now
is the mystery that could fill a whole library
much less an arbitrary stanza

But of course you already know about that
from your own random suffering
& sudden inexplicable bliss

I suspect Mississippi will provide its next generations less suffering, say hallelujah. Also less bliss. Brand-name America is on its way, the real invading army, and its hostages are being held in pizza parlors and twin cinemas from Corinth to Natchez, from Hernando to Pascagoula. If there are any poets among them, it will be interesting to hear what they'll have to say.

THE PHIL HARDIN FOUNDATION
AND THE
MISSISSIPPI WRITERS SERIES

IN 1964 Mr. Phil B. Hardin of Meridian, Mississippi, established an educational foundation. At the Foundation's organizational meeting, Mr. Hardin made the following statement:

My material wealth has been principally acquired by the operation of my bakery business in the State of Mississippi and from the good people of that state. For a long time I have been considering how my estate could best be used after my death. I have finally conceived the idea of creating a charitable foundation through which the bulk of my estate can be used for furthering . . . the education of Mississippians.

Upon his death in 1972, Mr. Hardin willed a portfolio of stocks and bonds, as well as the bakeries, to the Phil Hardin Foundation. The directors of the Foundation use income from these sources to make grants intended to improve the education of Mississippians. Since the transfer of Mr. Hardin's estate to the Foundation in 1976, the Phil Hardin Foundation has distributed over 5.4 million dollars for this purpose.

In 1983 the Foundation directors authorized a challenge grant to support the publication of the series of anthologies entitled *Mississippi Writers: Reflections of Childhood and Youth.* This series recognizes the accomplishments of our state's authors. The series also introduces young Mississippians to their state's literary heritage, perhaps providing thereby a "shock of recognition" and the transmission of values revealed in that heritage: family, community, a sense of place and history, the meaning of justice and honor, the importance of enduring in the struggle for just causes, the significance as we live out our lives one with another of "courage . . . and hope and pride and compassion and pity and sacrifice." By so doing the series may help young Mississippians come to grips with the complexities of Mississippi culture and heritage and of the larger society that now more than ever impinges on this place. As importantly, the series may help forge a sense of common identity and interest.

The Phil Hardin Foundation is honored to join with other Mississippians to make possible the publication of the *Mississippi Writers* series. Mississippians can accomplish more working together than working alone.

C. Thompson Wacaster
The Phil Hardin Foundation

The Following People, Organizations, and Businesses Generously Contributed Funds to Match the Challenge Grant Awarded by the Phil Hardin Foundation

Dr. and Mrs. Joe Bailey
Mr. and Mrs. Charles G. Bell
Ms. Jane Rule Burdine
Mrs. Roberta J. Burns-Howard
Mrs. Betty W. Carter
Centennial Study Club (Oxford)
Mr. Henry Chambers
Coca-Cola Bottling Co. (Vicksburg)
Mr. and Mrs. Sam W. Crawford
CREATE, Inc.
Ms. Carole H. Currie
Mr. and Mrs. Glen H. Davidson
Mr. and Mrs. William Deas
Mr. and Mrs. Herman B. DeCell
Mrs. Keith Dockery McLean
Mr. and Mrs. Robert B. Dodge
Fortnightly Matinee Club (Tupelo)
Dr. and Mrs. Jan Goff
Dr. and Mrs. William Hilbun
Mr. and Mrs. Howard Hinds
Mrs. Mary Hohenberg
Mr. Irwin T. Holtzman
Mr. Stuart C. Irby, Jr.
Stuart Irby Construction Company
Dr. and Mrs. David Irwin

The Honorable and Mrs. Trent Lott
Mr. and Mrs. T. M. McMillan, Jr.
Miss Marjorie Milam
Mrs. Blewett Mitchell
The Honorable G. V. Montgomery
Mrs. Gaines Moore
Mrs. L. K. Morgan
R. R. Morrison and Son, Inc.
Mr. Richard A. Moss
National Association of Treasury Agents
Mr. William M. Pace
Mrs. A. E. Patterson
Dr. Max Pegram
Mr. and Mrs. Jack R. Reed
Dr. and Mrs. Pete Rhymes
Dr. Stephen L. Silberman
Mr. and Mrs. Bill Spigner
Mr. and Mrs. Landman V. Teller
Dr. and Mrs. P. K. Thomas
United Southern Bank (Clarksdale)
University Press of Mississippi
Mr. and Mrs. Harold Wilson
Mr. Sam Woodward

MISSISSIPPI WRITERS
Reflections of Childhood and Youth

Communication

Now we dial the phone
but Aunt Callie still yells into it
and ends every sentence with a question mark
as if she can't believe that all her words
can get through those little wires

But back then we stepped out and pointed our voices
across the hills

Whooooeeee

It would follow the bottoms and up the next hill
and in a few minutes
it would come back from Cousin Lester

Whooooeeee

When there was trouble
Uncle Vee would blow the fox horn
or ring the dinnerbell
and someone with a car would come
not knowing the problem but that we needed a car.

When Uncle Vee yelled or blew the horn
there was a message to send

> *Don't you boys be out there*
> *yellin' up somebody*
> *'less you got somethin' they need to know*

But we'd yell
and the old folks would know we were just yelling
and let it go
our high voices somehow falling short of the next hill
the dogs not even coming from under the porch.

Weeks would pass without a real yell
then it would roll up the hill from Cousin Lester's

Whoooooeeeeee

And Uncle Vee would step out on the porch
and cup his hands and answer

and turn his head and listen
nodding at the message I could never understand.

It's how we heard Cousin Lottie got snake bit
and James Louis came back from the Pacific

It's how the fox hunts were arranged
and the hog killings set

They yelled about babies born and people cured
about fires and broken bones and cows loose and dogs lost
the words always short and spaced
for the distance they had to travel.

Now there are the wires
and Aunt Callie still yells for the distance
and looks at the phone
holding it so her eyes can aim the words
through the instrument and across the hills
where they are to go.

The Snakes

There were snakes
my god there were bad snakes
but we didn't see all that many
except in Aunt Callie's imagination
under every log and in every brushpile

> *Now you chirren watch*
> *you'll step on a snake*

We knew them all
the copperhead/rattlesnake pilot/highland moccasin
(all the same snake)
plus the gentleman rattlesnake
who would always rattle before he struck
and the treacherous cottonmouth
hidden beside the path waiting for the chance to bite not run

> *Cottonmouths got to discharge that poison*
> *so they got to bite somethin' or somebody*

And there were copperbellies not poison but mean
and after Uncle Vee killed them
he pushed their heads into the soft mud with a stick
deep so half the snake was in the hole

It's a sign our family
killed the snake

And there were good snakes especially the king snakes

You ought to see him kill a bad 'un boys
wrap hisself around that other'n
and squeeze him to death

But we killed them all
because a snake was a snake

Well I couldn't tell, Uncle Vee
they all look bad

There were spreading adders that puffed and hissed and acted mean
but couldn't hurt you
and rat snakes and bull snakes and hog nose snakes
and chicken snakes that ate our eggs and baby chicks
and when you reached into a nest on a high shelf in the chicken house
an old settin' hen might peck you
or it could be a chicken snake
so sometimes eggs in a high nest would go rotten
because we'd all think the next day's cousin would get them.

There were blue racers and black racers
and one time rabbit hunting
Uncle Vee and Cousin Lester saw a racer and kicked it
like when they were boys
and it curled up in a ball
and the other one kicked it high in the trees
it staying in a tight little ball
then both running for it and Cousin Lester kicking Uncle Vee
and they both falling in the leaves

Won't that kill the racer, Uncle Vee?
Sure will

And glass snakes that broke into pieces when you hit them
yes, really into sections
each one wiggling on its own

You leave him alone boys
he'll get back together
no matter how far you scatter them pieces
take one a mile away he'll get back together

One day on the path to the spring
Jimmy Lee and I saw a hog nose snake swallowing a toad
so we watched him do it
throwing his jaw all out of joint
the toad kicking his legs and hopping
making the snake's head jump off the ground
like a snake with hind legs in its head
then when the toad was inside
we killed the snake and cut him open
and the toad hopped away.

But the mean snakes were moccasins
even the un-poison ones
the brown water snakes at the swimming hole
that come toward you with open mouths hissing

> *They got a nest here somewhere boys*

and we always argued whether they could bite you under water
and we never found out.

After Aunt Callie got bit by the copperhead
all the men went hunting for bad snakes
with hoes and some shotguns
They turned over logs and whistled at brushpiles

saying a long straight whistle will bring them out
and at the end had killed hundreds of snakes
bad and good
and we measured the longest ones
and some of the boys skinned them for belts.

Then we didn't worry about snakes for a while
and hoped maybe they were all killed off

> *They'll be back boys*
> *they were in the Garden of Eden*
> *and they'll be back here*

Grave Digger

His name is Otis Cox
and the graves he digs with a spade are acts of love.
The red clay holds like concrete
still he makes it give up a place
for rich caskets and poor

working with sweat and sand
in the springing tightness of his hair
saying that machine digging
don't seem right if you know
the dead person.
His pauses are slow as the digging
a foot always on the shovel.
Shaking a sad and wet face
drying his sorrow with a dust orange white handkerchief
he delivers a eulogy

   Miz Ruth always gimme a dipper of water

Then among quail calls and blackeyed susans
Otis Cox shapes with grunt and sweat and shovel
a perfect work
a mystical place
a last connection with the living hand

Genealogy

You are
in these hills
who you were and who you will become
and not just who you are

   She was a McKinstry
   and his mother was a Smith

And the listeners nod
at what the combination will produce
those generations to come
of thievery or honesty
of heathens or Christians
of slovenly men or working

   'Course her mother was a Sprayberry

And the new name rises
to the shaking of heads
the tightening of lips
the widening of eyes

   And his daddy's mother was a McIlhenney

Oh god a McIlhenney
and silence prays for the unborn children

those little McKinstry Smith Sprayberry McIlhenneys

> *Her daddy was no count and her daddy's daddy was no
> count*

Old Brother Jim Goff said it
when Mary Allen was pregnant

> *Might's well send that chile
> to the penitentiary soons he's born
> gonna end up there anyway*

But that lineage could also forgive
with benign expectation
or transgressions to come

> *'Course, what do you expect
> his granddaddy was a Wilkins*

or

> *The Whitsells are a little crazy
> but they generally don't beat up nobody outside the family*

or

> *You can't expect much work out of a Latham
> but they won't steal from you*

In other times and other places
there are new families and new names

> *He's ex P&G
> out of Benton and Bowles
> and was brand management with Colgate*

And listeners sip Dewar's and soda or puff New True Lights
and know how people will do things
they are expected to do
New fathers spring up and new sons and grandsons
always in jeopardy of leaving the family

> *Watch young Dillard
> if he can work for Burton he's golden
> but he could be out tomorrow*

And new marriages are bartered for old-fashioned reasons

> *If you want a direct marketing guy
> get a headhunter after someone at Time Inc.*

Through it all
communities new and old watch and judge and make sure

the names are in order
and everyone understands

All Day Singing with Dinner on the Grounds

1

There were old men with ear trumpets
who patted their feet against the rhythm
and sang notes melodious only to themselves
sitting near the front on an aisle
where some young cousin or nephew had led them.
Snuff staining the corners of their mouths
tobacco breath filling the rows around them
they stayed there most of the day
but the rest of us moved in and out
and new groups came
in cars and trucks and yellow school buses

> *Here come*
> *Mr. Sanford Hale*
> *and the Philadelphia singers*

Coming to the singing convention
coming from three or four counties away
on dusty roads over hills and through bottoms
in heat that made the radiators boil
and fresh ironed shirts go damp and wrinkled
in heat that made the britches stick to our legs
when we got up from the hard oak pews.
Coming to sing
in duets and trios and quartets
and some soloists like Miss Ernestine Lee
whose face had the light of God in it
when she sang How Great Thou Art

> *I declare*
> *you can hear Jesus*
> *in her voice*

And some congregation singing
different song leaders from different churches
taking turns

Now we gonna ask
Clyde Wyatt of Bethel Baptist
to lead this next one

And sometimes they'd get up a quartet
from different churches
always discussing who would sing lead and who would sing bass

Now you come on up here Leon
and you too Hamer
and you sing alto Mr. J.W.

And after two or three false starts
they'd sing all the old ones
all the ones everybody knew and heard on the radio
every Sunday morning before church
On the Jericho Road and
Take a Little Walk with Jesus and
My God is Real and
I Saw the Light

Sometimes they'd make all the ladies sing a verse
or all the children
or all the folks over sixty
Then between songs there'd be testimonials
or one of the preachers would lead a prayer
because all the preachers from all the churches came
and led a prayer before the day was over.

2

Late in the morning
by some signal I never saw
the ladies began to leave the church and go to the cars
and get baskets and sacks
and head to the dinnergrounds,
big gray tables under the trees
or sometimes rough lumber nailed between the trees,
and spread starched table cloths
and decide somehow among themselves
where the meat would be
and the vegetables and bread
where to gather the cakes and pies
and jugs of iced tea.
Then someone would let the songleader know

and he'd say that dinner was ready
and everybody would go outside and have another song
and a prayer
then start along the tables
smiling at their neighbors
thanking God for the day
spooning their plates full

> *Now you boys just keep back*
> *and let them ladies go first*

It seemed all the food in the world
fried chicken crisp and soggy
country ham and sausage in biscuits
deviled eggs and creamed corn
and blackeyed peas and okra
and green beans and sliced tomatoes
and corn bread and spoon bread
and all manner of pies and cakes
stacked apple pies and Mississippi mud pies
pound cakes sliced thick with strawberries and cream
big wet banana cakes
and coconut cakes you ate with a spoon.
And the ladies would watch to see
whose dishes got eaten first

> *Miss Nora*
> *you just can't make enough*
> *of them old time buttermilk pies*

and smile and say how this wasn't near as good
as they usually make.

3

Then the singing would start again
with people coming and going
with men and boys standing outside the open windows
rolling cigarettes from little sacks of tobacco
picking their teeth with black gum brushes
and spitting into the red powder dust.
And later in the afternoon
we'd go off into the pines behind the church
and throw rocks
and shoot green plums from our slingshots

and not really listen to the singing any more
but hear it anyway
and the motors starting
and the people getting on the schoolbuses
and our names called when it was time to go.

Baptism

He waded into the cold water up to his knees
then across a sandbar and into the current
and turned and called to us
and suddenly the swimming hole was different.
We'd been there for a thousand swims
but it was different
colder maybe
swifter
deeper
surrounded not by boys and girls in swim suits
but by Sunday dressed ladies and coat and tied men
singing

> *Shall we gather at the river*
> *the beautiful the beautiful*
> *river*

And we moved in a line
barefoot and in white shirts and wash pants
the girls in dark colored dresses
which would not show through when they got wet
Across the shallows onto the sandbar
and from there went one at a time
in the name of the father, the son, and the holy ghost
to be put under the water
his arm behind our shoulders
and his hand over our mouth and nose
and our hand on his hand
For only a few seconds but it seemed longer
longer than any time when we had jumped or dropped from a vine
longer than when we swam underwater to scare the girls
longer than we thought we could ever stand
but he pulled us up
and said amen and the people said hallelujah
and our mothers hugged us as we went wet onto the bank.

Then he came out of the water
and we sang On Jordan's Stormy Banks I Stand
and he lifted his arms over us
all shivering there
the water draining from our pants cuffs
dresses clinging to the girls' legs

And said some words
about our sins washed away
and cleansed in the blood
and born again
And told us we were saved
and would go to heaven
and have life everlasting
and many other important things
we remembered for a long time.

Death in the Family

1

People hug us and cry
and pray we'll be strong
and know we'll see her again someday
And we nod and they pat and rub
reassuring her to heaven

> *She's with Jesus now*
> *no suffering where she is*

Then sit on hard benches and sing
of precious memories how they linger
and farther along we'll understand it

> *Cheer up my brother*
> *We're not forgotten*

The preacher studies his Bible and stares at the ceiling
and the song leader in his blue funeral suit sweats
and strokes the air
with a callused hand

> *We'll understand it*
> *all bye and bye*

And powdered and rosy cheeked
Miss Anne sleeps in an open coffin

the children standing tiptoe to see through the flowers
but scared to go near and drawing back when lifted
And the choir brings a balm in Gilead
and a roll is called up yonder

> *When the trumpet of the lord shall sound*
> *and time shall be no more*

And big men shake heads white at the hat line
while women weep and flutter air with palm leaf fans
And later we stand amidst the stones
by the mound of red clay
our eyes wet against the sun
and listen to preachers and mockingbirds
and the 23rd Psalm

2

Men stand uneasy in ties
and nod their hats to ladies
and kick gravel with shoes too tight
and talk about life

> *Nobody no better'n Miss Anne*
> *No Sir*
> *No Sir*

Smoking bull durhams around the porch
shaking their heads to agree
and sucking wind through their teeth

> *Never let you go thirsty*
> *bring a jugga tea to the field*
> *ever day*

They open doors for us and look at the ground
as if by not seeing our faces they become invisible
There are not enough chores
so three draw well water
and two get the mail
and four feed the dogs
and the rest chop wood
and wish for something to say

> *Lester broke his arm one time*
> *and Miss Anne plowed that mule*
> *like a man*
> *put in the whole crop*

And they talk of crops and plowing
of rain and sun and flood and drought
The seasons passing in memory
marking changes in years and lives
that men remember at times
when there's nothing to say

3

Ladies come with sad faces
and baskets of sweets
teacakes, pecan pies, puddings, memories
and we choose and they serve
telling stories and god blessing the children

> *I declare that Miss Anne*
> *was the sweetest Christian person*
> *in the world*

Saying all the things to be said
doing all the things to be done
like orderly spirits
freshening beds from the grieving night
poking up fires gone cold
filling the table and sideboard
then gathering there to urge and cajole
as if the dead rest easier on our full stomachs

> *Lord how Miss Anne would have loved that country ham*

No sadness so great it cannot be fed away
by the insistent spirits

> *That banana cake is her very own recipe*
> *I remember how she loved my spoon bread*
> *She canned the berries in this cobbler*

And suddenly we are transformed
and eat and smile and thank you
and the ladies nod and know they have done well again
in time of need
And the little girls watch and learn
And we forget the early spring cemetery
and the church with precious memories
and farther along we do understand it
the payments and repayments
of all the ladies that were and are
and we pray ever will be. Amen

ANGELA BALL

Surgery

for my mother

Easily, I slip Reception, steal
through the dazed bright factory,
the night hospital—past the empty
stiffness of wheelchairs and stretchers, rooms with people
half visible in beds, the bright stillness
of shelved equipment,
the whole air how it is
after something falls—
and find you just back
from Recovery.

A long time ago, this morning
you wheeled away
under the single wing
of a sheet—a delicate work
about to be unveiled.
After two days at the mercy
of clock sounds and the tall
sharp window that made you feel
like a timber
chopped through, about to fall
to a sky sailing peacefully
into nowhere—where you are now
alone. I can join
hands with your absence, your lost
voice asking water, your lips
cupping what I can offer:
ridiculous, tiny, pink sponge
on the end of a stick.
Your face all flatness
and depth taken over
with reflections facing
the wrong way, the white
of every color; the immense
specific gravity
of your body laboring behind
a thin dense curtain. Your absence
occupied by pain: its blank

engine pounding toward
and toward you
with the air, your body
its track, its grooved
shadow, the ear asking the ground
is it still coming, the dull unshaken white at the edge
of the river sunk
under the trestle, the weeds
bowing and scraping, the trembling
dust motes, the hand
pulling back a curtain
like a dog-eared page.

And all the places that are
without you: lemon groves
above the sea swimming
hard in a hard rain, swamps
hung with glittering
moss, pools of white dust
gathering stars,
mountains facing ruins
of mountains, a fir tree
flaring with blackbirds.
Level bare woods, footpaths
strutting the edge of fields,
the feet of cattle
ribboning a savannah
to a volcano,
cities with lights
like the paths of cemeteries
and constellations,
an open railway carriage
drawing up at the sea with people
who've never seen
its shining pages
turn, who stand gazing, and
a tribesman explaining, "We do not need
to go to sleep hungry with
this mountain of ours."

And the things you wanted: college
and clothes. You stand
in a narrow mirror stroking
satin over your head, lending it,

for a moment, your shape.
And the red of the dress
flames to itself and the blue
floats in the dead shadow
of the rack while you rest
a year with your illness,
graduating from high school
alone, your scholarship lost.

Still with you:
your pity for the string
of a snake you found
in the house one day
and killed quickly as you could,
with a spade.

Your patience with spring
making a kite of the air, swooping and floating; with summer,
quietening: glisten of blackberries,
hollows companioning smoke.

You walking the long hill under
a snowstorm to wrestle the TV antenna
from the wind and calm
the picture.

You a child at the opera house,
standing up alone
to say your speech—all words
inside and moving toward
you like lights to make
complete brightness.

The first cry
of your first child—what
happiness, and nothing
to answer with but snow
like a sift of messages,
water so blue, pine
with a little crown that waves
like a plume.

Your letter to me: "I remember
when you were small the many times
you came to me with love."

In this distant room
I stay a few hours holding your hand,
your place, saving it for you
until you come awake.

RANDOLPH BATES

Anglicized and now known as Dauphin (daw' fun) Island, *Ile Dauphine* is in the Gulf of Mexico off the Alabama coast. In 1699 a French-Canadian explorer named it *Ile Massacre* because of the scores of human skeletons he found on its beaches. After he died, his brother changed the name in an effort to console the young dauphine who was mourning the death of her mother.

Dolphin Island

The summer that x-rays found shadows
swimming in my mother's lung, I stayed here,
at her father's house, in a place I mistook
to be named after dolphins, a haven from sharks.
No bones lay banked in the sand, just trash
and bleached ship boards, things I still see
strewn beyond the three of us, as we wandered out
where the salt heat was hard to look through:

Grandpa's a small man. He waves his cigar.
James, the black giant who stinks of storage and port,
is clowning before him. Grandpa shows fists,
then starts to shout *right!* and throws dollars
for each of the heavyweight champs that we name.
One of his biceps can dance like an egg.

James' wine-yellowed eyes seem to reckon my winnings
and how he might steal them. Nights he dreams sharks
at his cot, acts twice shrewd when I pay him
to give me his chore dragging in crab traps.
He'll never know the charm isn't his:
I've seen dolphins passing these breakers.

Other days crest into afternoon.
Three minds awash and nothing to say.
Grandpa's the lord in scenes James rehearses.
I think about wrecks, beasts, and beasts' play.

Today we dragged the traps in at sunset
near dolphins rolling down the shoreline.
Our son cried *sharks!* He wouldn't believe
what I told him. Not even at our bonfire—
until I drank wine, and mixed facts with myths
about dolphins and whale talk. His eyes leaped
at the waves when I described the shark's brain,
but the word *bottle-nose* made him smile again.

The island's other names remained buried.
Acquisition, slaughter, the bereft dauphine,
they're tales for different seasons; for tonight
we've had pleasure, years make it clear:
crabs' claws, the weather band, stars,
Radio Mystery Theatre in darkness,
then baseball from Texas and cards
with cracked faces in sepia light.

My shadow on the screens of our rented cottage
now reflects the depth of this moonless night
before I give it back in watery toasts
in the names of slaves and dead kin.
Nothing left but to re-cover the children,
then come to sleep at their mother's breast.
I clasp her bones as the Gulf crashes.
Creatures, leaving voices, circle our beds.

CHARLES GREENLEAF BELL

The Tower

We are nearing the town. First of all I see the tower
That brought the electric lines from Arkansas.
We had climbed the trees and hung ropes for the plunge,
One best of all at a blue-hole, where we would swing
And drop to the round water like a stone.

The courthouse summoned next and gave no ease
Until we had scaled the roof and spire and pole;
But the three-hundred-foot tower was challenge still.
The pillars were sheer cement; we cut a tree,
Propped it in the mud and worked to the steel.

There the ladders began; we climbed and climbed:
It seemed the earth was round and the air thin
Before we came on a platform swaying in the wind.
Current hummed in the wires, incredible power
Of the fire-liquid spilling across the stream.

And we were there at the copper veins of that blood.
It was not the heart leapt only; I climbed the last rail,
Hung by the knees over reeling earth and air,
Daring the comrades, who would not take that dare
From a fool whose eyes loved danger like a girl.

The river coiled beneath its triple coil.
The flat land breeds a hunger for the heights;
And what is climbing and the work to climb
But the moment of vision, here at the last verge
Of the wide water, dreaming of the flight down?

The Break

It is good sometimes to grasp our helplessness.
We went one night to see them hold the levee.
The slope burned with torches: in light and dark
Men struggled, brown and white, with bags of sand,
Building the top, or below, where it seeped in a boil.

Fires hissed in the rain, a steady rain
Blown on gusts of wind from the raw west.
The waves lapped at the ridge and as we looked
Reached higher and higher, land-exploring arms.
In two days it broke and the home sirens screamed.

School was finished; farmers poured to the town.
The protection levee was being closed. No one
Thought it would hold but the engineer, a man
Who was always sure and always wrong. He had built
The city streets with ditches that bounced the cars—

His own device for drainage; in a flat land
They could never drain themselves. Widow Archer called
From her yard: "D'ye think he'll hold the water, Judge?"
"I doubt it," my father said. "He should," she cried,
"He's held it in our streets these twenty years."

Harder to keep it out than in; the river came,
Sat a while at the gates and then crept through.

Who could forget the longing of that night,
Or how, at the break of morning, down the street,
Those silver lanes of liquid ran like a dawn?

Gar

Shorty, the minnowman—first settlers gone to seed—,
Calls me to fish in Lake Lee. We drive in the dark.
By dawn we are tied at the willows. The sailors' warning
Flutes the green depths with red. Soon rain is falling.
We sit in a steady drizzle as corks go down,

And bland white perch come slithering through the air.
And now I have hooked the fish I strangely admire,
Tremendous thing, old prehistoric gar,
With armor plate and alligator jaw,
Who steals the bait, sweeps off, and breaks the line.

The fishermen all hate this fossil sign
Of the swamp past we share. My father would stave
Their heads, or if they were small, crack the bills
In his hands, cursing them as the devil's spawn.
And once near here we found old Foster seining,

The big net filled with spoonbills, catfish, drum;
And in their midst an alligator gar
Twice the size of a man was plunging wild,
Ripping it all to shreds. They hauled to the shore,
And Foster stood, a shape of violence,

The revolver crashing in his lowered hand
As he pumped the slugs into the dark wallowing form. . . .
Now all around us the water works with gar
That rise and belch, sweep oily tails. Demons
Of the South, you are strong; time is yours; you will endure.

The Circus

Where all those houses are was a wide field
Filled with goldenrod; across the canal
The canebrake began and stretched to the wood,
Dark reaches of swamp oak; and every fall
The circus came and set up in that field.

The train arrived in the night; we heard the whistles;
Then with the dawn we could see the painted carts
Rumbling along the street in front of our house,
The swaying elephants and the caged lions,
And curtained vans with the still sleeping stars.

In a little while a tent with many flags,
Like a dream city, rose white in that field;
And our sidewalk was lined with Negro stands:
Fried chicken and biscuits, cold drinks, cakes and pies.
Then the leaping life of acrobats and clowns,

Lion-tamers with curled whips, moustached and proud,
The beautiful ladies on horses, in diamond gowns,
And on into dark with music, lights and crowds.
It was a concentration of all the fire
Down the roads of time, the traffic of man;

And then in the hush again the rumbling wheels,
Rattle of hooves and swish of elephants,
Dim in departing night, and with the dawn,
The empty field, the trampled goldenrod,
And a boy standing alone as dusk returned.

Moundbuilders

In an Indian burying ground where the spade turns savage
Bones we bury our outnumbering dead.
They by the river cleared a few fields in the great
Web of forest where bayous pulsed and returned,
Overhung with trumpet vines bright as cardinals.

A little way to the north is a group of mounds,
Pyramids of earth where the temples stood
On gaudy heights round which they danced in plumes—
First stirrings of form against these shifting floods.
We dug there once and uncovered giant bones—

Cattle, no doubt, but for us they were primitive men,
Looming in the golden dusk like myths of the dawn.
And who knows if such too, touched with Mayan fire,
Would have conquered the forest for another day than ours?
They were too slow; we came and took the future.

Now far to the south I have seen in a cypress swamp
On a dwindling reservation tired Indian hulks,

Empty of meaning, and thought of the childhood dreams.
Destiny is a cruel driver. Take up his proud
Yoke, not proudly. We are the moundbuilders now.

Even in this liquid land and its night grave
Of white and red, we raise beacons of form,
Crown the dissolving with earth and marble mounds;
And the lighted road, reaching for a strand of steel,
Bridges the old river, in whose arms we drown.

KATHERINE BELLAMANN

At Moon Lake

If you have never seen a heron's flight
Beneath the moon, across a Delta lake,
Nor watching breathlessly, have seen it take
Its dreaming way through the mysterious night,

Then you have missed the ultimate delight
Of those more fortunate who would forsake
The world of commonplace, that they might make
A world replete in dreams however slight.

Legends of clouds, sharp etchings of the trees,
And silences lit richly with star-shine,
And sarabands of silver mosses seem
But beauty's incantations; surely these
Will bend the jeweled air to some thin line
Of melody that will complete the dream.

The Bayou

There's something much too sinister and sly
About the inky bayou's dim retreat.
Beneath the Gothic roof where great boughs meet
Too dense for faintest glimpse of sun or sky,
No little winds go whispering by;
The air seems waiting for the startled beat
Of bird-wings, but the silence is complete
Save for a distant loon's distracted cry.

Still, I would gladly follow where it leads,
Disdaining threat of danger; venture through
The emerald tunnel seeking for the key
Which locks its secret, slipping through the reeds,
Hoping I may surprise it, find the clue
To that unearthly jeweled mystery.

LERONE BENNETT, JR.

Blues and Bitterness

For Billie Holiday

Ice tinkled in glasses,
froze and rolled away
from hearts
in tombs where she slept.
Smoke noosed,
coiled and dangled from ceilings
in caves where she wept.

I woke up this morning
Just befo' the break of day.
I was bitter, blue and black, Lawd.
There ain't nothing else to say.

In saloons
festooned with trumpets
she prayed—sang
love songs to dead men
waiting with hammers
at the bottom of syringes.
She sang it in a song
before Sartre put it into a book.
She was Bigger
before Wright wrote,
was with Nekeela
in a slave coffle,
was stripped, branded
and eaten by the sharks
and rose again
on the third day in Georgia.

I wondered why God made me.
I wondered why He made me black.
I wondered why Mama begat me—
And I started to give God His ticket back.

D.C. BERRY

On Reading Poems
to a Class at South High

for Davy

They sat there stiff as frozen fish in a package.
A girl in mirrored sunglasses curved my face in stereo.

Before class she'd asked if I could poetrimatize her.
My two Groucho noses shot out of her eyes.

I heard the muffled communiques fish make in aquariums,
the doiks and boings they send up in cartoon bubbles.

    For the icy crack in my voice,
    I was getting back doiks and boings.

I was picking up speed, the room had momentum.
The bell rang and the door flew open.

    They drifted to another class, I suppose,
    and I went home, where Queen Elizabeth,

my cat, met me
and licked my fins till they were hands again.

Shaving Daddy

I pulled up the sack of skin on daddy's throat
to tighten the three-day beard.
Daddy stretched out the rest of the slack
by jutting his head like a mule toward the foot of the bed.

His lathered chin was a horseshoe
slipping off his face even as I scraped.

Why shave at all once beyond the cliche
That was a close shave? I didn't ask.

Daddy says reasons are fences with one-way gates:
they never let you in, they only let you out.

No need to ask. We have enough fences, enough
excuses between us already. I washed up.
The fewer the questions, the fewer the excuses,
the closer I get on the distance between us.

Annette

I realized Mother wasn't Mother but somebody else
when she sent me a check signed only Annette.
She'd forgotten the rest. I said it outloud to test it,
to get a sense of who she was as Annette,
as, no doubt, she wrote and wrote and wrote it,
as schoolkids do, to get a sense of herself, herself,
looping and darting the curlicues of her name
as if some signature might explain the mystery,
the loops and curlicues of every Annette
looping and darting about each time like a different kite
on a different string, each Annette equally senseless.

I forged my last name on the front of the check,
first time I'd ever forged my own last name,
then slashed my speed doodle on the back,
illegible as a cut worm with suddenly two threads of identity.
My face floated up in the cashier's window.
She approved of all my darting loops and slides.
I bought a kite.
The string tied it not to the ground but to the sky.

Climbing the Family Tree

I whipped Davy too hard with a switch.
Before asking his forgiveness,
I thought I first ought to forgive myself.
Teach us both a lesson,

or we were back up the family tree
to where we once were in the Old Testament,
where Anger One begat Anger Two, and did beat him,
and Anger Two begat and did beat Anger Three.

Davy chomped down on his pacifier
like it was a pink cigar and went to sleep.

I sat on the ladder in the dark tool shed,
where I used to nip from daddy's half pint.

He never whipped me because he never knew
where his swig had stopped and mine had begun.
First, to forgive myself, forgive but not forget.
I had all the time it would take—ladder rungs
that keep the legs apart also keep it together—
to climb out on the limb of the prodigal son.

Grandma's Pet Wild Rabbit

He hopped like the last grains of popcorn,
erratic, always one more final hop,

    each up jerky as a hiccup,
    each down soft as a parachute.

Then there he sat, no painted eggs, no picnic basket,
no plastic grass, four feet without any luck,

    grandma's pet wild rabbit,
    the back of his head framed in my slingshot,

. . . not a rabbit exactly,
like a chocolate bunny is a rabbit but isn't.

He dropped like an amputee's useless sock.
I cut off a foot for good luck anyway.
Grandma's gravel road drained away.

My head is still framed in the sling shot;
the Easter rabbit hops out of a black stew pot.

MAXWELL BODENHEIM

Rattle-Snake Mountain Fable

Rounded to a wide-eyed clownishness
Crowned by the shifting bravado
Of his long, brown ears,
The rabbit peeked at the sky.
To him, the sky seemed an angelic
Pasture stripped to phantom tranquillity,
Where one could nibble thoughtfully.

He longed to leave his mild furtiveness
And speak to a boldness puzzled by his flesh.
With one long circle of despairing grace
He flashed into the air,
Leaping toward his heaven.
But down he crashed against a snake
Who ate him with a meditative interest.
From that day on the snake was filled
With little, meek whispers of concern.
The crushed and peaceful rabbit's dream
Cast a groping hush upon his blood.
He curled inertly on a rock,

In cryptic, wilted savageness.
In the end, his dry, grey body
Was scattered out upon the rock,
Like a story that could not be told.

Daniel Boone

You were dressed in leather pants,
With moccasins upon your feet,
And on your head a round
Coon-skin cap stood, and the tails
Of the cap dropped to your back.
You had a flint-lock rifle in your hands,
And a powder-horn hung from your belt.
Kindness and savageness
Rested on your rough and hairless face,
And the paradox resembled
The wilderness through which you strode.
Something variable, strong,
And irresistible was held
By your hooked nose, eyes, and wide, close lips:
Something like the weather—
Wind, and rain, and sun,
With nought but trees and earth to beat against.
Behind you an Indian lurked,
Peering out from a bush,
With feathers sticking straight from his hair,
And naked save for loin-cloth and war-paint.
He held his tomahawk
Poised, and aimed it at your head,
And my heart began to jerk,

Like a fast but crippled acrobat.
I was a boy of twelve
Then, and you were standing
Pictured crudely on the page
Of a hectic, clumsy booklet
Sold for ten cents in a candy store.
Yet, in the moment when I saw you
Threatened, strong, and alert
In the wilderness, an instinct
Told me that you were a poet
Forced to use his eyes and muscles
In the place of words and spoken rhythms—
Writing one long poem
On a space of ground
Afterwards known as Kentucky.

THEODORE BOZEMAN

Pocket the Blues

Blues is a pocket knife
an exposed blade
close it
put it away

blues is a knife
that slices the heart like a pie
and eats itself up
while starving others

it causes sunset
midnight sky
black stormy clouds
Shango & Ogun crying tears—
like rain hell-hard rain
iron droplets
it also burns
and peels tears off the moon
makes tears bleed
and jails joy—
joy, a vampire in a coffin
during a sunny Spring day

slip it into your back pocket
please, pocket the blues blade

blues fingers your heart
on Muddy Water's guitar
and Bessie's mamaly moans
for a righteous man's loving
is explained
in Trane's
soprano sax
shrieking like Amtrak
from Mississippi
to Chicago
or elsewhere
or anywhere
rather than to self-pity

somehow, a soul
got to become Gemini
and run inside its own mouth
for Canada
from America
and find Africa

> *o fly hurricane*
> *across*
> *the plantation*
> *of the mind*

TV Child

The television has
white arms
and hands on the head
of a black child

the black child has a t.v.
guide
in his hand, saying,

> "Mommy,
> can I look at this
>   this
>   and this . . . and
>   this . . ."

CHARLIE R. BRAXTON

Say Hey Homeboy

(For Sterling Plumpp)

say hey homeboy
what's happening
up there in the big ole windy city
where the cold hawk blows
and the music flows mellow steady
like cool sweet muscadine wine in the summertime
from down home blues to modern jazz
i heard you hear it all . . . live
at least one hour a day
five days a week
working laborously on a bluesy feeling
taking notes & trapping them into feets
as opposed to measures
while forging metaphors into rhythmic beats
of iambic & troachaic pentameter
your words wailing from between the pages
of history
bring the whole world a little closer
to the pain the anguish & beauty of a native son
just a few generations removed
from the chains that bind the flesh
but not the spirit
for your spirit moves through
the timeless magic of the mojo hand
as it writes your message
under your name
in the burning sands of time
this is to say
go on homeboy
take it on further
and bring us all on back home
to the red clay hills
of mississippi

Childhood Remembrances

i remember w-a-a-a-y back
when i was young
the make-believe games
we played for fun
like hopscotch and hide-and-go-seek
the roving reporter-the man on the street
i also remember
how crowded it was
when we played house
we shared the crib
with the family mouse
now we weren't rich
so we couldn't afford
no pool
instead we danced in front
of the hydrant
to keep our cool
i remember trading bottle taps
for ginger snaps
sitting on the corner
popping paper caps
with rocks
(we couldn't afford guns)
naw i never played cowboy
(we couldn't afford the hats)
but we played cops and robbers
and wore funny mask
made of brown paper sacks
the rich boys from across the tracks
laughed at us
(as if we were fools)
but it never bothered me
in fact it was cool
because my heroes
were never cowboys

Jazzy St. Walk:
An improvisational poem

hip hitting riffs
split my brain on past
the sullen refrains
of trane's free jazz movement

going on and on and on and on and on

and now
even though i don't know exactly
where it all begins
or ends
      i do know that i've
spent decades untold
doing a old blues walk/dance
                    down these old mean & empty streets
sweating between the sheets
of satin dolls and many moochers
singing good night irene
'cause papa's got a brand new bag
of rhythms (& blues)
rocking and rolling all the way live
down mainstreet harlem
by way of muddy springs mississippi
you see
contrary to the all popular belief
jazz aint no kind of music
it's an artful way of life
spiced like a pickled pig tail
steaming on a peppermint twist stick
        dig what i mean

YEAH
i walk alone along
these rough rugged robust roads
                  of jazz
the same damn way
i walked the dirty/dusty rows of cotton way
back
    down in the
              deep
                  deep
                      south

nobody knows the trouble i've seen
glory glory
hallelujah
lord have mercy . . . mercy . . . mercy
hallelujah

see you don't know what
it's like to live a
lyricless life of a poet
in exile
        lost   &   wandering without vision
with only the bittersweet
rutabaga memories of life
back home

HOME

                where the heart beats
                tom tom voodoo chants

HOME

                where a small pin in
                the bottom of a rag
                doll is a sudden sharp
                pain in the ass of
                masta jack

HOME

                where shango's hammer
                swings like basie's big
                band on a one night stand
                in a funky joint north of
                gutbucket u.s.a.

i say

YEAH

i do walk alone
along these pitch black back streets
crying & bleeding blue/jazzy sounds
from the raw pockets of my fatal wounds
i plead for ancestral elders wisdom
to close the gaping holes
in my soul before
i expose too much
        too quick
        too soon

for these old angry streets are just
too too mean to be seen without
an axe to grind behind . . .
if you dig my meaning

Working the Nightshift

(at B.C. Rogers' Chicken Plantation)

3 o'clock monday evening
just about the time
when most of your workingclass brothers
begin to think about quitting

you enter the plant dog tired
from a long weekend of trying
to forget last week's work
& yesterday's bills
that are still overdue today

but the pungent smell of dead chickens
instantly becomes bitter reminders
that your cutting career at B.C. Rogers
is far from being over

to think
yesterday you were a high school/college
graduate with big dreams of being
a big man in a small town—
your town

but it aint your town
& cuttin' stinking dead chickens
really aint your kind of a job
but it's the only job you got
& thank God you got one
(I aint) the guy up the street doesn't
& neither does the girl next door
but B.C. Rogers Chicken Plant(ation)
is hiring & firing
new slaves to fill new slots
left by old
slaves whose hands are bloody raw & tired
of slaving for minimum wage
while the rich folks in Pinehurst
eat fried chicken, baked chicken, broiled chicken

chicken cacciatore, chicken-alla-wendy, chicken—
alla-king
& poor folks eat chicken feet, chicken necks
chicken gizzards, chickenstew (with no chicken)
chicken backs
SAY WHAT!? CHICKEN BUTT!!!!!!!!!!!

don't you wish that all rich folks
would turn into a plucked chicken
& fly into a vat of hot grease
& let us poor folks eat good for a while

BESMILR BIRGHAM

The Will's Love

love God—
                my mother said
He who shut the Lion's mouth
and sealed the flames to their own burning

"the soul is like a little bird in His hand
a bird that lives in a wild briar tree"

love Life—my father said
laying the map out
                green-red mountains
                blue-yellow sea
the soul is a migrant
roe-bird that nests on sea rocks
a hawk   a falcon—
                        an eagle
or a "splatter-wing parrot
that only at night sleeps in a tree"

it took
my childhood before I could see

each one
said the same
                I am

                love me

The Sevier County Runaway

an ad in the paper, 1843

                        two negro slaves
                        one old
                        an ear cut off—
                        the other 'cropped'

                        color:
                        deep black

                        he took nothing
                        his name: BOB

                              the young negro
                              left on a horse

an old black man with his ears cut
walking through these bottoms
wading the Costock, river up—
an old black man
sleeping under a big sweet gum

hurrying through the pines
breathing the air i breathe. here

his ear holes listening. i touch the side
of his cut face; i see his black face
crying
the anger in his eyes is dark as the
wolf's. the accusation of his eyes

looks out from the dark yard
of this house. an old black man
dead,

lying deep in the wood, his black body
on the black earth. he is covered in leaves
he does not hear the young man

                        riding, riding

To the Unwritten Poems Of Young Joy

1
that were.
that were not abstract as language is abstract
that did not demand description

from an animal age
the cry of the young wolf
the joy
of the wolf

a cat-joy sharpening its claws

not aware of sound, the joy of great waves
hitting the beach in storm
and the joy of unity

i try to bring a unity to myself
to all the figures i am

relationships

the human bonds that have broken the crystal
the learning that has torn
                            like wind in heavy
leaves, shattering their substance
emotion that is not pure

i would lie as a red leaf lies
fallen on the ground

the joy of the rock
that is past the joy of the shaping of the
rock

2
    joy is born in the heart
it is born in the seed, and past joy

there is observance

the cry of the old wolf
is a cry of knowledge

yet, in winter, how the old ones' cries at the breaks
of our pasture
can pierce the heart—

the old wolves coming deep from their safe lairs
to hunt, to kill, to ravage the herds of
sheep, cows in huddle, cows
their bellies full of the young

blood on the ground when the calves come, the wolves
crying
to get in to them

they smell the blood on the ground
the animal cries
are cries of terror

the written and unwritten poems past the point of
wonder
are poems of love
and poems of terror

that are
the structure of language

The Figure's Math:
eight and four

from Nursery Rhymes

eight a beautiful year—
knowledge sits a fat bird
with its belly its head
                    round with knowing

and four a time of wonder
not as many fingers as a hand
but square as a box—and inside
the box's wonder

twelve
(one and two
a mad fox running in the wood
and two hind racing after)

together to make a greater count:

  when the heavy bird
  droops his eyes wings shut, sits
  a dry stick on a dry limb crying

in a still room, without
madness or fox or tender hind
where figures walk their stark shadows
the dead,

move over the mind

Morning of Love

I wake. the earth turns around

in its spheres; working all night
we sleep in light-held exposure
exposed to sound in all the singular
varying
areas, gypsies of pleasure; the map

fills with our campfires. the breaking
surf forms and reforms, a tearing apart
of dreams and suppositions, waves washing
cooled to shore, turned shoreward
to rush back in pushing undertow

flotsam, washed on the reefs, held
to the rocks; the moon against the still
darkness
makes its count of days, an ultimate
repetition. love, a cycle that will not

last as long as the moon, becomes
dispersed as the stars, when the wild
winds rage. Now
we sleep without consequence; settled
inland, we watch the migrating birds

   crying in flight
and our own cries echo through this
house, a solid place. the eyes
slowly have lost their visions of earth
—when
will the hurricane come? wings of song
consumed in the billowing care that wastes
and tears away, dries up the heart

yet, in the imagery of sleep
we are children again, abandoned in
innocence;
our bodies touch in an everlasting

remembrance of isolation and disclosure

VIRGIA BROCKS-SHEDD

Southern Roads/City Pavement

SOUTHERN ROADS
>   Held me virgin and
>   barefoot in the dust
>   that circled up to cover my face,
>   my hair, and engaged my nostrils
>   to inhale the dust of life
>   for me to become when I am dead.

MY SOUTHERN DUSTY ROADS
>   Led me from the deep piney woods
>   of my shacky home to the
>   pavement of Highway number 49
>   to see cars going to or coming
>   from the city 30 miles away;
>   waving my blackberry buckets,
>   hoping the riders would stop
>   and leave fifty cents for
>   my three hours of picking, and dodging snakes,
>   and getting untangled, while
>   envisioning money to leave
>   at the white folks' store
>   for nickel bars of delightful
>   but seldom had candy bars,
>   and then go home and say to
>   my daddy's widow,
>   "Mama, I made some money today."

MY SOUTHERN ROADS
>   In the little world of my life;
>   didn't know our folks could not afford
>   to take us to see the city streets;
>   I wonder now if I knew they existed;
>   and we thought everyone was like us,
>   except the folks in cars;
>   and me and my sisters and brothers
>   were jumping up and shouting everytime
>   we saw Black folks in cars as we
>   exclaimed which car was our own;
>   the cars, passing us, and now I recall,
>   some riders, glancing with pity

at those poor, poor children,
and stopping to buy our
fifty cents syrup bucket of blackberries.

The only other world we knew was
in the cowboy movies that we saw
in a tent during one season on unused,
unplowed dusty or grassy grounds,
because it was early 60s before we saw
television regularly to reject
our own lives, to imagine ourselves
dancing to Welk's champagne music
and wearing fine clothes.

SOUTHERN ROADS

That held and carried us barefoot
and occasionally with new cheap shoes
to school and our country church,
where we tried to look and be
without sin and important, too,
among those who were; and,
trying to get to heaven in one day
from the preaching and shouting and the
baptizing in our white sheets of goodness;
and going back home just before night
to play, fight, court and whisper
and glance and touch the boyfriends
and girlfriends we paired with unnoticed,
we thought, by our parents, and grandparents,
and aunts and uncles and senior cousins
who told us ghost tales and
superstitions and family histories,
as we listened to fox sounds and panther wails
and saw community, not homebox, entertainment
in pennies disappearing from and reappearing to
my daddy's hands while he lived to 1951

To wake and kill home raised chickens,
and cook them on the fires we stoked
in our wood stoves; pick greens, pull corn,
pick plums; stomp on clothes in a big tin tub,
stir them up in a big black pot,
and wait for hog killing time when we knew
we would eat homemade skins and the pig's feet;

and when with no meat, have homemade
buttermilk and cornbread

SOUTHERN ROADS
In the grassy, dusty paths that led
to Mrs. Eleases's house, Mrs. Clara's
and Mr. J.P.'s, Mr. Horse's,
Lynette's and Nooky's, Herman's and Billy's
on rutted walkways, or little craggy clay hills,
leading to springs of water for drinking,
branches of water for washing the clothes
from the bodies, the lives of sawmill, paperwood
workers; men touching women and children in the
new corners of our everyday life,
after our mommies came home from cleaning
the white folks' homes and our daddies bringing
very tired bodies home in their overalls
on

SOUTHERN ROADS
A peaceful haven for
floating southern spirits,
rejuvenating their times when they
physically touched the soil,
protecting living lives in the
meekness of us as we moaned together
in blackness of nationwide black care and
love for the Emmett Tills and the
Mack Charles Parkers; and, saying
deeply inside of us,
"Lord, have mercy; please have mercy."
And cry and shout at Mahalia's throaty notes
singing, "Precious Lord," and to later
feel the fleeting joy when we would
wind and grind to the lightning music of
Brother Hopkins or scream in pleasure
to know that B.B. was singing about women
who could love and cause or leave misery.

SOUTHERN ROADS
Leading to death in the lynch sites of
forest of trees; to burial grounds in rivers,
in the soil of dams; in carports and living
rooms of modern homes; in unpillowed beds

on railroad cars; on lawns adjacent to
dormitories; in the paved streets of cities,
at Parchman, Whitfield, and even the whiskey stills

SOUTHERN ROADS
Tapping and rooting and growing to and with
the lives that left for Chicago, L A, New York,
the army, Oakland, Detroit, Milwaukee,
the street corners, bars, heroin, coke—
the best of life, we thought, in escape from

SOUTHERN ROADS
I miss you since all I now touch
is asphalt or concrete or carpet;
gritty dust, not the fine kind
that blew with the clean winds through trees,
or kicked up with dusty barefoot feet
in the rows of fields we chopped to
make food for ourselves or money for the others
who hired us for $3.00 a day,
and then to shop at their stores for processed
foods we thought better than our natural
homemade brands or the fish we caught and ate
from creeks and natural lakes.

SOUTHERN ROADS
I now seldom walk anywhere,
but I do drive back to visit
the roads of my youth;
touching the soil, bringing some of its rocks,
its dirt to my city street;
and bringing the memories and the caresses
of the senior ones and the younger ones
who never left whom I see
still shaped and living in the
southern dust, home with me.

SOUTHERN ROADS
From the dust of you I have risen,
and have come and produced from me
two other lives to replenish you, too,
along with all the juniors from my sisters
of every race;
children to teach us loving and how to care
as those who were taught before
to care for the present us.

And, I wish to leave you naturally made
by bare or animal skinned feet;
to leave you laying paths to a world of peace
in unpaved, unpolluted by concrete and asphalt,
and gasoline and machine air;
and that airplanes will always pass by you
and not land too near;
that the blues and spirituals you give
will be orchestrated by southern homing birds
which won't ever have to fly away;
all creature; including me, who need you
to remain dusty or muddy when wet,
just dusty or muddy, good southern roads.

SOUTHERN ROADS

Foundation of my life,
holding all that made me,
my expired families and friends,
my ancestral anchors, so far
from where I am now.
But, what sorrows at each birth
these ancestors must have given in hopes
and prayers that the children
of black lives and black spirits
would have lives better than their own . . .
to try and not ever miss the early lives
of their scrotums and wombs which had died
from disease or natural miscarriages;
yet,

SOUTHERN ROADS,

You've paved a permanence in my life,
for I am bounded by gentle southern spirits
that travel you, too, and still,

SOUTHERN ROADS,

You will lead those to me
when I lie still, covered in death,
under southern love,
returning myself to you,
O precious southern soil.

JONATHAN H. BROOKS

Still I Am Marveling

(After reading Countee Cullen's "Yet Do I Marvel.")

My friend, you marvel how this thing can be,
A blackened bard is told to sing; and I
Am moved to supplement you; I muse why
And when Apollo's rare proclivity;
How he can master ample nerve to try
This way of beauty, knowing full well, Ay!
How, begging, Homer died. I dimly see,
Since it is proved that dye of any hue
Does not impair the essence of a thing,
How two of equal gifts and chance may do
An equal deed. Still I am marveling—
How one black poet ploughs the whole day long
And burns the oil of midnight for a song.

ISABELLA M. BROWN

Prayer

I had thought of putting an
altar here in the house,
just a small corner.
Anyway, I usually fall down on my knees
anywhere in the house.
I get on my knees and bow down
without thinking anything sometimes.
I say sometimes
God, here is my mind.
That's a good prayer
because during these times
there is almost always none.
So I ask God to hold my mind
and lead me in His path.

It sure is raining hard today.

WILLIAM BURT

Hank and Peg

He was as skinny
As I was
But wiry
The kid next door
Who was everything
Summer was made of
White t-shirt
Freckles
An ugly crew-cut
An uglier dog
A red bike
Without fenders
His name was Hank
Together
We cultivated boredom
As though it were
A rare orchid
In the shade
Of the carport
Beside the fallout shelter
Beside the house
Where his family lived
The pavement there
Cool to the touch
Was a hot-bed
Of get-rich-quick schemes
And Charles Atlas ads
Experiments with firecrackers
That didn't go off
On the Fourth
And still didn't go off
On the twenty-fourth
Experiments in creative talking
Backwards
Who could talk the longest
The fastest
With water in your mouth
Warm hose water
Acting out the final scene

Of Bataan
Careful not to die
In the oil puddle
Acting out
Godzilla Meets Werewolf
While the sun
Not even moving
An inch
Baked front yards
And gnats crawled the lips
Of the ugly dog sleeping
Her name was Peg
And she was old
Before there were
People on the earth
There was Peg
Toothless
Panting
We thought she was smiling
It was canine air-conditioning
We thought she was a bulldog
She was a Boston Terrier
Ugly, bloated, unafraid
Even of death
Which was on her
Like a smell
Bored enough to provoke Peg
We would grab at her club feet
And make fun
Of old Peg
Old blind Peg
Old fat Peg
Until a death-rattle snarl
Became a neckless lurch
Peg gummed the air
And sometimes
An inch of finger
Reminded her
Of the taste
Of sweeter days
Peg the fighter
Triumphant
Cat killer

The world
May not remember
But the heart
Never forgets
And so it is
That I recall
Mississippi summers
And a carport
And the sound of a screen door
An aimless whistled tune
I would look out the window
There was Hank
Coming through the hedge
Peg at his heel
And the day would begin

Mamaw and Frank

Proud woman
My Mamaw
She stood out
Among the poor people
Of Clarksdale
Like a diamond
Among stones
Severe
Straight-backed
She prepared to go
To the post office
As a soldier
Prepared for battle
Black cotton dress
Buttoned at the throat
Her long witch's hair
Carefully pinned up
Before the dresser mirror
She pulled herself tall
Turning this way
That way
Glaring
Daring the mirror to say
One blessed thing
Proud woman

My Mamaw
Stern
No time for foolishness
Rigamarole
She called it
Mamaw never in her life
Said I love you
But she wrote it on every moment
We spent together
In her living room
Dark and cold
Playing cards
Telling ghost stories
Giggling with excitement
Precious thing this
Silly childish love
Between a little boy
And an old woman
This stern old woman
In her black cotton armor
With her old cardboard Bible
And her steadfast distrust
Of all grown men
Mamaw's husband Frank
Was homely
And cross-eyed
But soft inside
Like the sweet potatoes he grew
All the neighbors
Would say
Mr. Swayze
Oh I hate to ask
But this back of mine
So if you would
Could you possibly
See your way clear
To carry me here
Carry me there
Do this
Do that
Do the other
Oh thank you
Mr. Swayze

What would we ever do
Mr. Swayze
Rigamarole
Mamaw would snort
They're just making a big
Fool out of you
Frank Swayze
And he would duck his head
Pained at displeasing her
I loved Frank
Who smelled of tobacco
Which he hand-rolled
Or else spat
Into a peach can
Frank never had two dollars
At the same time
His whole life
But he jingled with pride
At the Chinaman store
And bought me bright red sodas
I thought Frank was rich
Mamaw snorted
And leaned back in her rocker
And opened her Bible to Revelations
She read about Satan
Coming to earth every thousand years
Last time it was Hitler
She told me soberly
Now it's Martin Luther King
I said nothing
I knew she was wrong
And it was the worst kind of knowing
Like a place inside me
That couldn't get warm
I was twelve
Past easy reach of childhood
Mamaw looked at me
Over her Revelations
With a look she reserved for the neighbors
And grown men
I'm not really older
I wanted to say
I'm just bigger that's all

Frank came home
From the Chinaman store
Drunk as a boar
He vomitted on the linoleum
Mamaw rose indignantly
You're killing yourself
She scolded
One more can of beer
And you'll be dead
Frank Swayze
Dead
A drunkard
She followed him
Into the kitchen
Don't put that beer
In my box Frank Swayze
Look at you
How much did you spend
On that slop
He bent beneath her words
Like a hatless man
In a rainstorm
Falling back
Against the sink
Seeing the can there
He tore it open
Reared it like a weapon
I
Flew
Through
The
Air
Grabbed it no I cried no
What are you doing
He said dully
I'm taking it you'll die if you
Drink it you'll die
What do you care he
Said not letting go I
Care because I love you
I cried and the can
As cold as anything
I'd ever touched

Came away
From his hand
I poured it
Down the sink
Mamaw helped me pour
Them all down the sink
And later
I lay awake
In the dark
On the couch
In the living room
Remembering
Card games
And ghost stories
Giggles of excitement
And sodas of bright red
Forever gone
Forever cold
Like the place inside me
Aching dully
I knew it would never
Get warm again
Not really

JACK BUTLER

Preserves

Great love goes mad to be spoken: you went out
to the ranked tent-poles of the butterbean patch,
picked beans in the sun. You bent, and dug
the black ground for fat purple turnips.
You suffered the cornstalk's blades, to emerge
triumphant with grain. You spent all day in a coat
of dust, to pluck the difficult word
of a berry, plunk in a can. You brought home
voluminous tribute, cucumbers, peaches,
five-gallon buckets packed tightly with peas,
cords of sugar-cane, and were not content.

You had not yet done the pure, the completed,
the absolute deed. Out of that vegetable ore,
you wrought miracles: snap-beans broke
into speech, peas spilled from the long slit pod
like pearls, and the magical snap of your nail
filled bowls with the fat white coinage of beans.

Still, you were unfinished. Now fog swelled
in the kitchen, your hair wilted like vines.
These days drove you half-wild—you cried, sometimes,
for invisible reasons. In the yard, out of your way,
we played in the leaves and heard
the pressure-cooker blow out its musical shriek.

Then it was done: you had us stack up the jars
like ingots, or books. In the dark of the shelves,
quarts of squash gave off a glow like late sun.

That was the last we thought of your summer
till the day that even the johnson grass died.
Then, bent over sweet relish and black-eyed peas,
over huckleberry pie, seeing the dog outside
shiver with cold, we would shiver, and eat.

Ember-whistle

It was late at night, and winter coming,
and frost had settled on the stiffened grass.
There was no moon, no nearby city's glare
obtained, and in that black and country field
everything in him that depended on light
I had half-lost. Under the still, sharp stars,
we stacked cut thorn, exhaling ghostly plumes.
He sprinkled kerosene, and we watched the fire
roar and crackle, containing it till it died.

It faded low, and there was a half mile
of pasture-land to walk back home. We'd turned
to leave when he thought of something: taking
his pocket-knife, he cut a finger-length
of cherry, notched it, laid it in the coals,
and waited till it glowed.
                              "Ember-whistle,"
he said, and blew a note, holding it
with the point of his knife-blade.

We went on home,
past drifting cows, wrecking the fragile white
of the tilted fields with our heavy boots.

And till it too died out, I watched him lift
that coal, and put it near his lips, and blow,
and saw his face each time flame red and bright.

A Myth of Snakes

(And Something Better)

I think I may have heard the legend once,
dozing while the preachers jawed past midnight
in Dad's livingroom, a fable like slanted light
under a bedroom door. What with accounts

of glass-snakes fractured at their brittle joints,
hoop-snakes that bit their tails and rolled in flight,
snakes that stung like scorpions but did not bite,
and still less textual creatures and events,

all witnessed, actually witnessed, by someone there
or on a church field—
                    That *must* be when I first heard
how great clear globes of gum sometimes occurred,
rolled year to year in lake-beds like marbles in palms.

We found one last summer, bumping in shoreline calms
like God's transparent, floating brain. I swear.

Stuck Tractor

Not to make too much of a tractor, but
there it was as I passed the boy-scout hut
(I was running to do my heart some good),
sunk to its axle-bones in garden mud,
like an ancient beast attempting to clamber
up out of a tar-pit. And I did remember,
walking to where it waited for a rescue-try,
a notion I don't use, but keep on stand-by.

The top of the ground was solid to the foot,
though damp enough to take a track or rut,
but somewhere one or two feet down changed state.

It must have been all that rain back in December,
and then our sandy substrata—good for timber.
Not so good for gardens or tractors, though.
The treads had scooped up quicksand glop like dough.
I got a sudden image of Jasper County
about as permanent as a butter-pat at ninety,
or stable as the skin on scalded milk.

I had a dream once of that disturbing ilk.
A floating island—sunlit, raftered shops,
a curious industry, or craft, perhaps,
that filled their wooden bins with heaps of crystal
like the jeweled pips that fall to may-pop pistil
and snow-flake in a child's kaleidoscope.

Like an idiot, I stuck a pencil in it, and up
sprang a silvery gout and we started to sink.

I'm too realistic to really think
we float like a rug on a swamp in a fable.
I'm sure we stand both on solid and stable
sand and sand-saturated high-water-table,
the sort of sealed and happy paradox
that fills astronomy and geology books,
and never raises any question of what's real
till broken into by a point or wheel.

The Buzzard

What do you do for a buzzard with a busted wing?
After all that pity for a crippled fox,
it'd be bigotry not to help the thing.
They held it in the field glasses from the front door—
death's authentic dark gargoyle, all right,
trampling the hilltop over the mailbox.
Was there something in the graveyard it was waiting for?
—And then they saw the one wing dragging in the dirt.
He put on his boots and his jeans and his checked shirt,
and took two towels in case it wanted to fight
(to wrap his arms up in like a falconer's),
and strung his neck with bumping binoculars.

It was a pleasant hunt in the downhill light,
an excuse to visit the creek and look at roots
where the floods had laid them bare as old men's veins,

and think what had its warrens where they wound,
and think of spiders wintering underground—
but always there was that buzzard shadowing his thoughts,
and nothing but finding it would really do.

They met at last in a stand of green bamboo
sprung up from rubble-heap hillside moraines:
crack-leathered shoes, the burst hull of a tire
whose sidewall held a little stagnant rain,
half-buried bottles dreaming in their moss,
tin cans brittle as beetle-eaten pine bark,
and one dead buzzard, maybe, by the time it got dark.

A green light blossomed frailly in the cane
that meant, he knew, the red sun's bulge and loss
unseen, a sky like fire's exhaust on fire.
The moment prompted: the two of them began
a halting and intermittent stampede
that only ended when the creature ran
headlong into a forgotten fence's wire
a tree held partly out of earth, and so
ensnarled his neck he could not get it freed.

He squatted for a look in the last grey glow.
That wicked, rumpled beak, the naked head . . .
Was it like a hawk? And if so, how much?
He put out a hesitant, trial hand,
and jerked it back in an electric dread
when the buzzard shifted. It might have been,
no matter what he would have let on then,
his own death he put out a hand to touch.

That was before he was able to understand,
before they'd left it in the tub all night
as in the mind's aseptic analysis—
one wretched blot on all that glaring white
every time he came in and switched on the light.
He'd torn a T-shirt into strips,
held the knot with his teeth and breathed through his lips,
but hadn't had the nerve to call a vet.
He would have bet whatever you wanted to bet
not one would have been willing to handle *this*.
Who would believe him if he were to swear
this oddment, fragment from that broken vortex,
that black, revolving augury in air

that sends such shudders through our orderings—
see how he ducks at a fancied attack?—
is just a poor, big, worried-looking chicken,
a bureaucrat, and black-robed clerk, with wings?

In the morning they transferred it to the shed,
where it remained and did not seem to weaken,
and showed a stomach for the dog food they fed
(no need to worry whether it might spoil).
But one day he came out, and there it was, dead.
And so he had another guilt on his head—
to have forced it from a proper funeral-soil
and made it die in prison on a dirt floor,
lightless but for chink-dazzle as the sun went lower—
to carry with him into how many springs,
into a life that seemed wider and more gentle,
if somewhat lonelier and more accidental,
stopped in the woods by the whump of big black wings,
his kinsmen laboring upward from their soup and strings.

The Kid Who Wanted to Be a Spaceman

For Larry Johnson, Mississippi's first star-poet, who watched with me one afternoon in Arkansas the airplane creatures of another and watery dimension

When I was a child, I wanted badly to be a spaceman.
That was before the government took over and called them astronauts.
I was the last child born before television.
I used to listen to "Spaaaaaaaace Puh-*trol*" on the radio.
That radio was the size of a jukebox.
It had flanged, rounded cones for knobs, and its interior
glowed more strangely than fireflies.
I did not know what lay behind the fabric of its speaker,
what impenetrable mystery.

I was probably the only kid in Enon, Louisiana
who wanted to be a spaceman.
This was before Sputnik.
I invented Enon, Louisiana's first, last, and only
Secret Squadron Chapter, and flunked the physical I thought up.

Everywhere I went I would start a club.
We were going to the moon.
I drew rockets in class, rounded cones with flanges,

I filled their outlines with blunt-cornered squares labeled "Fuel," and
    "Oxygen."
I figured it would take a million dollars.
We were going to get the money from La Tourneau, another mystery,
who lived in Vicksburg, and tithed,
according to Southern Baptist legend, not one-, but nine-tenths of his
    millions.

I figured I could talk him into it.

None of it happened.
There's no way you could believe how serious I was.

I used to lie on the hood of the car after prayer-meeting
staring at stars
while the grown-ups talked under the pole-light,
my back warm from the engine,
imagining all upside-down, hanging by my skin over deep galaxies,
longing to roll and see them under me as well.

The stars are not decoration: they are heart-broken love.

I wanted so badly to be a spaceman.
I became a Christian by accident at six—I'd only stood to ask if this was
    the invitation,
but they thought I was coming forward,
and then I saw my mother weeping in terrible relief and they were
    shaking my hand,
and it felt good to be congratulated for my moral courage,
and I kept quiet.

All this in a revival in a shotgun shack of weathered rough-cut lumber in
    a cotton field.

How can I tell you what happened to my religion
when the robot in *The Day the Earth Stood Still*
lifted his master in a gesture like the *Pieta*
and took him back to the flying saucer and brought him back to life?

So, science-fiction and scripture,
straight A's and daydreams in the red-dirt hills and the delta,
the strange, deflected resultant of desire:
these led me inexorably
to broken song, the musical names of the constellations.
I'd thought I was science-minded
because in the 4th grade I shaped from modelling clay,

the sort given at Christmas,
four ingots like quarter-pound sticks of butter, one red, one blue, one
    green, and one yellow,
the best Tyrannosaurus Rex.
He was green outside because green in *Compton's Pictured
    Encyclopedia*—
but transected, what swirl, what rainbow!
True, after a myriad revisions
all went brown as the threat of entropy—the act that made the rainbows
    eventually unmade their possibility.

And so it was the poetry that stirred me, the wonder of science,
and the numbers and formulae meant no more to me than the band of
    numbers on the radio,
though many of them are still with me—MM'/d^2, for example,
an allegory for love as Heinlein had a character say in a little paperback
    called *Universe,*
with Joe-Jim the two-headed mutant rampant on the cover.
The numbers and formulae, I repeat, were only arcane jargon,
and I gradually discovered,
blaming myself horribly, that I would never be a scientist,
and still more gradually admitted it to the world.
Neither will I live on a plantation again
or write the fiction that Faulkner wrote.
I am doomed to envy the root-eloquence of farmers,
the dumb luck of those trowel-tongued test pilots who first tracked up
    the moon.

And yet, this very evening, swimming at B.A. Steinhagen Lake,
the sun like a ball of blood dropping,
the rose, the cerulean, the auric and just plain green tints rippling and
    mingling where my stroke broke water,
the air all smoke and distance,
a barrage of bubbles trailing up like pearls to trouble my face
from the cleft between thumb and forefinger of each hand
as each dove into the blurred green depths
like a man falling from orbit . . .

Once as I rolled for breath from that underworld
there bulked on the swell of my passage
the bulbed silhouette of a free-floating clump of water-hyacinth
like a piratical alien ship
flagged with aleph and zed and hove to,
and in that moment I knew that it was such a ship,
that all seed is such cargo,

that all journeys occur in a dangerous, lovely world with no bottom,
that I am and have always been
a traveller among, and a poet of, stars.

The Edges, the Fractions, the Pieces

When I use to work deferential equations
I had a neat sheet I kept track of it on
inking in ordered chains of tuneful logic
like dew collecting on a latticework
or sugar crumbling grain by grain to nectar
but when the next change stumped me as it did
more times than I'll mention, out came Stubby
the friendly yellow #2 chewed pencil
with round blunt lead and sweat-stained foreskin wood
long unwhittled in the sharpener's whirling knives
and eraser's thin brass jacket bitten flat
to raise just one more day's meniscus of correction
and out came Oscar the mangy scratch-sheet
and all his hay-pile fat comedian friends
glad to see me as always and so we romp
we tussle in the briar-patch scratchy grass-fields
until a girl without an ounce of fat on her
strides by in a pure white muscular gown
and I am dressed in wedding-white for church again
with an ink string tie the height of fashion
over the starchy ruffle of my beating chest
when I use to work D for any ol' equations

ROBERT CANZONERI

To a Campus Tree in Spring, Seen Out a Second Story Window

Only your middle shows from here, green starred
Big branches, solid trunk. I climbed you raw,
As a savage boy, hugged your rough bark.
But, older now, I'll climb you felled and sawed,
Walk up stairways under a shingled roof
More solid than your sky of summer leaves,

Four floors above root ground to our highest room.
And if your twig-top green still higher lives
Than I, I'll tell you of less academic
Buildings built of sand-lime fusions, steel,
Your wood, and the clay you cling to baked to brick:
Structures that stand more than ten times as tall.
They know of soil: to sweep; of rain: to shed.
We let you stain our rooftop with your shade.

Cleaning Up

(Nina)

At her age, she doesn't dip
Her hands into the sink,
But stands at arm-stretch
Dripping suds, and talks:
"My teacher's the nicest thing!
I mean, she has to get mad,
But she always says she's sorry
Afterwards."
Shouldering hair from her eyes,
She squints at a foaming dish
And then straight-arms it clean.
"Some teachers
Just leave their yells in the children."

The Day the Cold Came

Football lights drew bugs of summer;
where were the southward geese?
Apple sprung to bloom again, and gum trees
leaved, the damned instinctive fools.
Gardeners cursed the burlap
weekly rotting by azaleas
under no frigid siege.

Our craving had the edge
of fresh tub ice.
The midnight bark of shivering dogs
struck us as nice.
Winter's dark discomfort
of bulky clothes

we lusted, and approaching numbness
from our toes.

The day it came we dared it. After work
we walked the early dark on sidewalks, jerked
off our gloves and barked our kunckles hard
against the tight tree bark—and then forgot
that kind of foolishness.

　　　　　　　　Under the graphic
mercury vapor lamps we saw a man
of pumps working an anti-freeze device
long-hosed at a lock-jawed car.

　　　　　　　　Name
the perversity by which the moon incensed
us, rising tropic yellow like a lion.
We stopped and stared it up in cold denial,
watched it pale to silver, chilled, convinced.
We flipped it like a dollar over our shoulder.
Nobody, we could swear, was ever colder.

Mississippi

That Grand Old State of Mind

(Citizen, tell me,
What is your favorite tree?
"Magnolia is the bes',
Ah guess.")
Unlike oaks
Magnolias are a hoax
Of expense
That doesn't quite convince;
Not so coarse
As pines and sycamores,
Nor so trim
As poplar girls who swim
To stay slim,
Magnolia matrons corset
Up like hoarse
Harridans whose sole defense
Is pretense,
Whose gaudy brooch provokes
Canvas jokes.

(Now that you've heard from me,
What is your favorite tree?
"Ah tol' yuh.
Magnolia.")

Bird Dog Man

The bird dogs had the run of their long pen
And ran, now and again,
But most of any summer afternoon
Dug in and slept
Or crept up on suspecting birds, who soon
Enough—just as a bird dog broke and leapt—
Flew from the hurricane
Fence squares they perched within.
It seemed a ritual until
One bird remained as planted for the kill
And one dog found his fill
Of feathers in the teeth and on the tongue.
He was well trained, though young
And full of open field trial fantasies:
His jaws could gently seize
Quail flushed and shot before him, leave no trace
Of teeth where pellets tore to tender lace
The fragile skin.
This bird had none of the dying heat nor thin
Folding of wings nor stiff
Unmoving legs nor the heart-thumping tinge
Of blood: it squawked as if
Such breach of the expected might unhinge
Both brain and jaw: it dug
With claws and beat with wings until the dog,
Eyeing its fellow dog, let the bird go
Between them on the grass.
Two bird dogs can harrass
One bird too wet to fly, or flustered so
Its wings won't work.
But what initiative to kill might lurk
Unpurged from wolf-old hearts
Had no chance to emerge.
The dogs clashed in a flurry, and the bird
Footed it through the fence

And crossed the yard, chipping at every hop
In crippled grackle outrage at his abuse.

The man comes with a crop
And curls the dogs down to his stolid shoes
Until they hold quiver perfect. He makes
Them hunch down in a tub
For soap and rinse and rub.
He locks their pen and gives the air a sniff
And squints up at the sky.
He will hunt birds when grass is frozen stiff
And all the leaves are dry.

ANNE CARSLEY

Demesne

Flat gray Delta land in winter
   falling before my wheels
As I have fallen before its spell.

Drab little towns have white-brown backsides
   between flicks of dusty neon.
They are cicada skeletons in spring.

Rooted to the clay, loam, riverbanks and shale
Bound to the muddy swath, an ice torrent, the Gulf, a puddle
Secured by roped honeysuckle, green hung kudzu, a moss fall
Held by names that mesh the generations, a white column, Indian
   trail, cotton field hut, or a sad train
   Enduring land and impermanent villages,
   Broom sage, muscadine vines . . .
So, I, captured by birth and caught to light
   Hold this Mississippi land.

The Natchez Trace

Called, I came.
Beckoned, I followed.
Coming at last to the haunted crevice
   of memory, into the hammered land of
   that great river whose name is a lift
   in the heart.

Sodden broom sage where the crows sit,
Cypress knees in the swamps where the outlaws hid,
   Plaques, cars, tourists, legislation,
   Past and present and future
In the dreaming Southern land.

It coalesces here, melds.
History and thought are met
   in that cleft hidden by blackberry
   bushes and green fields beyond.
Wholeness in the sunlight.

Here.

Catalogue

I have clasped a bracelet
   Hung an earring
   Burned a curl
   Glazed a mask
In your name.

There is little I do not know.
Try me.
   Antietam and Gettysburg. The Elder Edda.
   Summerland and Alligator
   Gumbo receipes and oyster patties
   The Third Reich and the camps beyond the Styx
   Kama Sutra and the belly roll.
   In your name.

The silence of words done is between us.
Our fingers explore a city abandoned.
In my name.

Festival

Gumbo, crawfish, shrimp, po-boys, strawberries,
   fudge, shortcake, azaleas, rain, and beer forever.
Take a chance on the hundred pound cake?
Stick a pin in the inflated twenty foot Miller bottle?
That your kid squalling down yonder?
Move to that Cajun wail. Shake it on over.

In the whirl the fat lady dances.
Her flesh goes in ridges and bumps over hipbones,

around the stomach, down the thighs. Her beer is
about to spill as she holds it high.
She catches up the young man in one old hold and
bounces with him. His headband is loose and his grin
changes. He steps with her. Faster. Fast.
Shaking.

Her scalp is pale as a pink azalea in the shifting sun.
Arms that sag and face split by time.
Eyes that see now
And mouth red with berries.
with joy in now.
She is invincible.

Glory.

Menu

Saturday afternoon was chicken killing time.

"Go catch the biggest pullet and don't waste the corn."
I watched the doomed one and wondered what it was like
to have the sharpened axe waiting.
She gobbled, I swooped, missed, and we ran.
Chickens everywhere.
Dog waiting to grab.
Let it go; have a roast.
"That chicken ready yet?"
I caught a wing and felt it break. That would be mine
on Sunday along with the liver. All alive now.

They said giants and ogres ate you, just ran you down
and gobbled, kept the pot ready if they preferred
cooking.

"Hold the head steady now. Stretch the neck out."
I felt the eyes bat against my sweaty palm as the
yellow feet twisted and she whacked down on the
block.
Once the neck and once the feet, then the blood
is all over the grass while the body tries to join
up its pieces.
The head stayed in my hand and twitched.
Did it know what happened?
Would I have known?

Ogres eat children.
Everybody knows that.

"Throw that over to the dog. Come help me pick the
  feathers off."
She picked up the headless, footless thing and the
blood still came. It was on the chopping block, on
her and on me. We'd open the craw and find the grain.

Ogres are for Saturday night and Sunday company comes.
I still like chicken.
Dead, chopped chicken.

"Get two this next time. Grab their legs."
          Whose legs?
          What liver?
          I didn't know Prometheus was real.

HODDING CARTER

Flood Song

Lawd, but it's black, with nary star showin',
It's jes' like us was dead.
Light the fire, boys, and keep it going!
But, boss, it turns the river red.

            Ol' Mississip's a-rarin',
            She's growlin' and she's swearin'.
            Ain't that a body floatin' in the light?
            She's reachin' out an' snatchin'
            And she's keepin' what she's catchin'
            Cause she's gonna raise a ruckus tonight.

Jesus Marster, but these bags is heavy,
Cain't stop no river with san'.
Heave up, boys, and pile 'em on the levee.
Us is flirtin' with the Promised Lan'.

            Ol' Mississip's a-rollin',
            Got her spade an' goin' holin'.
            Looks mighty like she's spilin' for a fight.
            She's traipsin' down a-swingin'
            When she rounds the bend she's singin'
            That she's gonna raise a ruckus tonight.

Look up yonder, boss, them bags is shakin',
'Taint no use now, that's sho!
God in Heaven, the levee's breaking—
Boss man, let us go.

Ol' Mississip's a-rumblin'
Cain't you see them san' bags tumblin'?
She don't care if you's nigger folks or white.
An' when she starts to spillin'
She's ready for a killin'.
She's raisin' her a ruckus tonight.

Slave Story

"In 1872 the Negro and Carpetbag legislature voted $1,000,000 for gold spittoons."

At twenty-one Jupe ran away
To join the Yankee jubilee.
The word had trickled to Mount Pine,
Ole Abe had set the niggers free.
The hounds retrieved him in a swamp,
His master gave him ten yards grace
Then shot him just above the calf
To make him realize his place.

When Jupe was thirty he limped through
His state's once proud assembly hall
As legislator from Mount Pine,
And spat his plug-tobaccoed gall
Upon the tiles for they were white,
And meditated on new boons,
And though he voted aye for them
He never used the gold spittoons.

Four reeling years, and then the Klan
Rode through the state and dragged him out.
They strung him skyward by his heels
And beat him with a leaded knout,
And while he hung there, someone struck
His forehead with a pistol butt,
And when they loosed his inert bulk
The door of sanity slammed shut.

I can remember old Unc' Jupe
Who could remember nothing much,

But spat up at a spittoon sun
And dragged his leg beneath a crutch,
And foretold weather by the pains
That creaked along his stiffened knee.
And when he died the headline said
A faithful former slave set free.

Ashes of Sackcloth

When she was fifteen she last walked the tracks
To town to peer into the Bon-Ton store,
And covet the sheer pink things women wore
Unless their mothers patterned bleached-out sacks
That once held flour and such. The girl was slim
And tawny as a sunset, loving bright
Prohibitives. And so it was to him
An easy lark to coax her in the night.

Her mother found out first, and beat her blue,
And tore away the clinging little bribe.
She crept from home next day. A city's stew
Sucked her into its mess, in friendless gibe
At God the loving whose compassion lacks
Knowledge of flour and fertilizer sacks.

In Depression Time

How many in the family? Five?
Right here is where you sign.
Let's see your work card. Here's your meat—
Back there, don't shove the line.

> *Corn pone and bacon fat*
> *And limp grass for a hoss.*
> *Out yonder runs the river, boys,*
> *Let's beat the Yanks across.*

You need a pair of overalls?
No flour in the bin?
Three days a week will have to do—
Back there, stop pushing in.

> *Mired guns and broken steel,*
> *Old Stonewall, thar he stands.*
> *Hell, we don't need no powder, boys,*
> *Let's lick 'em with our hands.*

The seed won't come until next week,
There's talk of winter fuel;
Don't worry, we'll take care of you—
Back there, you know the rule.

>   *Ravaged field and blackened roof,*
>   *And faded calico.*
>   *We ain't in want of scarecrows, boys,*
>   *Let's plough another row.*

TURNER CASSITY

Cane Mill

In winter, through felled pines,
The clearing fills with still,
Flat haze. In blurred confines,
The lame mule turns the mill.

Sugars and resin, grain
By grain, burn toward their lees;
And where two smokes, one cane,
One pine, drift in the trees,

Dark residues foretell
Our season's heritage—
Where, through time's circling smell,
The slow mule plods toward age.

The Lumber Baron

The granite angel and the cast-iron fence
Share that neglect of death they would atone.
This gate, though it sequester decades hence
A chatelaine still wearing veils of stone,

Cannot ward off at last the toppling doom
Of seedlings rooted at her earthbound feet.
Now, young pines scent my grave with narrow bloom,
Spiced with the wood it yields. I find it sweet,

For all that I preferred to trees alone
A smell of sawmill smoke and turpentine,

The sawdust pile afire deep in its cone.
Sawdust and lumber, blood and yellow bone
That were my life, inherit from the pine,
When fires are gone, a fire, a breath not mine.

A Song to Be Vindicated

A little like the *Macon*, drawing-board baroque,
An ornate rocket ship knifes through the inked-in smoke,
Her life-class pilot faceless. Is it Flash? Brick? Buck?

And in that Art Nouveau control room, also steering,
Who, golden hair marcelled and earrings wired for hearing,
Stands by with uplift bra? Intrepid Wilma Deering.

Robot sunshine, real night, robot chaperon.
Insomniac Miss Deering dials the somnatone,
Upstanding Buck has two cold showers *and* the tone.

Then, a landscape littered with the shapes of crystals,
And a perfect landing (robot luck). No hostels,
No 4-H. Wilma, the disintegrator pistols!

Hawk-men seize us, giant lizards tongue our heels.
But Hawk-man One, the brute archangel hung with seals,
Leads toward the dark skyscrapers and the upturned keels.

An architecture early Chrysler Building, bongo
Drums its sole communication, and the Congo
Model for its rule—the yellow planet Mongo:

Reprimanded by the League, and one vast press
Of war lords. If its winds seem foul, its seas are cess.
Its present emperor is Ming the Merciless.

Can lonely Ming find happiness with Earthling lover?
His torturers think yes. Can Buck, so far from clever,
Implode the anti-matter soon enough to save her?

No. But Dr. Huer's flagship lands relief,
And crowns Buck Ming the Second—jockey strap gold leaf,
His theme song Siegfried's world-inheritance motif.

WW II in the City of Homes

Royal Netherlands Air Force is training a contingent of flyers at the Jackson Air Base. Most are from the Japanese-occupied Netherlands East Indies. Cadets wear the colors of the House of Orange. —JACKSON (MISS.) DAILY NEWS, December 1, 1942

It is a Shriners' Lodge where lodger rhymes with Nadja.
It is a dull, dull town; but so was Koeta Radja,

And the Hague is no Port Said. What one misses,
Finally, is some least sense of not-rose-bushes;

Of the life that is not pruned. So many Blacks,
Humidity so unrelieved, and still it lacks.

I train for war. However, love must first combat me.
Ten thousand powdered matrons throw their daughters at me.

We take drives. There is a park of sorts. Sumatra,
It develops, is a singer. Is Sinatra

Then an island? Yes, My Dear. A small, far island,
Just as this is (has been, will be). It is my land.

Our distinction is, we are antipodes
And know it. Far from Mean Time by the same degrees,

You don't. What are you taught at school? Drum majoretting?
Do our lands compare? Well, yes. The sun at setting

Has a look of one fruit drawn on blotting paper;
Mildew blurs the moon. At home, though, fruits are riper,

Mildew greener. So I had as soon not squander
These last days before my Orange wild blue yonder

Here in such a tame gray hither, but the choice
Is fate's, not mine. I hear fate speak. In Calvin's voice.

Hedy Lamarr and a Chocolate Bar

Showings are six a day, continuous.
No need to wait in line or be on time;
In any case the plot will be generic:
Boy meets. Scorning the concession stand
(I am austere, for not much more than twelve)
Unfed by choice I go to meet the dark.
Algiers a frame or two before the end,
And in her big close-up Gaby departs,

Rogue Helen at the railing of a ship,
To wreck the blood as on the wall of Troy.
It is a vision that transfixes. Gel,
Dead center in the aisle, I cannot move
So long as ecstasy stares out ahead.
The vision vanishes, and Charles Boyer
Comes on to suffer who cares what. By now
I am so shaken that I turn around,
Retrace my steps, and thank the taste of Mars.
If, showings later, I become aware
That my experience is every man's,
And every man, if *she* is on the screen,
Is rooted in the aisle as I was, too
Exanimate to stumble toward a seat,
It does not mean that under Mitterand
I womanize. And at our age who wants
Algeria. But I know what I know.
I have seen beauty stop men in their tracks.

Summer of 1942

OPEC an ogre far in future,
Mississippi in July
Props open doors and uses air
Conditioning to advertise.
A sidewalk by the theatres
(Majestic and the Paramount)
Is *Nanook of the North Goes South.*
Attractive, rival, fatal waste!
How we who pass are taken in:
Murmansk and the Aleutians, France,
The North Atlantic. Nanook, join!
And we who, Levite or the Priest,
Pass by upon the other side,
We too experience a draft:
Oahu, Iwo Jima, Guam.
There is an average, not hot,
Not cold, that now exempts us all,
If, coming after forty years,
It makes one value the extremes.
And though we pass, we form a queue;
Queue every one and feel the chill;

Pass; pass by. Every, every one.
My Lord Emir, unprop the doors.

CECILE BROWN CLEMENT

Lillie Learned to Read

When she was fifty-seven
Lillie learned to read
in community education.

Her fingers, colored like ripe eggplants
with pink bract nails, followed lines
Tuesday and Thursday nights for a year.
The tired desks were scarred
with hearts and initials and codes.

Lillie lived by cooking
in the day, shopping by pictures
of green beans on the cans,
pictures in the yellow pages,
her eyes like magnified black-eyed peas
consuming every clue.

At the third level
Lillie and her best friend Alice
graduated to the reading computer.

Each night Lillie reads her Bible,
each day her recipes. She has
a rich heart, a chocolate pie.
She hasn't read who is the President,
yet.

WILLIE COOK

Not the Starlights

That greyhound just kissed you on the cheek,
left you holding hands with a used samsonite,
and the yellow eyes in black concrete cliffs,
bottled up rainbows and fast breaking traffic
that do not notice you are not TV scenes in
Hill Street Blues. You are here. Wherever
your eyes drive you is the city. The night
has already booked a place for you. If you
don't accept, you can't leave yourself and ride
another choice out of town. Every street
corner houses a different colored trick, every
street vendor runs down different highs. Take
it before bedtime with a large glass of caution.
If what you run into and what runs into you
knock you out, you've hooked a live current, the
shock may wake you up before counting you out.

Wake

Nights passed come back tonight,
digging for the buried, living still,
wasting chorused moans
that will not put silence to sleep.

Monologs drive truth away,
set fire to fractured wants
lying numb under nickle-weighted eyes,
and a face comes clear out of pit,
speaking too far from my ears.

On the other side of breath,
dreams are born open-eyed,
looking for last year's loss
in the remains of rain'd out ash.

It seems then or now
that day would find this room,
walk in arm in arm with sleep
and wait for the wake.

Times come when time starts talking,
then another voice is heard,
beside me, truth is touched,
breathing up August midnight.

But more often, I reach out
and hold an armful of darkness.

55 *Confession*

I sat listening to words that were AWOL
in a Smack Oven stall, washing our throats
with suds. He was weighed down with a heavy
bag he wanted to hang on my line. My ears
dug the gravity, stuck behind his eyes, that
went featherweight in my head when the Teen
Queens got on the phone yakking about some
stud called Eddie, My Love. His thoughts saw
clear through my waiting, and decided I was
hitting it hard listening to him pour more of
himself out on silence. I emptied the last
of the suds in his glass to turn him on. I
was turned off by a chick in red that threw
my eye back at me. Back to taking care
business, I laid dead for the blood to run
down his mind and lay it on mine. I pushed
myself in his head, looked out of his eyes,
saw myself working on a face that said, I
know where you're coming from, to the sounds
made by the glass striking his lips. When he
decided he had dished out enough, "Please, Eddie,
don't make me wait too long", the grip on him
left and a grin parked in its place, like I had
played, Say twenty-three Hail Marys, run over
the rosary ten. His grin graduated to thirty-
two pearls as he laid a green leaf on the
confession table for another suds. I shook
him off. I knew you would see it that way
blew a bad breeze, and we walked out into the
shower of the Lynch Street sun. Before we
divided Dalton, he clamped a vice on my mitt,
saying, If anything ever hits you, I'm around.

CAROL COX

Listening to James "Son" Thomas Sing Delta Blues

I think of blooming roots,
                    waking spiders,
          bulky rusting stems;
of the digging and sorting
spring will do
if left alone.

Son Thomas singing on this
watery March night,
          thick enough to fill up warehouse doors,
fine screens built all over town
to keep out growth:

he tells us what it is
          he's broken open every hour,
but not how many silver fingers
were replaced
after the ruin became too clear.

Silver Pins

she keeps lined up in rosewood drawers,
(slivers of pearl and dark red stone),
and sometimes gently to herself
pulls out the great-aunts' names:
Carrie, Annie Lizzie, Eva,
Ginny Mary, Fannie, Sally—
and feels the restfulness of netted hair
held in a knot
and thin blue dresses
moving down the wide front porch.

The smell of distant rooms
comes in too close;
this smokeless room, empty of another life,
can hold too much—
a pear tree heavy as the dead,
the tea cakes chocolate-drenched,

a broad front hall held deep in summer noon.
Her arms are heavy
in the present heat,
her mouth is full of whisperings
and songs: I've learned one anxious fact,
I'll hold to that,
I've seen the way it wavers in the light
and edges out the dark,
sharply,
broken and regained.

Perhaps you'll all come back.
I'll make iced tea; we'll water ferns;
the back porch steps will blister,
and then heal.

In the Fifties

1   Daughters

those sweet-faced fifties girls,
their twirly skirts and certain skin,
how they loved to dance!
they swept on past their cheeky parents,
kicked the heads of yellow day lilies,
skipped on toward the glowing trumpet vine—
gangway for colors, seasons at the throat.
the hotter summer grew,
the flashier they spun,
the more evaporation nourished the earth.
sit down in Mississippi
and you might miss it all,
or you might *get* it all,
just as chilling a thought;
the music sent it on along.

at ten-going-on-eleven, only a hint of dread
bore in:
they had Elvis and an endless life.

2   The First Time

Deep in the throat of summer in the south, 1956,
my mother kneels along the curving zinnia bed,

my brother slaps basketballs back and back again,
I lie on the hot sidewalk with a new beagle puppy.
We are all past speaking,
captives of the sun and milky air,
the loose, damp weather moving under our skins
and leaving us full as melons—
our bones seem lost.
The morning tilts toward noon:
some movement on the street,
a vision through the haze, the steaming atmosphere:
a huge blue Oldsmobile, Mrs. Haynie's car,
creeps along the curb.
The windows are rolled up!
She sits with other ladies, eight rouged cheeks,
and waves, in splendid quarantine.
My mother murmurs in astonishment.
We rise, approach them, eye their powdered arms at rest,
their pale silk dresses floating on the seats,
and then—a sheet of icy air escapes,
the window down lets out its precious passenger,
it smacks against my open mouth.

* * * * * * * *

At night I lie awake beside my radio,
warm air soaks up the sounds
of early, jubilant rock'n'roll—
like fireworks, flashes coming rapidly,
guitar, piano, threatening wails,
a dizzying glimpse of something out there
my imagination barely touches on
and has no words for yet—
it's here and not-here,
mystery of place, a cooling hand on hot asphalt,
a promise no one gave.

In the Room of the Civil Rights Exhibit
at the Old Capitol

Picture of a bombed-out church:
is this a ruin? Like an old plantation house
collapsed from rain and termites,
drifting toward the grass?
Mothers and daughters in feathery skirts

murmur that they never saw.
The barbed wire is a mystery.

Generals stroll among the population everywhere,
their rage an elevated state
no longer needing definition.
The bombs this month, in April,
shower casually,
like roses dropped along the porch.
Each one engenders more—
to keep the flowers coming, pick the heads.

The armies surge with youth,
and more mistaken pictures in the mind—
this rock is bread,
a river turns to steel,
a fragment on the ground is gold,
or bone, or language given form.
The children pick up everything.

The cool halls where the photographs were brought
make ticking, foreign sounds;
underneath run solitary paths.
Time may play the friend to ignorance,
a day may hold a waking dream
in which a memory moves into flesh,
becomes routine; we hold it out; it's what we have.

HUBERT CREEKMORE

To the Very Late Mourners of the Old South

Come—decay has crushed your crinolines,
forgetfulness has rusted over the graces
of your courtesy. Too long your faces
now have poured their maudlin might-have-beens
in tears upon the fond remembered scenes
that make the artificial wreath time places
on your tomb of adolescence. Stasis
of perception is all this weeping means.
Come—forget the feudal charm of days

you never can resuscitate, and gaze
upon what breathes in vital beauty here
before your backward turning feet. A near
and burning loveliness you trample down
to hold upon your head this martyr's crown.

Encounter with a Dog

Because my eyes struck his, the hound has paused
half in flight, lest I throw a stone
for his temerity. He would have nosed
my ankles at a kindly gesture; drawn
my heart (had I not pondered pedigree)
so great his timid loneliness and hope.
If I can feed his mouth he does not know,
nor if my social class is good to keep.
He merely warms his instinct in my look,
fancies rubbing at my legs; waits
(long after I have turned) with an ache
of fading hope; then derelict, foots
away. His instinct twists beneath no ban.
Foolish dog to waste such good on man.

JOHN CREWS

Caught Caught Caught

You were the first caught, John Hindman,
running up the brick steps on Locust Street
caught caught caught.

Others were caught on their way to reform school,
parachuting into Mausers at Normandy,
in the warm waters off Solomon,
by a Georgia police bullet.

We smaller ones cried
I draw a circle on your back
then ran and hid close to home.
Rough Ganymedes played caught
caught caught naked in the Y pool.

But that hot August night the dark was close
and the bigger faster boys played
caught caught caught
away from home and refined play.

They chased you down streets through yards between houses
stirring up the August dust your black hair flying wet
sweat popping on your temple wrist and the calf of your leg
running through hedges and gates scaling cement walls
knocking over cans running on porches
dogs barking cats scattering grownups cursing.
You were determined not to be caught.

Then the race up the steep steps, broken and red teeth,
not making it to the top not hearing the dark cry
caught caught caught.

Sabbath Coin

You were foreign to me, yet kin and dear:
Jewish, aristocratic, and austere;
gray hair, China blue eyes, powdered,
sitting in silver state amid
the mahogany and cut glass
during those Sabbath visits
by James and me to your hotel suite—
far removed from Farmer Street "One-and-Over,"
peg, "nigger shooters," Chinaberries,
and porch voices from behind the four o'clocks,
greeting passersby with, "Ain't it hot?";
remote from Christ Church plain song and faith;
high above the Y's disciplined shouts.
We sat and talked: "How's Aunt Annie?
How's Evelyn?" We reached into our pocket
of things and pulled out small change: school,
family, illness, Sunday rides,
and walks to the cemetery. You opened
the ancestral trunk and I gazed
at a Joseph coat of things and breathed
the must of memories: Torah, yellow
fever, and your travels to fjords
and pyramids. Then we had chocolates.
You reached into your purse and extended
show fare. The audience was ended.

Though you have been dead forty years,
though the hotel no longer exists,
you live on in a lighted niche
of my days: seventh floor, end of the hall;
foreign, aristocratic; kin and kind;
handing out Sabbath coin to two small boys.

JACK CROCKER

Bear Hunt

for my grandfather

He watches in the dark for dawn
To give the trees single shapes,
The leashed dogs jerking him
To the trail where bear stink
Lies heavier than bear walk.

"Now, Mr. Knight, be still,"
The nurse says, watching his heart
Fire and misfire.

Reading the tracks he sees the dogs
Drift back whipped and dazed
From charging a dogwise old bear
Too big to run, who strolled
Into a swamp, backed against a cypress,
And swatted away whatever lunged—
Except the bearwise old bitch
Who keeps her distance and yelps.

"Fibrillation," the nurse says:
Shock. Raised voltage. Shock.

He lets go the dogs and listens
To their high belling thin out
And dissolve, circling the scent
Like confused blood nosing veins.
He waits, leaning against the silence,
And hears the old bitch stymied,
Singing.

"No," the doctor says. They stop.

Lost in dogsong he trails through
Palmetto and wild fern into a wealth
Of swamp to where the old bitch stands
Silent, fixed in the awful stink.

HENRY DALTON

Hill Born

We are the hill born. Townfolks gawk
At us on Saturdays
And keep their distance. They smile at our talk
And look down our country ways.

Our bodies are shaped by rocky slopes.
Our thoughts are bent to the plow.
And we are slow of speech. Our hopes
Are such as hills allow.

The taste of pine is in our wells,
Its biting green on our sky.
We are born to love hill tastes and smells.
Wild grape and crab apple are wry.

When joy is a flower or grief's a nettle
Our words pull up to a halt.
Don't smile, townfolks. If we talk too little
It's not our fault:

For hills are possessive, hills are bitter;
Hills are jealous of their young.
Folks blame it on the cat—but I know better.
The hills got our tongue.

Spring Songs

1   *The Assault*

He never knew what hit him:
                          the snake
that boiled up when we turned a plank
while mending the garden fence.

Pieces of him fought back,
then lay still again . . .

For our mother (still seated)
had gone at him with the axe.

2   *The Hawk*

The hens and chickens
were still noisy:
                    our mother
still by the watershelf
where too late
she had run to scream at the hawk:

that   mission accomplished   was east east
            flapping from sight.

3   *Snakes Go to Bed Early*

Go ahead. You're not too little.
You know cows don't find calves in hollow logs.
The cows won't be much further.
                                Go ahead.

You're past the purple ironweeds.
You're under the sweetgums along the east branch:
where
        like you
                    snakes go to bed early.
Only—they don't still see the sun. They sleep
their own dark and smile.

Go ahead. You're a big boy.
                            Your tall brother
is with you. The cows can't be much further.
The branch is dry now. Wade the warm sand.

    The snakes won't uncoil.

ROSALIE BURKES DANIELS

Ballad of the Sandrock

Dusk broomsage whispers
gray/red of hills that
blend into black/bleached
Lobutcha swamp of
loam creekbottoms where
crawfish work in the night
raising bubbly towers
    or back slow
through shallow waters
filled with hornyheads—
little fish left over
from that virgin age.

They sweep flecked white sand
with fan of fin pink/red
gills torn with bent pins
guts filled with
dragonflies & puny worms
dropped from
Nanih Waiya willow
under wild rose sun.

Biloxi Beach Drama

The moon,
silver tomcat,
struts across the still night—
the waves, disturbed, throw nightcaps
at him.

JEAN DAVIDSON

Constellations

The scrim stretched from post to post
across the path where the gate should be,
shivered with the force of each word we whispered
as we knelt close to the small brown spider
(we called it "she") who wove her opalescent maze
with frenetic chasing like a violinist's fingers,
as if she were inspired by a Vivaldi opus to spring
and nothing so mundane as the need for a place
to catch and eat her supper.

One high, sustained note pulled our eyes toward the hill
where what we thought was a copse of briars
swayed and blossomed into several camouflage-suited gnomes
(the gnomes were our children, missing since noon)
who zigged and zagged down the wooded path
in a protean gambol led by my red dog Toro,
the youngsters' hair glazed a uniform yellow by the shaft
of sunlight which had wedged through the cover of leaves
only seconds before.

Our wanderers joined hands and swerved into one
perfect question mark before they uncurled
and slid toward camp on the backs of their gridded heels,
a haze of dust against the web as I yelled "Watch out!"
And in the next instant the lattice, still intact, shimmered
like an aurora in a wake of solar wind and the spider
paused for a wink in her almost completed hub.
Then I was knocked off-balance and became part of a
thrashing, bellowing, disheveled lump of folks.

Boot, nose, canteen, hand, we jostled ourselves
into circles within circles around the campfire
which simmered our evening meal of bread and stew.
"Are they real?" our small fry babbled. "Are they good?"
Red, green, blue-veined pebbles,
some with glints suggestive of gems,
spilled from their fleece-lined pockets into the space
which separated us from them.
We picked up each stone and rolled it in our palms.

We held each nugget high to catch the last rays of sun,
scrutinized them all through our magnifying glasses,
scraped them with our knives, touched their smooth planes
with our tongues to enhance subtle patterns
and fossils of shells from an ancient sea.
"Jasper," we pronounced. "Copper, azurite, pyrite, mica."
"All real," we promised. "All good."
"But is there gold," the youngsters fretted, "or silver?"
And they abandoned the treasures in favor of stew.

Later we rested in down-filled bags, warm and plump around us,
tarpaulin screens secured to pine trees
to shelter us from the night wind;
and we watched for meteors, traced our fingers
from star to star to find the constellations:
Orion the Hunter, dog at his heel, the Big Dipper, the Pleiades;
and I recited myths I had heard which explained their being.
Then the children concocted new patterns and stories,
combinations growing more outrageous as they rambled on and on.

I was about to comment on all the things we never see
but think we see because of the trails they leave
when I looked at Toro who snuggled close, his head on my arm,
and he raised his head to look back at me.
Cricket and frog sounds had begun to crescendo,
and the fire which was down to one ember popped and hissed.
Instead of speaking I closed my eyes, burrowed deep
into my nest, and listened to my breath as it mingled
with that of my dog and of my sisters, nieces, nephews

scattered on the dark ground around me.

L. C. DORSEY

Silent Communication

Today I saw a poem—
    a funny white female poem
riding on the 14th St. Bus.
She looked out of place—
    but not because of her white
face.

It was her orange hair
and clothes in Black.
It was her black and green
eye make up.
It was her diaper-pin
earrings.
But most importantly,
the difference was the
yellow diaper pin
fastened through her cheek.

Now people on the 14th
Street buses are not generally
readers.
We are lookers.
But today everyone's head
was buried in a book
or magazine
or newspaper;
As if to say that they
did not find orange hair
and a diaper pinned
cheek quite extraordinary.
But then He got on the
bus.
Circa: Junior High
Reality: Black down to
earthism.
He checked out the orange
hair.
His face was a study
in confusion, disbelief, and
awe.
Like wow! A diaper
pin through the cheek!
Reality touched him:
But that's not right?
Does it hurt?
He touched his cheek.
He turned his attention
to the rest of the passengers.
What is this?
Everyone was reading!!
He looked around frantically

as he silently screamed for someone to
check out the lady with
the orange hair! Check out
the diaper pinned cheek!

He looked for affirmation
of his sanity.

His desperate eyes met
mine.

The silent questions
were there.

Silently I gave him
the answer:

"You are O.K. and I am
O.K."

"The orange hair is
not part of our
reality"

"The people on the
bus see her, but they
refuse to give her the
satisfaction of acknow-
ledging her orange hair
or her diaper pinned
cheek."

His eyes told me
that he understood.

We both watched the
orange hair studiously ignore
our stares until he left the bus.

He waved to me from the
sidewalk.

The orange hair got off next.
I hoped he'd catch the
bus and I could find out
his name.

I never saw him again.

Sybil Pittman Estess

The Country Idiot

Not many remember him anymore, my cousin
who had epileptic fits in the bottoms of holes
and other abysses he had to be in
by necessity—like the life he was in
with no means to control. No medicine
that they could pay for or wanted to know about
for their son named Leon in that land, at that time.
Now that he is little more than a vague memory,
I still see the country men taunt him
to climb down the fresh-dug well
late that night. He swallowed his tongue
and his mouth foamed
when the loud crowd turned its head. I remember
the giggles, the jests, and how he grinned afterward,
as if having come through some trial,
some accomplishment. And it was:
his mere living. Another extravagance
from my red rural past—like my grandmother's house
with no bathroom, no electricity;
like the king snake she found in her dresser drawer once.
And like Leon's two brothers, also dead: one in a carwreck,
drunk doing ninety; the other burned
in the gasoline housefire.
(He only wanted to clean the paintbrushes
near the heater.) Each grave has a picture by their
mother, my aunt. I was seven
and fresh from town when I fled,
so late, from Leon in black water
to grandmother's bedside for her to cover
my eyes from Leon whom I hated,
Leon, who never missed Sunday School
once in his thirty-one years. Full mid-moons,
now I fear him.

WINIFRED HAMRICK FARRAR

Remember Corn Fields?

Remember corn sprouts silvery green in spring—
Teasing invitations to jays and crows—
And weird concoctions created to ring
Our fields, protect the newly mounded rows
From greedy beaks? Do you remember the stalks
With their blue-green leaves, broad sibilant tongues,
Sighing, whispering, their silky songs on our walks
Down the path while we swore the corn had lungs?
Remember too the raspy sound of dry
Blades rubbing themselves in sorrowing wind
In late September under leadening sky
When we walked at twilight feeling the end
Come on? Remember shivering with the chill,
Dreading something awesome beyond our will?

WILLIAM FAULKNER

Mississippi Hills: My Epitaph

Far blue hills, where I have pleasured me,
Where on silver feet in dogwood cover
Spring follows, singing close the bluebird's "Lover!"
When to the road I trod an end I see,

Let this soft mouth, shaped to the rain,
Be but golden grief for grieving's sake,
And these green woods be dreaming here to wake
Within my heart when I return again.

Return I will! Where is there the death
While in these blue hills slumbrous overhead
I'm rooted like a tree? Though I be dead,
This soil that holds me fast will find me breath.

The stricken tree has no young green to weep
The golden years we spend to buy regret.
So let this be my doom, if I forget
That there's still spring to shake and break my sleep.

From A Green Bough

We sit drinking tea
Beneath the lilacs on a summer afternoon
Comfortably, at our ease
With fresh linen on our knees,
And we sit, we three
In diffident contentedness
Lest we let each other guess
How happy we are
Together here, watching the young moon
Lying shyly on her back, and the first star.

There are women here:
Smooth-shouldered creatures in sheer scarves, that pass
And eye us strangely as they pass.
One of them, our hostess, pauses near:
—Are you quite all right, sir? she stops to ask.
—You are a bit lonely, I fear.
Will you have more tea? cigarettes? No?—
I thank her, waiting for her to go:
To us they are like figures on a masque.
—Who?—shot down
Last spring—Poor chap, his mind
. . . . doctors say . . . hoping rest will bring—
Busy with their tea and cigarettes and books
Their voices come to us like tangled rooks.
We sit in silent amity.

—It was a morning in late May:
A white woman, a white wanton near a brake,
A rising whiteness mirrored in a lake;
And I, old chap, was out before the day
In my little pointed-eared machine,
Stalking her through the shimmering reaches of the sky.
I knew that I could catch her when I liked
For no nymph ever ran as swiftly as she could.
We mounted, up and up
And found her at the border of a wood:
A cloud forest, and pausing as its brink
I felt her arms and her cool breath.
The bullet struck me here, I think
In the left breast

And killed my little pointed-eared machine. I saw it fall
The last wine in the cup. . . .
I thought that I could find her when I liked,
But now I wonder if I found her, after all.

One should not die like this
On such a day,
From angry bullet or other modern way.
Ah, science is a dangerous mouth to kiss.

One should fall, I think, to some Etruscan dart
In meadows where the Oceanides
Flower the wanton grass with dancing,
And, on such a day as this
Become a tall wreathed column: I should like to be
An ilex on an isle in purple seas.
Instead, I had a bullet through my heart—

—Yes, you are right:
One should not die like this,
And for no cause nor reason in the world.

'Tis well enough for one like you to talk
Of going in the far thin sky to stalk
The mouth of death: you did not know the bliss
Of home and children; the serene
Of living and of work and joy that was our heritage.
And, best of all, of age.
We were too young.
Still—he draws his hand across his eyes
—Still, it could not be otherwise.

We had been
Raiding over Mannheim. You've seen
The place? Then you know
How one hangs just beneath the stars and sees
The quiet darkness burst and shatter against them
And, rent by spears of light, rise in shuddering waves
Crested with restless futile flickerings.
The black earth drew us down, that night
One of the bullet-tortured air:
A great black bowl of fireflies. . . .
There is an end to this, somewhere:
One should not die like this—

One should not die like this.
His voice has dropped and the wind is mouthing his words
While the lilacs nod their heads on slender stalks,
Agreeing while he talks,
Caring not if he is heard or is not heard.
One should not die like this.
Half audible, half silent words
That hover like gray birds
About our heads.

We sit in silent amity.
I am cold, for now the sun is gone
And the air is cooler where we three
Are sitting. The light has followed the sun
And I no longer see
The pale lilacs stirring against the lilac-pale sky.

They bend their heads toward me as one head.
—Old man—they say—How did you die?

I—I am not dead.

I hear their voices as from a great distance—Not dead
He's not dead, poor chap; he didn't die—

JACK FENWICK

Reverend Cole's Epistle

In a frozen field fifteen miles out of town,
We worked through a gray morning,
And at noon,
Laid down our axes and hooks
Between the smoking brushfires.

A small church stood nearby,
Derelict in the weather,
A cabin of God, deserted,
With no lock on the door.
We took refuge there from the wind,

And sat on rough boards with lunch pails
And thermos jugs.
I went to the pulpit,

Looking around for some sign of sheltering hope
For weatherbeaten prayers.

The pulpit was a board
Nailed on a two by four,
Primitive as the manger and stable,
And a folded piece of paper
Was wedged in a crack,

Left there by some lonely pastor,
Like a letter in a bottle
Drifting through winter in that sacred shack.
The note was as crude as the place.
I had to patch words to read it:

"I come," the preacher said
With his painful pencil, "and I come on time.
Sorry none of you are here.
Hope we get together someday
And work for Christ. In His love. Reverend Cole."

WILLIAM FERRIS

For Amanda Gordon

who

killed: Possum with hoe,
At night,
Alone.

sewed: Colored worlds with,
Scraps,
From cloth of white and black people,
Their shirts, sacks, curtains,
Frozen together.
From perch in Hamer Bayou—gold.
From evening sun—blood red.
From storm—purple.
Her vision of hours pieced together.

sang: Ring the bell, I done got over.
I done got over at last.
My knees been quainted with the morning dew.

Head been bent in the valley too.
Her song.
Her song by birthright.

stood: Statue tall,
Eye fixed,
And rang sound and color together in final statement.

CHARLES HENRI FORD

"One day, one day"

One day, one day
calls the other days away.

Not as the dog of morning
trees the cat of afternoon;

but as watching time in a well
sink with its arms around the moon.

One moon, one face,
to other suns and jaws give place.

The Overturned Lake

Blue unsolid tongue, if you could talk,
the mountain would supply the brain;
but mountains are mummies: the autobus and train,
manmade worms, disturb their centuries.
Tongue of a deafmute, the lake
shudders, inarticulate.

You are like the mind of a man, too:
surface reflecting the blue day,
the life about you seemingly organized, revolving about you,
you as a center.
but I am concerned in your overthrow:
I should like to pick you up, as if you were a woman of water,
hold you against the light and see your veins flow
with fishes; reveal the animal-flowers that rise
nightlike beneath your eyes.

Noiseless as memory, blind as fear,
lake, I shall make you into a poem,
for I would have you unpredictable as the human body:
I shall equip you with the strength of a dream,
rout you from your blue unconscious bed,
overturn your unconcern,
as the mind is overturned by memory, the heart by dread.

Somewhat Monday

there is a hill here and the green blades slyly with nostalgia
a mockingbird says *aw now aw now* with eyes congealing drops of sweat

i find no fault with the snakes lovely
or why reproach a petal for its perfectness
there are worse things than a hawk's swiftness
there is an icy image latent and the phlegm of drudgery in
throats and throats

Reptilia

The way a tongue darts from a crack in chaos. The way nothing is ever the same. The way you do what you find yourself doing. The way nothing matters. The way sleep rusts the soul. The way nothing is ever understood. The way sleep sharpens time. The way nothing happens. The way she poisons a cup of coffee. The way nothing can help. The way he walks. The way nothing was said. The way babies are born. The way nothing changes. The way it starts to rain. The way nothing could be done. The way to make love. The way nothing stays still. The way roads go winding. The way nothing remains.

The Dead Spring

By whose order does the drizzling eye,
A winter wound shrinking in the glare of spring,
Fix the game blood galloping, galloping
From head to foot of the sad spraddling farm?

Let the smoke flurry though it leave the lungs
Crisp as cinders, charred as twin stars
Lured from their orbit by the voice of the void.
Let the clouds play as if nothing were decaying!

I sing the dead spring fooling us all with flowers.
I praise the gruesome hour,
Fascinated by the dangle of its own bones' music,
And the wind, that infinite corpse
Whose ghost is now perfume, now rot.

I am sure I heard the rat of death last night
Drilling the last door of the heart's desire.
I am sure that he will get what he was grinding for.
Spring is not my cat.

JOHN P. FREEMAN

A Barn in the Morning Light

Across the field the early sunlight blows
Like a hot wind fanning the barn.
Along the east wall the planks brighten.
The leeward side remains dormant in shadows.

Light dances on the corrugations
Of the roof as on ripples of pond water,
As though the heart shimmered with fire,
Or currents of brilliance arced across the brain.

And yet we know more than one side of things:
The sun scalds its portion of the sky,
A flaming mouth whose breath blisters the eye
Or skin it touches. Paint is peeling

Back from the boards, exposing the undercoat.
The far wall grudgingly lets go of night.
As the sun rises, shadows shift their brute
Weight around, away from the heat of light.

The Sycamore

Nothing else in nature could seem
as bleached as the dead sycamore
towering over the sweet gums
and beeches by my neighbor's creek.

When I first noticed the tree, I thought
it had its own kind of beauty:

the stark clarity of its form
exposed, the solid strength of trunk.

But I never saw a bird's nest;
there was no foliage to shelter
the young from the sun or predators.

And as the months passed, I missed
the seasonal greens and golds. It stood
white as bones whether violets bloomed
around it, or black-eyed Susans, or gentians.
It was in the grip of perpetual winter.

One day I crossed the field and stood
by its roots, and looked up into bare
limbs from which the background blue
of the sky was falling away forever.

RICHARD FREIS

The Beach Hotel

As civil as a sky by Tiepolo,
these brilliancies of gold and white and blue
pavillion formal gaieties below.

Sand and scrub Versailled: a turfy view,
a tailored esplanade of lawn, thick
walled against the sea's ferocious hue.

The slatted palms' cicada whirr-and-click
spins thin gold for the ear, spills latticed light,
a drifting tesselation; on the brick

umbrellas diagram ellipses, bright
shade, where patient fathers mime dismay
as children breast tame waters in delight.

Only the braided snakes of light at play
beneath the pleated surface of the pool
blaze shapelessness, as if tides ebbed away

had stranded on fixed coasts of will and rule
blind beasts of dream. Their phosphorescent dance
enciphers there in random, bright renewal

the sea's fierce reveries of change, of chance.

Tornado Warning

Immobile in thick air
the trees rest, leaf on leaf;
fixed as a photograph
we sit, hushed with fatigue.

Wind soft as the break
of light on leaf and skin,
directionless, gathers.
We shiver in the calm.

Abrupt, on the mute air
a siren etches fear:
we wait upon a headland
along the edge of storm.

The air roughens, hoarse;
the sky congeals to black;
thunder cracks like cannon;
rain flails like the sea.

Wind, water, thunder
mock identity;
form blurs back to chaos,
landmarks slide away.

Ruin's ancient voice
hovers on the pulse.
As bearings disappear
we crouch in shaken earth.

ELLEN GILCHRIST

Sharecropper

I receive from the landlady seeds tools stock
credit for food and usable living quarters
In her son's arms for hours I stop dying
My shack has cardboard windows
A kitchen without knives
When you get free come running over the roads
third porch from the fork
the one with the jukebox

the old grave half-crazy dog
asleep by the screen
If I am away wait in the swing
look in the milkcan for a message
I'll be down by the river
washing fingerprints from my dresses

The Best Meal I Ever Had Anywhere

At the wonderful table of my grandfather
Bunky got the high chair
Dooley got the Webster's Unabridged Dictionary
and I got the Compton's Pictured Encyclopedia
Volumes A, B, D, and E.

The best meal I ever had anywhere
was one Sunday Pierce Noblin
wired the salt shaker to a dry cell battery
Dolly got a fishbone caught in her throat
and almost died
Sudie went into the parlor to sulk
and when no one was looking
I stabbed Bunky in the knee
with Onnie Maud's pearl handled wedding fork.

There Will Be Seven Fat Years

for Don Lee Keith

Pierce Noblin was the only boy
in Issaquena County to make
a skirt out of an umbrella.
He forced Melissa Harbison who is a cripple
to wear it in a play.
He told her if she didn't wear it
he would drown her in the river
with a crowbar for an anchor.

The play was the Old Testament.
Melissa played Uriah's wife
and doubled for a harem
in the closing scene.

The play was in a treehouse
Pierce stood out on a limb

with his arms folded
telling the Pharoah about this dream

and spread his flannel wings
and when
the first deus ex machina
in the Delta failed, he fell
and broke so many separate things
he got to spend the whole sixth grade
in Memphis, taking dope,
being fed from trays,
and writing off for autographs
from an automatic electric bed.

Where Deer Creek Runs Through Cary

Pierce Noblin and I sold snuff
at the store on Saturday.
We knew all the names by heart,
Bull Durham, Garrett's, Tube Rose.
Snuff came in tiny cans,
in drawstring bags,
in brown bottles.
I knew when I dipped
I would dip Sir Walter Raleigh
from a silver can, his plumed hat
in his aristocratic hand,
his scarlet cloak ready to drop
before the queen.

Baby Doll was there,
two hundred pounds of woman
with the pin that said, REMEMBER,
then a real pearl, HARBOR.

Our cousin Charlie ran the store.
He sold hair pomade
and ginger cookies from a bin.
On crowded afternoons
we let the German watchdog in.
Charlie stood by the cash register
cracking jokes, fingering the blackjack
that lay beneath the folding money
in a velvet sack.

SID GRAVES

H. Desoto: Notes from a Diary

Environs of Quizquiz, Mississippi (1541):
As an object lesson and Necessity,
Thirty warriors were decapitated
Nineteen women raped and
Twelve kept

The torch put to temple and town hall
Or to that part thereof which would catch

Grain taken eaten fed to horses and hog
Destroyed or sullied
A half dozen boys misused
Several score scattered with their faster sisters
Four left dead more mutilated

Twenty men branded
Eight dismembered six garroted
A quantity flogged. . . .
> *We call, now, a city & a nightclub*
> *With your given, a county and car*
> *With your surname and you a hero*
> *Whose course, like history,*
> *Is charted in varied accounts*
> *As true vein of blood*
> *In truth's own torn body.* ○

DOUGLAS GRAY

Mosquito Man

It was a time when only insects,
plants and children thrived—
August, blazing hound star nights.
Roaches swam in lemonade pitchers;

hydrangas swarmed around the porch.
Grownups limp in chairs and suits
fanned themselves with the evening news.
No meals were cooked and no beds made,
since no one slept. Outside, at liberty,

we played war from moonrise to moonset,
smeared ourselves with real blood.
Black, white and Choctaw,
country club churchgoer and pulp mill hand
scratched at the common itch.

One hero stalked among us: Mosquite Man,
the fog-maker who brought
the best and only dreams.
We never saw his face

but Wednesdays in the droning Mississippi dusk
he came billowing clouds of DDT.
Then how the neighborhood was changed—
the grass all gone,
pines, sky and houses blotted out.

It was battlefield or moor
or Heaven's Gate. The vision burned
at our eyes
as we ran lost to each other
and immune to home, that other life.

The Reluctance of Spring in Ohio

Back in Mississippi,
back in what used to be home,
the buds have already fallen from the trees
and are making nasty brown stains
on my mother's Toyota.
"I'm having to keep the doors to the house closed,"
she tells me, long distance,
"because all that awful yellow dust
keeps blowing in."
Winds howl through the wire,
as in the mouth of a cave,
and in the confusion of voices between
I hear a man say that his son's been released
from Parchman prison,
just in time for Easter.

In the early morning
the air is heavy with promise
hanging like a thread of spit from a cow's lips
that always seems about to break

in the wind
but never does.

At school, the student on the front row
wears a bowling jacket and talks through her nose
to the boy on crutches.
His sweatshirt reads EPISCOPAL WRESTLING.
Her voice rattles the windows of the room
like a strong gust rolling down from Lake Erie.
The buds on the trees outside
hang eerily still,
unchanged for a week now.

Just before the bell
the others shuffle in like convicts,
leaving the door open for latecomers.

ROBERT HAMBLIN

Requital

Old man.
I watch you straddle
the barbed fence,
ache yourself over,
limp through bitterweeds
and piles of manure
to the pond below.

I follow,
wrestling with fishing rods
and tackle box,
dutiful son
if no longer a child,
fitting my path once more
to the diminishing measure
of your step.

We are different now,
you see that as well as I.
Still, each year we return
to this place to enact
the ancient ritual.

Today, though,
I leave the fishing to you;
I have other game to catch.
Careless of the lure
bouncing quietly on the water,
I watch you across the narrow lake
and recall how once there was
between us more than water,
a gulf too wide for casting.

But that was long ago:
today I sit idly
and trace my sinking youth
in the wrinkled absolution
of your face, grateful
for the armistice of age,
the peace that somehow survives
the rage of passion and regret.

Like that bass there,
which you now lead thrashing
across the violent wave
and lift with still strong
and steady hands into
the splendid, sun-splashed air.

RABIUL HASAN

Night Blooms

1
For weeks I have shut myself away from you.
I shine like an old moon, my one-half always dark,
My other half I cannot see beyond the Mississippi Delta.
Chickweeds and lamb's-quarters sway around my yard,
Like them I live a life so treacherous without you.

2
Outside my study the stars weave into a frieze, a flambeau
In the sky. How wonderful to be staring
Into this deep, hollow and timeless space around, lost somewhere
In this churning sound and silence, and the body, starved,
Hunkered inside an old pickup hurtling down the driveway.

3
Minutes later I see them, with awe and delight,
Along the turnpike toward Greenville, Mississippi,
Outstretched for miles across the open fields,
Like fantastic monarchs, like shining swords,
My fair-haired mutes in the moonlight.

BROOKS HAXTON

Justice

I'll have to look up the name of the son of a bitch
Who tried to pick that fight in the locker room
With James Cole. James was a skinny black kid—
Half-pint smart-ass, like me—and we were friends
In a friendship that had to be complex
Since he was one of the first few black kids

In the all-white schools. Sometimes in homeroom,
Which was Chemistry Lab, we'd share a table
And snide remarks, and if some people thought
We were laughing at their expense, that was
Because we were. I remember a girl
From Teen Club came to collect donations

For the Homecoming Dance. I asked her, nodding
Toward James, were they keeping the niggers out.
She was embarrassed to say, and I
Was never again invited to Teen Club
Affairs, not even my own Graduation Dance,
Which I considered an honor not to attend.

James was getting dressed out, joking with me,
When the kid whose name I've forgotten said,
"You think you're hot shit." "No, man, I don't think
I'm any kind of shit, I swear." James wanted
To turn it into a joke, but he failed.
"I'd say you're shit." This almost syllogistical

Repartee was interrupted by Malcolm
Davis, with whom any life-loving redneck
Would not want to fuck. Yet Malcolm, though angry—
And he was losing his patience in general—

Kept his voice calm: "White trash," the locker room
Got quiet as catacombs, and Malcolm

And James were the only two black kids around,
"Why would you pick a fight with James here seeing
As James is so much smaller than you? Couldn't be
You're a coward, could it? A . . . peckerwood
Coward? I'm your size. You're not picking a fight
With me. Why is that, white trash? Might get hurt?

"Look. I put my hands behind my back, OK?
Now, you want to hit somebody, hit me."
What's-his-name, who seemed to have lost that sense
Of an imperative vengeance devolving
On him, now stammered excuses, backed off.
How did you get away with it, Malcolm,

Not to get away with it after all?
Was it three years later I saw you, saw
On the *Delta Democrat Times'* front page
After sentencing for armed robbery,
Fist overhead, your face? Manslaughter, was it?
The clerk at the Chinese grocery store died,

Or. . . ? Forget it, Malcolm. I can look it up.

Recess

I feel it now, that rage I felt at seven,
The time I wanted revenge on Larry Ables.
What did he do? I can remember only
My rage stalking the second-grade playground,
Clenching my fists to summon up the picture
Of Larry Ables in full repugnant detail.

He wasn't a bad-looking kid, not even
Detestably handsome. Tall and freckled,
Red-headed, with new jeans and a plaid shirt—
Country come to town, polite and shy.
Still I remember my fury, clenching
And unclenching my fists, furious with myself

For not knowing where I should hold my thumbs
When I punched him. That was it. With myself.
Larry might not have known he had done anything.
He kept playing freeze tag while I stalked.

And what could I do now? I didn't want
To hurt him or be hurt. I was afraid

Of how I felt, afraid to break the rules,
Afraid to call attention to myself,
Afraid what Mrs. Rowell would say, what
Other kids would think. I didn't want to care!
And my rage was as enormous and as painful
Even as fear. I tightened my lips

And told myself I would act in so daring,
So just, and so effective a way that no one
Would challenge my seven-year-old independence
Ever again. Not ever! Never! The bell
At the end of recess rang, and I stood
Under Mrs. Rowell's right hand, first in line.

I Live to See Strom Thurmond
Head the Judiciary Committee

Greenville rhymes with "teenful" in the native speech.
I belonged to the Teen Club there one year.
The Teen Club had been formed to keep school dances
White now that the schools were two percent
Desegregated. I knew that. I knew
It was inexcusable to belong,

But dances were the best place to take girls,
Still I hated the dances, and I quit.
At the Klan rally outside town one night,
Shelton, Grand Imperial Wizard, spoke.
I was there with integrationist friends.
We didn't call attention to ourselves,

But watched them burn a fifteen-foot-high cross
Wrapped in burlap and doused with gasoline.
There were women and children there in hoods
Picnicking under the flames, and smoke you could taste.
Shelton said that seven Jews in New York—
Who ran the world—had been sending firearms

To the Catholic priests in the South. Yeah,
The Catholics stored them all in the basements
Of churches, and then the beatniks and SNCC-
Working communists came to give the word

To the niggers to pick up their guns, and,
Brothers and sisters, in sweet Jesus' name,

Will you be there to stop that massacre
Now that we know the truth? Flames on the cross
Were dying along its arms, when somebody
Snipped the powerline to the stage, and the lights
And the mikes and speakers went dead, and people
Held guns in the dark when it started to rain.

The Conversion Shift

After he'd had the Hurst Conversion Shift
Put into our parents' Buick Special,
Ayres and his friend Dwight took Louis and me
Snake hunting one day on Old Warfield Road
Where the barrow pits were a garden for water snakes
And the road had a good quarter-mile strip marked off.

We'd been looking to catch a mud snake,
The red and yellow pattern on whose belly
Made it our most brilliantly marked species.
Having caught, though mud galore, no snake,
Louis, Dwight, and I were muddy enough
We couldn't ride in the car, so we perched

On the trunk lid, banked at an awful pitch,
With no toe-hold, and no hand-hold, and Ayres
Set about taking her through the gears. I sat
By Dwight, my redneck bodyguard from rednecks
Who would have been happy to pound the shit
Out of a nigger-lover like me, but knew Dwight,

Unlike me, weren't no nigger-lover and
Fought back. At the lunge into second gear
When I started to slide down losing my grip
On the chrome trim of the rear window, I
Asked Dwight, did he have a good hold? He said,
"No!" through clenched teeth. There was no question about it.

I was gliding down slowly away, hands
Slipping with mud to smear the coppery
Finish when we lunged into third. At what?
Ayres said the optimum speed for the shift
Into third was around fifty. Therefore,
At an optimum speed of, say, fifty or more,

I was about to touch down, backflip down
Old Warfield Road in hysterical fear.
Dwight watched my skidding hands accelerate
Into frenzy. Looks met one last time.
With what blue eyes love nearly threatening
Eked out my poor courage to say goodbye!

Pond

When the water scalded in the shallows
and the mud closed on our anklebones
while sunken leaves gave up the gas
of their long rotting underwater,
in a cow pond, horse pond, full of the flop and urine,
we would swim even when August
raised steam rank as the ripening of a body.

After a dry spell when the clay red surface
sank in and the deeper green tinged
water oak and live oak leaves reflected,
when the torso of the cottonmouth behind the stob of head wedge
curved twice into the zero visibility of one foot under,
turtles tilted in their disks of darkness
in and out of sight,
the elegant slider with red earmarks, stinkpot, cooter.

Cat with wide head narrowing into body,
largemouth big as a newborn, bluegill, punkinseed,
the minnows everywhere, the tadpoles,
gnats in tall clouds, cruising dragonflies,
the damselflies adrift and horseflies circling,
skaters, striders, over the water scorpion's slow motion,
plunge of the diving beetle, giant waterbug (that prowler,
one-fanged, forelegs built to spring their deathtrap on a fingerling),
bullbats striking the double trail across still water with their wingtips—

into this the pack of us boys went splashing, laughing, shrieking curses,
down the bank where Zion's congregation
sanctified these waters with baptizing,
sang hymns, preached waist deep with white robe floating,
where in worship children of my mother's father's grandfather's slaves'
   children
still on that same bank stood witness, witnessed also
by jackmule, jenny, bull and steer,
mare and foal, and turkey buzzard miles up circling,

witnessed by the little bossman in the congregation,
witnessed fear struck in a child's eye when the large hand closed
on mouth and nose to pull her under.
"No!" the eye said,
but she went down backwards, bending backward at the knee,
the waist, resisting, stiff, she could not swim,
but gave herself into the preacher's hands,
she clutched his wrist, hands bound, was taken under,
and the congregation did not speak,
the preacher looked down at the surface,
and O Lord we saw where she was gone
into the mud cloud in the water. Gone.
Her mother wept. I wept. I did not know her.
Gone too long. Gone one whole second. And another
second. Second. And the congregation went down
in our souls we went down in broad daylight
where we could not breathe
we held ourselves too long
too long till she rose up again and all saw
she was shaken
O Lord
by the Power
all stood shaken by the Power
which with first breath broke among us
into the sung praises.

Down that same bank now in cut-offs, tearing into the water,
rousing cattle egret, killdeer, kingfisher,
and green and great blue heron,
watched by the indifferent mule and mallard,
by the suspicious goose, we
hedonists of twelve, of thirteen, fourteen, fifteen,
came to swim.

we the guilty children, smokers of cross vine, trumpet vine,
dried corn silk, coffee, smokers of the bad cigar shoplifted,
keepers of hidden knowledge
we cult worshippers of forbidden pictures,
car thieves, kleptos, came, unbridled,
watched by draft horse, by beef cattle, watched
by nanny goat with two weeks' kid for our next Cajun cookout,
cut loose from our parents, came to swim,

where, Fafa warned us, one boy drowned when they were little,
died not understanding in the eighteen hundreds what occurred

was for the sake of stories to be told us lately
although none of us would drown or ever die
so that the boy's death had been truly pointless
which would ever be incomprehensible to elders
more so the more serious the Presbyterian
until the world was lost on deacons
such as he
who said interminable grace at breakfast.

So we listened
and tore straight down into the pond
where we would dive for bottom
where the dead boy was
my now dead grandfather's lost friend
inhabitant of the cold
that gave us gooseflesh even in the heat of August
keeper of the soft mud melting from the hand
before it made the surface
child mired where the oak limbs snap that dull snap
under the drone of engines worked into
and over the near country
under the hot world cold in an impenetrable darkness.

Landscape with Figures

Lonely white boy home from college takes big family car,
Takes Leica, takes light meter, drives far off, far out, far,
Far from town, takes county roads, takes time, late afternoon,
To watch midwinter light change, sees black girl on foot alone.

Vast, empty, flat, straight-furrowed, flat, flat land,
All four ways barren to the dark fringe of horizon scant
with locust brake and brake of baldy cypresses.
West one mile, straight, down two-lane blacktop, her house is,

A shack. Bare chinaberry tree in front with tire on rope,
Distant one mile, is in detail visible. Her school bus stop,
Back east one mile where this road humps up into that,
Is visible. Midway they meet. *Where this white boy at?*

She waits while he rolls down the window till he says, "Hello.
Mind if I take your picture?" She means yes, still she's screaming,
    "No! No! No! No! No!"

Breakfast ex Animo

The red-tailed hawk perched in the toothache tree by the front porch
Faces me over morning coffee.
Three deer sail through the back row of sweet corn,
Clear the top strand of barbed wire,
Take five quick bounds apiece in the dewberry briars,
And break into the dark woods each with two flicks of her tail.
The coons retire from their crimes at the hint of dawn,
Still there is one dragging a cornstalk through the fence backwards
With both hands.
On the powerline two doves coo aloud, chortle to themselves,
And resume necking.
Venus rises.
The armadillo that lives under the woodpile
Cruises the Jerusalem artichokes for tubers.
"I'm helpless before coffee," I confess to the hawk,
Who recalls,
Miles down, on some hillside,
Some fool avenging himself on nature
With his pump-action twelve-gauge,
Me.
Taking flight with a pounce towards me,
She veers low into the close growth of the gulley
With slow strokes
Maneuvering
Through thickets where no bird that big could fly
While one aerodynamically unfeasible housefly
Dive-bombs my scrambled eggs.
Aurora,
Readying herself in the black treetops,
Releases her long waves of light
In the limpid ultramarine
Like a red laden brushtip touched to one edge of a wet page
And the cock goes crazy.
Can't the frizzly rooster announce dawn to the frizzly hen
Without heralding doomsday
Or the shambles?
"So much, doves, for the bucolic breakfast,"
I nod, grabbing my cane
As I round the corner for the henhouse,
Where,
According to the rooster,
Snakes, foxes, nutrias, and opossums contend,

And the catamount routs all for the spoils,
But the catamount,
Alias bobcat, alias painter, screaming painter, alias lynx,
Whether in ectoplasm or the flesh,
Rarely shows his small, sleek, whiskery, malignant head,
Although one centenarian neighbor of mine,
Henry Davis,
On sleepless nights the final five years of his life,
Could hear, far off, a painter scream
In the old peach grove near Second Creek
Where his and his first wife's house used to stand,
And where their twelve—sometimes he said twenty—
Children were born.
Back at the obstreperous henhouse,
I spot atop the gatepost
A Komodo dragon-like lizard, three inches long,
And he spots me,
He does eight rapid push-ups while his neck puffs out
Until a pink madras coin protrudes under his chin.
The staccato puck puck puck scream
Keeps repeating itself inside the tiny coop
While outside,
Having latched the gate,
I stand still,
Bois d'arc cane in my right hand,
Momentarily to collect my wits.
No, I am not awake.
I come barefoot, prepared to meet a rattlesnake,
Ready to beat mama possum with a cane,
When any numbskull would have boots on and a gun.
Wait.
The weathered, guttered, knotty, foot-wide
Cypress planks of the henhouse,
Streaked before sunrise with dew,
Might well admit a snake,
A small nutria, not to starve,
Could claw, gnaw, scuttle, and squeeze in,
But no possum, I'll assume, and doubtless not the lynx.
The chickenyard scent of guano and dust soaked with dew rises
While all Earth is still,
Wind, pond water, dark woods,
Cloudless blue, green, rose depth in the East,

All still,
Except, inside the carpentered box, behind the rustic wooden latch,
The puck puck puck scream and loud beating of clipped wings
Invisibly made by the frizzly rooster with horrific regularity
As by the works of an apocalyptic metronome.
The frizzly hen looked fine last night,
Hypnotized,
When I lifted her to add four eggs to half-a-dozen she had laid.
Six days ago I put the porcelain doorknob in her nest,
Imperishable egg, to make her set,
And she, obediently fecund, far, albeit, from intelligent, complied,
Now while I turn the latch and while the frizzly rooster evokes
Erebus, Nemesis, Nyx, and all their cohorts,
The dire demiurges of the dark,
I conjure scenes of mayhem:
Friz, her saucy, tousled head
Drooped on the near rim of the nest,
The mangled neck,
Her viscera depending from an open side
Upon the doorknob and remains of eggs,
While her assassin,
Valuable pelt all caked with slime,
The nutria—to an Araucan, coypu, here, the devil rat—
Springs effortlessly from her nest
To scurry,
A tight squeeze,
Out the same hole where he weaseled in.
But nutrias don't eat eggs,
Much less kill hens.
I crack the door,
And while the rooster screams his head off
I deliberate.
The striking range of the pit viper—
Whose heat-sensitive pits,
Behind the eyes,
By now would have detected my warmth
On the far side of the door—
The striking range, I say, of this pit viper—
Whether moccasin or rattlesnake—
Equals the extension of the letter S suspended in the upheld neck
Or one third the spine's length from head to tail.
The longest rattler I've seen had twelve rattles
And he measured more than six feet,

A foot longer than myself at that time
When we hunted rats in the same barn.
The morning we met I took aim
And blew the knothole out between his eyes
With one puff of long rifle rat shot.
Now, to that snake's equal, coiled on Friz's nest,
An eyeball at the crack of this door
Is no kindred creature
But a target,
As the apparition of the head's wedge was to me,
Reared,
One yard from my knee,
The flickering, olfactory tongue tasting my flesh
In the calm heat,
Each brow bone, arch for an obsidian pebble set in gold,
When an unearthly trill
Ascended
From the shaken tail
On freezing spiral tracks around my spine.
I tear open the door
And the frizzly rooster barrels past my leg into the yard crying,
"PAHCK puck puck puck puck puck
PAHCK puck puck puck puck
PAHCK puck puck
PAHCK puck puck puck."
He runs and his head bobs
While his legs volley his speeding bulk around the yard,
Wings flapped for balance,
And his holding pattern looks like the collision course of an electron
In the wrong shell,
But I can't be bothered,
Because—
Though with Friz frozen
On the head of the snake
I can't tell which kind,
Diamondback rattlesnake, or gray rat snake, or copperhead—
I know
That the jaw,
Having unhinged itself,
Is at work to swallow or let go of that last egg
So he can leave,
Because snakes listen for vibrations,
And he,
His belly's auditory membrane to the ground,

Has known
Since I first twisted the latch
That I am here.
Friz cocks her unkempt, characteristic frizzly's head,
Not stirring feather one below the neck,
And catches me with a quick beaded look
That says,
"Hold it, peabrain
If this son of a bitch is deadly
The one dead will be me,"
And her gaze plunges
Like that of some frizzly prophet
Surveying
From Moab
Judah to the utmost sea.
What's visible,
With drab chains of geometry draped down its length,
Too red to be a rattlesnake,
The wrong shade for a copperhead
Too fat to be a copperhead too,
I'm nearly certain,
Is a gray rat snake,
Although a copperhead could be that fat
Pregnant,
She, the most treacherous of the pit vipers,
Being the unsnake-like one
Who bears an already poisonous brood of six alive.
I feel certain that it is a gray rat snake,
Yet while heaven goes red
On a blue field etched with small violet clouds,
Though nearly certain,
I still wait
Until I see the head.
Friz meanwhile seems to have attained satori,
Or at least the sorrowful, rapt look
Mary gives
In the annunciations
Where she's said to have foreseen the Passion,
Which leaves me as an annunciating angel
Flourishing a bois d'arc wand for lilies,
And the snake, apparently, must be the dove.
The rooster's quiet outside
And the customary doves call.
Miles off

An early lumber truck winds down toward first gear
On Springfield Hill.
Inside an east-facing henhouse blanched cypress boards redden.
I begin to doubt
My savoir faire with snakes,
Because this one has had time to drop egg
And haul ass
And here he is.
I pin his back with one end of the bois d'arc wand
And simultaneously
Out of nest and shadow
Emerge head and anfractuous tail,
Fangless, without rattles,
To investigate and wrest off the cane.
I can relax.
Even when he rears to strike
And vibrates his tailtip
Between dry cypress boards,
Aping his more musical cousin,
Even though he must be five feet long,
I know
That he's all show
And when I reach to take hold of his neck
He wallops into my left thumb so hard
The impact jars my hand,
And he hangs on.
In criminal code
Assault is the mere threat
And battery, the beating,
But to be hypnotized and bitten
Before breakfast
By enormous
(Even nonpoisonous)
Snakes
Is no crime
But a nightmare.
In the nightmare,
While the yawning head glides
Toward my knuckle
An officious, cosmopolitan agent in the brain
Transmits, without authority,
Alarming messages
To the incredulous, provincial muscles of the thumb.

"Out of the way, boys. Withdraw. Watch out now! Dodge! It's . . ."
The gray rat snake,
Here in his capacity as chicken snake,
Having acted in a tour de force
As thumb snake,
Writhes off the crane,
Lets my thumb go,
And heads out the knothole beside Friz's nest,
Not hurriedly,
Nor with malevolent phlegm,
Like the pit viper,
But with fluid and exact economy
Until the swallowed egg a foot behind his head sticks.
On both sides of my knuckle
Horseshoe-shaped rows of toothpricks
Leak like the riddles from six dozen lancets
Until red drops drop from my thumbtip
Onto the red tinted dust floor.
Day breaks.
Phoebus squeaks by the horizon.
The snake battles in vain to break the swallowed egg,
In vain
Because the egg is not an egg,
Is nothing to be swallowed,
Is
The antique porcelain doorknob from Friz's nest.
Below the flattened ovoid bulge
The metal stem stands out,
Drawing the cream-colored skin of the belly so taut
That scales bend,
Separate,
And the convexity
At the rounded head of a small subcutaneous screw
Shows.
Darwin would have deemed this feeding pattern
Maladaptive,
Hence unlikely to enhance the species,
Save by proving fatal,
Thus removing feeble genes from the genetic pool.
Failed long since as a naturalist,
I learn
That the henhouse I built in the wilderness
Is not less
Than Plato's Cave,

And the oblivious serpent therein eats the bogus egg
Only to find his way prevented
By the very implement of release.
My thumb smarts, still I feel profound.
The snake looks unenlightened though,
And who knows
How callus-, fur-, and talon-eating enzymes
Handle doorknobs, if at all?
The four-foot rope of unavailing muscle writhes,
And when I grab the knob in my right hand
The body, looping my wrist,
Spirals up my forearm
Like a bullwhip
Wrapping itself around a post.
Pressing the knob to the knothole
So the head can't come inside,
While cool, peristaltic ripples fill my palm,
And coils tightening on my forearm
Call to mind
The reputation of the rat snake as constrictor,
I begin to smell
The newly released smear of musk
Fortified with guano
Lacing the air.
Day is full-fledged.
Clear light strikes the bleeding thumb
From which a warm drop plummets
Onto the bare, sensitive ramp of the left foot.
I tug the knob,
But the snake latches himself on the far side of the board
And the scales
Caught in the cypress's grain
Tear with a dry whisper.
I try twisting the knob
And the snake comes unlatched
By what looks like a mechanical function
Absorbed from the doorknob's former life, as,
In one groundbreaking experiment,
Worms "learned"
The reticulum of an unfamiliar maze
By eating other worms
That had learned first hand,
Or

As the reader of a poem
May be said to learn
The arcanum of the gray rat snake at dawn
Without bothering to acquire
The bitten thumb.
I pin the head now with the cane in my left hand
And take hold of the neck.
Friz,
Who has kept put,
Angling her gaze with pert accuracy,
Watches me back out,
Snake upheld in the wilderness,
And begins shifting her eggs
For an even seat.
Summer leaves and grassblades revel
In the early light
To the revival music of an insect orchestra
Performing the most recent overture
To their serenade.
Traffic picks up on the Liberty Road.
In the spirit of things
I go down through the woods
Past flower- and thorn-bearing vines
Into the dark tangle of choked weeds
To celebrate
The ceremonial release of the gray rat snake at dawn,
And on the clay floor where the shadows are,
Where the cool mist hangs,
I leave him,
Motionless and alert.
He could die.
He could come back.
He could learn
Never to steal eggs from a frizzly hen.
And the doorknob, like Jonah
When God took pity on him and Nineveh,
Could be found in mullein
Near dewberry bushes in bloom, or purpled with sweet fruit,
By some untraveled cowpath,
Probably not.
Probably,
When I get back to the front porch,
One fly

Will be sampling the congealed grease on my scrambled eggs,
And the armadillo that lives under the woodpile
Will be sleeping.
The doves will have alighted elsewhere,
And the coon, gone.
Venus will have slipped into the blue folds of translucent sky,
And I will find myself at breakfast,
And begin.

KENNETH HOLDITCH

Red Clay

Standing in this city garden
sipping tea in strange company,
something—the smell of moss?
the mole on that girl's cheek?
that whistle of a distant train?—
has turned me back and in and . . .

And so we stand again upon the hill,
for whom this time (that time) I cannot see—
"Hill of Heaven" Cousin Someone called it
(near to heaven, Uncle said, as I will ever be)—
almost two score years ago
and I a child.

So real: the embracing smells: new shoes (Red Goose)
and new turned earth (red clay)
which I can almost reach to touch,
to crumble in my boy hands,
and Brother West intoning Calvinistic grief,
some woman's sob, and wind, cold,
echoing grief in the cedars . . .

But look away from assembled kinsmen,
above and under ground and in between,
across the valley to the north,
the pines, devoured by kudzu vines,
the wilderness beyond—

Until the first explosion of the clods upon the box,
then all and each again interred
safely within the mounded past.

JOYCE HOLLINGSWORTH-BARKLEY

Old Mag

The first black woman
I ever knew
came in the back door
of Granma's kitchen.

I touched her hand
and looked at my finger.

Born the year of
the Surrender
was the only birth date
she could remember
as she muttered over
turnip greens in the sink
or grumped her way
to the ironing board,
her sword tongue switching
inside her teeth.

Old Mag,
why are you so mean?
Why do you swat at me
when I reach for tea cakes
to stomach ache on
in the Chinaberry tree?

Why are your eyes
gnarled like that
when I'm sitting
on the doorstep
and it's time for you
to throw out dishwater?

Is it because I wondered
if you'd rub off on me

or because no other white child
ever touched you?

Eva

Winters
when old Eva
came to milk the cows,
            she wore
her dead husband's overcoat,
its pockets torn
across the edges
by hands gripping
deep down the change
she got for going
stall to stall.

It was the only coat
we ever saw her wear
and wondered what
            she wore
when he was living
or if she wore a coat
            at all
in the cold cuts of winter
and the fickle fall.

Perhaps he stayed at home
            'till,
her milking done,
both of them
could share its warm.

White High Tops

When they drank
they talked about the Depression
and how they took their last fifty cents
to buy me baby shoes.

I'll bet those shoes
were laced white high tops
            and never polished.

Shoe polish cost five cents
and five cents bought
      fresh greens for three folks.

I'm glad there was no money
      to bronze baby shoes
and put by family photographs
on a table Grandpa built.

My guilt needed no small monument.

M. CARL HOLMAN

Picnic: The Liberated

Enroute to the picnic they drive through their history,
Telling jokes and watching the road, but averting their eyes
From the rows of sun-flayed faces barely darker than theirs
Through which they pass like foreigners or spies.

The children play word games, count cows, inspect
Their armament of softballs, glasses, rods and hooks,
Survey the molten prairies overhead for signs of rain,
Retreat like crayfish to their comic books.

Grown-up laughter dwindles; they enter the wool-hat town
Like a gangster funeral, under the chastening eye
Of Confederate cannon, depot, First Baptist Church,
The white frame hospital that would let them die.

But out of sight is as safe as out of mind:
Dust lifts a protective screen half a mile down a winding road
Opening into a grove of pines, the green lake beyond
And the smoky pungence of barbecue as the cars unload.

So the long day blossoms in the sumptuous shade
Where the velvet-limbed girls parade their peacock beauty
In slacks and shorts, ignoring, excited by the clashing glances
Of waspish wives who lose track of matronly duty

And the men rotating their drinks in dixie cups,
Absently talking of civil rights, money and goods
But stirred by audacious dreams of rendezvous,
Boar-ramping conquests deep in the secret woods.

The tadpole hunters soak their shoes at the scummy edge
Of the lake where a boat capsizes but nobody drowns.
The badminton birds veer off course toward the tables
Where the gold-toothed winner grins, the loser frowns.

The sky contacts, the country dark creeps in,
Flicking a chilly tongue across the grass.
Uneasily the motors cough, headlights blink on,
Goodbys go flat, and tempers turn to glass.

Their tags are passports as they straggle home
To sprinklered lawns on Circles, Lanes and Drives,
Claiming once more the preferential signs
With which the Southern city stamps their lives.

Deep in the night the wind walks past the lake,
Leaps the pinewoods, lays an impartial hand
On cannon, croppers' shacks, touches at last
The handsome mortgaged houses where they sleep—
Mounting their private myths of freedom and command,
Privileged prisoners in a haunted land.

Mr. Z

Taught early that his mother's skin was the sign of error,
He dressed and spoke the perfect part of honor;
Won scholarships, attended the best schools,
Disclaimed kinship with jazz and spirituals;
Chose prudent, raceless views for each situation,
Or when he could not cleanly skirt dissension,
Faced up to the dilemma, firmly seized
Whatever ground was Anglo-Saxonized.

In diet, too, his practice was exemplary:
Of pork in its profane forms he was wary;
Expert in vintage wines, sauces and salads,
His palate shrank from cornbread, yams and collards.

He was as careful whom he chose to kiss:
His bride had somewhere lost her Jewishness,
But kept her blue eyes; an Episcopalian
Prelate proclaimed them matched chameleon.
Choosing the right addresses, here, abroad,
They shunned those places where they might be barred;
Even less anxious to be asked to dine
Where hosts catered to kosher accent or exotic skin.

And so he climbed, unclogged by ethnic weights,
An airborne plant, flourishing without roots.
Not one false note was struck—until he died:
His subtly grieving widow could have flayed
The obit writers, ringing crude changes on a clumsy phrase:
"One of the most distinguished members of his race."

Rebecca Hood-Adams

Cotton Choppers

Brothers,
Barefoot in the summer sun,
We lean against our hoes,
Chopping childhood into seasons,
Sharing shade,
Working weeds,
'Til Mama calls
For collard greens and cornbread.

Berry-browned
We grew cotton-tall,
Stalk-straight,
Squinting beneath straw toppers,
Teaming with the spirit
That slipped away to city life;
Country boys,
The farm was all we knew.

Diphtheria

Seventh summer
Sister took sick,
Hottest time I ever knew;
Sweat beads choke my neck
And dust devils dance
In fields behind the house.

Back of the buckboard
Raymond, Baby, and me
Sit quiet,
Even Dolly is sad-faced;

Secrets everywhere
But no one tells me.

All the way to Aunt Pet's
Papa never says a word;
He reins up sharp,
His shoulders shake
The one time Raymond coughs.

Sister sleeps with me
Since before I can remember,
Aunt Pet says crawl in beside her,
But I fidget until dawn;
Dreams of fever
Flash through sleep,
Striking Sister like a lightning bolt
That hit old man McWilliams
But never touched his horse;
I hear the grown-ups talk,
Some mystery, says they,
The way God chooses children.

T. R. HUMMER

Hanging Fire

Little Willy's daddy used to hang him
Up in a croker sack over a slow fire
When he was peeved. He'd throw
Wet leaves on the flames till the smoke came thick,
Then get the sack swinging—he didn't want
To burn the boy, just make him think—
And as Willy swung, his daddy would swing
A piece of one-by-two at him, aiming for the rump
Which sometimes he didn't hit quite right,
It being neither here nor there.

Every time Willy came out of the sack, he came out black
With soot, black with bruises, blackhearted,
Wouldn't talk for days, I couldn't tell him
Willy, it's wrong, you feeling that way
Like his mama did when he went back to the house.

I couldn't say anything to him. I'd just watch
That woman scrub for hours at his stubborn body,
Her black arms sweating, swearing as she scrubbed
That if it was the last thing she ever did
On this good earth, she'd make him shine.

Night Burning

In the night meadow, grassfire burns
My eyes till only the shadows
Are good to look on. It takes
Care to make a fire that touches
Only what you want touched.
It takes a life of burning
And knowing what to burn.

One night when I was a child
I woke to the changing
Light of pasture fire. I turned
To the window, saw
Lines of flame sweep
My father's dark fields.
I thought, what if he loses it,
What if it breaks away,
What if everything burns?

I saw my hands catch fire,
I touched the sheets, the quilts,
Let go of it, let it rise
Into the rafters until
The black roof split
And the October sky
Opened to nothing I could name

And in that moment of joy
When I did not know who I was
I saw my father walking
Over the fields, the blinding
Torch in his hand falling,
Touching, rising—the earth
Around him turning
Dark and light.

The Shell

What I found
In the dark of the woods,
In a creek
Cut deep by spring
Runoff, I took
And hid from my father
Who would covet it

And call it his own.
It smelled of that old
War I dreamed of nights
When my spirit grew older
Than itself with remembering.
I found it buried

In the blood-red
Clay of the creek-bank,
Dug with my hands,
Pulled it free, washed it clean
In red water, dragged it
A mile through timber,
A mile through pasture,

Then lay in the haybarn
Beside it till sunset
Touching the pitted
Iron of its casing
While, far off in dark
Trees, thought I saw

Shapes of men marching—

But my father's voice called me
From the barn and the story
I had heard all my life
Without learning: how armies
Met on our field
And camped here in sight
Of each others' fires, waiting—

How in the woods with them,
The north woods just yonder,
My great-great-grandfather
Slept without learning
Where he was until sunrise.
Then he woke and saw

His own farmland. I found once
The shed full of junk
My father's plow snagged:
Musket-balls and-barrels,
Coat-buttons, shoe-buckles,
Wheel-rims, and a man's
Legbone he pulled
From the stockpond, hooked
Deep in the marrow-hole.
So I came back

At sunrise to what
I had buried in the hay
Of my father's barn, brought it
Out into the light,
Knelt there beside it,
Ear to the iron,
Tapped it and heard
Voices, the bugles,
Hugged the shell close

As I ran from the cover
Of trees and remembered
The shape of this field—
Knew for one moment
As the cannon spoke
What was mine, what was waiting
In this dark earth, buried
Alive, alive.

A Crazy Girl
Brings the Rural Carrier a Dime

Every day she meets me at the mailbox, holding
Her hand out. It's not the mail she wants.
I've tried to give it to her, but she won't
Take it—just stretches her arm toward me, unfolding
Her fingers from the palm. And there's the dime.
She wants me to have it. I ask her *What do you need?*
She won't answer. She reaches toward me, shaking her head
Like there's something we both know. Time after time

I've shrugged my shoulders at her and driven on.
A ten-cent stamp, a cigarette—nothing satisfies her.

Every day, no matter what, she's there.
God, the way she looks, waiting for me in the rain!
Once I thought she followed me home. I started
To take her in my arms, hold her: *Is this what you wanted?*

The Rural Carrier Admires
Neil Varner's Brand New Convertible

On Main Street, right in front of the Ford place,
Neil Varner's convertible sits, as well as it can
With no front wheels, hardly any front end,
The engine in the front seat, and in the space
Where it should be, crushed metal, not an inch
Left smooth, that used to be hood, grill, and bumper.
The windshield's gone. There's dried blood everywhere.
But they say he walked away drunk, without even a scratch.

Look in the back seat, somebody says. I look.
There's nearly half a cow back there, the butt end,
Cut off neat above the legs and nestled in
The black vinyl cushion. Black Angus. Black against black.
They say he was doing ninety when he hit her.
They're still looking for the head. It could be anywhere.

The Beating

Everybody knew Clifton Cockerell was not half bright,
But nobody knew his passion
Till we found him on the playground back of the junior high
Carving names on a tree. His poor secret
Stood no more chance of staying one

Once we had it, than Clifton did of knowing
Why we cared—but we couldn't let it rest
Till everybody heard it, especially the girl, who was pretty
And thought he was some brand of animal. We'd sing
Their names together every chance we got, impressed

With her way of changing color, like some
Exotic lizard trying to disappear,
And forgot about Clifton pretty much till he came on us
Sudden one afternoon, wrathful and dumb
And swinging a length of cable. It wasn't fear

That defeated us. It was surprise
That it mattered so much what we'd done.
How could we know? He'd been one of us all our lives,
So close it was hard to see how he'd beat us
This once: he was already man enough to think he loved a woman.

So he came down on us sudden, boys,
All of us, and he gave us a taste of the hurt
We'd live to know another way: how love
Can be wrong and still be the only joy
That's real: how, when we come to it,

We stand amazed but take the blow, transfigured, idiot.

Sorrow

When my grandmother was dying
She could forget
Everything she hated,
How my grandfather laid
His hard farmer's hands on her
And wrung out sons:
How she loved her sons,
But how bitter the act of love was,
Why she was a dark
And melancholy woman.

Maybe joy is a matter of losing
Your earthly connections,
Maybe only then can you love
Clean, without hatred or desire.
Once when I was a boy
I was walking in woods
I thought I knew, near dusk,
And suddenly everything went strange,
The light, the leaves on the ground:
Shadows pointed east
So I walked west, the way
I thought I had to go,
But nothing came clear,
Nothing but sunlight burning
Through oaks, blinding me
Until I found the shadow
Of one trunk to walk in:
I followed it, came

To a young tree, took it
In my hands
Like a woman's waist,
Forgot to be afraid, not caring
As long as I held on.

My mother told me this:
When my grandmother was dying,
She turned to a nurse
And asked *Are you my child?*
The nurse said *No*.
My grandmother took her hand,
Held on hard: whispered *Well*
It doesn't matter then.
It's all right.
Yes. All right.

ANGELA JACKSON

Make/n My Music

my colored child/hood wuz mostly music
   celebrate/n be/n young an Black (but we din know it)
     scream/n up the wide alleys
an holler/n afta the walla-mellon-man.

sun-rest time
my mama she wuz yell/n
   (all ova the block
      sang/n fa us
ta git our butts in
      side.

we grew up run/n jazz rhythms
    an watch/n mr. wiggins downstairs
      knock the blues up side   his woman's
           head
we rocked.   an the big boys they snuck
an rolled   dice/   in the hallways   at nite.

i mean. we laughed love.   an the teen
    agers they jus slow dragged thru smokey
               tunes.

life wuz a ordinary miracle   an
have/n fun wuzn no temptation

we jus dun it.

an   u know
i think we grew.   thru them spirit-uals
        the saint-tified folks wud git happy off
        of even if we *wuz* jus clown/n
        when we danced the grizzly bear an
        felt good when the reverend
        wid the black cadillac   said:

        let the holy ghost come in
        side you

that music makes you/feel sooo/ good!

any how   i wuz a little colored girl
        then . . .

so far
my Black woman/hood ain't been noth/n but music

        i found billie
                holiday   an learned
                        how
                        to cry.

Greenville

        mouth/greasy
        and diaper/wet
        me./in a oldmans thin arms wrinkledwarm
            and brown
            full of granpapas foodandfussin
            bout them kids
            leavin this here littlebaby
            by herself

    and my brothersandsisters
    skippin down the road like
    duststorms skippin like

    dizzy dazzlestones across the water

    i couldnt catch up with.

Home Trainin

my father never did
heal my smart talkin
mouth. no matter
how many pursuits

aroun and unda the kitchen table
with belt or extension cord.

i had two smartin legs
        and ass
but my mouth
        continued to sass

mary mariah

my grandmother
mary mariah is sitting
by the window
her face   etched smooth
                into the day
        in her cheek/bones i
        see my aunt
bee bee who died when she was a little
over thirty   i see my aunts
bay-suh maude mary and hattie
and some of aunt jenny too
                i see
the young lines of my sister
bettys face

mary mariah is sitting silent
by the window   carrying generations
in her bones.

Early Evenings

early evenings and the streetlights
not yet on
we carry/d the backyard
to the front
cement
and study/d the street
while jumping double dutch

or irish in case of tie
waiting for the seven fifteen
bus
bearing our mama

bus rush by kicking dust and paper
and us all raggedy
me. a rather wild child
racing to the corner

mama would wait out a light
and rest
            her shoppingbag
we would rip it from her and
worry
it
for a surprise
empty or not
            there was a happiness:
the gift of her
brownred/yellow and laughing
                        weariness
rests easy in our eyes. . . .

The Charmed Circle

tumbling like charms from between our motherslegs
we'd fall

our father
was singing
strings and knocking
songs on wood in

talismans

the woman gourded us
in her warm

palms
guarded us in her breath
of
night wishes
&holy numbers

she rolled us
in a circle of milk
& marrow kneadings

cast us in the center of curses
where
brother/backs hunched against the grindingstone

while *their* sons
stalked concrete
she threw us skilled
as pennies
              to meet the street

and the man
gambled goods&
calloused hands
for a living

tumbling like dice from between our mothersthighs

we spun
fierce

given
in a pact of seven
daughters
&sons
as a pair
of eyes

remember the firstborn who died
                        without her births rite?

she rolls my mothers
memory
in the mississippi dust

my father plucks and knocks her hidden bones
                              roots now.

where
time falls and
            fails
beneath the central soil.

we are not defeated.

George, After All, Means Farmer

he carried a tomato plant &
watermelon
across the daydream highways and no stop sign ever touched him
he would not wait
there is one line in the palm
of his hand
it is thick as blood and crooked and crowded
against callouses
one line that is heart and life and a head

elaborate as the green that stalks into soft red moons

ambiguous bleeding that wants to be fruit
& vegetable
the way insanity wants genius save for cruelty

and this is in his hand
the bloodline let loose

his caring is locked into the soil
and somedays i believe i must leave it there

it is most sure of itself
when red roses unpeel and threaten the discipline of winters
my father's flesh indelible

hunched over a handplow
in eulogy for his father's flesh, in fear
that all of his line would waste like a watermelon flung against the earth
and the meat broken from tenderness
& bleeding in splits like fruit too soft from too much sun

too long a time alone grey
he hunches against the handplow. he is turning to grey and metal

as if he has known his earth's cruelty
a long long time.

What I Said As a Child

What I said as a child I say
as a woman:

> There is romance in common
>   movement
> of sound and sand.
>   Religion of a
>   kind, is
>   true, affirmed.

> Ours is the worn water and ripe fire, leaves
> that burn alongside the road
> into
> smoke
> thick as Nigerian oil. A cover
> for magic and skill

> We balanced a house of extended families
>   atop our heads.
> The music drifted down
>   around our faces.
> Wind crossed our cheeks
>   in scarifications.
> Spirits feathered around our waists
> and fell to our knees;
> a dance
> of prayers   that I said as a child

I say again:

> We walked in the air of the ancestors,
> hot, and tight
> like
> the space between two breasts. A crossing
> of tongues
> in the middle of an African night

> The future is a quiet bed, a spread
>   of hunger, and fallenwish
>   is mystery to divine:
> a drum technique
>   hidden in a man's hands.
> We sit on the edge of our own echo, and craft.

What I said as a child I say as a woman:

We are from a house of balance and control.
The road ahead is burning smoke and oils.
What comes after is an act of will.

Lagos, Nigeria

Why I Must Make Language

For
A Voice
 like a star.
 Shining.
 With points to pierce
 space,
 and be
 simple, superb
 clarity.
Incandescent.
Some thing
a child might carry
down the black hall,
and make peace with Mystery.
Or woman
into a wooded place
where she may see
the shapes and
names of trees.
Anonymous awe be called
Glory.
Or man
might seek
in the cave
of a woman
and see the writing
on the wall,
and find some
Luminosity.
Ancestors may descend
on streams of light.
Or
all look up
and listen
deep
into the night.

The wild
and civilized
Sky.

Dr. Watts Meets
the Man with the White Liver

1   Dr. Watts
    (for Joan, Jeff, and Phil Cohran at
    the MBTA in St. Louis)

It is the song every soul knows.
No one knows where it began.
If they did they'd go there when it goes
home.

The throat becomes a cowrie shell
the moan slides through crooked, crowded
with sorrow alive as joy
and joy sounding sorrow sounds.

"Where you from, Dr. Watts?"
say the sister on the mourners bench.
"Hold my soul, Dr. Watts,"
say the deacon in the amen corner.

Dr. Watts open his black bag
dark as a cola nut
divinities come rising out.
He got the death rattle in his dark bag.
He got the love cry humming out the womb
and the scrotum.
He got the grave sinking in the soil and the
weeping over it.
He got the waterbag bursting and the birth canal
groaning wide to holler out
arrival.

Back through Middle Passage the Church say amen
and the midnight days of crying
over the tumult water, chaos in the crests,
death in the lowdown leeside of these cruel
mountains of water
in a black canoe of longing sound travels.

Delicate the kiss, nose-touching breathing in, home again
"Where you take me, Dr. Watts?"

"Home again."

"Amen. Amen."

It is the song every soul knows.
It is the song every soul knows
to travel in the hum,
                    the groan,
the long way
home.

2   The Man with the White Liver
    (for Josephine Sankey)

He got the thang make a woman cry out in the night.
The man with the white liver
he the killin-love giver.

His first wife die smilin,
say hand me my comb so I can comb
this hair befo that man get home.
His first die smilin,
sit up in the sheets
say hand me my comb
before my husband get home
so I can live in his arms
forever. She smilin
reachin and dyin
for the man
with the white liver.
He the killin-love giver.

He second wife die dancin
cross the street dreamin he
standin on the other side
heard him whisperin her name
in the broken car horn
carried her own way from here.
She dancin like Dunham in the middle
of the street dreamin her name on his
sweet, thick mouth, lift her
dress above one knee, raise the
other hand high-swearin she hear her name

in his juicy-dreamy mouth. She
wave to it
and git
hit.
Car with the broken horn
carry her own way from here.
She dreamin about a man
with a white liver. You know him.
He the killin-love giver.

His third wife die like a coffee cup
first thing in the mornin
she dark and laughin when he stirrin her up,
die with a silver spoon in black brew so strong
the spoon stand up
in the cup
first thing in the mornin she die
like maxwell house good to the last drop
people say they read the grinds in her eyes
grinds say lord have mercy I love me my man
with his white liver he the goodest love giver.

He got the thang make a woman cry out in the night.
He got the thang make a woman rise up light as light
and slide through blinds like sunshine.
My girlfriend's mama tell Angela stay away
from a man with a white liver
        when she find one
        run
say girl stay away from a man with a white liver
he the killin-love giver
His love take the life
from every smilin wife
he have one behind the other
linin up for lovin
like lambs to the slaughter.
I'm tellin you like I tell my own daughter:
Stay away from a man with a white liver
who make yo liver quiver yo nose open wide
yo heart stop dead in the middle of his rockin ride.

He the killin-love giver.
He got the thang make a woman cry out in the night.
His shoulder the last thing she see.
His coffee cup the last thing she ever be.

3   Mules and Woman
    (with respect to Zora and
    the Ground of the African Church)

Sorrowtalked eye-to-eye forgiven is no mere burden.
The one who sings is no mere beast.
The one who slip the harness of the horror stands alive as earth.

Today I can watch the wind and it is blue smoke.
I shake myself inside my dress, consider rain and choose Shine.

I was walking down Mississippi River Street
                and a ghost stopped me.
No one could see it but me,
standing in the middle of the sidewalk
smilin at a haint with his hat in his hand
        instead of his head when he can tote that too.

        When one mule die
        the rest neigh-cry
        till the wagon take the dead thing away.

        Mississippi River Street rampant with noise,
        radiant, won't hold still.
        But I have walked on blue black water.
        Watched dead rise before the wagon came.

        Everywhere I see mules,
        open mouths sing blues, then be human, then
        beyond.

Funerals, weddings, baptisms
I take off my skin, hang it up
like a soaked quilt to dry the tears
and sweat from feeling. I stand naked before Church,
holding Dr. Watts closer than my sagging, girlish breasts.
My soul wear no clothes when she sing.
It is all being in love with more than one
man who is one whole man you can look into his eyes
without blinking.

                Where would I go to hide?
Dr. Watts standing with my skin hooked on his finger
and I am next to him solid and living the song with no words
that every born again mule knew in death and in life before
birth, now hums true again hot in the chest and throat
breaking natural out the mouth like breathing.

Where would I go to hide?
Sit down, rock my soul like my baby and Dr. Watts
climb in my lap and moan for the milk no mother can buy or borrow
only make in hearts of her eyes, in lines of the palms of her hands.
And where would I find lines with no skin?

Where would I go to hide?
I tell you I am living now. Like in Mississippi
Grandmama's bedroom sitting on the high bed you could break
                    your neck leaving
Cousin Chubby said fried fish, greens and cornbread was
good eatin. I am good livin. Blue smoke watching,
naked, haint-smiling, entertaining Dr. Watts, dreaming
of a man with a white liver who can't kill me
who love mulish women, hainted ones, I am the sainted one
naked with no sense of memory but good like God rocking
hums in my lap and looking for no hiding place even if
wind be blue smoke hurricane and I make red milk
in the hearts of my eyes and reach out my lifelines to
a hopeless haint I can stand myself

Naked now where would I want to go to hide? from this
funeral wedding death and birth baptism
the sliding tears washing my soul cleaner than
Dr. Watts whistle or the look in a sweatin man's
eyes when he lookin at a perfect, brutal, sun
killing him with living while he lick his lips and dream
of water, then put his shoulder behind a woman
guiding him while he dig in and groove the earth to the quick
deep endless quick.

Where would I go
Where would I go to hide this
yes-crying love yielding beyond flesh yet
subsumed by sweat

Where would I go naked so
following blues and Dr. Watts
like a double-seeing shadow
standing before you with only blue smoke
between us
humming yes and yes and yes

subsumed by sweat and yielding
beyond mere flesh.

AUROLYN JACOBS

I want to name my children after poems

I want to name
my children
after poems,
after words that
rise and dance warmly
on cold windowsills,

after phrases
that fight the zig zag
wonders of black
man
   hood
      hooded in old stories,
            folk tales
                  and voodoo chants,

after poems that
flow warmly like re-heated soup
and hot evenings in
June,

poems that
steam up pain-glazed eyes
of old women
removing age,

poems that
fight like trapped animals
in free zoos,

poems that gobble down
freedom like
mad dogs at a
family picnic.

I want to name
my children
after poems
that drumbeat
the sun from
her hiding place
opening

her legs
for one more
day's work
day's struggle

and because I
feel sometimes
we are only
making tiny motions
against a whirlwind,

I'll name my
children after
poems.

it ain't hard being a woman
just time consuming

I am used to the
callouses on my hands
and my heart,
the cracks in my dreams.
I know the bowed heads
of the womenfolk,
and though it was
a bitter lesson
to learn,
I learned it well.

There is never
enough time
for the things
we need,
golden times to think,
spirited times
to remember ourselves
before motherhood
and marriage
and long winters
with no rent money.

If our demands
are too strong
it's just that,
we have always

dedicated ourselves
to a heritage
that kills us.
Quickly I say
my prayers.

Wilma

her ashened hair
like grey hanging moss
rushes from crinkled
black skin.
brown stalks
for fingers,
reach out
like an open field.

her dreams go riding
beyond the gravel road,
beyond the red clay walls
that stand to box in
her tears,
brown tears,
rolling dreams
down her face,
a lost antique.

forgotten
left sitting in the shade
of a decayed oak tree,
she is riding down
the highway,
in a car with
no wheels,
forgotten.

Joan Johnson

Elegy for the Girl Who Died in the Dump at Ford's Gulch

1

They forbade this place alone to us. My parents,
Ever reasoning, ticked off the dangers: snakes,
Tangled in the kudzu; rusted nails, refrigerators
Like coffins; ivy blisters; tramps; potholes;
Broken glass. A girl had died there once, slow
Smothering when a clay bank collapsed on her. Although
I did not know her, I practiced holding my breath
For weeks, glad at last of my lungs' helpless force.

2

Hide and seek held such dangers. Pop the whip thrilled
With its cruel gush of breath from the centrifugal
Whump of the end body. Scissors, paper, and stone
Left me bruised for days with punches from bad guesses.
I had wretched from dizzy whirling on a dare. In truth
We were watchful of the jagged, the creeping, the hidden
Places when we plundered that gulch like a foreign country.

3

In the shell of a Hudson I found a Victrola
And twenty-seven records. My sister danced
Like crazy with me, giggles stitching our
Guts when the voice wound down. We swigged
An inch of gin judiciously, chewing wild mint
To kill the smell. We shrieked at a snake
Skin, the gulch bottom sand fooling our silly eyes
With glitter so that we thought we saw it
Slithering. We cast off a broken doll, the skull
Of a cat's carcass, and a string of green glass
Beads to make the dry skin whisper with a stick.

4

Dared, I could not refuse to fondle it, like paper,
Like strands in Mother's wig, like the taste
In my mouth when I held my breath too long. My parents

Would have warned me that where there is a skin
There is a snake. Dead girl, your lesson was
Against hiding in shaded caves. Those games taught me
To turn over warm rocks with a long stick, the shape
Of poison ivy leaves, the racket like flies that swarms
In my head when I've spun too long. And, yes, you taught
Me to be glad of seeing gold spots from looking
At the sun, glad of wary parents and quick lessoning.

LARRY JOHNSON

Once

Once, in 1949,
in Eastabuchie, Mississippi,
while my fingers were rooting
a gritty carrot from the earth,
there was a blast, a roar
louder than that first helicopter
I had seen a month before.
I wasn't there to see the flash
of red and black in the tall magnolia,
or hear the spang of feathers
on the tin roof of the garage.
All I did was run to the yard
and discover, nestled in my grandfather's hands,
an ivory-billed woodpecker, dead,
punched through with shotgun pellets,
a thick gout of blood staining its beak,
blood bright as its head or a magnolia seed.
The rarest creature of earth,
and I saw one, fallen to earth,
but less precious to me than the helicopter
which had sliced and dipped so silverly.
"I wanted you to see it," he said.

Near Eastabuchie, Mississippi

1

This pond. A gray, manmade cup
sunk in a field surrounded

by pines. That child, we know,
fell from the bitterweed edge,
floated that day, threshed, and sank
as if flying; he looked up, certainly,
and saw his cries become silver globes
as the sky was whirled and sucked
into flawed milkglass—a dense
congealment of light, water, breath.

None of us ever knew this child
except as his drowning relates
to our own curdled vision of death;
we can even think of him as recalled
to some prenatal world of dream . . .
say he faded, painless, insane
with the pressuring quiet—a syrup
of pine-close, cricketless green—
the turgid center of our eye.
But what would all of that mean?

2

Now we walk toward the trees. Near the path,
the old Gunn place slants through the weeds.
A gnarled, gray house shows its ribs
as its builders might, lying in the earth.
Split shingles invite the thick moss
to thread the roof over, the porch
has aborted into the field,
kudzu snarls round the outhouse.
Should we care what this ruin held?

The Gunns. No faces. They were born here,
and too quickly we can categorize
their lives: how they axed out the trees,
saw the gravel roads mire, and the cows
swell with their calves and disease,
watched the *Grapette* and *Clabber Girl* signs
flake in the heat and lean.
We admit that the sky they breathed
was blue, clean, smelling like earth
in the Genesis they read and believed—
but some of us probably will think
of plowing-sweat, green bitter milk,
Mason jar whiskey and knives,

or a black man, naked and tied,
being hanged from a tall, scaly pine.
Our child, that unscaly thing,
slid out—but the Gunns, who lived here,
had seen 78 years worth of something
he avoided; and we, in our way,
think we have, too—could their death
have been fluid, then? What was it like?
Retribution? An absence of cars?
A collage of this house, briars, and sweat
in a black scripture of pine needles and dung?
What would you say of it? Like the door
of the outhouse meshed over with kudzu,
you inside, your stinks feeding the green?

Emory D. Jones

Whitey Remembers

1

Brown slapped the Board
And got our attention.

Boy,
You had been only
Southern scenery
Squatting in squalid shacks
That rimmed rows
Through which you dragged
Your autumn afternoons.

We thought
You'd keep your place
Forever.

2

Little Rock surprised us
With pigtailed pickaninnies
Parading down guarded corridors.

Too long, you sat
In the back of lunchrooms, buses.

Through torrential thuds
Of Selma billy-clubs,
Snarling police dogs,
Pussle-gutted curses,
Martin touched us
From the Birmingham Jail.

3

White citizens counciled,
And thirty-two
African Baptist Churches
Burned, Baby.

Freedom's children marched,
Consumated brotherly love
In a Philadelphia dike.

Little George stood in the door,
And Robert waltzed with Ross
While Meredith reeked riot,
Lorded slums—
He got a butt full of buck-shot
For his pains.

4

Panthers prowled Oakland avenues,
Chicago caverns—
"Hot breakfast for the people;
Cold steel for honkies."

In Tennessee Stokely burned,
Baby, burned
While H   Rapped out in Maryland.

5

Sheeted knights rode nightmares,
Flared with flaming crosses
Weather-warped cabins
Cowering in cotton,
Martyred Medgar, Malcolm X.

Burn, baby—
In Chicago, Detroit,
Washington, Watts—
Burn.

6

Martin marched over the mountain
And saw the promised land.
His monument—a Memphis motel.

Cleaver cooled his soul, brother;
And Huey's ashes fertilized
Chicago's Southside slums.

7

Red-necked dragon spawn ride again,
Solicit support at road blocks,
Heft ax handles and .410's.

8

Neatly balanced actions affirmed
The bus question either way.

Why bother us now
With Okolona cheerleaders?

MARGARET KENT

Living with Animals

*It has been said that dogs drink at the River
Nile while running along that they might not be
seized by crocodiles.*

These mornings I lie awake listening for signs
of life in the house: the scurrying of mice
in the eaves, the tick of birds in the gutters,
the sure-footed step of love outside my door.
Grumbling, I rise. The darkness has washed me
clean of shadows. I am a groundhog emerging

on the last day of the year, squinting down
light tumbling in pieces behind me, shapes of
where I've been, no idea of what's to come.

Of a concrete nature, it's Sunday: ribs and
God and rest, the long slow grinding down of
afternoon, the inevitable ride toward darkness,
animals fading in the fields, at the sides of
roads. We cross the bridge to Arkansas, our
hands in our laps, the radio playing hymns,
"this blinding light that comes with love"
is nothing now, a failure, the sad overloading
of the heart's circuits, this dark house
condemned by love, condemned by love.

It is another light that divides us now, clear
shapes again in the fields, in the mirror, at
the edge of roads: yellow dogs, for instance.
their fur muddied and bedraggled, casualties
of the river, perhaps, or of morning: how when
I see white teeth bared sideways to the sun,
the pale conversion of tongue to dust, the
befuddled cowlick along the spine, I think of you,
how we outran the danger but surrendered to time.

It is growing dark. At the edge of the fields
the levee rises like a brown serpent feeding on
fireflies. Our separate lives, I suppose, have
never stood much of a chance. But think of
the animals we have known and feared and
nurtured in this black of night and know
fear leaves us all head down at last, running
blindly along some river and always alone.

At home in my room I listen: the pear tree
outside my window is a blasphemy of evening birds.
They chatter as if daylight had never before abandoned
them. I think it is so. Sometime later, I make tea
and write you these words: in a forest of peccaries,
a wart-hog is the sole dissenter. In a forest of
wart-hogs, a peccary is a welcome sound. In a forest
of both, bread crumbs make not a hair's breadth of difference.

Watching the Island

For David

1

That afternoon I drift toward the upper lake around
    Archer Island,
take the route through the trees, cleared by fishermen
    after the storm.

Of all passages, this one is the quietest: the boat's motor
    vanishes
behind me; turtles, their brown heads rising twig-like
    above

Distant logs, sit motionless, their shells drying in the sun.
    And
overhead the translucent haze of cottonwood fills the air,

Rising and sifting the light until it falls on the dark surface
of the lake like snow: a false winter in mid-July. And I
    think, then,

Of that real winter in the doorway of the house on
    Manila Street
when, reaching up to a woman in a dark coat, I found
    strange

Melting flakes of white on her shoulders as she lifted me
    into her
arms before she was gone.

2

And of all afternoons, this one is the quietest: fishermen sit
silently among cottonwoods, anchored in shadow.

The blue glint of dragonflies floats on the surface of the
    water;
the boat moves soundlessly among trees.

And then, around a fallen live oak, I see it: the buoy
    that marked
the channel near Archer Island in my childhood,

Stranded among the storm's debris, its wooden battleship
    hull
upended and rotting, its blinking light now half
    submerged and dark,

And I remember those nights on the concrete spine of the
    levee
in my father's old Ford, the cold metal of the fender pressing

The backs of my thighs, my knees, my feet dangling in
    the dark: how
I looked out at that beacon that signaled the water's edge,
    land's end

And thought: it is the only island I know, and more distant
    than any star.

3

And coming home at dusk, the boat adrift on glass, a
    pool of light
drying inward towards darkness, Archer Island soundless
    to the west,

A ragged fire of trees against the waning light; cars on
    the levee distant,
blinking, the channel dark, its buoy vanished among
    cottonwoods,

I think of my father's eyes, the color of the river; my
    mother's hair,
auburn once, a whole sky giving up light, and know I
    am moving

Still toward some island, childless and coming home
    through the dark,
wondering: how can I take these colors, this light, this
    long day
home with me?

ETHERIDGE KNIGHT

A Poem for Myself
(or Blues for a Mississippi Black Boy)

I was born in Mississippi;
I walked barefooted thru the mud.
Born black in Mississippi,
Walked barefooted thru the mud.
But, when I reached the age of twelve
I left that place for good.
My daddy he chopped cotton
And he drank his liquor straight.
Said my daddy chopped cotton
And he drank his liquor straight.
When I left that Sunday morning
He was leaning on the barnyard gate.
Left her standing in the yard
With the sun shining in her eyes.
And I headed North
As straight as the Wild Goose Flies,
I been to Detroit & Chicago
Been to New York city too.
I been to Detroit & Chicago
Been to New York city too.
Said I done strolled all those funky avenues
I'm still the same old black boy with the same old blues.
Going back to Mississippi
This time to stay for good
Going back to Mississippi
This time to stay for good—
Gonna be free in Mississippi
Or dead in the Mississippi mud.

The Bones of My Father

1

There are no dry bones
here in this valley. The skull
of my father grins
at the Mississippi moon
from the bottom

of the Tallahatchie,
the bones of my father
are buried in the mud
of these creeks and brooks that twist
and flow their secrets to the sea.
but the wind sings to me
here the sun speaks to me
of the dry bones of my father.

2

There are no dry bones
in the northern valleys, in the Harlem alleys
young / black / men with knees bent
nod on the stoops of the tenements
and dream
of the dry bones of my father.

And young white longhairs who flee
their homes, and bend their minds
and sing their songs of brotherhood
and no more wars are searching for
my father's bones.

3

There are no dry bones here.
We hide from the sun.
No more do we take the long straight strides.
Our steps have been shaped by the cages
that kept us. We glide sideways
like crabs across the sand.
We perch on green lilies, we search
beneath white rocks . . .
THERE ARE NO DRY BONES HERE

The skull of my father
grins at the Mississippi moon
from the bottom
of the Tallahatchie.

Connecticut—February 21, 1971

The Idea of Ancestry

1

Taped to the wall of my cell are 47 pictures: 47 black
faces: my father, mother, grandmothers (1 dead), grandfathers (both dead), brothers, sisters, uncles, aunts,
cousins (1st & 2nd), nieces, and nephews. They stare
across the space at me sprawling on my bunk. I know
their dark eyes, they know mine. I know their style,
they know mine. I am all of them, they are all of me;
they are farmers, I am a thief, I am me, they are thee.

I have at one time or another been in love with my mother,
1 grandmother, 2 sisters, 2 aunts (1 went to the asylum),
and 5 cousins. I am now in love with a 7-yr-old niece
(she sends me letters written in large block print, and
her picture is the only one that smiles at me).

I have the same name as 1 grandfather, 3 cousins, 3 nephews,
and 1 uncle. The uncle disappeared when he was 15, just took
off and caught a freight (they say). He's discussed each year
when the family has a reunion, he causes uneasiness in
the clan, he is an empty space. My father's mother, who is 93
and who keeps the Family Bible with everybody's birth dates
(and death dates) in it, always mentions him. There is no
place in her Bible for "whereabouts unknown."

2

Each fall the graves of my grandfathers call me, the brown
hills and red gullies of mississippi send out their electric
messages, galvanizing my genes. Last yr / like a salmon quitting
the cold ocean-leaping and bucking up his birthstream / I
hitchhiked my way from L.A. with 16 caps in my pocket and a
monkey on my back. And I almost kicked it with the kinfolks.
I walked barefooted in my grandmother's backyard / I smelled the old
land and the woods / I sipped cornwhiskey from fruit jars with the men/
I flirted with the women / I had a ball till the caps ran out
and my habit came down. That night I looked at my grandmother
and split / my guts were screaming for junk / but I was almost
contented / I had almost caught up with me.
(The next day in Memphis I cracked a croaker's crib for a fix).

This yr there is a gray stone wall damming my stream, and when
the falling leaves stir my genes, I pace my cell or flop on my bunk

and stare at 47 black faces across the space. I am all of them,
they are all of me, I am me, they are thee, and I have no sons
to float in the space between.

Ilu, The Talking Drum

The deadness was threatening us—15 Nigerians and 1
Mississippi nigger.
It hung heavily, like stones around our necks, pulling us down
to the ground, black arms and legs outflung
on the wide green lawn of the big white house
The deadness was threatening us, the day
was dying with the sun, the stillness—
unlike the sweet silence after love / making or
the pulsating quietness of a summer night—
the stillness was skinny and brittle and wrinkled
by the precise people sitting on the wide white porch
of the big white house . . .
The darkness was threatening us, menacing . . .
we twisted, turned, shifted positions, picked our noses,
stared at our bare toes, hissed air thru our teeth . . .
Then Tunji, green robes flowing as he rose,
strapped on Ilu, the talking drum,
and began:

kah doom / kah doom-doom / kah doom / kah doom-doom-doom
kah doom / kah doom-doom / kah doom / kah doom-doom-doom
kah doom / kah doom-doom / kah doom / kah doom-doom-doom
kah doom / kah doom-doom / kah doom / kah doom-doom-doom
the heart, the heart beats, the heart, the heart beats slow
the heart beats slowly, the heart beats
the blood flows slowly, the blood flows
the blood, the blood flows, the blood, the blood flows slow
kah doom / kah doom-doom / kah doom / kah doom-doom-doom
and the day opened to the sound

kah doom / kah doom-doom / kah doom / kah doom-doom-doom
and our feet moved to the sound of life

kah doom / kah doom-doom / kah doom / kah doom-doom-doom
and we rode the rhythms as one
from Nigeria to Mississippi
and back
kah doom / kah doom-doom / kah doom / kah doom-doom-doom

Once on a Night in the Delta:
A Report From Hell

for Sterling Brown

Gravel rattles against the fenders of the van
The River flashes in the distance.
The wind is thick with the scent of honeysuckle.
The road from Greenville curves like the sickle
Of the new moon, now hanging over east Texas.
Moun' Bayou sleeps on a straight street.

The poor live on both / sides / of the tracks
In this town peopled by Blacks.
Tho the bloods / now / pack pistols
And rap on two-way radios,
And the homes of a few are spacious and new,
With sunken patios;
Tho the dice are / shot / thru a leather horn and
The whiskey burns my belly in the early morning,

We still shuffle in lines, like coffles of slaves:
Stamps for food—the welfare rolls and the voting polls.
We frown. Our eyes are dark caves

Of mourning.—So I'd like to report to you, Sir Brown—
Fromaway / down / here—
Mississippi is *still* hell, Sir Brown—
For Me and ol Slim Greer.

SINCLAIR O. LEWIS

Anyone Who Rejects Me Gotta Be Crazy

Anyone who rejects me
   has to be crazy, honey
I am black and beau-ti-ful
I am strong
   Strong and indestructible
As I walk you can see the
   rhythmic history of my proud People
   in my steps
Baby, I am Saturday Night decked out in
   Sunday's best.
Sugar,
Anyone who rejects me   Has gotta be Crazy.
I am exhaultation
I am celebration time, celebrating
   my blackness
Honey, I'm the Congo
         The Nile and the Mississippi
I'm dark and mysterious
Sugar, I am something else
   and
Anyone who rejects me
Has gotta be Craaa-Zee.

R. G. LOWREY

Remembrance of Things Past

1

It happened before you were born,
Before your father was born,
I who am old can scarcely remember it.

It was morning. The light was yellow on the road,
The horse's hoofs plopped slow in the yellow dust,
And Mother flicked the whip

To make him go faster.
It was thirteen miles from our house to the station.

I said "We are going to Grandmother's house."
Mother did not answer.
She flicked the horse again with the buggy whip.
It was a big, bay horse with a black tail.

I do not remember who else was in the buggy;
I do not remember anybody,
But there must have been somebody—
The horse did not go on the train;
He had to go home again.

The train ride must have been
Like any other ride;
Its scenes are not among the things I've kept.
Lulled by the wheels on the track,
It may be that I slept.
Maybe I sat by the window
And watched all kinds of things go by outside—
Trees and telephone poles and pasture grass
And cows that ran away when the train passed.
Maybe I was too busy
Looking to notice that Mother was not looking.

I do not remember how
We got to Grandmother's house.
I guess there were horses—Uncle Henry with
The span of grays and the hack.
But when we got to Grandmother's house, I remember
There was a block of ice as big as two
Cardboard shoeboxes on the kitchen table—
There in the hot summer at Grandmother's house
Where the pond did not freeze even in January.
The ice had come a long way on the train.
It was a marvelous thing—
Blue and transparent except
When you stood in the right place, where the light crept
Across its face like silver.
I wanted to taste it, but
They said, "No! Grandmother
Is sick, the ice is for Grandmother."
They went where Grandmother was and shut the door.
There was nobody left for me to play with,

Nobody paid any attention to me. I wondered,
If I got sick like Grandmother
Would *they* give *me* some ice?

Mother came back to the kitchen.
She said, "We don't need to keep the ice any more."
She chipped a piece of ice and gave it to me.
I wondered why she was crying.
The ice was cold on my tongue.
Then the ice was not cold any more,
It was not even there—
Just water, flat and tasteless.
I went to play in the yard.

2

Miss Jarman had geraniums with dark
Red blossoms and a delicate smell in the leaves.
She said if I would bring a can and some sand
She would give *me* a geranium cutting.
I went to the gulley where they kept the cans
And the sand. The red wasps had
A nest in one of the cans.
A wasp sat on my ear.
I went home, screaming.
I remember the wet cotton and the smell of ammonia
But not the geranium cutting.

3

One time I was nine years old.
There was a girl. She wore
A crisp, white dress patterned with blue flowers.
Her hair looked soft as corn silk; it looked smooth
To touch. I wanted to touch her hair, and I
Was terrified because
She might not wait for me,
She was older than I was.
I prayed that she would wait for me. God said,
"I am your Father, I know better than you."

A long time afterward,
After I had met and married your Grandmother,
After your father was bigger than you are now,
I met a woman in a far, strange town.
She said, "Remember me? I am Doris."

She was fat, with a pale, blotched skin and a double chin.
I did not remember her.
I did not want to touch her yellow hair
Stretched thin across her scalp.
She was not the Doris I remembered.

BIRTHALENE MILLER

remembering who you are

big mama come out into the yard.
one leaf left clinging, shivering to
the hickory nut tree.

it fall to the ground.
big mama stomp on it. hard.
scrunch it beneath big, bare feet.

a chicken hawk sailing high, sailing free.
a gun shoots and it falls.
i see it fall. to the hard, cold ground.

i feel it fall.
a rock. in my heart.

big mama say, men.
she spit it out
like it's weevily corn bread, bad tasting
in her mouth.

she been walking low, shuffling, head down—
hanging.
daddy come in last night. late again.
smelling of hussy perfume. again.

big mama run him out with her razor that lay
always warm like love against her breast.

she walk tall now.   a woman.   and proud of it.
she say, girl, always remember who you are
and then nobody can take you from you.

mama walking tall and remembering who she is
and me walking beside her and wondering who
i am and who i will be.

i think of the one-eyed man
one brown real eye, one glass blue one
what always stands on the corner and winks
at mama as we walk by.

i wonder what his name is,
who he is.

WILLIAM MILLS

Politics

John Farrell's woods
Were pushed down today.
Everybody from all around came
To see the machine.
The driver
Pulled levers, touched buttons and
The big cat responded,
Ripping and shoving.
He was fast.
Charley Ben and I walked up close,
Treetops slapped down.
The driver nodded,
Shifted the thin cigar
To the other side,
Spun off, ground shaking.

John Farrell needed more room.
You can see the reason.
But I looked at Farrell's woods
At my feet,
I saw spilled eggs and circling,
A rabbit running.

Still, it's something a man has to face.
John Farrell needed more room.

Unemployment

A young hound howls.

I am almost slumbering
In a rocking chair.
The soft rain pats
A Mississippi road.

I feel like the road.

Cock

Many mornings
The neighbor's barnyard cacophony
Has served as the final wedge,
Splitting an aching head
Whereupon the halves of the head
Have fallen to the bedroom floor,
Severing the memory of last night's fun.

This morning (the moon gone,
The sun not yet ready to make its move)
My dark was such I couldn't
Find the clock,
Leaving me uncertain hours
With no vouchers for courage,
When a proud young cock's crow
Served notice to the world at large
And his hen house in particular
That sun or not,
Here was his solitary
Announcement to the dark.

Silhouette

When I was six and plundering primary school
The week long, my parents kept me to yard
Till supper and bed. Saturday, though, it was over
To John B's for ball and bat or soldiers

The Germans the bad ones again. Released from school,
Loose from my own yard, from my mother's eyes,
Away from the teacher's eyes where I tried to keep
The capitals big and the long words on the pages.

One rainy Saturday, the mother of John B,
If not to be saved by bayonet or ball
Was not to be subdued. She took out
Scissors and paste and thick construction paper.

Was this to be school again? No. One, then the other,
Laid his head down while she traced around them,
Then cut out who we were, the scissors snipping
Around the top and the eyes, over the nose,

The lips and chin, down to the Adam's apple.
(So much attention paid, so much demanded).
How I marveled at the artist of that afternoon,
And marveled at me, the way I had never seen me.

She pasted this white image on a sheet
Of black paper and stuck it on the wall.
No one could read my eyes, a statue's eyes,
And I have not since seen so clearly what I am.

Our Fathers at Corinth

*for William J. Mills, Co. A., 24th Mississippi Infantry Regiment. Died June 18, 1862.
Buried in an unknown soldier's grave, Enterprise, Mississippi*

"Let the impending battle decide our fate, and add one more illustrious
page to the history of our Revolution, one to which our children will
turn with noble pride, saying, 'Our fathers were at the battle of
Corinth.'"   *P.G.T. Beauregard, General, Commanding*

Winter in Mississippi and your sons stand before you,
All of us together now, here between Chunky River and
Okatibbe Creek. You lie unmarked in these four hundred
Gray stones, still in formation and like enlisted men
Everywhere mostly unknown. It was this
That haunted your children,
That we didn't even know your name,
Only that you never came home.

The specter of our forgetfulness drove us
To front porches of the old of Greene County
Wanting to put a name to your wraith,
An end to our neglect.
As we rocked our way to eighteen hundred and sixty-two,
A hundred-year-old cousin remembered
You had walked the long way to Corinth.

That your young son got a licking
For trying to follow you.

She also said your name, great-grandfather.
With this we followed you to these cracked stones.

The records showed it to be
A late spring of blood.
You clustered at the courthouse
With your brash and ruddy cousins
Come to watch the lieutenant dressed in gray
Come to hear him talk about the fight.
He spoke of April at Shiloh and the butcher's bill,
Of General Johnston dying,
Of Mississippians buried there.
He spoke of Halleck with twice our number
Moving on Corinth.
He read a letter from Jeff Davis:
"Beauregard must have reinforcements . . .
The case of vital importance.
Send forward to Corinth
All the armed men you can furnish."
What parts of the late spring day
Warred in your Anglo-Saxon mind
As you moved slowly from the dock
of rhythmical certainties in Greene County
To the caesura of war, that pause
As the blood boils before its final thickening
Before it is left to cool in Corinth, in Enterprise?
Young yeoman, rude in your blue eyes,
Straw hat cocked in the county's latest style
Was it defense, not wanting to miss the big event,
Or just being shy about staying home?
No matter. You walked to Corinth. You went.

Well, not being cavalry because you had no horse
Means nothing to us now who conjure your ghost.
We have been mostly the infantrymen
Of the country's armies—Hill 209, Hill 800.
Yes sir, they have numbers.
We feel the earth as we walk to the world's wars,
And remembering, we return to care again,
Planting the seeds to tide us until the next
Rearing of the Apocalyptic face.

In the middle of May you found yourself
Not only in Company A, but in Polk's First Corp.
You also found what enlisted men know—
Being scared is only half.
There was typhoid, measles, and dysentery;
Also nothing to eat.
Instead of the clear water of the Chickasawhay
Here muddy, stagnant holes
Held what there was to drink.
How you soldiered and how you died
We don't know. Diaries tell us
What days it rained. We know Polk's Corp
Was beyond the entrenchments skirmishing day and night.
Everyone prepared for the coming fight.

As always the enlisted men were the last to know—
All units would fall back to Tupelo.
Perhaps this was your last bright sight
As the torches were put
To the trunks and tents, the blankets and beds,
As eighteen thousand in hospitals moved
Farther south.
No great battle, just plenty dead.

Grandfather, as you leaked away in June
Did you think at all of generation?
Your wife even then carried a son.
Did dreaming take its hands and urge you
Past Corinth to her labor to come,
To us, unnumbered, unknown
But coming, grandfather . . . coming.
Your blood may have thickened in Corinth
Yet your seed twisted to a birthing scream,
Your blood surged to now,
Surges like a sea in my head
Even as it may have spoken to you lying there
In your cocked hat,
Now tipped to shade your eyes, now tipped to die.

What now for the unknown soldier?
Somewhere in this plot of four hundred Confederates
Your bones stopped
But your blood salts leached the ground
On their way to the Chunky and Okatibbe,
On down the Chickasawhay, past the summer corn,

And the homestead you left unfinished,
On to larger holdings. Your salt blood
Moved now down the Pascagoula,
Out to the Gulf of Mexico, out to the salt seas
Embracing the earth, holding us all.
Your home is large now, your wraith has a name.
You rest in your sons
Who must keep you to keep themselves.

KAREN L. MITCHELL

The Eating Hill

Going to get some eating dirt, special dirt
For my mother.
Going to take a pail, a fork
And dig in the special ground,
Until the pail is full
With baked brown, sweet soil.

Grandma took me to the brown hill, eating hill
When I was much younger.
We the dust, ate the dirt
When very cooked
In Grandma's great wood oven.

Down the well, the deep well
I went to get some rain water.
Passed lined clothes, wet clothes,
Passed great-aunt's cabin
Snatching her great red rose.

Take a honeysuckle, take a blackberry,
Must take a pail of rain water
And sit on the eating hill, special hill
Until my heart stop running,
I stop racing,
Quiet, so quiet
On the eating hill.

Closed my eyes, my brown eyes
And watched the colors bleed in darkness.
Did I hear birds? Grandma's voice?

Or was it my grasshoppers
Singing behind my shoulder?

Don't sing too loud, my Grandma's still.

"Nothings like eating dirt,
Nothing's quick and easy to fill,"
My Grandma said, sitting on the eating hill.

Great, great, great, who?
The water restored my lips.
Remember, remember, remember, when?
Grandma, you remember
Us laughing on top of
The eating hill.

Touch, your wrinkled touch
Rocks me in your arms.
So quiet,
So pretty,
This red rose
Fading in my arms.

My torn dress, flower dress,
Blows in my small face.
Laughing sister, younger sister,
Come to me
And let mud mix with our lace.

Cool water.

Chopped wood burns
Cold rooms.
Laughing sister, sleep next to me
Living under covers.

Beans in the garden,
Oil lamps in the box,
Green leaves in my hands crumble,
Red berries grow smaller.

Too dark my dear,
My Grandma dear,
To eat with you much longer.

She is mine,
Moving,
Old sister,

Old mother,
Brown-eyed dirt, lovely dirt
Waking in my arms.

Mother, mother
Grandma said
Don't take away eating dirt, special dirt
From me, to me,
Eating dirt
Would stay.

So I must climb the eating hill, special hill
In the morning.
Must walk the road, the path
Slide between trees, cedar trees
And clear caves by mid-morning.

Black Patent Leather Shoes

Slipping in my black patent leather shoes
Papa would make sure they reflected
Me
Not caring how many times they were
Used
He would make me put them on
With laced stockings
I never danced in those black leather
Shoes
Only studied their simple details:
Black
As black as my hair they surely were
With three straps, that held me there, and heels
Stacked
And I could not wear my black leather
Shoes
Everyday, but only once or twice a
Week
And he would make sure black polish was
Used
Papa would make sure those shoes
Reflected me

Birmingham, Alabama: 1963

The choir kept singing
while the preacher screamed through the walls
Miss Anderson testified that she
was cured because she believed
and we all got the Holy Ghost
drinking his blood
eating his body
I clapped my hands and cried "Jesus!"
saw Baby sleeping on Mama's lap
his dime rolled into the aisle
"Glory!" Miss Anderson cried "Glory hallelujah!"
and then I heard a sound
saw my pink dress tear
something colored my stockings my shoes
I saw my black face split
heard feet moving
"Mama!" I cried
and we four went up
with the dust

Don't come to this wake
or touch this small cold body
lying in velvet
I am Job's children
dead from the Lord and Satan's wager
dead when the wind closed its eyes
and smote the four corners of the house
I have been left dry
without knowing why
I have not read the papers of Birmingham

Braid my hair
in the rain-washed morning
I want to come back to you
stand beside the stove
and watch you stir steam
curl my finger around your ear
and make you hear the beating inside you
I want to breathe through the pores of this wood

I keep hearing the choir sing
Steal away, steal away, steal away to Jesus
I keep hearing the preacher's sermon

"So young! And she's gone!"
Steal away, steal away home
"She didn't become that doctor!
She didn't marry and have that child in her arms!
Then grow old and rock another baby!
She was killed in a church in Birmingham!"
"Lord!" Miss Anderson cried "Lord have mercy!"
I ain't got long to stay here
I am Job's children
Steal away, steal away home

CHARLES MOORMAN

September Song

And has the summer passed at Lux without
    A single shimmering afternoon or languid
    Evening? I remember—what? Only flaccid
Hours of numb routine, on weekends bouts

With dead machines, on holiday the lines
    At airports inching irritably along.
    Listening to the river now, its song
Entices me poetically to pine

For childhood summers, for the wicker sofa where
    I read *The Prisoner of Zenda* twice
    One endless afternoon too wet for base-
ball; Or to sigh for summer's tragedies:

For Pickett waiting that July day for leave
    To charge, for Roland dead at Roncevalles,
    And for "a summer's day" when Satan fell
"From morn to noon . . ., from noon to dewy eve."

But all this sensitive despair, I feel,
    Is not the summer's fault, nor am I sure
    That Pickett, Roland, Satan found their gore
So glorious. Vanities flock to fill

Our heads with feldspar dreams, and the least fox
    That roams these woods knows better than to piss
    Away the present conjuring the imaginary kiss
Of chimerical summers. The swirling river mocks

The Prisoner of Zenda, Pickett's charge,
   The lot. Troy having fallen, all flesh is grass;
   And so these August, gewgaw symbols pass,
Cheap jingles by the Woolworth heart writ large.

Oh, September river, surely here at Lux
   You may baptize our foppish ironies
   To faith in what survives the obsequies
Of wit, the steady current beneath the flux.

SANDRA NAPIER-DYESS

The Gravel Pit

When she was little,
he would drive them,
her and her cousins,
squealing along the very edge,
commending them all into God's
hands while dipping one wheel
into the pit.
Later she wondered
was it a gamble everytime
whether they came driving back
over the red gravel to the house?
He took no blame, it was in the breed.
His ancestors, proud possessors
of one brindle mule and a suit of clothes,
would range back and forth
over state lines
dodging debts and
making grimeyed babies
old at twenty-five.

JOHN NIXON, JR.

I Remember 1929

I remember 1929.
The cotton gins went Boom-boom-Boom-boom-Boom.
At five, in Mississippi, I was fine.
Hot noons, that summer, in the dining room

They let me sip diluted home brew, though
My mother was the most belligerent dry
The world has known. Daddy built bungalows.
My sister, cutest gal in junior high,

Had cut her curls "wind-blown" and had a pink
Silk hat with glitters on it. Black Aunt Ann
Died and was buried with some pomp. I think
Boob was my favorite funny paper man.

Our neighbors in the vast brick house across
The road imported bands from Memphis twice
That year for dances. Sweating brine, a horse
Brought us a wagon, an ice man, and some ice.

The cotton gins went Boom-boom-Boom. One fall
Day Mother took the bottled brew behind
The barn and smashed it there. And that was all
The crash I heard in 1929.

Ornamental Knowledge

To have fed the oval hunger of his skull
With a dull flow of useful chemistry
And mathematics only would have starved
The boy for life. Bored by the practical
Rules for survival in a world forever
Changing its rules, his mind yearned constantly
For purely ornamental knowledge. Never
Tempted by basket ball, he memorized
The sovereigns of medieval France,
Their queens, their wars. He found the early Louvre
More to his liking than the school gymnasium.
For who with half a feeling for romance
Would travel with the team to the next county
When he could much more glamorously move

Across the centuries beside the ninth,
The sainted Louis toward Jerusalem?

The boy would not. He painted on his skull
Sufficient scenes from Gallic history
To make a whole existence colorful.

Miss Maggie and the Voices

On anybody's roster of old girls
Not readily forgotten in our town,
Miss Maggie's name is tall. When she came down

From her last bristling day at the switchboard,
Her business frown still on her, she was through
Forever with wrong numbers and the new

Dumb operators, through with thirty years
Of disembodied voices that barked, purred,
Shouted, or whined. Lord, what she *had* endured.

Good-by. Good riddance. So Miss Maggie walked,
Idle and ponderous, around the square.
With high-topped shoes on, with her faded hair

Mannishly bobbed, she had clumped forth at last
To face the voices. I can see her yet,
Pausing immensely in a tangled street—

Propped on her cane, letting the traffic swerve,
Miss Maggie, scowling, whom the voices made
Leathery, acid, lonely, and unafraid.

A Niche for the Architect

Custodian of wars, keeper of kings,
Mr. McLyle, plump as his histories,
Presided over four of my winters. Things

On which he and the text saw eye to eye
Were limited. Caesar and General Lee
They both considered brilliant boys, but I

Mostly recall with what heretical mirth
Idols were yanked from pedestals in that class
And groundlings elevated from the earth

To take their place. Ah, what a pantheon
Mr. McLyle devised (installing fools
And sages, pirates and patriots, nuns

And courtesans), delighted to erect
This better heroes' hall for us. Now we
At last must make a niche for the architect.

LEWIS NORDAN

He Fishes with His Father's Ghost

After his death we wade together
Chest-deep in a cold river. He smiles
And winds a silver thread
Into a silver reel and lands a fish.

Next I catch a fish and put it with the first.
They lie behind us in a wicker creel
Dying. We cast out again and again and
Catch other fish. They also breathe the killing air.

Mother said he was not tender, she said
There never was so sexless a man.

I look back and see my fish have human faces,
Dwarfish arms and legs; his are sleek and bloodless,
Their flesh impersonal silver.
Grieving, I catch other demi-men.

When all are cooked and crisp
He eats whichever are closest to his reach.
He ruined everything, my mother said.
He was not tender. I cannot love his memory.

I wade again into the same water
And again he casts beside me.
Again his fish are silver and mine
Dwarfish monsters. But now I know

They love their torture.
They love my grief.
All lie squeaking and beating their legs
And arms against the earth.

My first silver strikes the final cast.
It leaps at the end of my silver thread.
I wind my silver reel, and I look
At my father, who is proud of me and not tender.

The fish's sweet flesh dissolves
Upon my tongue. With warm white bread
I sop the last sweetness from the pan.

STEPHEN OWEN

Confessions from Childhood

(Class Reaction to *Lord of the Flies*)

1

With chairs in a circle
We become an island
Staring deep into chasms
Of ourselves.

From the fear and anger
So shallow in our flesh
The beast awakens
In confessions from childhood:
Stories of hanging sisters' dolls
With jump ropes,
Aiming toy pistols
At heads that spout
Blood mushrooms,
And exploding firecracker bombs
In cat skulls.

The beast lunges,
Digging out our backbones,
Leaving them snarled vines.
Our flesh rages
While our spirits cower
In the mouth of pig lore.

2

Afterwards on our island
A final wave breaks
Covering us with shame
And wonderment.

The beast recoils
And settles back
Under our quivering flesh
While in animal silence
We sit afraid
With human masks
At our feet.

PATSY CLARK PACE

Distant Kin

In Mississippi, historians record only facts,
The gathering time and place of distant kin.

But cousins at reunions drink water
From a shallow well with a dented dipper.

As the young explode conversations
The summer sun wilts white roses
Which girls cut short-stemmed
To pin in their hair. The boy cousins
Boast their hunting skills,
Then show trophy scars
Where fish hooks tore the flesh.
The explanations are electric.

At Mississippi reunions, the distant kin
Discuss the kinship, exact cousining.

The dinner under the trees is over.
Only the flies stick and stay
Where chocolate cake ended the meal.
Gold watches signal the quieter drone
As second hands sweep the last tale.

In Mississippi, old wrinkled women smile
And feel a cousin's kiss, remembering.

Saigon Sky

A memorial poem to the heroism of black Mississippian PFC James A. Woodruff, killed in action in Viet Nam June 1, 1969, and awarded the Silver Star posthumously for gallantry. "Saigon Sky" was inspired by the dignity of his monument and the quiet peace of his grave site in Odd Fellows Rest Cemetery, Aberdeen, Mississippi

I saw him fall—
Pressed down by the big blast
Into the Saigon Cemetery
As if the burial and the ritual of dying
Were reversed. The sand filtered,
Sifted, spattered a thin pattern
Over his drawn face.
The blue lips and green eyes
Were all of him.
The twisted, crumpled HE
Bled slowly at the edges
Until the sand darkened,
Leaving him like a paper man
Who would blow into the March sky
And float there endlessly—
Tied to earth with one slender string.

LINDA PEAVY

Some Keep the Sabbath

You squirm and wiggle on my lap
sweaty as I, your cotton skirt, like mine
clinging to legs and thighs, your hair
a wet blur across your scalp, your spirit
strangely weighted by the atmosphere.
Your eyes take in the rows and rows of people.
Families with mannered kids and cooing babes
old men who wheeze, women whose palsied heads
are bowed in prayer or raised in praise.
You will bring questions to me.
The singing, broken harmony, uneven unison
the words so unfamiliar you make no attempt to follow,
listening instead, as my strange alto confidently moves
with organ's plain, slow steps, piano's bright accompaniment.

Your eyes most often go that way.
The hands that play those keys are hands whose warmth you know.
The sermon, spoken by a man younger than I
yet years more fervent, the sermon bores you
so you squirm and bounce and do the things
no four-year-old who's used to church would do
and I, knowing you've given my secret out
contemplate the comments that will
buzz along the rows of butterbeans
rustle in the cornfields
and flit around the corners of Cox's grocery.
The invitation hymn begins,
oozing about us as we cling
to what is still familiar—just each other.
I find one hand touching your shoulder
feel my knees tighten around your legs
only the limp cotton of our skirts
knowing the desperation of my grip.

Poem for a Sister Three Decades Dead

Long before I knew
you were not like the others
death had come to seal your secret
in a metal box. We kept you there at home
set your small casket on a satin stand
and let you lie in state within
a picture-window frame. My scout troop
came to say goodbye and I could see
upon a wave of green their faces,
sad as mine, for all the loss
was not their own. You alone
were tearless on that afternoon,
a waxen doll of six-month size
your tiny arms outstretched
as if inviting life to take you up again.
At ten (the age I was when you were put away)
my daughter's playing with the baby clothes
my mother swore no other child would wear.
She's dressed her best doll in a pink knit suit
whose rusty snaps have left their stain
on all they've met inside that drawer.
Once more a waxen doll is framed inside

a picture window, snugged in the yellow blanket
in whose flannel folds they brought you home
and took you back again.

Dark Quartet

1

Wirey, black as charcoal, coming just to Mama's shoulder,
Iva plied her piling hoe as well as any man,
peeling rough grey bark from off pine pulpwood's sticky surface,
mingling its pungent turpentine with unfamiliar odor of
Bull Durham, spat in long, brown streamers
through her gold-capped teeth.
An outside worker, Iva came only as far as our back porch,
filling her Mason jar with lukewarm water from
the faucet by the steps.
Once I brought a tray of ice cubes out to her.
Soon we noticed ragged bachelor's buttons
by the dripping outdoor hydrant—
a silent, nodding gift from Iva's hands.

2

O.D. was ironing, cleaning girl
("girl" though as old as Mama and outweighing her
by forty pounds or so). Out on the breezeway
she would iron for hours, her bare feet flat and
two-toned brown against grey cement floor.
Too shy to talk (she always said "too busy")
she'd sway and hum over my dad's rough work shirts,
smoothing her iron now and again against the bough
she'd broken fresh that morning,
sending its clean pine fragrance through
the heavy summer air.
Once when a sudden storm blew up
she stopped her ironing, sought the refuge of the kitchen,
tossed apron back over her head, and rocked and moaned until
the jagged lightening came no more
and thunder's threatening roar became
a safely distant rumbling.

3

"Miss" must have had another name
and Charlie, too. But I knew nothing more
in all the years of interaction with the two.
Granddaughter of a slave owned by my great-granddad,
she stayed, as had her father, serving the white folks
she had always served. My grandma's cook,
her cleanliness was never even questioned,
in light of which I never understood
the scolding that I got one day
for eating sweet potato pie warm from her own wood stove.
I never understood because it tasted even better there, somehow,
served in the tiny room whose only light
was from the coal-oil lantern
whose fumes gave off the perfume
Aunt Ebie didn't want.

4

Creamy brown and smelling of lavender dusting powder,
Louella, with a dip of snuff discretely tucked
into her lower lip, came to keep the children.
Upon her broad, white-aproned lap
we sat to hear the stories she would read.
She was the only one who could—
but then we didn't think to question why.

The Telling Tree

"I'll race you to the telling tree,"
she called past clang of recess bell,
then sped to be the first of three
to claim the oak whose tangled roots,
sprawled angular as spiders' legs,
were shelter enough for secret things.
Shedding thin coats, they dropped onto
the hard-packed clay, legs out,
backs leaned against worn trunk,
coats snugged across them, blanket-like,
till yellow-brown plaid, dark navy, and red
were spread from root to rough, gnarled root
against the late November chill.
With only their faces out and free

there at the base of the telling tree
they shared the things they could not share
anywhere except that place.
Fran's mother was having a baby again.
Lee's dad had beaten her til she screamed.
Norma Jean's brother was back in jail.
And everyone knew that Freddie would fail
third grade and have to repeat next year.
And maybe you didn't go straight to hell
if your teeth touched the host—
but maybe you did,
and for other things, too. On and on
the secrets flew—nobody caring if anyone knew
all that they had to say to be free
there in the roots of the telling tree.

WILLIAM ALEXANDER PERCY

Home

I have a need of silence and of stars;
Too much is said too loudly; I am dazed.
The silken sound of whirled infinity
Is lost in voices shouting to be heard.
I once knew men as earnest and less shrill.
An undermeaning that I caught I miss
Among these ears that hear all sounds save silence,
These eyes that see so much but not the sky,
These minds that gain all knowledge but no calm.

If suddenly the desperate music ceased,
Could they return to life? or would they stand
In dancers' attitudes, puzzled, polite,
And striking vaguely hand on tired hand
For an encore, to fill the ghastly pause?
I do not know. Some rhythm there may be
I cannot hear. But I—oh, I must go
Back where the breakers of deep sunlight roll
Across flat fields that love and touch the sky;
Back to the more of earth, the less of man,
Where there is still a plain simplicity,
And friendship, poor in everything but love,

And faith, unwise, unquestioned, but a star.
Soon now the peace of summer will be there
With cloudy fire of myrtles in full bloom;
And when the marvelous wide evenings come,
Across the molten river one can see
The misty willow-green of Arcady.
And then—the summer stars . . . I will go home.

Overtones

I heard a bird at break of day
    Sing from the autumn trees
A song so mystical and calm,
    So full of certainties,
No man, I think, could listen long
    Except upon his knees.
Yet this was but a simple bird
    Alone, among dead trees.

ERIN CLAYTON PITNER

Apples in October

for Brian

Munching apples
we linger on the steps in the sun.
For me the days plod downward
each in its own gray shoe of stone.

For you at four, the steps are a rubble
of roots and stone stemming
toward a corolla of leaves
cradling earth and sky.

All is here.

Seeds of light bursting
from the dark core of stone.
And in your hands apples
sunsoaked with juice
running down your chin.

To a Child on her Sixth Birthday

for Erin Abbott

You grow tall
in your blue velvet dress
demure as Alice stroking her cat.
A tortoise-shell cat sheathing his claws
at the merest clutch of your hand.

You grow, I shrink.
Somewhere betwen the least and most
of you, we meet.
Week by week, year by year, I come
yet each is the first. No inbetween
for child or beast.

You cut your eyes at me. They follow
their own caprice. Curious how eyes
of child and cat peer back at me unchanged.
That ancient ingenuous gaze transcending
all the woes of Eden lost, before the advent
of cudgel, whiplash and fang. The cat stirs
in your arms and hones his claws, daring me
to take a single step within your realm.

When first we met, you shrugged me off
with a swift invincible glance.
A child holding her cat before her
like a shield emblazoned upon the heart.

I retrace your footsteps, year by year,
as my own.
Somewhere between the first and best of us
both, we span the wall.

Wind Child

At ten, you are a poet.
You speak of crickets chattering
beside camp fires
and willow trees webbing the wind
with silver-green fronds
of lace.

The word *free* appears often in your verse
as you envision *gates of tomorrow.*

I probe each nuance with gentle fingers
but you shrug me off and slip away,
flexing your wings,
refusing to light on my palm.

Shush crickets
shrilling you to banked fires.

Shun willows
conjuring the wind.

Flee
while the day swings wide!

STERLING D. PLUMPP

Blues

Blues. And the morning lifts
night from its dishrag
of darkness, commences to moan
vines of light climbing
over the horizon
in a vested crimson summoning.
Blues. And the day arrives
spitting pieces of rays
on darkness in transitions.
Blues. And time wakes me
to another pain before executioners
arrive, with commands
from mythology to wipe me
from being. But I'm ready,
ready as anybody can be,
ready for you,
hope you ready for me.
I got ax-handled tears
in the ball of my hand,
drinking bruises and blood
in a alcohol vein,
ain't in no mood
for no jive commands;
ain't in no mood
for no jive commands.

Blues. When I got
out the womb. All red
and underfed. Couldn't lay down
cause the blues all in my bed.
I got this pinching memory
so bad/I don't know
'xactly what to do.
I call on god
but he can't answer;
I call on the devil
but he can't hear;
and I call on the wind
and it comes here. Moved me
round so long
that I can't rest at all.
Blues. I got this pinching memory
so bad/my mind notices
everything that crawls.
Blues. Won't somebody come
tell me the good news.
Feel so low/feel like an empty cistern
in a six month drought.
Everytime I try to move the dust
gits up and dances about.
I got the blues.
And if I forget, I got
everything to lose. But don't
git me wrong cause I ain't
gonna lay down dead. I will
just sing, feel pain, and keep
going ahead . . .

Clinton

1

Before me/taut pallets of smoke.
Day waking from pores like black smiles
Defying tenements' grasps. Rural town,
Your skies got the blues.
My longings like cigarettes
Come back for your deep sleepdrags.

It is inhalation, winged memoryreel
Of panoramic comfort that takes
My infancy again to diapers and dust
In the front yard. The song of flowers
Breathing windy perfumes agitates
The fever of sunshine. Escalators.
Your gullies and hills. I run
Through rains from tree
To tree when thunder and lightning
Lie bedridden. Spring.
I am looking out/on uncle's shoulders
Before feet can enroll in your rich embrace.
Funny. How old and young, men and women,
Animals and plants, come up with the sun
To darn the morning with laughter.

2

Talk between the people and the soil
Goes on in sermons by middlebusters
Solos by section harrows
Graces of cultivators
Shouts by swinging hoes
And confessions by hands and knees.
The little plants of cotton, corn, tulip,
Bean, turnip, and okra, open their eyes
To the sun and people bending.
Growth of the vines is a "hello"
Climbing to greet minstrel poles.

3

Night town, strange winds of mystery
Blowing ghosts of rising moons,
I rock in your harvested bosom.
My milk and bread in a bowl
Come through tar-tars from momma.
Hot cornbread crumbles like dirt clods
And makes the clabber bubble.
Before my bowl runs it over
I shovel my spoon to my tummy
And run to the pot before I do-dos
What I gotta do.

4

Dick Tracy chases Eighty-Eight Keys
Past Little Nancy and Slugo.
Cotton town, crossroads town
Of honeysuckle blossoms on fences
Like the faithful on the King's Highway,
Work is seed tonic, logical wine
Committed to the thirsty reason of men
Winning today's rib tips of command
With the swallowing of their labors.
Out cross blackness
Lightning bugs soul clap with stars.
In my heart I want sweetwater
And before I drink at prayer time
Momma says "She is your momma;
I am your grandmomma". I could not
Understand her meaning and my thirst
Became bitter mosquito bites. Shucks
In the mattress played hide
Tickling feathers in the pillow
So they flapped in my face. I lay
Listening to snores of unanswering walls.

5

Morning glories
Pull down music of work days,
Hometown, straw hat men
Walk with round women in ginghams.
I plow unfurrowed rows of my life:
Swinging in trees, sliding down hillsides,
And playing in cotton sheds.
My song of longing leaps
Through radios of your vistas
Like instant dreams in cups of sleep.
The mud and rains of freshness
Stroke my body like a do-right woman.
Black folks picking cotton
Hauling it to gins
Being cheated and whipped
Side their heads if complaints
Burst from sorghum lips.

6

Like a quail
I saunter down your dusty roads
Evenings and dare
Hound your paths, nights
When ghosts blow their cold breaths
In my face when I climb hills
And rinse me in hotness
As I walk in valleys. Rails
Crack with the Bugga Man's steps.
Darkness is a blanket. I touch it.
I cannot sleep anymore unless
My mind exhumes your covers
From the couch of memory.
Momma breaking clods to insert
Seed birth of promised greenness.
Years blink in the distance
Like comets. Yet my scope
Is set on fall afternoons
When leaves wear reddish brown
Shirts and bop to the ground.
Dew comes in mugs of fog
And the sun oversleeps
But goes to bed early.
Off in your nights frost
Becomes coconut of midnight cake
As we watch the simmon tree
For an old possum . . .

7

Today at the edge of light
I soar back to your horizon
Like wise lips hugging thighs.
This hedonistic kneeling of wonder
Yearns in my loins
Dry ice in time's hind pocket.
And I cannot but glory at the sight
Of yesterday rocking down
Through the perversity of my despair
Like an old Black man in a buggy
The bay mare trotting and
He sitting in judgment like Pontius Pilate.

Summer town, I walk out on your fingertips
Reaching for grapes and black cherries.
The bucket I carry in my heart
Is a memory vault. Cotton mouth moccasins,
Spreading adders, and rattlers
Coiling at your toes for granite peace.

8

I resound in your wide halls,
Dirt town, red clay boys
Throwing mudballs
Against banks and one another,
Men and women in rubber boots
Wading and making ditches,
And setting tomatoes and onions straight
On rows. I am pierced by brightness
Of momma's headrag and cleanliness of her apron.
Poppa's overalls are true blue
And patches have conspired
To conceal holes. Autumn.
Pecans rolling around
And hiding under leaves.
I stuff my pockets/eating
Until my belly aches. Castor oil
Invades my ancestral pride
To make my minutes loose.

9

Bad town, I see a white-faced bull
Snorting anger out his nose and pawing
With sturdy precision to zero his body in.
I want to follow a leader beyond clouds
To high nests. Thickets become my refuge.
I walk miles in them. Before long I hear
A bellow coming to the trees. I run
To our yard and enter the grave/wooden gate.
With the agony of black widows leaving grave sites/
Husbands in their eyes, I withdraw to bed
Being checked by a white face
And a huffing and a puffing in the ground.

Night loops of silence/I come to loiter
A black seed in a ripe watermelon. I sit

In tribute of backlogs filling cavities in walls
With rowdy heat. January weekends are great days
For sitting/talking/roasting/and drinking.
Jars of peaches are opened on homemade bread.
Friends and relatives drop by with news.
Extra plates come with bowls of gumbo.
Soppings go on in seconds and the cobbler
Is last to go.

I trot out in the wild wind.
Sable coffee of you stencils
My soul. School/blackboards, benches,
Tables, and toilets outside. Mrs. Latham
Sits watching mouths for gum and quick hands
For spitballs. I cannot go unless
There is an excuse me. Sumner Hill
Is white sides and a green top.
I put my lunch on a desk/then take
My initial wisdom strokes.

10

I come crying/dry leaves
In the wind. Suddenly back
Where lasses and cornbread are vows
Wedded to butter. A looking-glass
Reflects hours/sassysweet dust kissed rains
In times I hugged tight over potlicker.
Could it be/now I am away/far and older/
That joy I know is but a breeze
From clarinets swaying in ways
Only Al Green can feel to order
With his inside love screams?

I have known the arresting
Tender surrender of leaves and
Sap piping green monsoons on desire.
Have known my life is music baked
By fingers only Max-Roached-Monks
Taking C-Tranes can buy with salt peanuts
Of insight. My growing years gallop
Like hoofs of justice. Fear rides
In my veins/when I am jailed by Jim Crow/
When I remember Willie McGhee burning/
Remember Emmett Till drowning/when I remember

Those castrated by silent consent
Not to revel in songs of their manhood.

I sing in solitude; sing pouring
Ways into your gourds and I drink
Recognition. I sing to Holy Ghost
Years/Sumner Hill's diction in accents.
Daily immersion into what St. Thomas said
He thought God was all about and
Life supposed to be. My neck bending
From beads/rosaries saying any life
Without the Roman seal is lost.

11

What is this hip yearning smooching hot
In my breath with passion cut by young
Southern language? What is my life
But a little cup of knowledge? What is
Pain joy sadness love happiness
And despair but a gumbo of life simmering
In pots of your wonder days, nightchild town?
The winds and ways people move
Are scars drawn on your morning valley face
By diasporic singers crying holy blues.
Your lips bless my presence with Satchmo's
Embouchure, small town.

Where do the past's fingers end?
Is yesterday but today and tomorrow
Called in more intimate poetry?
Where is the when of this angling statue
Carved in man's memory as footprints
Of events loved? Where is your magnolia sweetness
To zip up my mind? The streets wind in tune
With pathologies. Crimes manufactured
From need. Songs blown by life. I uncover
Your legacy in the city. Death paints my reality
Before I can pull sounds into sonic graffitti.

12

Your morning peace still drums
Color into Chicago's climate. I go

From open diaries. High school with nuns
Bunnied up in blue. Boys and girls
From "better classes" riding bicycles
And thinking they in space ships
To power and wealth. I am lost.
Keeping somebody else's seven sacraments.
Worshipping fear. Running from everything real.
College is no better than grammar school
Or high school. Only signs of illness
Are less visible. I am in an asylum.
Poor light. Strangers block mirrors
And muddy the water. Songs I have
Drown in books. I am condemned
To repeat names of the dead.

Chicago. Winds bandaging wounds
On faces. Making the world go mad.
My campus after St. Benedict's rules
Tried to commit me behind bars forever.
Ten-hour days. Mail bags. People working
And drifting in confusion. Men fighting
Men. Letting the boy kick their asses
And keep them humping till their number
To move up on the plantation is pulled.

Vision is all life can ever be. Man rising
From clay to control the stars
Because he covets his shadow hovering
In clear days. My source. You are vision.
Back down in Mississippi. Vision. This thunder
Pounding in the music I live.

13

The army. I cannot even dream.
My vision so fixated on suffering
I nearly lose songs spread across decades
My steps took to ripen a music
That is sight. Vision/I say
Is all a poet is and all life is.
Vision is all I could hold onto.
I wake. Morning calling me/notes bopping
Blue and mighty loud in make believe soldiers
Grinding their lives in rinds. Marching

To whistles monsters are blowing.
And the sky is grey and crying. I rise
From government issued hurt laughing.
Tears walking down my face.

The world. A womb and I, bottled flesh,
Dependent upon land to uncork my soul.
Every thought I imagine is thrown
By hands of the land. That source
Naming me. That source I return to
When skin is torn, mangled and I possess
No mending arts. But what is life in armies
But baths in rusty blades? Father dies.
Words freeze in memory. Touch bequeaths ashes.
Silence. A shaky bridge I must walk in pain.
Father. Source blowing away from my anxious,
Grasping fingers.

14

There comes time I call my bonny.
Call my bonny back to me. Comes time
when I call pieces of my life. Saying I
Don't know what tomorrow may bring. But knowing
Unused scraps of my soul will moan
To rising suns. I left the army calling
My bonny without bones of your sounds
To heal my weary soul. Yet there comes time
I call my bonny. Bring my bonny back to me.
Visions in my presence are decadent
As rusted wires/wild around rotted wood.
I bring my bonny back. Chicago and the post office
Like hangnails. Everytime I move pain warns me
To stop. Everywhere I go cops shoot Blacks
Over water faucets; Blacks kill Vietnamese
For blood money. Dances in the streets revive
Old djs to spin jams for bold men rising
From fathers nursed on blueberry hills.

15

The sixties,
I told Black people, it would be all right
If they changed my name/changed my name.
Stokely says friends will not know you

If Black power change your name/change your name.
I said man, it will be all right
If it change my name/change my name.
King says your enemies will pursue you
If freedom change your name/change your name.
I said it will be all right
If it change my name/change my name.
The sixties,
I rise screaming from the dead
Cause I be so glad I change my name.
The sixties,
My blood running like it must have
When Gabriel, Denmark, and Nat realized long ago
That history cannot be put off.
The sixties,
Black people change my name.
I am touched by moanings in daybreak-talking storms.
The sixties,
Malcolm is executed
King is murdered
Little Bobby sacrificed
And Fred Hampton is assassinated.
I am touched. Fred lying in a box.
Country Preacher speaking from a nearby record shop
To the cold wet day.
The sixties,
I am touched/really touched.
A warrior lying with red books on his chest.
Panthers marching to push hurtsongs
From tomorrow's heart.
The sixties,
I remember isles of sweet livelihoods, black town.
I change my name in documents by fire.
People melting steel to take their shadows
And spin images from movement.
The sixties,
My people discovering tiers of their lives in flames.
Changing my name.

16

The sixties,
Youth says it can no longer be my friend.
My voice

Leaping with Black choirs.
The sixties,
I salivate/trying to lean with youth.
I slip into the seventies
To the present. Willie says will it be all right
If I change your name/change your name.
I said it will be all right
If you change my name.
He says the present will be a dangerous place
To live if I change your name/change your name
I said it will be all right
If you change my name. I awake
My past running along like Ellington songs.
The seventies,
My youth withering like love songs.
The seventies,
I will be all right/I changed my name . . .

I Hear the Shuffle
of the People's Feet

i am a name clanging
against circles

i go round
in what's been said and done
the old puts leashes
on my eyes
i go round
in tribal widsom

men walking from the sea
as if it is dry land
enter my circle
put me in a straight line
from profit to death
i turn from now
back to the past
they fold my future
in their bank accounts

they take me from hands
to memory

i move from knowledge
to obedience
i plant tobacco
i train sugarcane
i yessir masters
i go straight from sunrises
to death
when i remember
i chant shango
i sing ogun
i dance obatala
i hum orishas

i am folded in work
i get up
i obey
i rebel
i runaway
they beat production
from my bones
and track up my mind
with their language

after one generation
i go round in silence
while my children work
without ever knowing tribal hands
they echo my songs
until whips dull their voices

i survive dungeons
by singing songs shaped by brutality:
i sing new necessities
in a strange band
my songs carry
rhythmic cries of my journey
and when i dance
yes, when i dance
i revive tribal possessions
the elders' hands
twist my eyes on right
and let my body go

true believer, the whip
tells my mind

what to dream
i feel the blood of africa
dripping down my back

though my pride rises
in what i do
to destroy the masters' blade
sinning against my skin
true believer, i survive
yes, i survive, i keep going
though they take everything away
i survive america

my name is written
in blood-wrapped days
untold centuries of cruelty
but i survive
come into the union
through a crack
my fist made
i had experienced
breaking freedom holes
by laying underground railroads
by plotting at night
by striking blows

they closed equality's door
before i could enter
they sent me bluesing towns
facing hostility
with open-eyed moans
i get my woman
from the master's bed
but lose her to his kitchen
learn every road
from all my searching
and not one of them end at opportunity
they send me bluesing towns

when i get the vote
terror drives me into fear
the tar, ropes, and evil men
scar my name with blood

they puke their fright and weaknesses
on me
instead of on those who own our bones

though they slaughter
still they cannot stop my efforts
i survive
following rivers to cities
putting my story on brass and winds

i live tyranny down
by swinging with jazz
but the white man's word
places hinges on my sky
from the shadows
i hear plantations talk
the civil war
sets me free from legal whippings
but not from lashes

when booker t prayed conformity
at backseat rites
i could hear lynchees scream
i could hear frightened men cry
i walked with DuBois
at Niagara
they jailed my reputation
in smelly epithets
yet i survive their onslaught
distance between freedom and chains
is measured by steps from backseats
to defiance

i move by going
where there ain't no fields
going where bondage is to production
to the factory's commands
in detroit
chicago
cleveland and milwaukee
away from hot suns
away from boll weevils
away from droughts
to a new world

my music affirms demons
barking resistence in my veins
and i sing ragtime gospels
hi-de-hi-hos hoochie coochies
my girls and temptation walks

in leaving the land
my legacy is transformed
in citified jive sayings

they take me to the work line
but leave my freedom at the station
listening to rails retell the places
i have not arrived at yet
i am still motherless
yet a hip-cat-rhinehart-zoot-suiting
malcolming wolf-waters shoeshine stone
i am a bigger bad trigger greedy
no-name boy prowling chitown
they put ethel in my waters
and she emerges lady day
pestering orchards of my soul
she-goddess of this strangeness
lady instrumentalized voice
tingling new sounds in new times

what the whip and lynchings
didn't get on the land
hard work, high prices, and the hawk
took away on these streets
they send me bluesing towns
"i ain't got nobody/got nobody
just me and my telephone"
i burn from exploitation
i empty my soul on fads
powdery substances Messiahs stand on

i mau-mau stampedes
against racist stalls
bellowing "for your precious love
means more to me
than any love can ever be"
the work songs rise
to become freedom anthems

the Supreme Court hears my lyrics
and its laws change beats
"separate but equal"
becomes "equality for all"
malcolm speaks/speaks so sweet
i hear the shuffle of the peoples' feet
we move in montgomery

we move in little rock
we move
we move at sit-in counters
we move on freedom rides
we move
we move in birmingham
we move on registration drives
we move
malcolm speaks/speaks so sweet

doin the riot/i fall from new bags
with a world fighting back
in viet nam
in angola
in mozambique
in the panther walks
poppa gotta rebellion thing
momma wears a freedom ring
freedom rings
from every alley and hole
brother, come here quick
take this struggle stick
freedom rings
the get black
burning too
take all the streets
do the boogaloo
freedom rings
feel so good
black out loud
dancing in the streets
with the fighting crowd

doin the riot
the burning too
throwing molotov cocktails
making black power new

we move
malcolm speaks/speaks so sweet.
i hear the shuffle of the peoples' feet

NOEL POLK

I Make Love to a Fat Woman, ca. 1960

You laughed, full of yourself and of me so high

Above the seat, heft happily backward toward the moon,
And all your flesh like a water-filled balloon

Roiled like a coming tide while joyous I
Fondled your enormous implications.

We were fructifine; the plow I wield
First furrowed in your elephantine field:

Acres of prodigious ramifications.
O it was love I made and have made since,

Remembering what it was to be made prince
Of the amplest charms dark back seats have met

In all the years since blood and bone
Made jubilation out of lying prone.

It was hippopotamic, my pet.

I Sonned a Father

I sonned a father who would not be sonned, broke
My child's heart to show him blood that bade me
Insecurely sit where he could see
My courage running out toward his, accused
By keen investing eyes that could not bear
To see me err or give me grace to think
That I could be forgiven my uselessness.
I watched him grow, nurtured him patiently with
My need, accepted all he returned of love
Or judgment, and watched him die within a minute
Of the day he could have looked at me in peace,
Or not have looked at all.
                                    Unsonned fathers
Make their sons survive them: the final blow.

MARGARET PORTER

Sugarman

for my father, Davis C. Porter

who is that cigar mouthed man
beside the chimney
in khaki pants

sugarman?

you say i followed him
to the toilet
put too much salt in
his grits

where did he go muhdeah?

you say he sat with you
on front porches at night in summer
hibiscus stroked your nose
in rocking chairs muhdeah

who is that man who lured you
into his world at thirteen years
that man gray haired in khaki pants
davis muhdeah
dad muhdeah

he left you with stairstepped
children to remind you
of his eyes his hair
his perfect mouth
his temperament
a house with eighteen windows

that man in the ambulance
who died and left his photograph
on the shelf
why did he go
before i could remember
the smell of tobacco
in his mouth
the coffee on his breath
or taste the salt
of his sweat

or love him
or hate him

why did he have to leave.
my memory so early?

Reunion

mudeah sat on the back
all these years
widebrimmed hats
nods her head
on the last row
next to Hon
Kud'n Emma
Kud'n Roof
by the window
Ain Mattie sang
a song after prayer
meeting every sunday
children grew up
in those seats
in those songs
greasy foreheads
straightened plaits
ribbons glistened
since those years
the house collapsed
roses ran wild
wisteria choked the memory
dirty faced children
from the yard
come home again
front row, mudeah

SAMUEL PRESTRIDGE

How to Tell a Story

Jesus the South is fine, isn't it. It's better than the theatre, isn't it. It's better than Ben Hur,
isn't it. No wonder you have to come away now and then, isn't it.   —Absalom, Absalom!
William Faulkner

Unravel it
slowly, but tautly, the last strand
of rope, turning, turning, slowly separating
as the hero scuttles over the burning bridge,
the starlet in his arms. Then,
let everything crash down.

Say in 1933 a farmer with a lot of kids—
specifics and details—19 kids, all sons
to strap and carry, all deaf, all look-alikes,
planned Christmas on a cotton bale,
his last, and him with a large family,
though this needn't be mentioned again,
except to say, implicitly, how old
the man must be; the kids too, old enough
to have their own minds—not mean, but knowing
just enough to ruin Christmas.

He'd meant to swap the bale for gifts
and couldn't have them with him.
This too is implicit: *old enough to have their own minds*
demonstrates the use of idiom, succinct,
the twist of salt, adding authenticity.

By problem and solution, let the plot develop.
"He'd gotten up that morning
before the kids awoke. —This being a farm,
it would have to be, say, 3:00 a.m.,
the wife up too, cold breakfast, cold stars outside,
the bale already loaded,
and the hand-cranked, flat-bed waiting to be started.
The participle will imply that something's pending,
and the situation will create itself,
but also problems: "hand-cranked" denotes
the setting of the spark,
tinkering with magnetos, and the danger
of the crank kicking back, breaking your arm for you.

By now, he'd be in the yard,
trying to crank the sullen truck, when WHAM!—
a useful interjection, "wham"—
the crank kicked back and broke his arm.

Now, we forget Christmas and the bale,
everything but pain and the urgency
to crank that truck.
"So, he set the spark again . . ."

Here, pause.

They'll know what's coming, but won't believe.
Then WHAM! And understatement:
"He couldn't even raise his arms
to wipe tears from his eyes."

This may seem an ending,
but you can't just leave it there—
him, hopping around the yard, his arms twin trout,
Christmas pending, the kids asleep.
What happens next is toe-nailing,
a carpenter's effect.
"So, the wife woke up the oldest,
the dumb one, who could drive the truck."

The boy took out the spark plugs,
put them on the hearth to warm,
siphoned gas into a syrup bucket—
again, details authenticate—
took off the breather, put gas in the carburetor.
A cat jumped to the fender while he held the breather,
rubbed the syrup bucket, sloshing gasoline.
The boy got mad, ran the cat.
Here, quicken the pace.
The cat hid under a white pine stump.
They'll know what's going to happen.
The boy doused it with gasoline.
Here, the reader winces.
Struck a match.
Say "whoosh!"

The rest is denouement.
Talk slowly.
Be deliberate.

The fire-cat ran across the yard,
setting it on fire,
across the cotton bale,
setting it on fire,
into the barn where goats were kept,
setting it on fire.
And everything burned, even the goats,
and the boy stood looking dumb.
And the farmer, arms broken, couldn't even beat him.
And Christmas was potatoes buried in the yard.

Next, tie the story off,
relate your own life to it:
"The boy grew up to be the guard
at the Fox Run city dump, the image of his father."

To close, insist it's true.
That it happened in your family.
If there must be a moral,
let it always be the same:
God works in wondrous ways.

Now:

The Lord God, He Made All That Stuff

(for Mike Mills)

1

Aunt Boring rose early, no reason,
beat biscuits from a lump of dough
colored like her flesh and therefore
to be hated. Her husband also
rose then, never spoke, and heavy-footed
toward the gospel clang the kitchen made,
a quavering, my old aunt's jowls—
which is where it came from—
and clicked the radio to song
on top of sound. I hardly slipped
from light & into sleep again,
where Jesus saved Chuck Berry
and aunt and uncle hushed
into the one sound of my breathing.

2

A dirt-colored shed, reclining almost
falling atop Saul of Tarsus, Aunt Boring's
half-starved dog, to whom I'd field cold biscuits.
Honed eye on it, he'd run head up & back

right into shed-wall, bounce back yelping, snag—
mid-air—the biscuit, run, and hide. He knew
what next: Aunt Boring to see the noise.
Then, I'd watch the shed, the ruin implied by slow descent.

Taller, she saw the fields beyond: the usual
sun on morning pasture, cattle, blessed by her myopia,
with something like a grace. She said,
"The Lord God, He made all that stuff."

At five, I thought she meant the shed.
God, then, was my uncle,
who built the shed, let it fall, knew why,
who walked, just now, barnward,

a cloud of chickens at his feet,
a hundred feather-dusty angels
who knew the barn meant corn
for the first nine to arrive.

Speaking

Cooner Peterson never talked
about the time he split his chest twirling
chain saws like six-shooters
on a Coca-cola bet too long ago to bother with,
except he wouldn't want it told
and won't say why.
                    Nothing—
even on a bender, vanilla extract
bottles pointing out his trail,
and him sleeping beside our spring,
dreaming the rogue snapping turtle
that he said chased him up a bluff,
the neighbor's pot-shots at him
when he'd ride past on his tractor,
his mother, evaporating into cancer.

Even when we cleared scrub land together,
him on the odd side of a dead bois d'arc
we'd pull toward a brush fire,
his smell, cake batter and sweat,
his eyes latched to his shoes.

I wanted him to say something. He wouldn't
look at me, wet shirt still buttoned up against
an Alabama August, as it always is, even, I'd guess,
when no one is around.
                                        We threw the bois d'arc
on the fire and loafed. I heard from underneath
his shirt the saw
I wasn't there to hear, everybody yelling,
his heart, just wanting out.

The Outlaw Bonnie Parker
Advises My Uncle on the Advantages
of a Higher Education

At Captain Blue's, a daughter answered where
to take the two mares you stood keeping.
For what, she knew—you knew
                                        that & blushed
for the four of you. Then to the barn,

the holding pens, the stud in one &
in the next, a contemplative jackass.
What's easier than putting things
where they ought to be & stepping back?

Then, the pitch & nostril flare that is horses,
that is power, which is not knowledge,
but will do, since knowledge too
rimmed the eight white eyes & your mouth

wanting something to yell to meet half-way
the churning in the holding pen. Because
cattle are haphazard, chickens quick,
dogs obscene but prototypical,

but horses such that when suddenly a woman
watched beside you, you weren't surprised.
Brought back to *where*. Embarrassed, you looked
away, saw the Ford, Ray Hamilton

reclined against the windshield, a hood
fixture on coffee break; Clyde Barrow
in the driver's seat, watching you both
in bas relief against the holding pens.

She said, "Why aren't you in school?"
Then fifty years. A war, some wives, three careers—
the whole world shuffled like the cards
you've dealt me, soon knowing what I've got.

"So, I told her I knew to hitch mules
to a cultivator, how to set the sweeps,
how deep to plow for cotton. Wasn't much
else *to* know. I told her.

"She told me I was wrong. School was
valuable. She wrote poems, too. Beautiful poems
that rhymed right out & everything.
Sent one to the Dallas Morning Star

"telling how she didn't really smoke cigars
like everybody said. Sent it with a picture—her posing
with the corpses of two highway cops they'd killed,
her skirt pulled up to howdy-do. It was cheesy stuff

"back then. But she struck me as real good-hearted,
real concerned for what I knew.
Not much later, she was dead . . .
So anyway, I wish I had of listened. But I didn't.

"Now you gonna play those cards, or what?"
I leave two face down on the table.
So many *didn'ts*, uncle, absences all
filled with time & waking up

to find time there.
What was she thinking of,
with one hand on your neck,
nails slightly digging in?

Scenario in which My Grandma Feeds a Famous Indian

Diagonals of sunlight paint the kitchen.
Outside, a horse is snickering;
its reins trail through the window's space to him—

Geronimo, ex-renegade,
now a simple farmer
with a really spotty past.

He watches everything,
balanced in a chair with one short leg,
eating chicken with a hunting knife,
brown rice with his fingers.

My grandma is eleven, frying panbread.
She drops a speechless plate
The coffee boils; the kitchen's strange.

She told me how he thanked her
as he could, his face, a cracked brown bowl
held out for more.

It is a Sunday in October, 1908.
In the next room, her mother coughs
into a bucket. By spring, she'll be dead;
Geronimo, within the year.

What he was that day
has settled in her memory
like the plate she dropped.

Song of the Old Men's Noses

When Grandpa died, delirious,
my father wept. On the side-porch
of the hospital, his hands played death

mask to his face; his nose, snuffing grief
like a fine scent from his fingers.
And when he was himself

again, his nose had taken on the fierceness
of his father's later years,
as if eroded to the bedrock

mortal facts of death
and coming back from death
older and more cautious;

a nose not harsh so much as ready
for the scent of grief.
I say my family's standard nose,

though a friend insists
all old men look the same.
That's hard to believe!

All old noses growing fierce
with the same sad knowledge
of history's sleight of hand.

Still,
I watch: my own
grows longer, leaner.

What We Got Is Idiom

in memory of Don Wrighton

Because anybody can see and hear and smell and feel and taste what he expected to hear and see and feel and smell and taste, and wont nothing much notice your presence nor miss your lack. So maybe when you can see and feel and smell and hear and taste what you never expected to and hadn't even imagined until that moment, maybe that's why Old Moster picked you out to be the one of the ones to be alive. The Mansion, *by William Faulkner*

1

Driving from Oxford
there are words I say
evoked by land
Weyerhaueser's marred—
fallen trees,
unused, ghostly
even in strong light;
houses abandoned
for no reason I can tell
except that everybody ends
up going somewhere.

There are words—to say
them is to summon
the images
that pull nowhere
but backwards.

2

East of Pontotoc, there is always roadwork.

This morning, some scraping of machinery
and a dump truck blocking traffic.

The road's sloped shoulders here are
shaved down to a stubble
of gravel and red clay,
the overhanging pines cut back,
their branches strewn road-side,
then ground into an aromatic blend
that's sprayed to mulch the washed-out ditches.

The small stores here are petaled
with parked cars—those who work the road,
those in the community who've come to watch
the wrecking and repair,
as if it was something to buy.

The land, meanwhile, continues
drifting imperceptibly
through miles of limp barbed wire.
If it could talk, it wouldn't.
If it had wants, they would
be misinterpreted.

3

Last night, there was a party.
I told a story from Vermont,
how a woman said I'm lucky
to be from Mississippi—
"Such an ignorant, backward, violent place,"
she said. "You must have lots to write about."
"I just thanked her," I said, "because I realized
I was dealing with an idiot."

A woman listening stood, and then,
as if intensity could change a thing,
could change a bois d'arc post
into a Doric column, she screamed at me.
"She's wrong . . . That's . . . that's
just not fay-uh." She sat down then,
content with having ridden
those undulant, slick syllables
to a personal and palpable conclusion.

I understood her need—
the setting what her daddy said
against the thrust of hearts
beating only one direction.

4

There was a maniac who screamed
at disembodied voices
and nights he snored
lulled threat against them.

For years his voice, sand against a glass
that wouldn't give.

Nothing settled and then he was lobotomized.

"There," the doctors said and
charged the state and waited
as he mumbled at his stitches,
then louder, but more patiently
as, a cat's back brushing lightly,
the voices whispered now,
sighed to him as he sighed back
demure, subdued, persistent.

"What?"
he'd whisper. "If you'd just. . . .
A little louder please. . . .
I didn't quite. . . .
What. . . ."

5

The stories that we tell
fasten us to midnight
and the words of the chant
and for and against
the dark.
                    The reprieve
in anecdote is connection

to tradition

which is an aspect

of nuance

which is a part

of romance

which is marketable,

and a downhill grade to hell,

where Cerebus, wise-assed, unconvinced,
has three heads:
one to snap you coming,
one for leaving
and one for while you stand
to think, "Now what?"

He can be bought
with cakes the legends say,
or if you sing, the rhythms
of the chant will make him sleep,
if you're good enough,
and you can go
in to see the dead
and maybe even leave.

The dead, for all your efforts
still knock together,
the dog, asleep, is still
as monstrous
              as your song,
its last notes, fastens
to the rocks
like a lichen,
like a clam.

Everybody's got a story.

6

His dog went too, as was natural to dog & John Haines both
when John's mama sent him to the store, circa 1917.
John's daddy was a sharecropper, it was planting time,
and the grocer was a good man, mostly,
giving credit to the farmers who had no money, much,
until the crops came in. The grocer kept account, of sorts,
of what each tenant owed him, and they settled up
at harvest to the dime. The system worked
and hinged on the good will of the grocer,
and suddenly on John Haines' dog,
who loped into the grocer's,
braced forepaws on the cracker barrel's rim
and started gulping crackers.

John watched as the grocer watched
and kicked him when John didn't, then both watched
the dog roll yelping out the door.

John Haines grew pensive. "Don't you know,"
he asked the grocer, "y'ought not kick my dog?
Don't you know I got to whip you now?"
And he did and for a long time, and people stopped to watch,
though it wasn't wise to interrupt John Haines when he was busy.

The grocer too was occupied—dodging, keeping track
of things that John Haines beat him with and ruined
to charge back to his family's account:
two mops, plow lines, a coffee mill,
a slab of salt-cured pork,
and a jar of horehound candy
John took when he left.

John's mama tried to make the grocer understand.
He said he did, and then he cut their credit.

As mentioned, this was planting time—
the time before John Haines left home
was measured best by groceries.

And leaving town, John Haines stopped
to tell this to the grocer,
who, with business in his cellar,
needed all the doors locked to his store.

John Haines left a note and town,
came back in a year a slapstick comedian
in a jake-leg vaudeville show,
as befits a man with too honed a sense
of justice.

7

My uncle, telling me the story, said,
"You see, the sun don't shine on one dog's ass all day."

and later, to illustrate experience,

"I been further up under the house looking for eggs than you been from
home."

6

Wanting to assume a saying
stems from some event
gives absurdity a rationale—
The celebration evolves

into a summary
of what's being walked away from,
the very music of it
implying a connection
to a past that's, after all,
really no one's business.

It's riding out a notion
not to see where it will take you,
but because you know already—

where its from
what it connects you to,
though tenuously & wholly
by an act of faith

or imagination

or backwardness.

9

The dump truck clears the road,
and a flagman waves me on,
as I'm thinking of a friend who said
"Leave things where you found them
so they can keep their power."

I'm placed by more
than what I move through,
so it is not enough to watch

this morning's sun
deflected off the last panes
of a house that's been abandoned;

not enough to build a list
of things I will not celebrate.

The pilot car is leading me
through clouds of dust and light.

SUSAN PROSPERE

Silver Thaw

How cold the angels are—
so they come down to Mississippi,
their breath rising from the ice of their bodies
to frost the clover.

And they take the trees one by one
because they are jealous.
All night we listen from the screened porch
as the trees ice over and break,
their branches cannonading as the angels load them
with their terrible artillery.

My mother plays old records of Big Band music
and we begin to dance,
my father, my mother, my brothers, and I.
We are embarrassed
because we move together without grace,
but say it is exercise, after all, to warm our bodies.

We say tomorrow there will be firewood,
divinely prepared, throughout the forest.
It is only a matter of taking the flatbed trailer
and filling it with these offerings.
We discuss the blessed nature of destruction
although we don't believe it.
The angels are famous for their propaganda.

When Yankee soldiers camped in Christ Church
three miles down the road,
they played lewd airs and dances on the organ.
The angels must have heard them
and left this part of the earth.
The growing seasons are long now
and stretch into winter.

In June there will be sweetheart roses
along the whitewashed fences.
Years ago I saw my father pin one on my mother
as if it were a corsage she would wear
to enter the evening.
Her body was limber then,

and the angels would have envied her had they seen her,
dancing in the Bahia grass a private dance
that did not include my father
or any of us who watched from an upstairs window.
This was the province of the sacred,
and we begged her with rising voices to come indoors.

Farm Life

Our contract with this world is not complete.
The natural objects seem reticent,
the dogwood hesitates up and down the ridge
to open its skim-milk blossoms.
It is afraid of our disapproval,
or that we will be merely obtuse
in not seeing its analogies,
the petals rusted as if nailed shut all winter.
They are wallflowers,
so I assure them again that they are invited.

We will do so much for money.
My father allows the lumber company
to come in for selective cutting.
The trees hide behind each other
because they have nothing to gain by standing
on tiptoe, the graceful ones,
or at attention, those that are serious
and make efforts at subservience.
They only end up in other people's woodboxes.
I can promise them nothing.

Only the machines rest easy in the shed.
They know they will clear the fields adequately
and will turn chaos into saleable bundles.
This is farm life, where we work
at cross-purposes with what was intended.
The monolithic bodies of the cows turn shy
as we move across the grass toward them.
Ahead of us they mingle with the trees.
The calves unfold from their mothers' wombs
in the equivalent dark of the forest.

Once we cut a hole too large in the nipple
of a bottle and drowned a calf with nourishment.

My father and I are complicitous on this earth,
though there are things we don't speak of:
the way he stacks his pennies in regular columns
and places his shoes by the bed
as if he stood over himself while sleeping.
He knows the mimosa leaves will close
if he touches them with his hands,
that the earth as yet is reluctant to receive him.

Star of Wonder

My mother lights the pilot light
              that guides us from one Christmas to another—

to the drumstick and the cat stealing milk from the creamer,
       the India rubber ball and the Tiny Tears doll
                            rocking in the cradle.
What mechanism in our heads makes us lie back,
              open our eyes, and cry real tears?

Put
      away
            the toys;
                    we are grown now.
The sheriff's star my brother wore
                    to keep law and order in childhood
hangs between styrofoam angels
              on a tree we fell at nighttime.

Pass the sherry, please, around the green tin trailer
                            we haul the tree in.
Here's to sugarplum visions while my father has his eyesight.

Here's to a smile and a penny whistle, here's to a promise,
       to stars blown through the sky with peashooters at bedtime.

Crossing our paths, here's to the deer
                            captivated by our flashlights.

Good night.

We sleep in cigar box beds with four posts made of clothespins.
       Good night,
              good night to pick-up sticks and good night to my father
                    placing smoke capsules in the Lionel steam
                    engine.

He is taller than the train we leave on.

All aboard   All aboard
                    we go faster
                              faster
past the plastic houses and the bristle trees
                    into the darkness under the wing chair.

Sub Rosa

In the distillation process, what can be
extracted from subterranean waters
makes a slight list: my mother, the de-petaling
of a rose, and boarding houses.
In Tennessee even the darkness is a gradient
the insects climb, so when we grow tired, we rent rooms
at Red Boiling Springs for a whole season.
We say we have a suite for the summer
because the passage from room to room
takes us past the robins
as they flop against the earth,
having all day drained the chinaberries
of their spirits.
A boarder in the room next door has carved a mandolin
of an opulence we can't endure—
my brothers and I are only children.
While we are sleeping, the adults go down
to the healing waters to recover their losses.

My father drives my mother into 1934,
the stars fizzing over the top
of the open convertible as they head towards
the Peabody Hotel in Memphis.
They are dancing on the hotel roof
the night of their engagement,
chrysanthemums in pink and silver foil
lining the floor around them,
while the music of Buddy Rogers widens
like the Mississippi River towards Mary Pickford.
She has come tonight to join him,
her purse blooming
with tissues of blotted lipstick.
The small pressure of my father's hand upon her back
leads my mother into marriage.

They move together slowly, as the ducks,
gathered in from the fountains in the lobby,
rise on elevators to the hotel roof,
where they have flown loose into the present.

They settle on our pond as dusk
diffuses into the flowers.
Confederate roses grow redder in darkness;
all of us are older.
I watch my mother and father from the lawn
as they move into the kitchen,
though the light has made a double exposure,
casting the reflection of the garden on the glass.
They appear to settle their chairs,
not in the kitchen, but in the arbor,
the trees of papershell pecans enclosing them.
My mother, reaching into what she believes
to be the cupboard, will find it empty,
her hand drawing back from the bluebird house
suspended from the barbed wire fences.
In the bowl of his spoon, my father holds a rose
though he will not lift it.
The hour of secret consumption is over.
When darkness dissolves the reflection from the window,
I see them as I imagine they will appear
in the firmament—slightly abstracted,
caught, as they are, on the other side of glass.

Passion

For a dime in the 1930's my father bought a drawstring sack
                                    of chinas and cloudies
and knelt on the ground where a house had burned
to play marbles in the evenings with his brother and first cousins,
forming a circle inside the space marked on the property
by a cistern, a chimney, and gallica roses.
In the dusk he fired shots that sent his opponents into purgatory.

He taught us what he could of courage and the science of the earth:
of litmus paper turned pink by the juice of a lemon
or blue when dipped in water and bicarbonate of soda,
of mercury that scatters and convenes in a shivery dollop,
and the power of a gyroscope balanced on a string, wheeling
                                    down the airways.

What he didn't teach us is the mystery that holds a man
                      and woman together,
my brothers and I each with marriages dissolving.
The time my brother crawled under the house to fix the plumbing
in the wet darkness, he carried a pin up lamp shaded with roses.
I think he was drawn by something provocative that we haven't
   discovered,
the electrical current from the lamp charging through his body
until he cried out to register the pain
of that terrifying moment when the voltage lit up his life.

LaVine Rogers

Saturday Night

"It was a good corner,"
Mama said.
Goodness being measured by the thickness
Of the stack I sat upon—come midnight.
It was a good corner
The winds must have said
As they whipped down Capitol and Farish Streets
To meet.
I was the anchor in their game
As they rippled loose corners
The folds had left.
Mama was thirty, tall, and thin,
But she seemed never to feel
The night's cold winds.
The regulars came by, stopped to chat
As they exchanged a silver dime
For the pages of printers ink.
But regulars were few and
Never made a good night.
It was the red lights that made the measure
As Mama held the paper high—
Headlines glimpsed thru the windshield
More often than not
Made a sale
Only subscribers nodded a no.
Midnight closes a Saturday night

Leaving the corner barren
Of folk and sound.
"Was it a good night?" I asked
As Mama gathered the remains
Of the stack I had sat upon.
"Yes," she replied without sadness or joy
"We only have seven papers left."

PAUL RUFFIN

Cleaning the Well

Each spring there was the well to be cleaned.
On a day my grandfather would say,
"It's got to be done. Let's go." This time
I dropped bat and glove, submitted to the rope,
and he lowered me into the dark and cold
water of the well. The sun
slid off at a crazy cant and I
was there, thirty feet down, waist deep
in icy water, grappling for whatever
was not pure and wet and cold.
The sky hovered like some pale moon
above, eclipsed by his heavy red face
bellowing down to me not to dally,
to feel deep and load the bucket.
My feet rasped against cold stone,
toes selecting unnatural shapes, curling
and gripping, raising them to my fingers,
then into the bucket and up to him:
a rubber ball, pine cones, leather glove,
beer can, fruit jars, an indefinable bone.
It was a time of fears: suppose he
should die or forget me, the rope break,
the water rise, a snake strike, the
bottom give way, the slick sides crumble?

The last bucket filled, my grandfather
assured, the rope loop dropped to me
and I was delivered by him who
sent me down, drawn slowly to sun
and sky and his fiercely grinning face.

"There was something else down there:
a cat or possom skeleton, but it
broke up, I couldn't pick it up."

He dropped his yellow hand on my head.
"There's always something down there
you can't quite get in your hands.
You'd know that if it wasn't your first
trip down. You'll know from now on."

"But what about the water?
Can we keep on drinking it?"

"You've drunk all that cat
you're likely to drink. Forget it
and don't tell the others. It's just
one more secret you got to live with."

The Rolling Store

It came,
his grandmother reported,
as regular as Sunday morning service,
grinding up the gravel slope
to her mailbox:
"White as Easter and
long as the arm of God!"
And there on shelves
high as a tall man's head
lay trays of butter, sacks
of beans, printed cloth,
soap, nails, jugs of kerosene:
"All a body could pray for."

Asphalt lies to the mailbox now.
("The ride to the grave will be
quick and smooth," he has heard her say.)
Her kitchen stinks of disuse
and roaches haunt her shelves
where a few jars of beans and peaches
squat in dust.
("A body just don't need much any more.")

On a hillside two hollows over,
when the air is right and the
leaves are gone, he can see

from the porch the rusty rolling store
lying on its side like a brown severed arm
in a glacier of grass.

Batting Rocks

It is lonesome, like something lost,
this twist of body to send a rock sailing
from the slap of a piece of oak flooring.
Long-unused muscles try to remember,
the eye is unsure, the stance experimental.
But I will bat this tub of rocks, picked
one by one under the doubtful eye of a
clerk at the local concrete works who
shook his head when I told him my purpose.
I will fill this section of pasture, marked
for a baseball field, with liners and flies,
homeruns beyond the calf pen and barn.

Switching from left to right, I can
almost remember the boy I was, squared
in the gravel road before my father's
house, batting the lingering day away,
can almost recall the rosters I kept,
with names like Mantle, Berra, and Mays,
can know again the whir of a foul, crack
of a long drive into the deep fields
of my father's pasture and neighbor's yard.

Now, with my cows looking on like annoyed
neighbors and the light failing fast, I
toss up another rock, set to swing, then
bring the oak slat across in a level arc.
Wood and stone connect and the rock sails
high and away, beyond the peak of the barn.
It is a homerun, and I am satisfied. I
stand quiet and watch Berra, his short
legs churning, rounding third for home.

Jody Walker: The First Voice

Jody—the name conjures fawn and fowl,
the smack of scuppernong wine.

Strung in a row, we lolled each
morning, waiting for his bus
to reach school, our tongues
and fingers sharp to touch
what he delivered: blackberries
silver with dew and big as cows' eyes,
possum on a chain, ratsnake
around his neck, pickled
pig embryo, rubbers with spikes,
wines rendered from the wildest fruits,
the stuffed two-headed calf
John Parker threw up over,
owl eggs, flying squirrels,
dried bull balls black as coal—
his store of exotics as endless
as the earth itself.

Shorter by a head than most of us,
he had merely to wink, gesture,
cup a palm toward us and we
followed, older, younger, where he led.

He charmed us with tales
of coupling animals, showed us
how babies came to be, shared
photographs of nudes, taught us
how farm boys drove deep
into the soft of fruit and beasts.

His was our brightest sin:
Our dwarf god from out
as far as the buses could go
stepped down from his yellow
chariot, his hand beckoning.
His secrets burned in us;
each morning we grew in his flame
beneath the simple sun.

Frozen Over

In Mississippi I recall only once
how the cold came down like a lid of iron,
clamping the landscape, stilling the trees,
and all the ponds froze over: not

just a skim for crashing rocks through,
but thick and hard enough to walk on.
The gravel pit where we swam in summer
spanged and creaked as I edged out
toward the gray, awful middle where,
if I went through, no one could reach.
I moved like a bird coming to terms
with glass, sliding one foot, then
the other, holding back my weight
and breath until they had to come.
I could see, beyond the far shore,
cars moving on the highway, slowing,
faces in the window ringed with frost,
the little ones waving, pointing
to that child walking on water.

VELMA SANDERS

Ghosts

They sit like broken wind-up toys
On the porch at the nursing home,
Where jasmine climbs the posts
And trains screech by in the hot blue dusk;
But they still live in Midnight,
(Or was it Silver City?)
Where not much passes by
But dusty pick-ups hauling hoe-hands,
And not much blooms but cotton.

ROBERT SARGENT

Aspects of a Southern Story

1   The story as told

That this black Mississippi woman, untraveled,
standing on the beach at Biloxi, her first sight
of those rounded waters, nothing but water
to the sky's edge—
the small consecutive waves curling up
to her shod feet—
and she staring quietly a long time,
and finally saying slowly,
"Ain't near as big as I thought it'd be."

2   The usual telling

The casually dressed white people sitting around
in a southern living room, having their drinks and stories.
Somebody says, "Did I tell you about . . . ?" tells one,
then everyone chuckles, and that one brings on another.
They have this quiet, undiscussed bond: the stories,
usually humorous, some about blacks, not all,
are a way of viewing, and a way of telling each other:
we're all right, we are the story tellers, not told on.
They're fond of the butts of these stories: the ignorant black,
the old maid, the miser, the liar, the hypocrite:
we're here together, they are down there, be thankful.
"Now this black woman, you see, the Dade's nurse,
had her for a long time, they took her to Biloxi . . ."
Not "nigger," these days, usually.

3   The woman

Born in a shack by the Big Black River
into a large family. Name, Alberta Johnson.
After some years of one-room schooling,
was put out to work for the Dades, a rich white family,
as maid, housekeeper, cook, nurse, you name it.
Was honest, dependable. Loved by the Dade children.
Stayed on through the years. Self-respecting,
she was also somewhat outspoken—"speaks her mind,"
the Dades all said, tolerantly. There were, of course,
things not spoken.

4   The Trip

That year she was taken with them to Biloxi, wedged
on the back seat of the car with the younger Dades.
Driving down, there was talk: "Tell us, really, Alberta,
you never have seen the ocean?" "No," she grumped,
"ain't never see'd it. Ain't never wanted to see it."
Secretly, she did.

5   Why alone on the beach?

Mr. Dade, smarter than you might think him,
when he stopped the car, stopped the children from going.
"Let Alberta go. You've seen it plenty of times."

6   Alberta as stout Cortez

What wild surmise went glimmering,
when she came to that beach, her Darien?

7   Magnitudes

Protagoras taught we size things by ourselves,
saying, reputedly, "Man is the measure of all,"
and therefore Alberta, making her private appraisal
of the restless sea, its magnitude against hers,
doubtless thought it delimited, not so big,
and reported it thus: the size of the sea as she saw it.

8   Her posture

From the way she stood,
her shoulders back, head high, her face a frown,
surely she showed at least a touch of defiance.
Was Alberta playing folk-hero, defying the deep
by belittling its size?

9   The words she chose

Could have remained unspoken. Or replaced
by words suiting the occasion, with maybe a grin,
like, "Ain't that grand!"
and gratitude for the wondrous privilege granted
by Mr. and Mrs. Dade. Alberta, however,
independent as usual, said something different.

10   Alberta as fretted servant

Were her words a way of letting the Dades know,
as she had done in the past, her demand for respect.
But to save face for all, disguised
by a humorous grumpiness?

11   Alberta the performer

Was Alberta reporter, folk-hero, the fretted servant,
player of multiple roles, and all at once?

12   The Dade children

Later, alone with their father, said, "Daddy,
don't make fun of Alberta." He smiled and said,
"I won't tell it in front of her."

13   Back to the story

From all these ramifications, only the story,
pruned of its non-essentials, simplified
by multiple tellings, survives.

14   A loose end

In the story as told, her words were breathed to the air,
with no one to hear. But in fact,
the words were brought forth as they drove away,
when pressed by the children. Mr. Dade, you see,
knew as a southerner he had a *story,*
which, as southerners know,
is subject to rearrangement.

15   Things missed

BRENDA E. SARTORIS

Hawks Descending

Because there are no thermals
on winter days
when the breath hangs
grey in the air like ice,
hawks descend
to feed.
Risking their dignity
on fencepost and branch,
they glare disdainfully,
daring us to forget the days
when these rough pine perches
were the wrists
of kings and princes.

Skeletal Remains: Museum of Natural History

Even at rest
they are not quite just frames
for feathers and flesh, trellis-work
securing sinews, muscles, and veins.
Hollow, light, fragile as paper,
in imperceptible arcs they taper
toward aerodynamic implications,
recalling the hawk
poised on the edge of an updraft,
preparing itself for the plunge.
Now caught in a Plexiglas cage,
still these tenuous bones articulate
the eloquent silence of flight.

JESSIE SCHELL

Delta Summer

My grandmother likes to tell about
when she was young and thin and
the levee broke
and the flood came over
the leaning town
like a dirty wave,
toteing horses and shoes and rings
and a few Negro men
who happened to be there
fishing their supper
when the waters sighed
and rose up.
She likes to tell about
how she tucked up her long white
skirts and climbed barefoot to the roof
alone, to watch, like a bird, the river
suck through trees and how
she heard the cattle and chickens
choke.

My grandmother lies in her bed
like a bloated queen,
painting her pointed nails,
her hair the color of rust,
and tell me this,
her watery eyes
as soft as fish:
how the mud was black
on the gate posts for weeks,
and how ten children
drowned that day
in the middle of
the oak-lined residential street.
Their graves, she says, are
quaint black stones
that lie beneath the concrete wall
which keeps the waters neat
today.

To the Children Selling Lightning Bugs

They rush
against a glass dome,
wounding each other.
light dribbles off them
like blood.
Wings are eyelashes,
batting against light,
their own light,
bleeding.
Like bombers
kamikazeing into darkness
darker than they know,
they fall.
Their batteries slowly weaken.
Blink.
      Blink.
A signal to the fleet,
those sparks that hover safe
as neat harbor signs,
under the willow, upside
down beneath moonflower vines.
Blink.
We are breathing a curtain of air,
we are finished with flowers,
finished with leaves. Blink.
Our engines are leaking,
our muscles are torn
from the sleeves of our wings.
Come to us quickly.
Come.
We are burning alive
in this pouring light,
in our own sweet blood.

The Blessing

He is surrounded.
He knows he must yield.
His sons line up like hollyhocks
along this bed's bright field.
Their sturdy flesh blooms white

inside his eye. At his feet
a cluster of daughters spreads like
a ripe still-life. Their cheeks,
their breasts, the shadows cupped
into each nape of neck: they are fruit
he has grown, his tongue can almost
taste them.

One by one now we make a last procession.
To each, a Lear aged past all possession,
secure in this kingdom of pain,
he whispers: You. You were my favorite.
You were. Always.
It is something he repeats.
He savors the taste of our names,
though he will not recall this secret confession
when the next child enters.

I've heard his refrain, seen it laid
in my brothers' and sisters' palms
like a silver dollar. I bend to kiss
the tender spot beneath his starched
pajama collar. And know I'm too late.
You, he says. You.
He must convince me now,
but it is finished.

Father, Father, I want to say,
I will never complain.
That word alone is a blessing.
Your blood sings in my veins.

Zora

Rubbing the naked white of our legs
with her skinny black hands—
those bent licorice sticks
that flailed the waters
on our dripping heads—
Zora:
like a witch's pot,
like the infinite black under cellar stairs.
The terrible whites of her eyes
rattled the goard of her head.

She would promise
to eat us whole if we misbehaved,
to lick our white bones clean
in the light of tomorrow's moon.
She would soap our skin
with the scourge of her cloth,
and croon the ritual to its end:
singing to us of Jesus,
of all her friends,
who were washed in the blood of the lamb.

JAMES SEAY

One Last Cheer for Punk Kincaid

We never believed that any judge's word
Could send Punk Kincaid to Parchman Farm,
  But when Punk broke and wept
  On the last night of his trial a year ago
We knew that he was guilty as accused
And never again would we run interference
As he brought back a down-field punt
Or took a hand-off on a sweeper play
And moved on out into an open field.
Today we are watching Negro trusties
Drag a lake near Parchman Farm
For his body.
Word had come that Punk went down
To help recover a drowned man;
We drove all morning into the Delta
Thinking he might rise grinning
Near the sidelines
And josh about this trick
He had pulled
Or simply say the names of towns
He cruised the rustled cattle through—
Anguilla, Rolling Fork, Redwood, on to Natchez—
And with the Negroes from the boat
Gathered with us in a circle
We would help him mile by mile
Through the outlaw past.
They drag the lake with net and hook

But it will not give him up—
Below their boat
The drowned are running interference
For Punk Kincaid
As he returns a punt
From deep inside his own territory.

Grabbling in Yokna Bottom

The hungry come in a dry time
To muddy the water of this swamp river
And take in nets what fish or eel
Break surface to suck at this world's air.

But colder blood backs into the water's wood—
Gills the silt rather than rise to light—
And who would eat a cleaner meat
Must grabble in the hollows of underwater stumps and roots,

Must cram his arm and hand beneath the scum
And go by touch where eye cannot reach,
Must seize and bring to light
What scale or slime is touched—

Must in that instant—on touch—
Without question or reckoning
Grab up what wraps itself cold-blooded
Around flesh or flails the water to froth,

Or else feel the fish slip by,
Or learn that the loggerhead's jaw is thunder-deaf,
Or that the cottonmouth's fangs burn like heated needles
Even under water.

The well-fed do not wade this low river.

On the Way

This is the children's road.
No way to find it but with my sons.
The world is something else
when we get altitude.

Hard to see it otherwise
even when flying alone
on the pass they give me for the flight out.

We saw the dangers long ago
and found a song or a saying
to keep us free.

At the pound we say
every dog has his day.
It doesn't mean much but it gets us by.

The railroad crossing has a song *and* a saying.
You know the song
but this is the first time
the saying's found a page—
let the low side drag
we yell, looking both ways even on green.

If the sun finds an open blind
and shows us someone sleeping
we've got the right tongue to josh him with:
Frère Jacques, Frère Jacques,
dormez-vous, dormez-vous?
The best part's when we ring
all the bells on the hill.

After that there's the valley so low
you have to hang your head over
to hear the wind blow.
We get solemn on that one
but it doesn't last.

I think they already sense I'm the old cowboy
sentimental and silly to the end.
We learned a new one today
and here I'm still humming it on the solo run:
From this valley they say you are going,
I shall miss your bright eyes and your smile.

It All Comes Together
Outside the Restroom in Hogansville

It was the hole for looking in
only I looked out
in daylight that broadened
as I brought my eye closer.
First there was a '55 Chevy

shaved and decked like old times
but waiting on high-jacker shocks.
Then a sign that said J. D. Hines Garage.
In J. D.'s door was an empty Plymouth
with the windows down and the radio on.
A black woman was singing in Detroit
in a voice that brushed against the face
like the scarf
turning up in the wrong suitcase
long ago after everything came to grief.
What was inside we can only imagine—
men I guess trying to figure what would make it
work again. Beyond them
beyond the cracked engine blocks and thrown pistons
beyond that failed restroom
etched with our acids beyond that American Oil Station
beyond the oil on the ground
the mobile homes all over Hogansville
beyond our longing
all Georgia was green.
I'd had two for the road
a cheap enough thrill
and I wanted to think
I could take only what aroused me.
The interstate to Atlanta was wide open.
I wanted a different life.
So did J. D. Hines. So did the voice on the radio.
So did the man or woman
who made the hole in the window.
The way it works is this:
we devote ourselves to an image
we can't live with and try to kill
anything that suggests it could be otherwise.

Said There Was Somebody Talking to Him through the Air Conditioner

for Barry Hannah

1

There is always one fiction or another trying to trade for real skin
and bone, just to turn around and drive that taken character back over

the border into phenomena with the story everywhere around him alive.
The charge is to claim whatever needs to be freed from fact: road, ruin,
    stretch
of river known by heart, ring or pendant, torn flag, fist in the face, ticket
    stub,
family plot, love and grief so riddled one with the other there isn't even
    a choice.
The character he's become says he doesn't want to die, but he's got only
    one foot in the fiction,
everlasting, the other in the grave of this life. And he needs us
    conscripted alongside him.
The night I was making my way back to the old stars and bars
magnolias, for instance, just after turning off the hard road: the man
beside the bankrupt crossroads store wanted to put his story against my
    ear
like a cap pistol I couldn't quite tell from the real thing.
He thought when he flagged me down that they really were over there,
three niggers and a woman with a gun he said trying to break in his
    trailer
and kill him, the character he had been traded for.
It was textured true enough in the crack of open window I gave him
to hold me idling there with the woven thing of race, gender, hair
    trigger.
The story, though, plotted or not, has to follow out that stranded line
    and make it come true.
I know, I have tried to tell some stories and when he said they were
    going to kill him
I thought now how did he get out here to the road to wait beside Doty's
    store
if they're trying to break in his mobile home that's too small for more
than one door and within earshot of where he's standing?
But he had already forced the five of them—the traded character he had
    become,
the three black men, a starved white woman I would guess—along with
    a gun
through the thin passage and into the Volvo with me and my sleeping
    sons,
what is woven through my life like no fiction I could ever work on the
    loom of days
and nights left in this world. And let me tell you, old pilot
of the silent craft, I could not be sure.
I could not be sure if by my promise to bring help I was leaving a man
to be shot at the side of a gravel road or getting distance on a sickness
    whose fiction

could turn and align my sons and me with those figures triggering loss
as though there were no other word for them.
There was cotton on one side of the road and soybeans on the other, the
    bean field broken
by a creek running down from the hill where my sister Donna had left
    the light on for us.
You've winged home yearly enough to know the time and place.
It has a texture and our lives gain whatever is gathered in the separate
    strands.
I'd driven a day and a half from Carolina, breaking the trip with a stop
at the Knoxville World's Fair, *the one about solar* the man at the Holiday
    Inn called it.
I wanted my sons to believe the taped lecture in the elevator to the sun
    sphere,
something about all one people under the sun.
We could do that and still joke at lunch in the Japanese pavilion
about how the soy sauce for the teriyaki was probably from Donna and
    Danny's last soybean crop.
The fireworks the night before broke out in a finale of red, white, and
    blue
flagging the river running through Knoxville and they played good old
    Sousa on the sound system.
The man beside my car late at night wanted me to stand beside him in
    the only country
he could imagine.

2

My father said it seemed slow but happened in a flash.
He said he aimed first for the rising sun in the middle of the fuselage.
He said he followed the smoke of his tracers and found the target and
    worked a line to the cockpit.
He said he could see the holes one after the other until the pilot, in
    propaganda-cartoon scarf
and leather helmet, turned and looked at him just before the cockpit
    window spider-webbed.
He said he and some buddies were frying eggs when they heard the
    plane come whining in
to use the island as back-drop for a long low run toward the *New Jersey*
    out in the bay.
He said the pilot was zeroed-in on the battleship but strafing men and
    tents along its path.
My father ran across open space to get to a .50 caliber gun on an aerial
    mount,

and I see bullets puffing the dust of his camp like war movies he could
  walk out of and did.
My father said all this, it was not a fiction, the island was Okinawa, the
  pilot turned
and looked at him, he could see his strange eyes he said, it was not a
  fiction, the news-clipping
my infant sister Jackie chewed to a ball of gray pulp and made into what's
  now a family joke,
death we can laugh at like it is a sauce come to us in a bottle with
  strange characters
we don't know beans about.
My father calls them Japs and must hate them still, though he watches
  the Braves on a Sony.

3

Jess Sutton in the room next to my father's at the nursing home
told me that Negroes have changed the game of baseball, I don't know
  how,
but he could hardly bear what he saw when he came over to share the
  Sony.
I tried to move him to stories of the timber he and my grandfather cut
  when they were clearing
Yokna Bottom, hoping I'd get some whiff of Faulkner, but all he would
  say was
That Bill he was a smart man and start back in on blacks.
Plus I couldn't be entirely sure he wasn't sometimes thinking of a
  Faulkner
who owned a peach orchard near the old hunting grounds.
According to my father, Jess was seeing snakes in the weeks before he
  died.
I know the texture here is beginning to read like the worn rag of race
  and guilt
but I can't say that Jess's feelings for blacks made him see snakes at the
  end of life.
He once told me stories that were free of hate and held me rapt for
  hours on end,
as true as the grain of ash and hickory felled and shipped from my
  grandfather's mill
to Louisville Slugger lathes, oak and cherry, walnut unscrolled in
  Memphis for veneer,
cypress, tulip poplar, plain or fancy, you name it they cut it, waded
  sloughs

and hacked briars to get to wood backlogged for boats, common doors,
the kind of parquetry
that Jess got down on his hands and knees to see near Argonne in
wonder
only three days before mustard gas just about blistered him out of his
senses.
You'd think the latter would have given him characters and creatures
enough to fill any fiction,
all he needed to bring back over to help free the facts of loss, but what
doesn't get mixed
or turned tell me if you can, not forgetting the tricks and turns on both
sides of the border?
My father came home from war with only a few shards of shrapnel for
reminders
yet was left in a wheelchair for life by an ordinary accident in the
Everglades
where he was clearing a swamp to sell to exiled Cubans for raising sugar
cane.
The ever-smiling Bahamian I worked with there one summer called the
cookies we shared *sweet biscuits*
and sent money back for his wife's fare to Florida, but it turned out she
didn't want to come.
How answer love, or know what to any one person is sweet in the world?
I'd count it such
in the end just to recall something like the peach orchard I saw in bloom
one spring from a hillside,
or casting for pompano with my father on Sundays where the St. Lucie
feeds into the sea.
As though I'd written my own book, free of the strands that coil back
through dream into silence.

4

Doty told us later that the man had come to his room in back of the store
the previous evening
and said there was somebody talking to him through the air conditioner.
Doty let him in for the night.
In a pause in our talk of cotton and beans and needing rain, Doty looked
out to the creek
where deputies were shining lights for *three niggers and a woman with
a gun*
and said like somebody in local color fiction *They ain't nobody out there
in that field.*

5

I think of this country, rhythms and idioms like that: Doty waiting for
   the brief lull
to let us know there was no one in the field to fear and his way of saying
   it.
I think of the mixed texture of belief, how the measures of voices and
   motions register
and randomly become a way we think of ourselves, our time and place,
   how in the same breath
with that lull and Doty's words I could name billboards, Booth and Chast
   cartoons, Bugs Bunny;
I could name the copy of *Tom Sawyer* in grey slipcase my uncle sent
   from Marshall Field's, Roosevelt
and the Kennedy voices, Nixon, King in Birmingham; I could name the
   homogenous voice chosen for the elevator
tape unreeling a future we could dream for children, or Brando's funny
   fleering desperado lines
in *One-Eyed Jacks* and Ben Johnson getting edgier and edgier in the
   Mexican fishing camp
they're holed up in until Rio can get his gun hand back; I could name
   Nicholson sweeping the table clean
in *Five Easy Pieces* after arguing with the waitress about toast I think it
   was,
or my two favorite aunts in Memphis joking they'll pay in Yankee dimes
   for my chores,
or any of the voices and motions bidding from both sides of the border to
   be what we believe.
I think of how the voice that had been dubbed in when I saw Brigitte
   Bardot's breasts
was Hollywood French-accent and way out of sync, making the breasts,
   the first I'd seen
moving on film, even more isolate and without a history.
But I didn't object to any of it at the time, so dumb was my own
   chronicle,
and I could have come back over the border, I guess if the loss in my life
   had run deep enough,
believing I kissed those breasts and not my aunts' faces, Met and Lydia.
The other day the wind was in the pines and I was free to walk with the
   woman I love.
The dried thistle she put in my buttonhole was the grey of a soft wool
   you'd reach out and touch;
still and all, I do not know where we are going.

Sometimes simply her profile blurs all loss for me, other times there's
    the rage
of a scene: her in an embrace I can't tell from fiction, can't tell if it's five
    summers ago,
yesterday, next year, can't tell if it's my private version of the broken-in
    mobile home,
the voice coming through the second-hand Whirlpool cooling the real
    room saying
the toast half-eaten on the plate before me is poison and everything else
    in the world.
The couple in the apartment above my uncle in Chicago wrapped
    aluminum foil
around their legs and feet to ward off the rays he and the CIA were
    beaming at them.
Television correspondents in Alabama are standing by to film a man who
    called in
to say he's setting himself on fire somebody hurt him so.
I don't know if the correspondents see him as another burning car on
    Dukes of Hazzard
or a place in the long line of anchors and stringers waiting to break
    Watergate again.
I don't know if he thinks the flare of skin and bone on the screen is the
    only way to make real his pain.
I know you start hearing all the rhythms, mixing all the voices and
    motions, you're in trouble,
trying for your own embrace with history, with one person, with this
    promise-land,
with the wind that can go atomic out of the worn-out pines
down through your Volvo antenna where one man is firing into a
    playground in L.A.
and another is setting the new national record in a McDonald's in San
    Ysidro,
dropping Mexicans and Americans of all ages on the floor of his wrong
    fiction still clutching hamburgers.
On television his wife says it's President Carter's fault and it seems to her
    like being asleep
on the couch and waking up to a TV show, his mother left him at age 8
    and he lost his job.
He can't hear the elevator tape of all one people; he put on his
    aluminum boots and walked out.
He can't hear the plain talk of bankrupt Doty *they ain't nobody out
    there in that field.*

My young dog Moose, Shiloh's Golden Moose, was woozy and sick from
    motion,
not bad fiction, riding home out of the pines in the long foreign wagon.
Sometimes that kind of dog-level equation is the only way to figure
    things, where you know the answer,
dumb and sentimental, is solid ground for the little fellow and he doesn't
    have to worry
with the half-joke of history in his name or his buddy's, Stonewall
    Jackson Bear.
Other times all I know to do is laugh and lie about it, tell stories, when
    the truth won't work,
when too many rhythms start jamming the instrument that otherwise
    tells if the signal is fictive.
I know the pilot meant to kill my father I could trust the motion that
    brought the thistle
to my buttonhole the pond at Shiloh was left a bloody mess walking
    home after the war
my mother's grandfather had to have stone bruises lanced along the way
    because he had come clean
out of his boots and that is no lie my sister Donna left the light on for us
    my grandfather
had sawmills all over Yokna Bottom before he and Jess Sutton left they
    had found
a permanent place in the literature of the land you figure it out there
    were animals drawn
on the side of McDonough's Store with the names of hunters who had
    shot them bears and snakes and what
they called panthers the man heard voices talking to him there was
    something strange in his eyes
the cookies were sweet biscuits to Desmond like his woman made my
    aunts meant kisses when they said
Yankees dimes I drive a car from Sweden sometimes I do not know
    where we are going.

6

But let's say we've got them all in the cage for now—voices, snakes, x-ray
    waves, whatever.
Let's say they're with the diamondbacks my grandfather would put in
    burlap bags and take to Overton Zoo.
Let's say that all the way to Memphis I could hear them buzzing in the
    trunk of the old green Ford.
Let's say that after his donation was recorded at the "herpetarium" we
    would go to the Peabody Hotel

to drink coffee and cokes and joke with his friends from the Southern
    Lumbermen's Association
about the ducks waddling to the fountain in the lobby and I could forget
    the snakes.
Let's say that nobody but me knows if that's all lies or autobiography
and that right now what's important is the story has given us a way of
    containing things and continuing:
the snakes are in the cage with the mix of fictions we've named and not
    loose in the floor of the old Ford
like one was once and we know which is which.
Let's say it's important because the no less than life and death question
    we could pose here
would take a clear mind, no Mr. Snake-Eyes whispering through the
    Whirlpool,
no sentimental stories of grandfathers tipping doormen to get duck eggs
    for grandsons
to take back to Mississippi and how I raised a flock starting with that
    incubated egg.
That is, looking at it without tears or coils in our eyes, do we say the
    man's crossroads fiction had a gun
pointed at him because he must have wanted deep down to die, and do
    we say by the same thanatotic token
there are some walking dreamers who'd take the missionary position to
    mean it's not for life we love
and would with purpose suffer us all into what the doctor from Vienna
    once characterized
as the peace of the inorganic?
Or do we say the mind's various displacements and translations don't
    allow the grand answer?
Maybe it's one thing to be in aluminum foil overalls at the crossroads,
your handkerchief of loss in somebody's highbeams,
and another to be telling a story with something like a master race in
    mind
to the point of trying to turn brown eyes to blue with hypodermic dye or
    V-2s, and even another to believe
the little kamikaze fiction called *Floating Chrysanthemums* you've
    traded into
for the run to Okinawa behind the fighter escort my father is going to set
    his sights on.
Because if all of that and the fact of installing rattlers in the ruptured
    trunk of an old Ford
point to the same desired embrace I've got to forget how he and others I
    remember

seemed to love life and laughter to where you'd believe their charity.
My fourteen year old son told me the other day when we were talking
    about a science fiction movie
that he wouldn't too much mind going back to the Fifties to live because
    rock and roll would be new
and there wouldn't be the arms race to worry about and other things.
To turn it around I guess I'd have to get in a time machine movie and be
    fourteen in the Eighties.
For one thing, I'd want to know how often the time fused to my wrist
    would flash on me like that watch
from Hiroshima on the cover of *Newsweek* the week he and I talked
    about music and time and the movie.
For another, I'd want to know how much I believed the frail simple thing
    we let it rest on:
how you have to live in your own time and believe in the best people
    you can find.
It wasn't *A Farewell to Arms* by any stretch but I did think of that
    passage about only the names
of things having dignity and I tried not to embarrass us with too many
    things that didn't have names.
Nor did I want to get too confessional for comfort, about how most of my
    friends and I
at one time or another in the not too golden past would have taken a
    ticket to the Fifties in a flash,
though more for a different chance at love and clarity.
There's always another story that can be made of loss even if we're dead-
    set on losing the likeness as well,
and I'm not saying we are: I don't know what it means that a fair number
    of us can trace
the sad and paradramatic fact of near neural ruin to both the changed
    prospect of days and nights
remaining to make good and plots that now seem scripted to the notion
    there's nothing worth another chance.
Saying that, I see how easily it shifts from the private text, where I
    thought it had its only bearing,
to the common one weighing on my son.
I don't know when worry begins to go beyond tending a flock of ducks
to trying to name and place love and work and death in a story that has a
    future.
At my son's age I was barely free of Little Moron jokes, one of which
    comes to me now with a timing
I guess it's best to laugh at: the one about Little Moron throwing the
    clock out the window

because he wanted to see time fly.

Little Moron wanted to see time fly, old pilot.

And all this time I'm trying to think how even the simplest among us
   wants

a story that frees the body from the fact of itself, its own moment.

I am half blind, so to speak, and probably going deaf, a ringing in my
   ears only white noise will block.

The doctors cite time's famous flight, gunshot, chainsaws, rock concerts.

Once I was so close to the amps I could see the gray in Garcia's beard

and they jacked up *Johnny B. Goode* to where I couldn't hear anything
   but the Dead for days.

Your dead electric hero Jimi Hendrix played it another way, same
   lyrics—leader of a big old band,

country boy from way back up in the woods among the evergreens,
   maybe someday his name in lights—

but different texture, the tight braiding he made of the story and his own
   life.

There was a voice loosed in the man's head that night that wouldn't
   yield.

He wanted me to bring the white noise over the line to him.

He wanted me and my sons to cross over with his story around us alive.

7

Once a voice separated itself from a graduation party in the yard below
   me and I knew

without having met him he was the father of the friend we were
   celebrating.

I saw him only that once, which was also the last time I celebrated
   anything with my friend.

It was the pitch and timbre of place telling me who he was, the
   resonance of landscape known in the light

of seasons, a cadence falling always homeward, away from how my friend
   must have pitched and tumbled

to the small crater that opened for him over a land-mine the next spring
   somewhere in Vietnam.

I took the voice coming to me through the open window on the glass
   porch where I was tying my bright tie

back down to the party and my friend's father was the substance of it.

8

For two winters on their nights with me my sons slept beneath the pelts
   of whitetail deer.

Probably it started with the open sleeping bags they chose for bedcover,
    the memory of our voices
within rings thrown by fires of driftwood or downed trees; from there it
    was only natural
to take the pelt from the foot of the bed and layer it between body and
    down bag.
They took turns with the North Face bag we once spread for a meteor
    shower years ago,
the night I began the story about a cat whose tail caught fire from a
    falling star
and how it was saved: *The Cat That Wouldn't Scat, the Ball That
    Wouldn't Fall, the Car That Wouldn't Go Far,*
and the Clown Who Brought Them All Around. Long title.
I don't know why we'd work so hard to save the cat when we'd be
    hunting deer a few seasons down the road,
both here in Carolina and on the old hunting grounds only miles from
    Doty's,
but I don't want you trying to tell me why if you're wearing the fancy
    boots or some flashy coat of skins.
I guess if you believed to the point of weaving your own belt out of milk
    and bean curd and hemp
you could maybe make me feel that the difference matters in the time
    we take—an instant or the ages—
to kill the wildness, and you could talk from that domestic principle to a
    kind of holiness
I can't imagine right now—not having the story you'd need to tell.
Listen, we ate the flesh, we saved the pelts, if there's a bone left in the
    dog-yard it's fossil.
Field-dressing the deer, I sorted through the viscera to name for them
    lights, liver, heart.
Call it whatever you like, but it was something more than meat under
    the tilted mirrors at Food Town.
We are trying for a story that will bind the years, follow out the stranded
    lines of our first dreams,
and the pelts are part of the texture we can touch and tell.
If that part of the telling cancels out our story for anyone I care about,
    I'd say again that we watched
the night sky for its fire, we freed the ball suspended—it seemed
    forever—beyond the boy's open hands,
we walked the dogs.
It's a long story, parts of it as worn and gray as hooves, old roads, photos
    we keep in an album
for the sake of sentimental history, the news chewed to a pulp.

I do not know where it is going.
There was a time the meteors and seasons fell with a sadness I did not
    want my sons to see,
the gray filtering to their mother's eyes and mine as we failed.
Part of a story is how it is told in another, that reach of the voice with
    ways to imagine.
I know to trust the motion bringing the thistle to my buttonhole.
If I didn't want them fully given to their own time, that somehow they
    could find a different constellation,
it's not like I meant the only dream is in the lost circles of sacrifice and
    elementary wonder.
One way I can believe the simple tape droning up to the top of a world's
    fair is how the sun comes slanting
into the fiction of itself, the gold sphere of one-way glass we are in,
and there is no way out for it but in our breath and eyes, it seems, the
    light translated and joining
what we will see and say at night by the crossroads store or in the letter
with money and maybe sweet biscuit crumbs or on the face of time held
    half-cocked at the open window
as though all laughter is mad.
I looked in the man's eyes and could not tell.
But don't you see how they could hit on something else?
They could put the gun down and turn the old Whirlpool off.
They could go out by the water of the creek and wonder at the stars
    together.
And for a moment it would not matter where we are going, the voices
    gathering for the story to tell.

EDGAR SIMMONS

Impressions

When I was a child I gave a burning glance
To a footprint framed down in clay,
To the splayed sand tracks along the hot beach.
The outline of a leaf, skeleton of a fish
Each elaborated sweet against the globe—
Clocked me right out of time.

And tales told against the darkness
Were impressed with dusk and swallow twitter sky
Till the very birds danced upon the sill

And all the kings and statues of kings
Were with me and held my hand.

Early Passion in a Puritan World

I remember a story of my youth,
a whitewashed Thursday afternoon with
pale green lemon yellow lights flickering on and off
in the dusty, straw-backed railroad car, and my hands
finding a strange, unbelievably large, enveloping and
weirdly ennervating world of sex in one
girl
not buxom but sufficient
to altogether portray the very far side of
floating worlds in greens and yellows, of
pitch blackness; a girl sufficient for
Lethean voyage where peril and joy were
limitless. We strangely rocked in the dark roll and
whistle of a train bound mother safe, past
the gravel roads, riding its own severe track down
to New Orleans and the anticlimax of Mardi Gras.

This was the band trip and every pew in every
church was blown out of the window as if an
exhilarant pagan typhoon had washed the very clay
crust off the protestant south.

World of Child Drummers

in my zeal and showoffness
as a child drummer I would
drown out my father's mandolin

and he would shrink his merry tinklings until Columbia the Gem of the Ocean

sounded only in
his joking smile
that tried to tell me something of the way he
always had to
disappear
into the threadbare suit of his living
in order to make
me slick Jack,

saying, "It's a poor family that can't afford one dude,"

and yet he
was begging
for a chance to play.

At the Seed and Feed

Carrying his mandolin in the curve of the afternoon
Past the hot and shaded porch
Past flead dogs and the kings of bottletop checkers
Shooting their crowed eyes beyond their strawbrimmed hats
I followed my father into the dark of an old store.

Among men and tin and bottle goods
Among bonneted ladies with embroidery hoops:
White tambourines etched with blue flowers
We stood in Jesus-sweet gloom.

Now Father's wizard mandolin sings the store alive
The strings lightly throbbing,
Tinkling on and on, the frets marking his fleshy fingers
His notes like plums in the dark.

Soon a fox yelps down the evening
And cows loll home spearing from a covert of trees;
Now the piney church turns yellow for Wednesday prayers
And Father, slipping the pick under the mandolin strings, bows

Dwindling in the sun.

Sons of Sad Dreams

The night of the storm my smallest boy
Woke out of a damaging dream
And, finding with blind small hands
The hall's walls and finally my bed
Crawled in between the sheets.
"I don't want to die,"
He whispered hot against my back.
I turned and rubbed his head.
"I want to sleep with you,"
And I thought,
O sad,
You will
And rocked him
Held him not too fierce.

JES SIMMONS

Letters

After my father died
I got a letter from his war buddy
a fellow drummer at Keesler Field
"I have heard from Joe. I know he is in heaven. He says
he has a drum."

A grown cousin from England
who knew him as Cowboy Uncle Joe wrote
"Your Dad once gave me a Davy Crockett hat, a cowboy watch,
and a Roy Rogers shirt that I was never brave enough to
wear."

A man no one knew came up to me at work
he'd seen the obituary
"Your father and I were in AA together. I'll be looking
out for you now."

I'd like to ask them to meet me
one rainy afternoon for a long lunch
We could sit in a restaurant
overlooking the sea
and watch the rain on the water
unable to talk
about the man each of us knew

Old McGehee

my great grandfather
unnoticed as rug corners
was taken from bedroom confinement
and brought to the family room for Christmas
my father
finding no gift for him earlier
had fled to Rexall's late Xmas Eve
returning from raw-knuckled cold
with a box of chocolate covered cherries
Christmas wondrous to my eyes
Brach's magic inside bright cellophane
Christmas morning we children
huddled near wrapping paper shrubbery

were startled from gleaming toys
our starling-bright eyes
following great-grandfather's thin legs
wading to his chair
my aunt fidgeting at his elbow
the wrapped gift deposited on his lap
eagerly opened for him
adults bobbing about like pigeons
squeezing his shoulders
shouting knowingly at his ears
their fingers pecking the box
while great-grandfather
his head bowed
sat stiff as the ornamented tree
his hands quail-still
under torn gold wrapping paper

Indian Mound • Winter • The Search

Men planting cotton rows
would come to this pecan tree on the mound,
sole shade in acres of dirt
grooved to points at my eyes' limit.

This is my father-in-law's farm
deep in the Mississippi Delta.
This winter he is converting yet another
field into catfish ponds:
> two million pounds of farm-raised catfish
> swimming above cotton stalks buried,
> rotted in the soil.
"Don't plant 'em too deep, son."

> Among dried leaves on the mound
> I search for arrowheads, stone beads,
> and shards of pottery,
find where a scratching dog or possum
unearthed a brown bowl edge
becoming a dried out hipbone in my hand.

A distant cry, a hawk rides
the cold air, its spread-wing
shadow breaking
> out of hawk-shape
> on the rough-clod field,

reassembling itself in the packed dirt
floor of a newly-dug pond, then
> flowing over the mound, bending
> around me to weave itself
> into the gray limbs above my head.
Eyes that catch a mouse at 300 yards
are fixed like death on the bone in my palm.

> I drop the Indian bone to cover it
> with the black soil in which it cannot grow,
> filling in the deep claw marks
> which brought the dead to me.
Let these bones stay in the soil;
let the old tree remain on the mound,
the hawk steady over my head;
farm the soil in any way you can.
> let me connect all of this,
> walk away with all of this.

SUE SPIGNER

Grandfather

In his old-age summers, when there were too many of us,
We trapped him in the early evenings
As he sat on his cool front porch.
On that red-clay, day-baked hillside
No light shone but the moon.
We were at his mercy.
He told us tales we hated—and loved,
Stories of strange lights over buried money hoards
And phantom branches scraping phantom windows
Around a silver curve in the sandy road.
We eyed the spot from where we sat,
Huddled like chickens for warmth.
Our mothers choked back their anger;
We were too young to be frightened so.
He relished our fear and their anger;
Had he not created them both?

Revival

The August night was as hot and close
As a winter's feather bed,
Enveloping and smothering what it held.
Both doors of the church were thrown open
In a futile attempt to catch some shifting of a wind.
But the still air was the same everywhere.
The preacher's wet shirt and drawn face
And the limp print dresses in the rough wooden pews
Were evidence that grappling with the fires of hell,
Plus the surface heat,
Was an exhausting effort.

Sweaty babies lay on pallets along the aisles,
Sleeping with the total absorption of babyhood exhaustion.
But she held her child, too close for them both,
Fanning him with an advertisement
For the facilities of a funeral home 18 miles away.
If she had turned her head, she could have seen through the window
The few men of the congregation, sitting in the dim circle
Created by a 60-watt porch light on the church's plain white eaves.

She did not look.
Instinctively she knew
That this child's father, her husband, was not among them.
He was somewhere in the evil, secret envelopes
Of that steaming August night,
Reveling in his freedom from restraint.

She held the child so close
That his head stuck to her arm
And a tiny frown played between his brows.
She pulled herself up and revived her sagging interest
In the preacher's now hoarse roar.
If she were holy,
Would this child not be holy, too?

FRANK STANFORD

The Picture Show
Next Door to the Stamp Store
in Downtown Memphis

The movie has not begun.
Girls from a private school
are forming their lines.
They have long socks on,
tweed skirts, blue weskits,
berets. The colors
of God and their school
are sewn in their scarfs.

My money and my hand
are in a machine.
The cup does not come down,
but the ice and cola do.
I make a cup with my hands.

They stand there, moving
in one direction
like does in clover.
The nun tells them to form.

Why are they afraid of me?

I am holding my hands together
like a gloveless hunter
drinking water in the morning
or calling up owls in the forest;
I am holding my hands together
like a hunter in winter
with his hands in the water
washing away the blood.

Outside, a man with a lunch box
walks past the marquee.
His new stamps
fly out of his hands;
orange triangles from San Salvador
fly into the traffic.

I am holding my hands
like the nun.

Then fly over Front Street.
He is looking up;
other people are looking up.
The stamps tremble
like the butterflies
from the Yazoo Basin
stuck to the radiator
of my father's car.

The girls are in the seventh grade.
The backs of their thighs
and their foreheads are damp.

What are they learning?
Ballet? French?

The nun is on her toes.

Their booties dance
in the leotards,
rounding out like the moon.
They are making a debut.

The girls are following the nun
into the dark.
The movie is beginning.
The lid on the machine
comes down like a guillotine.

The Burial Ship

Jimmy's wolf died
it wasn't nothing but a cub
O.Z. built a coffin ship
he made it so the head could look out the prow
the river was going to be his grave
we held services there
everyone wore a black mask and we cut ourselves for old times' sake
he was laid away
buried in the little ship
there was no sacrifice no dead chickens
we broke a Nugrape bottle over the hull it was full
the ship was about four feet long
Ray Baby and I could have fit in it if we were dead
for sails we stole a tent flap
Six Toes painted it red with a black cross

each one dripped some blood over the wolf in the boat
Melvin said the cold weather set in
we brought the blind child with us to tell the fortunes of the future
he always carried a frog gig and wore a top hat
he reached out his hands and wiggled his fingers
that's the way he knew
he said I need two bits and a little music
he didn't talk right he made it all sound like a song
everyone had dirty white gloves on
we had a jug a guitar and a oil bucket
somebody said woe is the wolf
we thought we heard Mose playing a fife away back in the woods
I was on Ace comb and Stage Plank wrapper
Baby Gauge sang Back to the Dust he wailed
I wanted to sing The Blood Done Signed My Name but they wouldn't
    let me
the blind child said he'd have to go to Newport to see Aunt Caroline
    Dye
ashes to ashes dust to dust the devil be had if this old life don't get worse
it was getting cold
he said some river rat was liable to use the wolf for bait
better keep watch
the smoke was coming out our mouths
Jimmy wasn't shivering he was just staring at the water
I poked him to see if he was in a trance
he said come on O.Z.
they rowed out to the coffin the ship bearing the dead wolf
they set it afire and watched it burn
there was one big spark that cracked like ash in the dark
it must have been the wolf's eye
it kept on going towards the heavens
it was a shooting star

JOHN STONE

Losing a Voice in Summer

How many parts rumble it was
how much gravel
dark, light
I don't remember

and it won't echo for me
from the shower stall

though sometimes off the porch
calling my own sons for supper
I can almost

almost hear it

as if you had let it go
out of the corner
of your mouth
like a ventriloquist
without a dummy.

I have no recording

otherwise I would play you
in the shower, repeat you
off the porch

from the cat-walk
of the glass factory have you sing
Go Down Moses
over and over and

tonight
with the reluctant sentence
deep in my head at the hoarsest hour,
dumb and laryngitic and alone

I first understood
how completely I have lost your voice,
father, along with my own.

Piano Lessons

She wanted me to stretch my fingers
into next week   and next week.
I mean stretch them,
pull the tendons in their joints,
loosen bone from bone a bit.
My hands were too small
for octaves,
too little for recitals,
Chopin and Brahms,
which she would have had me
playing even now
except I escaped
by moving to a larger town.
Here she will never think
to look for me.
My fingers can be normal.
And I can disguise myself
as a clarinet,
march past her in the crowd
lining the street for parades
and blow her eardrums out
with a high held G.

Double-Header

Each and every one of us has got a schedule to keep.
—a truck driver being interviewed on radio

I've made it
have been left alone in the stadium
locked here after the baseball
twilight game, having hidden
where I won't tell

on a bet with someone I invented
and therefore had to win.
I can hear the Security Guard
locking up, watch him making his way out,
turning off the lights as he goes

toward home and supper, away from
the smell of popcorn and beer.
I can see him look

with a question at my car,
the only one besides his

still in the lot and see him
look back once at the stadium without
knowing or even thinking I could be
looking back at him, my face barbed
with wire. I turn now to the stadium

that is all mine, bought
with my money, purchased with
a three dollar ticket for the top tier,
the stadium that is coming alive again
with the crowd that is coming back

but of course isn't coming back
to watch me play, with DiMaggio in center,
Cobb in left, Hornsby at second
Rizzuto at short, and all the others
who have been tagged out more than once

themselves, and who will get me later
or sooner, trying to stretch a single
into a double, catching up with my lost breath
that I can remember now from when
I was eleven, with a stitch in my side

sprinting still in spite of the stitch
for the inside-the-park home run
I almost had when I was twelve
for the girl I almost got when I got
old enough but didn't know the rules

dusting my pants off now
to the music I never learned, for
the symphony orchestra I never conducted,
my hands rough with rosin
for the truck I never drove

and the fish I never caught
and wouldn't have known if I had
how to take him off the hook,
for my father who is in the crowd
cheering out his heart

but who of course isn't there
as I pull up lame at second

with a stand-up double
in this game that goes on for hours,
my hands stinging with the bat,

the All-Stars aligned against me
in this stadium I own for the night,
one great circle and inside this circle
this square that seems the only one
on this curving darkening ball of earth

or the only one anyway
marked by bases I must run all night
for everything I should
by now
be worth.

The Truck

I was coming back from
wherever I'd been when
I saw the truck and
the sign on the back repeated
on the side to be certain
you knew it was no mistake

PROGRESS CASKETS
ARTHUR ILLINOIS

Now folks have different
thoughts it's true about
death but in general it's
not like any race for
example you ever ran
everyone wanting to come in

last and all   And I admit
a business has to have a good
name   No one knows better
than I the value of a good
name   A name is what sells
the product in the first

and in the final place
All this time the Interstate
was leading me into Atlanta
and I was following the sign

and the truck was heavier
climbing the hill than

going down which is as
it should be   What I really
wanted to see was the driver
up close maybe talk to him
find out his usual run
so I could keep off it

Not that I'm superstitious   It's just
the way I was raised   A casket
may be Progress up in Arthur
but it's thought of
down here
as a setback.

Trying to Remember Even a Small Dream Much Less the Big Gaudy Ones in Color with Popcorn and High Ticket Prices

As soon as you wake up

but before the first photon
has leaped through the black pupil
to the back of your eye

before you sit heavily to the day
at the side of your mattress

be on the lookout:

your last dream may just then
be disappearing
into the kingdom
of your lateral gaze

You may be able to recognize
one of the full-blown characters
if you can catch sight of his shoes
the flare of her dress
the cut and color of her hair

Then there's always the possibility

that your dream itself
may pause a moment
to look back at you

rubbing the sleep from its eyes

wondering how it got inside you
as its mother warned it might

amazed
that it too ended up

so far from home.

A Word from the Teacher

In the first grade
for this unit
we are studying
The Age of the Dinosaurs
We are also making
an exhibit to be shown
at PTA

Everyone except Johnny
wanted to make
a Stegosaurus
or a Tyrannosaurus rex
out of clay

Johnny preferred to make
a Brontosaurus
which explains

why the demography
of our dinosaur population
may seem somewhat
out of kilter

Nevertheless
the whole class
has been involved
in this demonstration
and we are almost ready
to represent
several hundred millennia

using a backdrop of green
posterboard, the dinosaur
models, of course

and at least a hundred
small clay pellets
meant to be eggs
and not whatever
petrified else
you may have been thinking
they were

By working together
we have learned much
in the preparation
of this interesting exhibit

which may yet win
First Prize
and make our inscrutable parents
proud at last

We thought of having
special music
to go with our
display
but we couldn't agree
as a class

on just what kind of music
dinosaurs
might have preferred

while on their way
to what everyone knows
came next:

a big fat zero

To tell you the truth
the whole thing
leaves me
a little sad

the way
every day
always
somewhere

sometime
someone

is having to start all over

WILLIAM SULLIVAN

Beneath the Surface

Work behind him and supper ahead,
he sets out to trace one of those narrow canals
which divide fields of beans, rice, and cotton
into exact square miles of Delta farmland,
six hundred forty acres each.
Those same canals, binding for marvelous quilts
with swatches of green in all hues and degrees of intensity,
seeming so regular and clearly defined
are actually teeming with life:
rats, turtles of fifty pounds or more,
opossums, rabbits, nutrias, armadillos,
and snakes of unsavory length
scurry, crawl, and creep from them
onto the fields, fields to which a farmer
has returned after an absence forced by wet or cold
to find that morning-glories, coffee weeds, and cockleburs
have reclaimed the soil he had tamed
through weeks of work by his hands and tools.
Another farmer returns to a field
which lies hard by the river to find
it reduced to stubble by herds of deer
who take refuge behind levees on weekdays
but whose weekend appetite for soybeans is insatiable.

Portions of this land are allotted to housing
and one lap of his course borders the field
behind a slough drained and filled long ago
to provide houses for babies of the postwar boom.
From time to time these homes come up "for sale"
and remain vacant for months as families
fully recovered from the baby boom move up.
He has seen trumpet creepers slip under
and between the asbestos shingles

and in less than three weeks' time
remove and stack the two bottom rows
with unseemly method.
The abandoned and silent structures standing
naked against the warmth and rain of April
remind him of *National Geographic's* profile
of nature's darlings, beautiful cheeta and ugly hyena,
who take their warm meals
from the flanks of wildebeests and antelopes
whose herdsmates gaze on bewildered,
neither afraid nor astonished,
with blank eyes and blank faces
which do not show they even know
the pain of being gorged alive.
A turn toward downtown and this scene fades
to faraway in Africa.

Now he hears the broken laughter and cries
from the county jail
where men, whose bright nights paled into morning,
are recovering from drugs, alcohol, or broken things,
bones or promises, homes or hearts.

The jail behind him and heading for home,
he wonders how many men know or even suspect
that beneath the ordered surface of things
a terrible energy which brooks no nonsense
strives to overrule God's edict, to quench the light,
to restore a state without form and void,
to foster Chaos and Ancient Night and the Spirit
of God once more moving over the face of the waters,
silent.

GLENN R. SWETMAN

Uncle Bob

The absolute hippopotamus moment
of your laugh, and the echoing tune
of your greeting broke all the formal
hellos into instant askings about
everything. Your rough fisherman's hands, rough

as the hair on your knuckles, reached, touching
to all your kin. The chest-hair leaked over
the top button of your shirt, and your belly
hung like a portent over the world's strongest belt.
That day I met cousins I had never known,
and standing on the shore of your camp
I saw that the waters that touched your shore
touched every shore, and, akin to you,
I realized I was a part of ever.

A Little Sonnet on a Contemporary Subject

As Noah worked, his neighbor spoke: "A boat
    is not the answer. We must change the way
    men think. We must stop drinking wine. The day
must shine that fornication stops. To float
a good size clan, a man would have to tote
    more food along than he could store away,
    and if he were due for a longer stay,
he'd have to take in livestock—just one goat
but two of each clean animal. I would
    rather chant to end all sin than labor
        like an ant. Arks cause complacency and
encourage vice instead of good, and *could*
    rush us into flood!"
                        So spoke the neighbor,
and . . . Noah threw a drunk when he hit land.

D. L. TARTT

An Easter Egg Hunt

                In the photograph I have
My great grandmother, all periwinkle eyes
And gaiety in her lilac dress
Sits in a corona of light
Under the quince trees, watching us hunt
    For the eggs she hid. I remember
    The eggs, grass-green and coral,
    Sweating and heavy in my palm,

My scratchy white dress and the creases
  It left on my knees when I knelt.
Metallic ribbons
  Fluttered from the Easter corsage
  That we had given her.
I remember
  A dusty rain smell in the air, remember
  Plum blossom, apple blossom
  Honey locust, the lilies
  Running wild by the clothesline,
  The terror of the Judas tree,
  Mauve clouds and storms of blackbirds,
Great rifts of light, that still menace
Near the photograph's white borders

My grandmother is bathed in a tenebrism
Beneath the quinces, joyous
In the own pre-trembling of her bursting heart.
She would be dead in a month. Should we have known
From the signs and wonders in the sky? That day,
She sat laughing on the grass, alone,
Her legs tucked beneath her like a girl's.

JULIUS THOMPSON

Natchez

I hear
The train
Coming
& the night
Is only
Half-
Over
& someone
Is walking
By the tracks
Looking for
A star
Looking for
A guide
Looking one

More time
Before he
Turns into
Himself

HENRY TIM

If God So Loved His Children All that Much, Why Couldn't Uncle Ed?

1

1. If you have ever held a dying mate
2. in quaking arms and seen the light go out
3. of loving eyes, and felt the skin turn cold
4. then you will know
5. how Emma felt in eighteen ninety-nine:
6. Aunt Emma Lee, my Uncle Edward's wife.

7. We were the Lees and Lorens, puffed with pride
8. despite the shame that Uncle Edward caused.

9. We were hard working, saving, sober folks
10. who often boasted, "None of us has been
11. behind a pulpit, ever, or iron bars."

12. That quip about the pulpit simply meant
13. we didn't preach at waywards in our town:
14. the cigarette fiends, those who took a swig,
15. girls with bobbed hair, short skirts, and those who danced
16. stayed out past ten, and didn't come to church.
17. Most likely those who danced, played cards, and drank
18. (Hostetter's Bitter's was their alcohol)
19. thought we were phoney saints—and dull. Perhaps
20. we tilted somewhat to the cautious side
21. due to the rhetoric that our preachers used.

22. They spoke of heaven in a mild, calm voice
23. vaguely, it's true, but managed to convey
24. the notion that the risen could survive
25. in comfort there. Myself, I pictured it
26. much like a public park, with walks and trees
27. and wooden benches flanked by lilacs where
28. sweet souls could sit and gaze at salty saints
29. or watch the birds.

30.   But when they mentioned hell
31. they were volcanoes spewing fire and ash

32. and glowing lava. It was clear that hell
33. was no mere bonfire, but a holocaust.
34. I saw live naked bodies twist
35. in awful agony, but not allowed
36. to perish in those flames—they were condemned
37. to writhe forever in that hellish heat
38. where brimstone throbbed, and Satan in red tights
39. laughed, gigging victims into hotter coals
40. to suffer for their sins, neglect of church.

2

41. The fear of hell made kids accept their chores.
42. We never argued with our elders then.
43. We did as we were bid, and never whined.

44. We fed and watered horses, mules, cows, pigs,
45. goats, guineas, geese, New Zealand rabbits, hens,
46. fetched eggs, set hens or incubators, milked,
47. took eggs, cream, butter to the cool, dark cave.
48. (We sat on earthen benches there when storms
49. were threatening—mostly to humor mom,
50. the fraidy cat—. One night dad raised the door
51. peeped out. The sullen clouds were gone, the rain
52. had ceased, the air was still as death, the moon
53. shone through the crack. Dad raised the lantern, stared,
54. then froze. "I cannot see the house," he said.
55. Then mom and sister went to Uncle Joe's.
56. We males stayed in the barn and batched
57. while dad, the hired hand, rebuilt the house.)

3

58. Kids curried, harnessed horses, ploughed, harrowed, hoed,
59. helped sow the fields, made, kept the garden, helped
60. our mamas with their flowers, picked ripe fruit
61. (Elberta peaches, cherries, apples, pears)
62. which mothers jelled, preserved in Mason jars,
63. plucked geese for featherbeds and bolsters, pads,
64. shocked wheat, shucked corn, picked peas, tomatoes, beans,
65. cucumbers, watermelons, canteloupes,
66. chopped firewood, kindling, toted it and cobs.
67. (we used cobs soaked in coal oil to start fires.
68. Mom's fancy kitchen range was long and wide.)

69. We cleaned the barn, white-washed the chicken house,
70. hung wet clothes on the line, took dry ones in,

71. helped mama iron (but not the pleated skirts)
72. pumped water from the cistern near the porch.
73. We dug potatoes, peanuts, pulled up beets,
74. plucked radishes and onions, cabbages,
75. picked wild blackberries in the pastures, woods,
76. shucked off our shoes, ran barefoot in the burrs.

77. Come fall, we dug the sweet potatoes, pulled
78. sweet turnips from their beds, wheelbarrowed in
79. bright, yellow pumpkins; sacked, in nearby woods
80. pecans. Come frost, we robbed persimmon trees.

4

81. We kids ran errands, too, the year around.
82. We might trot into Johnson's store, in town,
83. to buy round steak (if company had come)
84. or mustard plaster for mom's aching back
85. (if poultices were needed, mom made them)
86. polish for high-topped button shoes, a brush
87. to slick dad's derby hat. But best of all
88. on dragging summer Sunday afternoons
89. to buy ice cream and pickles for ourselves
90. (though usually we made our own ice cream)
91. with two bits and a dime dad winked he found.

92. I was the one we got the pickles for.
93. Dad humored me, knew ice cream made me sick.

5

94. Sometimes we kids did chores for neighbors, such
95. as scything weeds, or raking, piling leaves.
96. (Sometimes we roasted winnies on the fires.)

97. I don't know why, but brother Floyd and I
98. were always asked, when the Chautauqua came
99. to take the handbills, leave them house to house.
100. And sometimes, when a tent revival came
101. evangelists would have some handbills struck
102. and Floyd and I would put them out in town.

6

103. One chore we never did perform; dad had
104. a chapeau brass he had inherited
105. and once a twelve-month he would take it down

106. and fondle it
107. then brush the lint away and put it back
108. beside a camera that made tin-types
109. beside another that used glass for film.

7

110. We were excused from chores when we were sick
111. as happened frequently; one of we four
112. (three boys, one girl) would have diphtheria,
113. the mumps, the measles, grippe, the whooping cough,
114. the snuffles, ring-worm, or the chicken pox—
115. Someone was sick or sickly half the time.
116. When mama thought we were malingering
117. she'd scold us good, especially when she
118. was plagued and cross with rheumatism or
119. neuralgia. Daddy was seldom sick.

8

120. When there was no more kids' work to be done
121. we helped scrub clothes on wash boards, plates in pans,
122. washed dishes, swept pine floors, beat carpets, rugs,
123. took baby, in her carriage, for a ride.

9

124. We had our play times, too. On grape vine swings,
125. yard swings and teeter-totters, swimming holes,
126. in catching crawdads, hooking fish (with worms)
127. in pitching horseshoes, playing run-sheep-run,
128. or hide-and-seek, or skipping rope, with tops,
129. jacks, marbles, mumbly-peg, in guessing games,
130. in wrestling, running relays, horseback rides,
131. in ante-over, cross-out, tug-o-wars.

132. On Saturdays we kids—each one—received
133. a nickel to be spent in town. We watched
134. the train come in, watched folks get off, get on,
135. we watched two men unload and load express
136. using a high-wheeled, wide-wheeled, hand-pulled cart.

137. After the drayman and the buggies left
138. we ambled back to Main Street. There, root beer
139. was what we purchased—at the pool hall, too,
140. (The soda fountain in the front, somehow,

141. made ten-and-twelve-year-olds feel like grown men
142. to be so near pool tables in the back
143. —partitioned off with walls and swinging doors—
144. where adult loafers cussed the colored balls.)

10

145. On July Fourth most kids received a big
146. round fifty cents to squander as they pleased.

147. On winter days, or rainy, we played Flinch,
148. Rook, Lotto, tic-tac-toe, or dominoes,
149. played hide-the-thimble, cranked the phonograph.

150. Come dark, we took to riddles, stories, songs.
151. Mom pumped and played the organ, sang along,
152. while brother Marden held the lamp aloft.
153. Some nights our dad would sit beside a lamp
154. and make his hands cast shadows on the wall
155. while we (his kids) would try to guess just what
156. each shadow represented: bat, or ball,
157. an H, an X, an A, a pair of eyes,
158. a wolf's head (upright thumbs made ears),
159. a question mark, a bowl, a rabbit, hen.

160. At nine each night we listened for and heard
161. the long, low, mournful whistle of a train.
162. Soon after, on a trestle, saw its lights
163. in brilliant windows, heard it moan again.
164. Then we would put our toys and games away,
165. sit down beside our mother and be quiet
166. while she recited ballads, told us tales,
167. or sang old folk-songs (she knew scads of them).

11

168. Thieves were unknown in those parts, in those days.
169. Nobody locked their doors, whether at home,
170. in town, or with some kinfolks miles away.
171. Sometimes a wagonload of country folks,
172. a farmer, wife and kids, plough, furniture,
173. spare horse, pots, skillets, vittles, harrow, scythe,
174. moving from one farm to another one
175. might stop at noon, at some farm house and find
176. nobody home, but enter none the less
177. use cistern, stove, and table, tidy up,

178. fill jugs with water, hitch, move on and leave
179. exactly what was there when they arrived.

12

180. Our food was phytogenic. Nearly all
181. lived out of gardens; home-grown vegetables.

13

182. We did not recognize the wrongs we did.
183. We thought we were God's chosen, without faults.

184. For instance, neighbors asked my mom about
185. a couple new in town. My mama said
186. they seemed like honest, decent folks,
187. then looked around. She thought none else would hear—
188. but out-of-sight I did—what she'd say next,
189. She bent her body forward, whispered this:
190. "They're *renters!*" (Not exactly hoboes, bums,
191. but renters! Renters! We looked down on them.)

14

192. Nor did we think too well of Mexicans.
193. A few resided at the edge of town
194. in well-kept shanties, mostly with dirt floors
195. kept hard and clean (they even swept their yards).
196. They had more flowers than the well-to-do's:
197. Zinnias, cana lilies, four o'clocks
198. sunflowers, roses, pansies, cactus plants.

199. The men worked on the railroad beds, changed ties,
200. repaired the trestles, checked the rails for breaks,
201. arm-pumped a hand-car up and down the line.
202. The women worked as maids, washed, ironed clothes,
203. diapered babies. Those mild Mexicans
204. were shy, polite; the gentlest folks in town.
205. I've never known why we looked down on them.

15

206. Though we were unaware of our own flaws,
207. Lorens and Lees alike, we hid one shame.
208. Edward Noble Lee
209. had married Emma Loren. Afterward

210. he did a thing no adults could approve.
211. Our parents kept it secret, locked away
212. behind tight lips from children years and years.
213. When Edward did it, I was not yet born.
214. I reckon I was twelve before I heard.

16

215. The telephone was born before I was;
216. before my cousins were, or so I think,
217. though there were sixty of us, later on,
218. including double-cousins, six of them.

219. The telephone! In horse-and-buggy days
220. it was more useful than in years to come.
221. Excitement crazed the people in our parts.
222. They wanted this new marvel.
223.   Those with means
224. pooled funds, set poles, built lines, got telephones.
225. that cranked by hand. Our signal was four rings.
226. The phones, most all, were wired to party lines
227. so curious neighbors often listened in.
228. We, curious cats, would often listen, too.

17

229. The telephone! It would envelop earth
230. Edward correctly thought. He saw a chance
231. to make a fortune for his family.

232. He put his entire future into shares.

233. The dream went sour. The company went broke,
234. owed awesome debts shareholders soon must pay.
235. (Some law, or some condition made it clear
236. widows and orphans need not share those debts.)
237. Now Edward suffered nightmares. In his sleep
238. he saw his children ragged, underfed,
239. uneducated clods, incompetents.

240. A brilliant man, his sons and nephews thought
241. (after the deed was done and they were grown)
242. Ed could have paid those debts, gone stoney broke
243. then started over, persevered, and built
244. another fortune for his family.

18

245. Aunt Emma searched his face, but never saw
246. how blown with foaming yeast her Edward was.
247. He took the shotgun one bright summer day,
248. said he was going after turtle doves.

19

249. The barn was quite some distance from the house.
250. When nearly there, Ed met his five-year-old.
251. He wrote and handed her a note. "Take this.
252. Go to the smokehouse, hand it to your ma."

253. The child saw something in her father's face
254. that made her own face blanch. She ran, she raced.

255. Aunt Emma read the note and screamed: "No! No!
256. Noble! Don't do it! Noble! NOBLE! Don't!"
257. Aunt Emma always called him, "Noble." She
258. preferred his middle name. She screamed, "Don't! Don't!"
259. raced screaming towards the barn but heard the shot
260. when only half way there. Her Noble lay
261. his temple shattered, in a pool of blood.

262. She took him, dying, in her trembling arms.
263. She held his body while it bled to death.

264. The town and doctors were ten miles away
265. and all those telephones were tongueless now.
266. The horse was out to pasture and the Doc
267. would have to come by buggy from the town.

268. What could she do but hold him while he died?

GLENNRAY TUTOR

There's a Boy

There's a boy
whirling around his
frontyard
with no fence and no
trees and no shrubbery,
with piles of junk his

dad hauled in and laid
around,
rusting, bent, sprouting
weeds.
The boy is whirling around
with a long string of
tinsel
that he must have found
among the junk,
and there's not
a flake of paint left on
the house
but
there's the boy whirling
around and around and the
tinsel is flying and
glittering
with blue sky and sunlight
and wide spring fields.

Flying Saucers and a Gila Monster

I've seen more flying saucers
than I have Gila monsters

I've seen three flying saucers,
one Spring night
lying in the frontyard
with my brother just when
the first mosquitoes were biting
and the sky was bright-weighted
with stars pulling it down close to us
They came up like three moons,
and just as quiet,
in formation,
low,
coming out of the southern black trees
and in fast smooth seconds
passing over us and on into the black north.

I've only seen one Gila monster,
in the Memphis Zoo,
behind a wall of sweat smudged glass
lying on a section of glue-fixed

colored gravel
beside a plastic pool of water.
And it might have been dead.
I watched for a long time
and never once saw it move.

On a Day of Good June Fishing Weather
A Dog Would Like to Be a Boy

A dog would like to be a boy.
You can tell it in the way
he barks to go with them
wherever they're going.
You can tell it in how he watches
them, intently, his head tilting
one way then the other,
as they snap together their fishing rods
and eat their candy bars
and drink their Cokes
and string together all the fish they
pull from nowhere, iridescent and flopping,
laughing and yelling at each other,
not paying the least bit of attention
to him
until finally,
at the end of the day,
letting him nose into the minnow bucket,
then standing, watching, shaking their heads,
not believing it,
as he eats what's left.

DOROTHY TWISS

Bossier City Saturday Night

On those hot nights we lied
to our mothers, crowded close
in old trap cars,
followed the Saturday lights
across the only bridge in town.

We sat distracted in the Old Dutch Mill
watching a woman bare her skin
and later saw her sit at the bar alone,
buttoned to the neck in black,
drinking her whiskey straight.
Wondering, we drove back
to porches unlit by dawn,
to mirrors holding older faces,
to smooth untumbled beds,
to later wilder lying.

OVID VICKERS

Lola Forest

We lived near
A Southern flag stop.
Two shorts, we knew
The dinner train would stop.
Through net curtains
We could see the platform.
The conductor stepped off first
and then Miss Lola Forest.

Miss Lola wore a cloche hat
And jet beads.
Her rouge was high.
Her lips were full, very red,
Pouting just a little
At the midday July sun.

A big patent leather purse
Under her arm
Had a gold L F on the front flap.
Even in the heat she wore gloves
And carried a little jacket
On her arm.

"Lola has come to see her sister,"
Mama said.
"Lola has seen a lot of men,"
Papa said.

Mama looked at Papa
And passed the squash.

Miss Pearl Parkerson

When high school was over
she took a test
at the county court house.
She listed the rivers and cities,
knew who Woodrow Wilson was,
worked the equations with ease,
and got certified.

They gave her a school
on the River road.
The first day
sixteen students came.
The youngest was five,
the oldest fifteen.

While some recited,
others did seat work.
The girls giggled,
and the boys were shy;
but she taught them all
to sing and to spell,
to read and to write,
to cypher and to parse.

Some summers
she went to the Normal,
but one day the state
required a degree.
Forty winters had passed
since she opened school
on the River road.
So, Miss Pearl went home,
sat on the porch,
and crocheted.

The First Amendment

Somebody came early to push up the windows.
Breezes seldom stir Kemper County July nights.

High hair is cooler; long sleeves are not.
Perspiration glistens on faces
where Avon never calls, and
a plaid and denim husband fans
a freckled wife and sleeping, breast-fed son.
"I don't know what you came to do,
but I came to praise the Lord."

Exhortation begins—Praise the Lord!
Sin is condemned—Glory Hallelujah!
The sinner is condemned—Washed in the blood.
The monotonic evangelist pleads.
Bless His holy name—Come forward—Receive!
Faithful hands go up, seekers seek.
The Holy Ghost falls on a woman.
A message in tongues escapes her lips.
"Cunama naught, cinima naught.
Shickey mo shi, shickey mo shi."

With darting tongue and Eden eyes,
the cottonmouth coils and uncoils
at the touch of the faithful.
"They shall take up serpents."
Glory, in the name of the Lord!
"If they drink any deadly thing
it shall not hurt them."
Glory, I see my sweet Jesus!
I've been to the water and been baptized.
My soul got happy, and I'm satisfied.

The evangelist, exhausted,
sweat-wet with exhortation,
sits slumped forward, half-hidden,
by a depression glass altar vase
of faded and dusty crepe paper daffodils.
The congregation moves to touch and talk
with those who received the spirit.
The rite of passage is accomplished.
Glossolalia reached.
The seekers join the saints.

Margaret Walker

For My People

For my people everywhere singing their slave songs repeatedly: their
dirges and their ditties and their blues and jubilees, praying their
prayers nightly to an unknown god, bending their knees humbly to an
unseen power;

For my people lending their strength to the years, to the gone years and
the now years and the maybe years, washing ironing cooking
scrubbing sewing mending hoeing plowing digging planting pruning
patching dragging along never gaining never reaping never knowing
and never understanding;

For my playmates in the clay and dust and sand of Alabama backyards
playing baptizing and preaching and doctor and jail and soldier and
school and mama and cooking and playhouse and concert and store
and hair and Miss Choomby and company;

For the cramped bewildered years we went to school to learn to know
the reasons why and the answers to and the people who and the
places where and the days when, in memory of the bitter hours when
we discovered we were black and poor and small and different and
nobody cared and nobody wondered and nobody understood;

For the boys and girls who grew in spite of these things to be man and
woman, to laugh and dance and sing and play and drink their wine
and religion and success, to marry their playmates and bear children
and then die of consumption and anemia and lynching;

For my people thronging 47th Street in Chicago and Lenox Avenue in
New York and Rampart Street in New Orleans, lost disinherited
dispossessed and happy people filling the cabarets and taverns and
other people's pockets needing bread and shoes and milk and land and
money and something—something all our own;

For my people walking blindly spreading joy, losing time being lazy,
sleeping when hungry, shouting when burdened, drinking when
hopeless, tied and shackled and tangled among ourselves by the
unseen creatures who tower over us omnisciently and laugh;

For my people blundering and groping and floundering in the dark of
churches and schools and clubs and societies, associations and councils
and committees and conventions, distressed and disturbed and
deceived and devoured by money-hungry glory-craving leeches,

preyed on by facile force of state and fad and novelty, by false prophet
and holy believer;

For my people standing staring trying to fashion a better way from
confusion, from hypocrisy and misunderstanding, trying to fashion a
world that will hold all the people, all the faces, all the adams and
eves and their countless generations;

Let a new earth rise. Let another world be born. Let a bloody peace be
written in the sky. Let a second generation full of courage issue forth;
let a people loving freedom come to growth. Let a beauty full of
healing and a strength of final clenching be the pulsing in our spirits
and our blood. Let the martial songs be written, let the dirges
disappear. Let a race of men now rise and take control.

Delta

1

I am a child of the valley.
Mud and muck and misery of lowlands
are on thin tracks of my feet.
Damp draughts of mist and fog hovering over valleys
are on my feverish breath.
Red clay from feet of beasts colors my mouth
and there is blood on my tongue.

I go up and down and through this valley
and my heart bleeds with my blood here in the valley.
My heart bleeds for our fate.
I turn to each stick and stone, marking them for my own;
here where muddy water flows at our shanty door
and levees stand like a swollen bump on our backyard.

I watch rivulets flow
trickling into one great river
running through little towns
through swampy thickets and smoky cities
through fields of rice and marshes
where the marsh hen comes to stand
and buzzards draw thin blue streaks against evening sky.
I listen to crooning of familiar lullabies;
the honky-tonks are open and the blues are ringing far.
In cities a thousand red lamps glow,
but the lights fail to stir me

and the music cannot lift me
and my despair only deepens with the wailing
of a million voices strong.

O valley of my moaning brothers!
Valley of my sorrowing sisters!
Valley of lost forgotten men.

O hunted desperate people
stricken and silently submissive
seeking yet sullen ones!
If only from this valley we might rise with song!
With singing that is ours.

2

Here in this valley of cotton and cane and banana wharves
we labor.
Our mothers and fathers labored before us
here in this low valley.

High above us and round about us stand high mountains
rise the towering snow-capped mountains
while we are beaten and broken and bowed
here in this dark valley.

The river passes us by.
Boats slip by on the edge of horizons.
Daily we fill boats with cargoes of our need
and send them out to sea.

Orange and plantain and cotton grow
here in this wide valley.
Wood fern and sour grass and wild onion grow
here in this sweet valley.

We tend the crop and gather the harvest
but not for ourselves do we labor,
not for ourselves do we sweat and starve and spend
under these mountains we dare not claim,
here on this earth we dare not claim,
here by this river we dare not claim.
Yet we are an age of years in this valley;
yet we are bound till death to this valley.

Nights in the valley are full of haunting murmurings
of our musical prayers
of our rhythmical loving

of our fumbling thinking aloud.
Nights in the houses of our miserable poor
are wakeful and tormenting,
for out of a deep slumber we are 'roused
to our brother who is ill
and our sister who is ravished
and our mother who is starving.
Out of the deep slumber truth rides upon us
and we wonder why we are helpless
and we wonder why we are dumb.
Out of a deep slumber truth rides upon us
and makes us restless and wakeful
and full of a hundred unfulfilled dreams of today;
our blood eats through our veins with the terrible destruction
of radium in our bones and rebellion in our brains
and we wish no longer to rest.

3

Now burst the dams of years
and winter snows melt with an onrush of a turbulent spring.
Now rises sap in slumbering elms
and floods overwhelm us
here in this low valley.
Here there is a thundering sound in our ears.
All the day we are disturbed;
nothing ever moved our valley more.
The cannons boom in our brains
and there is a dawning understanding
in the valleys of our spirits;
there is a crystalline hope
there is a new way to be worn and a path to be broken
from the past.

Into our troubled living flows the valley
flooding our lives with a passion for freedom.
Our silence is broken in twain
even as brush is broken before terrible rain
even as pines rush in paths of hurricanes.
Our blood rises and bursts in great heart spasms
hungering down through valleys in pain
and the storm begins.
We are dazed in wonder and caught in the downpour.
Danger and death stalk the valley.

Robbers and murderers rape the valley
taking cabins and children from us
killing wives and sweethearts before us
seeking to threaten us out of this valley.

Then with a longing dearer than breathing
love for the valley arises within us
love to possess and thrive in this valley
love to possess our vineyards and pastures
our orchards and cattle
our harvest of cotton, tobacco, and cane.
Love overwhelms our living with longing
strengthening flesh and blood within us
banding the iron of our muscles with anger
making us men in the fields we have tended
standing defending the land we have rendered
rich and abiding and heavy with plenty.

We with our blood have watered these fields
and they belong to us.
Valleys and dust of our bodies are blood brothers
and they belong to us:
the long golden grain for bread
and the ripe purple fruit for wine
the hills beyond for peace
and the grass beneath for rest
the music in the wind for us
the nights for loving
the days for living
and the circling lines in the sky
for dreams.

We are like the sensitive Spring
walking valleys like a slim young girl
full breasted and precious limbed
and carrying on our lips the kiss of the world.
Only the naked arm of Time
can measure the ground we know
and thresh the air we breathe.
Neither earth nor star nor water's host
can sever us from our life to be
for we are beyond your reach O mighty winnowing flail!
infinite and free!

Molly Means

Old Molly Means was a hag and a witch;
Chile of the devil, the dark, and sitch.
Her heavy hair hung thick in ropes
And her blazing eyes was black as pitch.
Imp at three and wench at 'leben
She counted her husbands to the number seben.
   O Molly, Molly, Molly Means
   There goes the ghost of Molly Means.

Some say she was born with a veil on her face
So she could look through unnatchal space
Through the future and through the past
And charm a body or an evil place
And every man could well despise
The evil look in her coal black eyes.
   Old Molly, Molly, Molly Means
   Dark is the ghost of Molly Means.

And when the tale begun to spread
Of evil and of holy dread:
Her black-hand arts and her evil powers
How she cast her spells and called the dead,
The younguns was afraid at night
And the farmers feared their crops would blight.
   Old Molly, Molly, Molly Means
   Cold is the ghost of Molly Means.

Then one dark day she put a spell
On a young gal-bride just come to dwell
In the lane just down from Molly's shack
And when her husband come riding back
His wife was barking like a dog
And on all fours like a common hog.
   O Molly, Molly, Molly Means
   Where is the ghost of Molly Means?

The neighbors come and they went away
And said she'd die before break of day
But her husband held her in his arms
And swore he'd break the wicked charms;
He'd search all up and down the land
And turn the spell on Molly's hand.
   O Molly, Molly, Molly Means
   Sharp is the ghost of Molly Means.

So he rode all day and he rode all night
And at the dawn he come in sight
Of a man who said he could move the spell
And cause the awful thing to dwell
On Molly Means, to bark and bleed
Till she died at the hands of her evil deed.
   Old Molly, Molly, Molly Means
   This is the ghost of Molly Means.

Sometimes at night through the shadowy trees
She rides along on a winter breeze.
You can hear her holler and whine and cry.
Her voice is thin and her moan is high,
And her cackling laugh or her barking cold
Bring terror to the young and old.
   O Molly, Molly, Molly Means
   Lean is the ghost of Molly Means.

Kissie Lee

Toughest gal I ever did see
Was a gal by the name of Kissie Lee;
The toughest gal God ever made
And she drew a dirty, wicked blade.

Now this here gal warn't always tough
Nobody dreamed she'd turn out rough
But her Grammaw Mamie had the name
Of being the town's sin and shame.

When Kissie Lee was young and good
Didn't nobody treat her like they should
Allus gettin' beat by a no-good shine
An' allus quick to cry and whine.

Till her Grammaw said, "Now listen to me,
I'm tiahed of yoah whinin', Kissie Lee.
People don't never treat you right,
An' you allus scrappin' or in a fight.

"Whin I was a gal wasn't no soul
Could do me wrong an' still stay whole.
Ah got me a razor to talk for me
An' aftah that they let me be."

Well Kissie Lee took her advice
And after that she didn't speak twice

'Cause when she learned to stab and run
She got herself a little gun.

And from that time that gal was mean,
Meanest mama you ever seen.
She could hold her likker and hold her man
And she went thoo life jus' raisin' san'.

One night she walked in Jim's saloon
And seen a guy what spoke too soon;
He done her dirt long time ago
When she was good and feeling low.

Kissie bought her drink and she paid her dime
Watchin' this guy what beat her time
And he was making for the outside door
When Kissie shot him to the floor.

Not a word she spoke but she switched her blade
And flashing that lil ole baby paid:
Evvy livin' guy got out of her way
Because Kissie Lee was drawin' her pay.

She could shoot glass doors offa the hinges,
She could take herself on the wildest binges.
And she died with her boots on switching blades
On Talladega Mountain in the likker raids.

Big John Henry

This here's a tale of a sho-nuff man
Whut lived one time in the delta lan'.
His hand was big as a hog's fat ham
And he useta work for Uncle Sam.
His gums was blue, his voice was mellow
And he talked to mules, fellow to fellow.
The day he was born in the Mississippi bottom
He made a meal on buttermilk and sorghum
A mess o' peas and a bait o' tunnips
And when he finished he smacked his lips
And went outside to help pick cotton.
And he growed up taller than a six-foot shooter
Skinnin' mules and catchin' barracuda
And stronger than a team of oxen
And he even could beat the champion boxin'
An' ain't nary man in Dixie's forgotten

How he could raise two bales of cotton
While one hand anchored down the steamboat.
Oh, they ain't no tale was ever wrote
'Bout Big John Henry that could start to tell
All the things that Big Boy knowed so well:
How he learned to whistle from the whippoorwills,
And turned the wheels whut ran the mills;
How the witches taught him how to cunjer,
And cyo the colic and ride the thunder;
And how he made friends with a long lean houn'
Sayin', "It's jes' John Henry a-giftin' 'roun'."
But a ten-poun' hammer done ki-ilt John Henry
Yeah, a ten-poun' hammer ki-ilt John Henry,
Bust him open, wide Lawd!
Drapped him ovah, wide Lawd!
Po' John Henry, he cold and dead.

The Ballad of the Free

Bold Nat Turner by the blood of God
Rose up preaching on Virginia's sod;
Smote the land with his passionate plea
Time's done come to set my people free.

    The serpent is loosed and the hour is come
    The last shall be first and the first shall be none
    The serpent is loosed and the hour is come.

Gabriel Prosser looked at the sun,
Said, "Sun, stand still till the work is done.
The world is wide and the time is long
And man must meet the avenging wrong."

    The serpent is loosed and the hour is come
    The last shall be first and the first shall be none
    The serpent is loosed and the hour is come

Denmark Vesey led his band
Across the hot Carolina land.
The plot was foiled, the brave men killed,
But Freedom's cry was never stilled.

    The serpent is loosed and the hour is come
    The last shall be first and the first shall be none
    The serpent is loosed and the hour is come

Toussaint L'Ouverture won
All his battles in the tropic sun,
Hero of the black man's pride
Among those hundred who fought and died.

The serpent is loosed and the hour is come
The last shall be first and the first shall be none
The serpent is loosed and the hour is come

Brave John Brown was killed but he
Became a martyr of the free,
For he declared that blood would run
Before the slaves their freedom won.

The serpent is loosed and the hour is come
The last shall be first and the first shall be none
The serpent is loosed and the hour is come

Wars and Rumors of Wars have gone,
But Freedom's army marches on.
The heroes' list of dead is long,
And Freedom still is for the strong.

The serpent is loosed and the hour is come
The last shall be first and the first shall be none
The serpent is loosed and the hour is come

Jackson, Mississippi

City of tense and stricken faces
City of closed doors and ketchup splattered floors,
City of barbed wire stockades,
And ranting voices of demagogues,
City of squealers and profane voices;
Hauling my people in garbage trucks,
Fenced in by new white police billies,
Fist cuffs and red-necked brothers of Hate Legions
Straining their leashed and fiercely hungry dogs;
City of tree-lined, wide, white avenues
And black alleys of filthy rendezvous;
City of flowers: of new red zinnias
And oriental poppies and double-ruffled petunias
Ranch styled houses encircled with rose geranium
And scarlet salvia
And trouble-ridden minds of the guilty and the conscienceless;

City of stooges and flunkeys, pimps and prostitutes,
Bar-flies and railroad-station freaks;
City with southern sun beating down raw fire
On heads of blaring jukes,
And light-drenched streets puddled with the promise
Of a brand-new tomorrow
I give you my heart, Southern City
For you are my blood and dust of my flesh,
You are the harbor of my ship of hope,
The dead-end street of my life,
And the long washed down drain of my youth's years of toil,
In the bosom of your families
I have planted my seeds of dreams and visions and prophecies
All my fantasies of freedom and of pride,
Here lie three centuries of my eyes and my brains and my hands,
Of my lips and strident demands,
The graves of my dead,
And the birthing stools of grannies long since fled.

Here are echoes of my laughing children
And hungry minds of pupils to be fed.
I give you my brimming heart, Southern City
For my eyes are full and no tears cry
And my throat is dusty and dry.

For Andy Goodman—Michael Schwerner —and James Chaney

(Three Civil Rights Workers
Murdered in Mississippi on June 21, 1964)
(Written after seeing the movie, Andy In A.M.)

Three faces . . .
      mirrored in the muddy stream of living . . .
young and tender like
quiet beauty of still water,
sensitive as the mimosa leaf,
      intense as the stalking cougar
      and impassive as the face of rivers;
The sensitive face of Andy
The intense face of Michael
The impassive face of Chaney.

Three leaves . . .
      Floating in the melted snow

Flooding the Spring
oak leaves
one by one
moving like a barge
across the seasons
moving like a breeze across the window pane
winter . . . summer . . . spring
When is the evil year of the cricket?
When comes the violent day of the stone?
In which month
do the dead ones appear at the cistern?

Three lives . . .
   turning on the axis of our time
   Black and white together
   turning on the wheeling compass
   of a decade and a day
   The concerns of a century of time
   . . . an hourglass of destiny

Three lives . . .
   ripe for immortality of daisies and wheat
   for the simple beauty of a humming bird
   and dignity of a sequoia
   of renunciation and
   resurrection
For the Easter morning of our Meridians.

Why should another die for me?
Why should there be a calvary
A subterranean hell for three?
In the miry clay?
In the muddy stream?
In the red misery?
In mutilating hatred and in fear?
The brutish and the brazen
without brain
without blessing
without beauty . . .
They have killed these three.
They have killed them for me.

Sunrise and sunset . . .
Spring rain and winter window pane . . .
I see the first leaves budding

The green Spring returning
I mark the falling
of golden Autumn leaves
and three lives floating down the quiet stream
Till they come to the surging falls . . .

The burned blossoms of the dogwood tree
tremble in the Mississippi morning
The wild call of the cardinal bird
troubles the Mississippi morning
I hear the morning singing
larks, robins, and the mocking bird
while the mourning dove
broods over the meadow
Summer leaf falls never turning brown

Deep in a Mississippi thicket
I hear that mourning dove
Bird of death singing in the swamp
Leaves of death floating in their watery grave

Three faces turn their ears and eyes
sensitive
intense
impassive
to see the solemn sky of summer
to hear the brooding cry
of the mourning dove

Mississippi bird of sorrow
O mourning bird of death
Sing their sorrow
Mourn their pain
And teach us death,
To love and live with them again!

Ballad of The Hoppy-Toad

Ain't been on Market Street for nothing
With my regular washing load
When the Saturday crowd went stomping
Down the Johnny-jumping road,

Seen Sally Jones come running
With a razor at her throat,

See Deacon's daughter lurching
Like a drunken alley goat.

But the biggest for my money,
And the saddest for my throw
Was the night I seen the goopher man
Throw dust around my door.

Come sneaking round my doorway
In a stovepipe hat and coat;
Come sneaking round my doorway
To drop the evil note.

I run down to Sis Avery's
And told her what I seen
"Root-worker's out to git me
What you reckon that there mean?"

Sis Avery she done told me,
"Now honey go on back
I knows just what will hex him
And that old goopher sack."

Now I done burned the candles
Till I seen the face of Jim
And I done been to Church and prayed
But can't git rid of him.

Don't want to burn his picture
Don't want to dig his grave
Just want to have my peace of mind
And make that dog behave.

Was running through the fields one day
Sis Avery's chopping corn
Big horse come stomping after me
I knowed then I was gone.

Sis Avery grabbed that horse's mane
And not one minute late
Cause trembling down behind her
I seen my ugly fate.

She hollered to that horse to "Whoa!
I gotcha hoppy-toad."
And yonder come the goopher man
A-running down the road.

She hollered to that horse to "Whoa"
And what you wanta think?
Great-God-a-mighty, that there horse
Begun to sweat and shrink.

He shrunk up to a teeny horse
He shrunk up to a toad
And yonder come the goopher man
Still running down the road.

She hollered to that horse to "Whoa"
She said, "I'm killing him.
Now you just watch this hoppy toad
And you'll be rid of Jim."

The goopher man was hollering
"Don't kill that hoppy-toad."
Sis Avery she said "Honey,
You bout to lose your load."

That hoppy-toad was dying
Right there in the road
And goopher man was screaming
"Don't kill that hoppy-toad."

The hoppy-toad shook one more time
And then he up and died
Old goopher man fell dying, too.
"O hoppy-toad," he cried.

A Poem for Farish Street

1   The African Village

In our beginnings our Blackness was not thought so beautiful
but out of bitterness we wrought an ancient past
here in this separate place
and made our village here.
We brought our gifts to altars of your lives
with singing, dancing, giving,
and moved stumbling stones into the market place.

Dark faces of our living generations
hear voices of our loving dead go echoing
down corridors of centuries.
For those who suffered, bled and died

Let this be monument:
the passing throngs parade before our eyes again.
Our children playing here
Our neighbors passing by;
the daily swift encounters hear
and whispering in alleys,
dark corners of our lives
resuscitate.

In this short street a class of Africans create
A jungle world, a desert and a plain
A mountain road, rain forest, and valleys
green and sweet.
We touch the earth and sky and flowers bloom
around our quivering feet.
Sunshine and rain
beat on these stones and bricks,
and wooden window panes.
Green grass grows scantily
and skirts the blackened pools on
muddy streets.
Thundershowers, snow, and sunlight
stream through an open doorway—
Syrian butcher in his bloody apron;
Green grocer with his sidewalk wares,
And hucksters riding wagons down this road
With a cry
for everyone to come and buy.
This is a place of yesteryears,
forgotten street of dreams.
The stardust shines
into the crevices of dingy lives
and gleams across our listlessness.
Oh! hear the song
go whistling down the empty years
and let the afterglow
of all my hoped tomorrows
fall on my lonely shadow.

I'll hawk your dreams,
your broken stars of glass
I'll paint your visions
on a rainbow road
that shines across dark starry skies.

2   A Patchwork Quilt

This street is like my grandma's patchwork quilt
Kaleidoscope, appliqued with multicolored
threads of embroidery.
A golden sun, blue skies, carpeted with the greenness
the yellow, the red, the white, the black, the brown, and the checkered.
Bright gingham, fine silk and satin and linen cloth
patterned patches on the faces of these people
the Chinese laundry-man
Black cobbler
Green grocer
And down the street there used to be
a livery stable with a brown Indian man.
Now there's a taxi stand.
Once street cars passed along the side
Up Capitol
to where black slaves built the Capitol
the mansion for the governor
and over there, the city hall.
They made these bricks and laid them too
Not knowing some day they would meet
As Black and Tan in 1868.
This patchwork quilt is stitched with blood and tears
This street is paved with martyred Black men's flesh and bones.

3   The Crystal Palace

The Crystal Palace used to be
a place of elegance
Where "bourgie" black folks came to shoot
a game of pool
And dine in the small cafe
across the way.
The dance hall music rocked the night
and sang sweet melodies:
"Big fat mama with the meat shaking on her bones"
"Boogie woogie mama
Please come back home"
"I Miss you loving papa
but I can't live on love alone"
The Crystal Palace
Used to be
most elegant.

4   The House of Prayer

Two undertaking parlors on this street
close to the House of God
have witnessed all the shame of Farish Street.
In another life sister Sadie Lou
was like that gal from Madame's Fancy House
Bawdy Belle with her tight spanky-baby dress
her cigarette
her blood-red pasted lips on a clown's face
high heeled shoes
and lacquered hair
and her shoulder bag
swinging down her hips
full of tricks.
Hey gal, what you sellling
On Farish Street?
And she laughs a hollow joyless sound
Oh, you know you know, I know you know–
Mary Mack, dressed in black
silver buttons
All down her back.
I like sugar
I like tea
I love pretty girls
And they love me.
Ask my mama
for fifteen cents
to see that elephant
jump that fence
jump so high
Touched the sky
Didn't come back
Till the fourth of July.

5   Small Black World

Fly away birdies, fly away home.
Pigeons roosting
Gray as the dawning
Gray as the winter morning
Fly away birdies, fly away.
All our history is here
all our yearning, dreaming, hoping, loving, dying

All our lives are buried here.
See that old blind man
He is led by a child
And his tin cup in his hand
jingles coins like bells of the Calliope
a monkey on a string dances to the tune
Of an organ grinder
Shrill paddy wagon rushing crowds
Drunken, stoned, and crazy
slashing stabbing knives and razors cutting throats
sirens screaming
lookers-on shrieking
scattering and disappearing
flooding bloody Farish Street.
While the shuffling feet of ghosts who are prisoners in the night
pass into yesterday.
On the corner grey stone rises.
A black man's name is on the building:
Federal building on his land
Like the Reservoir on black land
Like the river roads on black land.
I have walked these streets all over the world
Black streets, Farish Streets
where all the black people all over the world
have set up their shops
in the markets of the world
where we sell our souls daily to every passerby
and our children come to play in emptiness
and softly night falls suddenly.

6   Black Magic

There's a magic man on Farish Street
Root doctor, hoodoo man
Sells charms and potions
"Cross the river for liquor
And bring your own bottle to the party."
They are playing checkers in the twilight
Before the barber shop,
Before the beauty parlor
Before the drug store where the man sells magic:
Love charms and potions and good luck pieces,
powders, and odors, and aphrodisiacs
High John the Conqueror and

Sampson Snake Root;
Across from the YW and the YMCA
Where the saints go marching in
Where the street dead-ends
And the cemetery begins
The other side of the tracks
There's a man selling lucky charms
And he sells bargains too
Choose between God and the devil
Choose between flesh and the spirit
Choose betwen sacred and the profane
But remember, when you sell your soul to the devil
Prepare to live in hell!
Black man you know well
Lie down with dogs and get up with fleas
There's a man going round taking names
Lawd knows they scandalizing my name
I want Jesus to make up my dying bed
when they carry my coffin down Farish Street
pigeon-toed and wrinkled nosed
sidling up to fate.

7   The Labyrinth of Life

I have come through the maze and the mystery of living
to this miraculous place of meaning
finding all things less than vanity
all values overlaid and blessed with truth and love and peace:
having a small child's hand to touch
a kiss to give across a wide abyss
and knowing magic of reconciliation and hope;
To a place blessed with smiling
Shining beyond the brightness of noonday
and I lift my voice above a rising wind
to say I care
because I now declare
this place called Farish Street in sacred memory
to be one slice of life
one wheel of fortune a-turning in the wind
and as I go
a traveller through this labyrinth
I taste the bitter-sweet waters of Mara
and I look to the glory of the morning of all life.
AMEN. I say AMEN.

JERRY W. WARD, JR.

Your Voice

it's a magic thing,
sun and rain and poetry
flooding in my memory,
but all I can remember
is how you got over
a deep river
with amazing grace
and cured your blues
with natural rhythms

From Meditations on Richard Wright: Black Boy

some black boys go deep south,
chiseling attitudes,
rise to recognition
up north, somewhere,
somewhere up north
the compass cannot read.

some black boys stay deep south,
battling the cobwebs
of a long and lonely dream,
making something somewhere
somehow out of nothing.

and then,
some black boys
know deep south
and only be.

Don't Be Fourteen (in Mississippi)

Don't be fourteen
black and male in Mississippi
　　they put your mind
　　in a paper sack, dip it
　　in a liquid nitrogen
　　for later consumption

Don't be fourteen
black and male in Mississippi,
have two 20/20 eyes,
feet that fail to buck, wing, and tap,
a mouth that whistles
 they castrate you, wrap
 you in cotton-bailing wire
 while your blood still feels,
 feed you to the Tallahatchie
 as guilt-offering to blue-eyed susans
Don't be fourteen
black and male in Mississippi
 they say you a bad nigger
 named Bubba, a disgrace
 to the race in your first offense,
 and give you to Parchman
 for forty-eight years.
 You need, they say, a change to grow.
Don't be fourteen
black and male in Mississippi
 they say you a man at two.
 be one.
 when white boys ask
 why don't you like them,
 spit on them
 with your mouth closed.

Unentitled

Be content.
Nobody remembers
you, so they accept
you for what you are
not.

Be wild, if you care,
as an angel
banging at heaven's
back door.

Kiss the sweetness out of chaos.

Yestermorrow
you were securely
insignificant,

nothing less
than a pale shadow
of plenitude.

Now, if winter comes
to freeze-dry truth from air,
you can spring
like rain lilies
out of mud.

Everybody forgets
the blooming.
They marvel
over the green signals of desire.

Trueblood

trueblood, he never heard
of incest and such mess
and worried only about pests
in his cotton crop,
looked on chaos and survived.

trueblood, he always understood
what professors thought they could.
he dipped snuff, drank rotgut stuff
and bought what labor bought,
looked on chaos and survived.

trueblood, he never owned
a tailored suit, high-stepped
in cast-offs when he got 'em,
was the holiest deacon in the church,
looked on chaos and survived.

in all his ninety years,
trueblood, he never uttered
the blind words "I've arrived,"
cause he stayed at home,
looked at chaos and survived.

Fusion

(for Baron James Ashanti and John Wakefield)

Communed us green
with Guinness and black
from expresso. The snap
of conversation
polished us bright
as boots.

We made us
    wiser than
    words made us hear
    the aching universe
    made us see
    eternity's debate
    of rifle butts
    with bones
    we made us
    mankind song.

And, yes, we'd sing
again, again.
We'd chant Zimbabwe
so pure
the lasses of Aughrim
could cornrow
their souls.

There's holiness
in speech, in song,
I'd say, a sanctity
the unsuffered
must never touch.

Something in the Gulf

this land wanted more
than the brave Biloxi whipping
a fierce surprise
upon the peaceful Pascagoula.

listen. at this distance
you hear the proud destruction,
the tragic joy of the death song

when the buzz of sawmill
and the clank of steel on iron
escapes the shipyard crew,
conjoining in the ripples of the river,
sounding again the ancient sacrifice.

even now, our feet planted
like granite on the salt-scented coast,
we feel the primal motion
of a history webbed in guesses,
surmise a something in the Gulf
trawling endlessly for the absence of life.

for you, for me,
even now that mocking song
celebrates eternity
in humid mosquitoed night
as we listen to destiny
surge through our Mississippi minds.

The Impossible All These Years

Sometime before you hit forty,
you must step outside your bones,
audit the maze your flesh has made.
And be amazed how much consequence
morality has planted on your feet,
how much ambivalence is the harvest
of your legs, how much lost potential
is barned in your gut, how much
opportunity has leaked from your pores.

From the outside, the prospect is not pretty;
your living is like linen full of catfaces,
your presence is a penitentiary riot.
You are criminal, a critical case
of becoming the unregenerate image
of yourself; but finding peace in your planet
you stride back inside to praise
the impossible all these years.

Jazz to Jackson to John

(for John Reese)

movement one: genesis

it must have been something like
sheets of sound wrinkled
with riffs and scats,
the aftermath of a fierce night
breezing through the grits and gravy;
or something like a blind leviathan
squeezing through solid rock,
marking chaos in the water
when his lady of graveyard love went
turning tricks on the ocean's bottom;
or something like a vision
so blazing basic, so gutbucket, so blessed
the lowdown blues flew out: jazz

jazz to jackson and
dust to dawn and
words for John

it must have been something like
Farish Street in the bebop forties,
a ragtag holy ghost baptizing Mississippi
on an unexpected Sunday, a brilliant revelation
for Billie telling you about these foolish things
back in your own backyard, angel eyes in the rose room,
Monk's changing piano into horn because it was zero in the
sun,
and around midnight there was nobody but you
to walk Parker and his jazz to Jackson;
yeah, brother, it must have been something
striking you like an eargasm,
a baritone ax laid into soprano wood,

like loving madly in hurting silence,
waiting to fingerpop this heathen air
with innovations of classical black
at decibels to wake the deaf, the dumb, and the dead;
because around midnight there was nobody but you
who dug whether race records were
lamentations or lynchings: jazz

jazz to jackson and
sunset to dawn and
words for John

movement two: blues people in the corn

steal away, steal away, steal away
the heart blow/horn blow/drum drop
to bass/five-four time beat
making a one o'clock comeback creep
behind all that jazz
beat—beepbeep—beat
steal way back to beginning
beginning
is the water
is the soul
is the source
is the foundation with my brothers
is Pharaoh jamming in the pyramid,
sketches of Spain for a night in Tunisia;
is MJQ, Tatum, Turrentine, Tyner,
the Jazz Messengers, messiahs, crusading
headhunters tracking down the mind

cause, Lord yes, all God's people got sold
and who'da thought
owning rhythm was a crime like stealing a nickel
and snitching a dime, when we had coffers packed
with golden music and time, golden music and time

sliding from the flesh, the bone, honeysweet music;
them lollipopcicle people
and they sardine ships
(and no music to speak of)
they stole it all and sold it all
for wooden nickles, for frozen dimes: jazz

behind all that jazz
blues people in the corn, in the vale of cotton tears,
blues people in the corn,
waiting, waiting, waiting,
wrapped in esoteric patience,
waiting to steal away,
steal away, steal away
soon as Miles runs down the voodoo avenue

with some jazz to Jackson
and pipes a private number
to call a tune for John

movement three: and this, John, is our new day

and this, John, is our new day.
never say goodbye to the blues that saw you through,
nor put down the spirituals and the salty sermonnettes
the drugs, the junkies, the jukebox juice, the sweat
and the pain of shelling hot peanuts, hot peanuts: jazz

and the jazz you gave to us
we give to you as jazz to Jackson and
because we really want to thank you
words for John

NAGUEYALTI WARREN

Mississippi Woods

If woods could talk
wonder what would they say.
Would they give away southern secrets:
tell of murders by knights in white sheets,
or of hounds chasing fleeing freedom bound
men,
or of trained dogs eating human meat?

If woods would talk
would they tell of burning flesh?
Would they tell how Black blood
fertilized their roots?

Woods won't talk,
but ancient tree trunks hold
the secrets of the South
in Mississippi woods.

Prayer

She knew prayer
Was the heart-felt longing of the soul,
But what her soul longed for

Was somehow unholy; ungodlike.
Somehow not like the god
She'd learned to serve in childhood's hour:
The great white father, gleaming so pure,
This longing in her soul was black,
Like the evil preached about on Sunday mornings,
Or the grime left in unclean clothes.
This thing—
This prayer within her,
Wanted nothing more than to feel
The presence of the Negro.
Wanted to feel the "everted lips, short,
Thick, nappy hair."
She prayed out loud to be
"Honest, decent, pure, innocent—"
But prayer, she knew
Was the heart-felt longing of the soul—

Southern Memories

Mississippi summer
delta sun burning black
hot white memories
of lush green
rope bearing trees
bringing death to Black folk
who dared to live free.

Nature Poem

Miss. Sunrise comes cracking her whip
Through the tall pines;
A fowl choir in harmony,
Serenades the new day.
And Sun burning suddenly hot,
Moves people quickly across the red clay,
In the Miss. morning—
This, a poem not 'bout trees,
Birds and sunrisin',
Is a poem 'bout the nature
Of an early sunshining,
Bringing black hands to white fields of cotton,
Burning hot sweat and maybe death
Before sunset.

NAYO-BARBARA WATKINS

A Frame of Mind

Written after the unprecedented 1979 meeting of a SWAC team (Alcorn State University)
and a SEC team (Mississippi State University) in a basketball game. The SWAC team won.

they sent
5 of our best
to tell us
SWAC
is inferior

like Wilma Rudolph
Satchel Paige
and Homestead Grays
were inferior

they told them
tell us
we were not
in their league

all the while
we shouted
who dat who dat
and the balls went
whoop! whoop!
talkin bout
whoop! whoop!
beatin them
whoop!
braves

brave
young blk men
stood in light
of history
to make   a point
to mark a mark
in time

whoop!
who dat
whoop! whoop!

who dat
young blk boy
come   from
shot gun school house
to intimidating halls
of ivy
saying
'league
is a frame
of mind

who dat
blk man
stand
in MS cotton fields
with the strength
of his ancestors
pumping in his veins
and the hope
of small blk colleges
and secondary universities
in his hand
dare shoot a ball
say
SWAC is BAD

who dat
little insignificant
blk coach
standing among
the giants
dare pull
a 8 second
whamee

whoop!
who dat
whoop! whoop!

whoop!
went that nigger's head
as billy club
come down
when he dare say
blk children
could go to MSU

whoop! whoop!
they cracked
his back
and tossed him
in jail
the price to pay
for his children
to go to school

so they took
5 of our best
and sent them
back at us
to say
their ivy halls
and integrated gyms
had raised our boys
to a league above
our boys
raised in blk school houses
in one room shot gun
institutions
of soul and heart
and guts and sweat
and patience and determination
our learning centers
with 2 bunson burners
and 2nd hand textbooks

but they hadnt
counted on
the Whitneys and
the Whitneys and
all the Whitneys
who give so much
with so little
and tell blk children
'league is a frame
of mind'

now go out there
and put the ball
in the hoop
whoop!
one for your ancestry

whoop!
one for your destiny
whoop!
and one for the boys
at MSU
who play fine ball
but may not know
this is for them too

and now lay
this one in
real easy like
MR Smith
so that all
will know
that league
is a frame
of mind
and that blk folks
can what they will
if they can
only dig it
and dig it
blk folks
as that ball goes
whoop!
in whatever you do

league
is a frame
of mind

what
  league
    you
      in?

  whoop!

A Picture of My Mother

i'd like
to show you
a picture
of my mother

if i could
paint it
you could
see it

but its hard
as hell
to paint pictures
of blk women
nigger nannies
strong-as-ox females

musty milky smells
lemon pies
and simple dresses
patting feet
rocking chairs
and sewing fingers

she was warm
her womb
her lap
against her breast
growing up
i'd come back
to touch the warmth

her do's and donts
linger in my ears
are imbedded in
my mind as they were
upon my buttocks

but i did not know her
we did not know her
knew none of them
mothers ancient
and eternal

we stand
reviewing their lives
at their graves
who were they
who was my mother

we knew her
mother

wife
friend
neighbor
comforter
nourisher
but knew not
the secret corners
of her mind
the sacred treasures
that loved and die
in her/with her
dreamy fantasies that
dared cross
her twilight

some hidden agenda
in her mind
some scheme
of how she wanted
things to be

i never asked
what it was
only tried to
escape it
as it prodded
and patted
my clay-like self
into something
only her secret
scheme knew

i never asked
why she raised
apron corners
to wipe tears
why she trembled
as i dashed
carelessly pass
her china-glass
dreams

she was mama
and thats all
i wanted

to know/
no i did not know her

she belonged to us
we took her
for granted
she asked
to be recognized
she offered humbly
her creations
of figurative meringues
and intricate flower beds
she sang a song
of full gutted hope
and praise
and we thought
it was all for us
she wove words
of wisdom and integrity
into simple sparrow-sweet phrases
we took for granted

now i want to paint
a picture
of her
for her
unto her holiness

the only picture
i can show you
of my mother
is me
and though i fall
for short
it is thru strokes
of self discovery
that i paint pictures
of my mothers
ancient and eternal

Mama's Children

Mama
my mama
your mama

our mama
his mama
her mama
we mama

our children gone
our children gone
our bright and shiny
futures of ourselves
gone

stolen from Africa
by slavers
oh, how i moaned
and groaned
over my gone child

ripped from my arms
on slave auction block
never, never
to be seen again
never to hear that sweet call

our children
our children
futures of ourselves

i remember
emmett till's mama
crying from chicago
to mississipi
to claim her little boy

i remember scottsboro
mamas and birmingham
sunday school mamas
soweto mamas and
haitan boat mamas

i remember mama
on television
talking about
her dead child
in atlanta, ga.

her child
my child
our children gone

i remember all
the mamas standing
watching, worrying
fighting back and dying mamas

i will remember
mama
my mama
your mama
his mama
her mama
our mama
mama in atlanta
mama in chicago
mama in little rock
mama in Africa

i will remember
i will remember
to guard mama's children
and when
somebody come
to do something
to mama's children

i will
shoot them
dead

Do You Know Me?

you cannot love me
if you do not know me
if you do not know why
my hands are calloused
and my feet are bunioned
and i smell not of rose waters
and oil baths

if you do not know why
my straightened hair
contradicts at the roots
and why my feet do not fit
very well in high heeled shoes
no, you cannot love me

you see, i sweat out
a sunday crepe dress
and my ample rear makes
a hemline lose its level

besides that, i take no pleasure
in sticking my pinkie out
while holding a cup of tea
and if you cannot understand
you cannot love me

i try to deal with certain customs
so as not to seem strange
but i really do prefer socks
over my nylons, multi-colored
wraps around my head, and i'd rather
leave the gap between my teeth
unchanged

it is utterly important
that you know these things
before you dive off
into some fantasy
of what i might be only to be
shocked by what i am

i must tell you i have picked
cotton and chopped wood
i have busted suds in iron wash pots
and i have obeyed masters
i did not want to obey

there are scars upon my mind
and bruises on my soul
mostly i try to forget
but when i remember
i am often bitchy

if you think you want to love me
you must know what turns me on
why i sing stirring grits
in my faded bathrobe
why i need to see you smile
and why sometimes i do not need to see you at all

you must understand that this outer image
is but a proper disguise

while i preserve and conserve
the real me inside

i am an African woman
and in the privacy of the private chambers
of my mind
in the intimacy of the intimate corridors
of my soul
when the doors to western civilization
are shut
i open the doors
to myself
and i am an African woman

"When Wells Run Dry—
For Muddy Waters and Associates"

Mississippi bluesmen Big Joe Williams, Sam Chatman, and Muddy Waters died within three months of each other in 1982–83.

who will play
a blues
for a blues people

who will sing
earth's salt songs
for earth/salt people

hard soil/long
rows/burning
suns/muddy
waters/of
mississippi songs

back breaking/cotton
high/spirit/low/lawd/
pockets empty/
mississippi flat/
delta songs

love aching/love
making/heart
breaking/boss
taking/songs
my daddy sang

who will ease
my pain and calm
my doubts and fears
when my baby. . .baaa
byee done gone

folk songs
just plain folk
songs/needing
songs/to laugh
and cry and poke
fun at overseers/songs

blues songs
for blues peoples
searching songs
seeking meaning
in futile labors
seeking endurance
under heavy burdens

friday nite fish
fry songs singing me
thru saturday's
jumping in the juke
joint songs singing
til monday morning's
blues blares songs

sometimes
i feel. . .feeee. . .eel
like a motherless
chile. . .a long. . .
along come pretty
baby. . .wid her high
heel slippers on. . .
saying daddy. . .hoochie
coochie daddy where you
been so long. . .mo
jo working. . .mojo
working on you

working. . .mojo
mooo. . .joooo
joe, big joe, where

you been so long
sam, don't ya know
i feel. . .sam,
i feeeeeel. . .
like i ain't got
nobody. . .to sing
the blues. . .to
play the harmonica. . .
and the guitar
and washboard
for my bluespeople
mo. . .jo. . .no. . .
mo. . .

who will sing
the bluuueesss. . .for
bluespeople. . .when
bluemen. . .done
gone. . .when
wells. . .done run dry
waters
will be missed

Missions and Magnolias

would that i could i'd write a poem
for a Black man, a teacher-woman,
5 astronauts, one also female, one somewhat Brown,
and the made-in-america towel of babel

it was hushed in the ole miss union
disbelieving eyes held to the horror
on television as we cremated them
in the sky that fell into the sea

outside magnolias sighed and swished
hooped skirts of evergreen
in the face of the cold clear sky
and we quietly remembered christa
who would have taught lessons from space

56 manned missions with a few women,
Blacks and Browns; america has asked the heavens
for answers we could not find on earth

now we pay a sacrifice of seven
while the media directs our mourning

but my thoughts will not be directed; they
soar thru the space of my mind like unmanned
space ships, reaching for reasoning, racing
to outrun the raw pain, seeking to know why
i am so troubled when magnolias sway undaunted

the teacher . . . this was the one with the teacher . . .
we wanted her to come back . . . and teach . . .
and teach . . . maybe she could've taught
about magnolias . . . we don't know enough
bout magnolias . . . magnolias and mississippi . . .
we don't know . . . we babel our hi-tech talk
but we don't know . . . just be babeling . . . building
towers and babeling . . . in mississippi . . . what's
mississippi and magnolias got to do with . . .
nothing maybe, maybe everything . . . peace on earth . . .

and i just read winnie mandela's book . . .
what's mandela got to do with it . . . nothing
maybe . . . maybe something on that shuttle
came from south africa . . . mined by Black
hands . . . don't reduce everything to color . . .
i was already feeling raw rage for winnie,
now this . . . missions and magnolias and mississippi
and mandela . . . lawd! the colonel hides
under magnolias and waves rebel flags
at Black boys and girls trying to be teachers
and engineers and astronauts . . . there you go
again, it ain't a color matter . . . he went up too,
didn't he . . . he was an american astronaut,
you know . . . guess we're equal now . . .
we die like them . . . not hanging from trees
like before . . .

we don't even know why magnolias
stand eternally green and sigh politely
as we dash foolishly to and fro
searching for answers to questions
we've not yet couraged to ask

they say we'll build another one . . . the goulish
and greedy await the contracts . . . the president
tells the children they too will fly into the sky . . .

the media shows the fireball again . . . and
again . . . will there be no peace on earth

who was mcnair's granddaddy anyhow . . . what
plantation was he from . . . did he know about
magnolias . . . will his grandson's ashes fall
from south carolina to south africa . . . really now,
must you always see everything in blk and wht . . .
my tears are quite colorless . . . i will cry . . .
i will cry but not today . . . today i am
mandela's mississippi cousin . . . and i need
peace on earth . . .

someday i will cry for america: her teachers
and astronauts and farmers and workers and
women and minorities . . . perhaps even her
colonels and presidents, so goulish and greedy . . .
i will cry but not today . . . today there are lessons
to learn . . . missions and magnolias and
mississippi and mandela . . . peace on earth.

EUDORA WELTY

A Flock of Guinea Hens Seen From a Car

The lute and the pear are your half sisters,
The mackerel moon a full first cousin,
And you were born to appear seemly, even when running on guinea
    legs,
As maiden-formed, as single-minded as raindrops,
Ellipses, small homebodies of great orbits (little knots at the back like
    apron strings),
Perfected, sealed off, engraved like a dozen perfect consciences,
As egglike as the eggs you know best, triumphantly speckled . . .
But fast!
Side-eyed with emancipation, no more lost than a string of pearls are
    lost from one another,
You cross the road in the teeth of Pontiacs
As over a threshold, into waving, gregarious grasses,
Welcome wherever you go—the Guinea Sisters.

Bobbins with the threads of innumerable visits behind you,
As light on your feet
As the daughters of Mr. Barrett of Wimpole Street,
Do you ever wonder where Africa has fled?
Is the strangeness of your origins packed tight in those little nutmeg
    heads; so ceremonious, partly naked?
Is there time to ask each other what became of the family wings?
Do you dream?
Princess of Dapple,
Princess of Moonlight,
Princess of Conch,
Princess of Guinealand,
Though you roost in the care of S. Thomas Truly, Rt. 1
(There went his mailbox flying by),
The whole world knows you've never yet given up the secrets of
    where you've hidden your nests.

JOHN MILTON WESLEY

Son Child

On a road in Mississippi
A dirt farmer stopped
Long enough to leave a son child.
A midwife's folly
Ended in a tear. Ten round
Fat fingers reached for
A hollow meat bottle
For lack of something else to
Do with a toothless mouth.
Out of a pregnancy, into
A cold world, free to stretch
Dared to move and demand love.
I never saw his face
Was told it was round and fat
And filled with false teeth
His fingers were also
Known to roam. He ran away
to avoid a steel cage and
An avocation of license plates.
In the years ahead, my brother

Would do his time.
Fats, was a big man the neighbors whispered
How could he be such a skinny child
And baldheaded.
Before the streets were named
And sewers were layed, when
Catfish washed up on the bridge
And the water rose.
Before Emmett Till whistled
At the white woman (they hung him for it.)
A son child left by a dirt farmer
Reached for something soft.
At two he knew the coal bin,
The blackness kept him warm.
Snow fell, Ice cream sat quietly
On the window sill. Hog killing time
Took his friends away. Only roosters
Remained calm and mounted feathered
Backs, crowing, then ran off
To the neighbors backyards. Pulling, scratching
Cackling chickens danced over brown eggs.
Sister Herron's cow kicked the bucket
All the neighbors came out to see
The truck with the pulley roll Bessie
Onto its back. Mr. Seals had a stroke
Coming up the street. He had promised to
Bring me cookies from the store. He fell
And never broke one.
Ruleville, a mainstreet town
North on 49-W, one policeman
Khaki and fat, spat on negroes
Ate their cooking, beat their men
Loved their women, robbed their children
Gave us their old clothes.
Shot-gun houses and shot-gun weddings
Married us to our turnrows, stuffed our
Noses with cotton, broke our backs
With haybails, turned our bright eyes dark
With corn whiskey, baked us browner
Than we were, bearing their burdens
In the heat of the day.
Saturday night, on "greasy street"
The pool halls filled with new crisp
Cotton picking money, full of Schlitz

Southern Comfort, and black berry juice
Wall to wall colored people, before
We were black, before we built toilets
On our front porches to save money
Running sewer lines to the back of the house.
Those were the simpler days of
Commodity lines, of surplus peanut butter
Raisins, and cheese, and milk and flour.
We moved up in line by trading cans of
Corn beef cured in salt and water.
Yellow meal seeped through holes left
In potato sacks. Sack dresses hugged
Our sisters shoulders and waistlines.
We ran for our lives from Klansmen
And tornadoes, high winds, and hail storms.
God caused everything life and death,
Beauty and ugliness, love and hate.
Compress whistles marked the time of day,
Crickets and church bells, whippoorwills
and fireflies danced and sang. Fish frying
Could be smelled for miles.
We were a backdoor people, we knew our place
It was behind the nearest white man, on
The back of the bus, through the kitchen
Waiting until, table cleaning time for
Cold rolls splattered with coffee grounds,
And meat left on T-bones, for negroes racing
With dogs. I once saw a vision of Jesus
Lying awake waiting for the cotton picking truck.
The voice of the driver made the
Sacred mouth move, in the steel cold morning hours,
"Come with me, come with me."
And a Billy goat waiting to be
Barbecued answered, "Baaaaa, Baaaaa, Baaaaa."
Short fat ladies, heads tied, gold teeth
Glistening, wrapped sweet potatoes, pork chop
Sandwiches, and teacakes in cellophane,
And climbed on the back of Ford pickups.
We went early to catch the dew-cotton,
And sunrise, while Jim Eastland, fat, racist,
And serving, chewed bitter round cigars
On Capitol Hill.
We were a beautiful brown hateless people.
Drowning in a sea of cotton, living on the

Leftovers of Bollweevils, and ladybugs.
A day was worth three hundred pounds, and
What honey-dew melons could be found.
Baby-Ruths, lasted all day, coca-colas were a
Nickel.
Those were the days this son child knew
Burned in his eyes by the sun. Chilled in
His belly by pump water. Etched in his soul
By fear.
Way, way back to where the memory fades,
And dissolves into misconcepts of freedom,
And white children, who loved us until
They were told to hate us, and keep
Their oatmeal cookies to themselves.
And they became "crackers", and we became
"Niggers", and before they locked our churches
At midnight, and burned crosses in our front yards.
Way before Wallace and the door, and Barnett,
And Ole Miss, before Little Rock, King, Kennedy, Watts,
And Selma, way, way back before they shrunk
The baby-ruth, a dirt farmer stopped long enough
To leave a son child, who reached for something soft,
And is still waiting to touch it.

Fannie Lou

Fannie Lou
walked with a limp
chewed tobacco on a toothpick
and told white people
"I am tired of being tired"
Before the bus ride to
Indianola to register,
and after she took back
her pretty round black face,
from Artra skin tone cream,
and she and Pap moved to town,
across the street from
The Church of Christ Holiness,
she became a legend in her own time.
Just imagine, one day in the fields
the next day at Harvard
or Coppin, or Princeton.

Then on Sunday, hers was
the biggest voice at
William Chapel M.B. Church.
I can hear her now.
   "thou my everlasting potion
   more than breath and life to me
   All along this pilgrim's journey
   Savior let me walk with thee."

"Bubba, you betta get on up here boy,
you know you gotta get that other hundred
and I can't help you today"
"un coming Ms. Fannie Lou, but
my back is hurting."
"Boy you ain't got no back
you ain't got nothing but a grissle."

Fannie Lou looked like a nanny,
was big busted, and
cooked the best chocolate cake
I have ever tasted in my life.
She died from lack of love.
What she wanted for her people
Ate her up on the inside,
While neighbors gossipped, and
spread rumors about
late night rides with civil rights workers,
and money for the poor.
While niggers too scared to help,
and too smart to be seen,
and take risks, hid,
until they almost beat Fannie Lou to death.

But, she kept on singing,

   "and before I'd be a slave
   I'd be buried in my grave
   and go home to my Lord
   and be free."

Disturbing the Peace

After the Milan brothers
killed Emmitt Till in Money, Mississippi,
the young black brother with the lisp

(the white woman swore he whistled),
they bought Michelle's Grocery Store,
across the street from us, in Ruleville
on the corner of East Weber Street
and Highway 49 W.
One hot Friday night, Lloyd Surney
a black man in his thirties
with the mind of a nine year old,
was slapped and pushed, and forced into a truck.
His mother, Ms. Tee Toe
came running up the street crying,
"Where is my boy, what is y'all done
done wit' my boy?"
She was arrested for disturbing the peace.

JAMES WHITEHEAD

The Young Deputy

It was Leroy Smith we meant to find
in the slough, the old river, with hooks
but didn't. It was two others, or halves
of two, the big man's torso, the small
man's thighs, which made the sheriff sick
in the boat. It wasn't one man no matter
how hard he tried . . .

Eaten by fish was one answer.
    Maybe gar. Drowned, with rope
    still strung from the thick wrist, and a little
    chain around the bottom's ankle.

(considering conflicting reports
of disappearance from various places
they might have been a dozen men)

Then it got to be a joke about
    the burial: one grave or two,
    since they'd got fixed as a single thing
    in everybody's mind. Smith,
    he never came to light, and it seemed
    to figure that the one good grave

could somehow cover all three—and more,
said a few with furious souls.

There'd be, I thought, if things were right,
a fine day of picnicking,
preaching to a big mixed audience,
and in the nearest pine one buzzard,
glossy, hunkering, with a confused gaze.

Two Voices

Taggart says he gives them what they want—
They come to him in the night blind drunk and broke,
And he sews them up free, without a shot.
With his coarse thread he has the art to raise
Great scars from ear to ear, and he does just that—
It's part of a ritual they've done for years.
"I send them proud to the fields and gins," he says.
"With their heads pulled back that way, those bucks are grand,"
He says. "They brag after all we did it raw."

Thompson says you can hear their cries to the creek,
And he nearly objects, believing the fish in their way
Are offended—or at least that so much yelling
Can make a cat hook-shy, and anyhow
It's always Saturday night and Sunday morning
After the tonk fights and when he fishes.
"And not only that," Thompson says, "it's giving
Sorry dreams to my children." And almost angry:
"You'd think a doctor and all, he'd think of his neighbors."

A Local Man
Goes to the Killing Ground

They formed the ritual circle
of Chevy trucks. Tracks were there,
worn tires, the still prints in the mud
and thin grass. My light could barely suggest
the glare that fell on the men they killed.

It was an intimate thing—
all of them drawn in so close
they didn't bother with guns
or the normal uses of the knife.
It was done with boots.

I walked around that quiet place
    and tried to reclaim the energy
    that must of course remain in the earth.
    It keeps the truth to itself
    as they will, when they stride out of court.

By then it was all grey, false dawn—
    and I thought it was like stomping
    a fetus in the womb, a little
    skin between the killers, the killed,
    for the dead were curled in their passive way.

He Remembers Something from the War

In Kansas during the war
    my grandfather made a big thing
    of a car left out in our alley—
*There's bullet holes and human blood
    so hurry up and eat your supper.*
And the whole world would jiggle a little
    like Jello, when he was nervous.
Mother and grandmother were gone
    to the movies to see my father winning
    the war in Europe—grandfather
    never went to the movies or church
    and for the same reasons.
*This is a lot like the real trouble
    your father is having in Germany,*
    he said, as we walked past our victory garden
    then down our alley.

The things themselves were plain—
    a blue Nash and a windbreaker
    stiff with blood
    but I wasn't scared
    even by the stain itself
    until he told the story
    about how for some reason
    a hitch-hiker had murdered a farmer
    then left the car and jacket in our alley
    after dumping out the dead farmer
    in the woods of northern Arkansas.

About the time the police arrived
    I asked why in our alley?
He was the only father I had
    those long years during the war
    my mother was gone to in the movies.

Later that night mother and grandmother
    scolded him for getting drunk
    because they didn't know the things
    behind the garden
    and wouldn't until the morning news
    that told another story
    which was a lie grandfather said,
    like Roosevelt.
Upstairs he staggered near the door
    outside my room and close to my bed
    where that night in a sweaty dream
    I saw a German soldier
    catching a ride
    with my own father
    in my own father's M-4 tank
    that was standing out in our alley.

He Loves the Trailer Park and Suffers Telling Why

A hopeful life is possible out here,
And sometimes nervous,
Though few of us will ever travel much.
Storm are what we fear.
Sometimes our metal homes are worse than thatch
Or mud huts or hide tents, when the wind comes.
Trailer Park Destroyed—a common line
Because nobody ever ties them down
The way suggested.

That's hopeful, true, a sign
Of basic piety, unworldliness
To help define the insane goings-on
You read about. Lives here are quite a mess.
We have a joke that goes, "We live in tin."

But still we have more fun than we do wrong.
We take a simple pleasure from the rain.

His Slightly Longer Story Song

She was older, say, thirty-five or so,
And I was eighteen, maybe. She was dark
And musical, I thought, out of a book
I hadn't read, Louisiana slow,
A chance to get my ass shot off or grow
Up quickly, outdistancing the nervous pack
Of boys I ran with. I was green but trick
By trick she taught where innocence could go
When what I wanted happened. Innocence
Or ignorance? or neither one? Or both?
She claimed she'd taken sweetness from my life.

She cried, imagining the pretty wife
I'd hammer with some grief. She said the breath
Of love—this kind—was mostly arrogance.
She'd drink and then she'd dance
Alone and naked to the radio
She said I was her baby. I said no.
She said in time I'd throw
Away her memory. I knew she lied.
I said I loved her body, loved her pride.

The Travelling Picker's Prayer
and Dream

Lord, forgive our drinking. Forgive our dreams
Of decency we can't shake off. Sisters
Are involved, and mothers, say our screams
That wake the whole bus up, and ministers
We come from haven't helped.

The poor are moral
But none of us have rotten teeth. Our teeth
Are good, washed by salt water. Fancy coral
Grows and forms what's called a barrier reef—
But what we're up against we can't be sure

Unless it is the sea, and the sea's too big
To drink to, and the sea's also impure
As Eve's mouth on the apple or Adam's fig.
Lord, a picker's dreams should not be cursed.
Remember the souls in the last hard town we blessed.

Pay Attention, Son

for Tom Royals and Sarge West

The things I've said were meant for praise
And I certainly never called you a liar.
All I did say was
It isn't possible in fact
To knock down flying animals
With a cotton boll—
And don't describe trajectories
Again. It's a damned good story,
Maybe the sort we have to have
To survive—
But it never happened—
And I know your daddy is stone deaf
And I'm sure it is his true belief
His word is all that killed that dog
Your mother spotted on the ridge—
I know that dog was killing chickens
And maybe did come howling in
To die without much blood. Maybe
It did flop down and die at his feet—
And I know he didn't see or hear
Your brother fire from the porch
At the same time
He slapped his old hat across his knee
And demanded, yes, in a voice to break
The meanest heart,
Death from the beast.
I'm sure he's positive that age
Has blessed him with a final power.
All I said was I don't believe
Your brother ever hit a dog
With a 22 at 500 yards
And I'll be glad to tell him to his face.
He missed or fell short.

A Natural Theology

Once again a spring has come around
And many of the best I think I know
Are going crazy.
                Light on the warm ground

Is almost God requiring them to grow—
Or, at least, to change—the usual song
And arrogant demand that nature makes
Of moral, thoughtful people all gone wrong
So far as they can see.
                    Their hands hold rakes.
They comb what later are attractive lawns.
They harrow in their ways, then drive the stakes.
Up which flowers and food will climb their dream
Of this one season right.
                    They pick up sticks
To make the whole thing work, then plant a tree.
Spring. Spring. They take it personally.

BENJAMIN WILLIAMS

And Not Just in Sorrow

And not just in sorrow
was slavery endured by our fathers
or the spirituals born
only to give a voice to despair.

And not just in sorrow
have we aspired to greatness
merging our jazz and blues
into the fabric
of human consciousness.

and not just in sorrow
shall tomorrow
and more tomorrows
simply rock for the ages
while the river Jordan
stands wide and deep
not to be crossed.

And not just in sorrow
did Martin Luther King
and Emmett Till dream
or Langston Hughes
listen to the caged bird sing.

John A. Williams

Before Electricity 1926

Out of a quieting chaos, a dominating dusk
There danced delicate as a firefly, a firespot.
(Much later I would consider caves at Qustul, Cro-magnon Man; ponder
Prometheus, think on Lascaux and the magic of firespots in lightless
places, lightless times.)
This firespot, more golden warm than a silver cold star, moved to meet a
sibilance—a soft and magical pop!
A swelling, stronger light, and Father's shadow
Stuck for seconds on the overpapered wall.
The ritual: rending holes in the darkness. The ceremony: the making of
light by dark old men to moor the sun in Sagittarius.

Otis Williams

The Blues Man

For B.B. King

He's Othello
And the world is his stage
Griot
Black Troubador
African Prince
He be
Blues Man
Prophet
Preachin' bitter truth
Blues flowin' from his vocal chords
like cool water from a Artesian Fountain
talkin' 'bout women watermelon meat sweet
Possum grape wine fine
Beale Street Maestro
Doin' a symphony with your mind

And the Blues stands up
walks like a natural man
Moanin' like a Baptist deacon at midnite
While

Transplanted plowboys in upsouth discos
Rub bellies with mello brown sugars
With toes dancin'
Black as Delta Gumbo Mud
Tappin' rhythm inside too tight
Platform shoes
The Blues Man
Plays on his guitar
Holds it close like a lover hold his lady
Plays it sweet n' low
Plays it soulful
3 o'clock Blues
'Woman Across the River'
'Sweet Sixteen'
'Got a job on the Cadillac Assembly Line'
'All I want is a little love'
'You known you didn't want me when
'You fell down cross my bed'
'And
'Rock me Baby Like My Back Ain't Got No Bones'

B.B. & Bobby at the Howard Theatre

Believers
and
Non-believers felt a common spirit
Love Gods congregated like friendly Ghosts
Amongst mortals
And
Blue Notes descended from Blues Heaven
Like indigo showers of soul
The reincarnation of Elmore James, Blind Lemon Jefferson,
Robert Johnson and T. Bone Walker,
Took place before the eyes of the multitude
The roll call resounded like volcanic shock waves of Blues. . .
Leadbelly, Bunk Johnson, Howlin' Wolf, Little Walter,
Ma Rainey, Sonny Boy Williamson, Magic Sam, Bessie Smith
The list goes on an on
Felt like hollerin' and cryin'
And carrin' on
While the Blues Prophet preached to his Congregation
Sang a four hundred year lovesong
For a African brother on a lonesome Shore

Did a thirty year encore to a one night stand
B.B. King played the Blues At The Howard Theatre
With Bobby Blue Bland standin' At the Crossroads
Rockin' in that same old boat
And
Visions of Mississippi Delta Nights
Cotton choppin' and Mule skinnin' mornin's
Flashed through my troubled mind
Unh, Unh, Unh,
Blues comin' over me
Like Flood waters risin'
Can't stand it
Can't stand it

About the Blues

If I could tell you how I feel
Then you would know what it is
About the Blues
But maybe your mind ain't tuned in
And maybe the blues don't move you
But they move me
Like the Holy Ghost moves a sinner
And I can't tell you how I feel
Cause it's a feeling that's private
Takes me back, way back
Every hurt, every joy, every tear I've shed
Flashes across my Mississippi mind
Just want to love my woman
Oh! . . . Turn me loose
Hurt me so bad . . . love me so good
Blues stay away
You hurt me, you hurt me, so good. . .so good.
Blues keep on risin' like a swamp fog

My Old Home Church
Bell Flower Missionary Baptist
Grenada Mississippi

The spirit wasn't always lively
in our church
Bell Flower Missionary Baptist

Use to stop by the Sanctified Church
On my way home
The Gospel Singin' made my soul shout
The Spirit hit me
The spirit was always live
And Movin' in the Sanctified Church
Like Christ was comin' in the mornin'

The big bass drum & tamborines
Kept the time
While the guitar and organ did their thing
And the congregation was singin'
Shoutin', dancin' rollin' on the floor
And 'speakin' in tongue
And the Spirit was movin'
Like Christ was comin' in the mornin'

But some Sundays
The spirit walked tall like
Moses walkin' on the water
in Bell Flower Missionary Baptist Church
When Mrs. 'Sweet' Clark would sing her song
"Its my Desire To Love the Lord"
Or
When my Aunt Arnada Purnel
Embellished the sound waves
With her favorite tune
"Christ is all This World To Me"
The spirit stood up and took note
Jus' like Christ was comin' in the mornin'

Sometimes you could feel it!
When Reverend Wm. H. Turner sang his song
Before he took his text
You could feel it
And when he preached all the way
From the pulpit on out to the mourners bench
Yes, you feel it
Like Christ was comin' in the mornin'

I get back home ever so often
Go out to the church of my childhood
All the old deacons are gone up yonder
Some old sisters are gone home too

Some faces are different
But the hymns are familiar
And jus' bein' there makes you feel good
Real good
Like Christ was comin' in the mornin'

Dixie Hummingbirds
A 50 Year Tribute

Other birds hush up
And
Listen
When they strike up a tune
When they sing
When they sing
Yes
When they sing
The old sparrow drops a tear
The chickadee and swallow
Take a seat and lend an ear
When they sing

Mighty voices
Them Hummingbirds
They say they're messengers for the Lord
Fifty years they've been his Disciples
Fifty years they've sung his word

Heard the word out on the hillside
Had to lay my cotton sack down
Everybody come to the meetin' this Sunday
Dixie Hummingbirds gonna be in town

Howard Carrol plays his guitar
Sweet as the sound of David's harp
And them others, they still singin'
Shoutin' and dancin', they still sharp

Beechie Thomas and James Davis
like angels voices hold the beat
James Walker and Ira Tucker
Singin' prophets sing so sweet

Willie Bobo has gone on home
To that great program in the sky

But now and then I still hear him
Singin' that bass that makes you cry

It all started in the southland
When they were young and in their prime
Runnin' for Jesus, singin' for Jesus
Now they're legends in their own time

Yes, they say they got voices like angels
Like the Heaven's bells they ring
But, them old Hummingbirds from Dixie
They don't fly, they jus' sing
They jus' sing

Fannie Lou Hamer

She was nothin' special
Jus' a Strong Black Mississippi Mother
Made from the Mighty, majestic mold
of
Sojourner Truth
And
When I remember Fannie Lou Hamer
I remember Ruleville, Mississippi summers
Choppin' cotton
Knee high to a tall man
Hot sun shinin' inferno blazin' down
on
Rows-long as I been gone from home
with
Coal dust Black Delta gumbo soil
Hot between my dusty toes
And a Oak tree strong woman
The rich heritage of African pride
Ragin' like tidewater in her Yoruba soul
It was freedom on her revolutionary mind
Leadin' my people out of bondage
Jus' like Moses
And
Befo' I be yo' Slave
I be buried in my grave
And go home to my Lord
And be free

South African Suite

Want to write a poem
For
The blacks of Soweto
Of
Nimibia & Mozambique
A summer western sky red
Sunshine
Poem
Freedom
For a Small child dead
Charcoal dust black
Sticky molasses dry red blood
Oozin' from peep sight tiny holes
In a hunger swollen stomach
A poem
Risin' up from the pages of history
Tree trunk tall
Mighty bush warrior tall
Beatin' bare fisted rhythm
On a drum tight barrel chest
Spreadin' the truth word
Transcendin' oceans
Cities, languages, minds, races
Declarin' simply
Freedom now!
Freedom now!
Want to do a Bluesful verse
For the African Princess
Whose proud lioness stride
Is betrayed by the too long sad
eyes
That reflect the midnite hour achin' need
In her firm oak bark colored loins
Created by too many 20 year long nights
With only her own heavy breathin'
And the Black of African nights
to caress her sensuous honey body
Man long time gone
Dead, in Jail, on a one way trip
In exile
Mighty warriors woman
Mighty warrior woman she be

If I could jus'
Do a revolutionary poem
For the Black students of Azania
The granite hard souls
The Buaxite fingers
The Copper faces
The forward thrustin' foot soldiers
Marchin' to the stacatto cadence
Of
No mo' bondage!
No mo' Appartheid!
No mo' Kodak ID card for me. . .!
No mo' auction block for me. . .!
Cause I got
The South African Blues
And
Chicago ain't my home
Got the South African blues
And
Chicago ain't my home
I can hear Mother Africa callin'
Son
You been gone, You been gone
Too long
Want to do a Universal Poem
About love
Speak in the mother tongue
Shout the word
From South Africa
To
South Mississippi
Same cold shackles
Decorate my whip scarred leg
Want to fill the gunsmoke air
With a soul stirrin' chant
A Negro Spiritual - a slow country Blues
A message in code to the people
A foot stompin' - hand clappin'
Tear Jerkin' Gospel Message
Singin' 'bout the struggle
Singin' 'bout livin'
Singin' 'bout Freedom
Singin' 'bout African People -
Freedom Now

TENNESSEE WILLIAMS

Impressions Through a Pennsy Window

1 Going Home

I knew more surely than the name of my train, *The Crescent*,
    that I was now deep in The South
when I was wakened this morning to see on a railroad siding
    as we pulled lingeringly out of a town with a
        Choctaw or Cherokee name
        an old red caboose
miniature cupola set like a coquettish bonnet on its
    low-peaked roof,
        a flirty bit of balcony on its tail,
        nothing appearing outmoded and retired,
not faded from red into dim, paint-peeling pink,

        But all freshly brilliant,
assertively, jauntily garish in the hot morning sun of Georgia
        seeming to call *Hurry back* in a Southern girl's
        honeyed drawl,

And I swear that for a moment and a half, with a pride
    that dismayed me,
        that shook me somewhere deep under the
        Mason-Dixon line
of my divided psyche,
    I sensed, I felt, nearly heard
the dreadful anachronism of The Rebel Yell!
    It made me wonder at blood . . .

2 Rival Breathers

How much vegetation there still is in the The South,
    the earth is overwhelmed with it,
devouring much of what we've been told is much less oxygen
    than the earth's air should hold.

And yet, despite Messrs. Cronkite-and-Sevareid's proper
    concern with ecology,
    I can't help feeling favorably impressed,
not because God is the unisexual propagator of all these
    generations of trees
and presumably of every citizen of the rooted,
    green-leaved kingdom,

It is, I think, only a moment of self-forgetful homage
to the licentious abandon and valor of all this vegetation,
    this flagrantly wanton display of woods in lustrous leaf
and weeds in vivid flower,
prevailing against the pests and the pesticides and
    the oxygen failing . . .

Descent

It was a steep hill that you went down, calling back to me,
saying that you would be only a little while.
I waited longer than that.
The thin-blooded grass of the hill continued to stir in the wind
and the wind grew colder.

I looked across the deep valley.
I saw that the sun was yellow as lemon upon the dark pines,
but elsewhere pools of cool shadow like stains of dark water
crept gradually onto the hill as the sunlight dimmed.

I waited longer. But finally I rose from the grass
and went back down the path by which we had come
and noted, here and there, your footprints pointing upward,
    narrow and light.

Nonno's Poem

from The Night of the Iguana

How calmly does the orange branch
Observe the sky begin to blanch
Without a cry, without a prayer,
With no betrayal of despair.

Sometime while night obscures the tree
The zenith of its life will be
Gone past forever, and from thence
A second history will commence.

A chronicle no longer gold,
A bargaining with mist and mould,
And finally the broken stem
The plummeting to earth; and then

An intercourse not well designed
For beings of a golden kind

Whose native green must arch above
The earth's obscene, corrupting love.

And still the ripe fruit and the branch
Observe the sky begin to blanch
Without a cry, without a prayer,
With no betrayal of despair.

O Courage, could you not as well
Select a second place to dwell,
Not only in that golden tree
But in the frightened heart of me?

Austin Wilson

Bus Trip

At dusk we left
Memphis
and all the way south
to Tupelo the drunk
sharing my armrest
(he stunk
of whiskey)
talked about the death
of his mother he was going to face
in Mobile.
All the way to Tupelo
he kept tapping the soft
spot of the baby's skull
whenever the mother
in the seat ahead lifted
the baby up to her shoulder.
Finally she caught him.
I played dumb.
She complained
and at Tupelo he was put off,
pleading about the funeral
waiting for him.
I saw him fighting
with the cop as we pulled out
of the Tupelo bus depot.

We made up the time
we lost in Tupelo
before we reached Birmingham,
losing an hour, though,
when we crossed into Georgia,
time I'll never make up
until I go west again.

Sonnets for My Son

1. Swinging My Son on His Birthday

I sing my year-old son the nursery rhyme
He seems a part of, swinging from this tree
That sways as if in wind. The chains keep time
Over his head, as I sing with gravity
Of Baby falling from sleep and boughs breaking.
I push my son away and back to me
He comes, this pendulum of my making,
His fall suspended, temporarily
Unaware of the pit. His swinging, shaking
The tree, speeds the leaves, fallen from their prime.
The seasons change too soon. We'll be waking
To winter before long. His birthday wanes.
I feel my age, caught by the leaves' pantomime,
By the melancholy metronome of chains.

2. Carrying My Son, Almost Two, on My Back
Through a Formal Garden

The other tourists on the path all smile
At how my son hangs on me. The straps bite
Where his restive bouncing pulls them tight.
I let him down to play in the glare, while
I find shade beneath a tree where a sundial
Is overshadowed by branches, lacking light
To mark the hours of both the day and night.
Here is a place I could almost reconcile
Myself and time, at least for an interim.
But I think how time will blossom in winter,
The dial's dark flower will thrive on shortened days
In the spidery shadow of the bony limb.
Even now time is working in the center
Of this garden: shadows move towards where he plays.

3. Teaching My Son, Just Turned Four, About Time

He doesn't understand how days make weeks
But he repeats our morning ritual
Of naming days, and by the words he speaks
He'll soon learn the strict chronological
Order of this world. The sequence of seasons
Will be demonstrated as repeated years
Define what now are only words, not reasons
He can understand for falling leaves. He fears
The trees are dying. They are playing dead,
I tell him; he seems to understand
Even though death is as over his head
As what I try to show (little hand, big hand—
His in mine) with the heirloom watch that when I'm
Dead he'll inherit (as I did) to keep his time.

RICHARD WRIGHT

I Have Seen Black Hands

1

I am black and I have seen black hands, millions and millions of them—
Out of millions of bundles of wool and flannel tiny black fingers have
    reached restlessly and hungrily for life.
Reached out for the black nipples at the black breasts of black mothers,
And they've held red, green, blue, yellow, orange, white, and purple
    toys in the childish grips of possession.
And chocolate drops, peppermint sticks, lollypops, wineballs, ice cream
    cones, and sugared cookies in fingers sticky and gummy,
And they've held balls and bats and gloves and marbles and jack-knives
    and sling-shots and spinning tops in the thrill of sport and play,
And pennies and nickels and dimes and quarters and sometimes on New
    Year's, Easter, Lincoln's Birthday, May Day, a brand new green dollar
    bill,
They've held pens and rulers and maps and tablets and books in palms
    spotted and smeared with ink,
And they've held dice and cards and half-pint flasks and cue sticks and
    cigars and cigarettes in the pride of new maturity . . .

2

I am black and I have seen black hands, millions and millions of them—
They were tired and awkward and calloused and grimy and covered with
   hangnails,
And they were caught in the fast-moving belts of machines and snagged
   and smashed and crushed,
And they jerked up and down at the throbbing machines massing taller
   and taller the heaps of gold in the banks of bosses,
And they piled higher and higher the steel, iron, the lumber, wheat,
   rye, the oats, corn, the cotton, the wool, the oil, the coal, the meat,
   the fruit, the glass, and the stone until there was too much to be used,
And they grabbed guns and slung them on their shoulders and marched
   and groped in trenches and fought and killed and conquered nations
   who were customers for the goods black hands had made.
And again black hands stacked goods higher and higher until there was
   too much to be used,
And then the black hands held trembling at the factory gates the
   dreaded lay-off slip,
And the black hands hung idle and swung empty and grew soft and got
   weak and bony from unemployment and starvation,
And they grew nervous and sweaty, and opened and shut in anguish and
   doubt and hesitation and irresolution . . .

3

I am black and I have seen black hands, millions and millions of them—
Reaching hesitantly out of days of slow death for the goods they had
   made, but the bosses warned that the goods were private and did not
   belong to them,
And the black hands struck desperately out in defence of life and there
   was blood, but the enraged bosses decreed that this too was wrong,
And the black hands felt the cold steel bars of the prison they had made,
   in despair tested their strength and found that they could neither
   bend nor break them,
And the black hands lifted palms in mute and futile supplication to the
   sodden faces of mobs wild in the revelries of sadism,
And the black hands strained and clawed and struggled in vain at the
   noose that tightened about the black throat,
And the black hands waved and beat fearfully at the tall flames that
   cooked and charred the black flesh . . .

4

I am black and I have seen black hands
Raised in fists of revolt, side by side with the white fists of white
    workers,
And some day—and it is only this which sustains me—
Some day there shall be millions and millions of them,
On some red day in a burst of fists on a new horizon!

Between the World and Me

And one morning while in the woods I stumbled suddenly upon the
    thing,
Stumbled upon it in a grassy clearing guarded by scaly oaks and elms.
And the sooty details of the scene rose, thrusting themselves between
    the world and me. . . .

There was a design of white bones slumbering forgottenly upon a
    cushion of ashes.
There was a charred stump of a sapling pointing a blunt finger accusingly
    at the sky.
There were torn tree limbs, tiny veins of burnt leaves, and a scorched
    coil of greasy hemp;
A vacant shoe, an empty tie, a ripped shirt, a lonely hat, and a pair of
    trousers stiff with black blood.
And upon the trampled grass were buttons, dead matches, butt-ends of
    cigars and cigarettes, peanut shells, a drained gin-flask, and a whore's
    lipstick;
Scattered traces of tar, restless arrays of feathers, and the lingering smell
    of gasoline.
And through the morning air the sun poured yellow surprise into the
    eye sockets of a stony skull. . . .

And while I stood my mind was frozen with a cold pity for the life that
    was gone.
The ground gripped my feet and my heart was circled by icy walls of
    fear—
The sun died in the sky; a night wind muttered in the grass and fumbled
    the leaves in the trees; the woods poured forth the hungry yelping of
    hounds; the darkness screamed with thirsty voices; and the witnesses
    rose and lived:
The dry bones stirred, rattled, lifted, melting themselves into my bones.
The grey ashes formed flesh firm and black, entering into my flesh.

The gin-flask passed from mouth to mouth; cigars and cigarettes glowed,
    the whore smeared the lipstick red upon her lips,

And a thousand faces swirled around me, clamoring that my life be
burned. . . .

And then they had me, stripped me, battering my teeth into my throat
till I swallowed my own blood.
My voice was drowned in the roar of their voices, and my black wet
body slipped and rolled in their hands as they bound me to the
sapling.
And my skin clung to the bubbling hot tar, falling from me in limp
patches.
And the down and quills of the white feathers sank into my raw flesh,
and I moaned in my agony.
Then my blood was cooled mercifully, cooled by a baptism of gasoline.
And in a blaze of red I leaped to the sky as pain rose like water, boiling
my limbs.
Panting, begging I clutched childlike, clutched to the hot sides of death.
Now I am dry bones and my face a stony skull staring in yellow surprise
at the sun. . . .

Haiku

For you, O gulls
I order slaty waters
and this leaden sky

The dog's violent sneeze
Fails to rouse a single fly
On his mangy back

An autumn sunset
A buzzard sails slowly past
Not flapping its wings

Coming from the woods
A bull has a lilac sprig
Dangling from a horn

From across the lake
Past the black winter trees
Faint sounds of a flute

The green cockleburs
Caught in the thick wooly hair
Of the black boy's head

I am nobody
A red sinking autumn sun
Took my name away

With a twitching nose
A dog reads a telegram
On a wet tree trunk

The spring lingers on
In the scent of a damp log
Rotting in the sun

The crow flew so fast
That he left his lonely caw
Behind in the fields

In the falling snow
A laughing boy holds out his palms
Until they are white

GAYLE GRAHAM YATES

Daughterlove

Old woman, old woman,
You did not bear me
But loved me-child, she-child
With the air in my face.
You sat by the creek bank
While I swam.
You made little dresses
In my size
And warm cookies
That fit my mouth.
Me-child is woman now
Distant from the creek bank,
And you stay close
Inside the house
With the cold oven,
Bending, halting,
Over your walker,
Faltering noiselessly
Over your grave.

I am woman
And run free
With the air in my face.

You gave me the air
And then your memory lapsed
Before I knew
To say Thank you.

How do I say it now?
From this distance
With this grief.

AL YOUNG

Birthday Poem

First light of day in Mississippi
son of laborer & of house wife
it says so on the official photostat
not son of fisherman & child fugitive
from cottonfields & potato patches
from sugarcane chickens & well-water
from kerosene lamps & watermelons
mules named jack or jenny & wagonwheels,

years of meaningless farm work
work Work WORK WORK WORK—
"Papa pull you outta school bout March
to stay on the place & work the crop"
—her own earliest knowledge
of human hopelessness & waste

She carried me around nine months
inside her fifteen year old self
before here I sit numbering it all

How I got from then to now
is the mystery that could fill a whole library
much less an arbitrary stanza

But of course you already know about that
from your own random suffering
& sudden inexplicable bliss

A Little More Traveling Music

A country kid in Mississippi I drew water from the well
& watched our sun set itself down behind the thickets,
hurried from galvanized baths to hear music
over the radio—Colored music, rhythmic & electrifying,
more Black in fact than politics & flit guns.

Mama had a knack for snapping juicy fruit gum
& for keeping track of the generation of chilrens
she had raised, reared & no doubt forwarded,
rising thankfully every half past daybreak
to administer duties the poor must look after
if theyre to see their way another day, to eat, to live.

I lived & upnorth in cities sweltered & froze,
    got jammed up & trafficked
in everybody's sun going down but took up with the moon
as I lit about getting it all down up there
where couldnt nobody knock it out.

Picking up slowly on the gists of melodies, most noises softened.
I went on to school & to college too, woke up cold
& went my way finally, classless, reading all poems,
    some books & listening to heartbeats

Well on my way to committing to memory the ABC reality,
I still couldnt forget all that motherly music,
those unwatered songs of my babe-in-the-wood days
until, committed to the power of the human voice,
I turned to poetry & to singing by choice,
reading everyone always & listening, listening for a
    silence deep enough
to make out the sound of my own background music.

1962–1967

The Problem of Identity

Used to identify with my father first making me want to be a gas station
    attendant simple drink coca-cola listen to the radio, work on people's
    cars, hold long conversations in the night black that clean gas smell of
    oil & no-gas, machine coolness, rubber, calendars, metal sky,
    concrete, the bearing of tools, the wind—true Blue labor Red &
    White

Identified with Joe Louis: Brown Bomber, you know They'd pass along
the mud streets of Laurel Mississippi in loudspeaker truck, the white
folks, down by where the colored schools was & all of us, out there for
Recess or afterschool are beckoned to come get your free picture of
Joe Louis, *C'mon & get it kids it's Free, c'mon naow*—What it is is
Chesterfield cigarettes in one corner of the beautiful slick photo of Mr.
Louis is the blurb, *Joe like to smoke too, see, and he want all yall to
follow right long in his footsteps & buy up these here chesterfields &
smoke your little boodies off & youll be able to step up in that ring
begloved & punch a sucker out.* It was the glossiness of the photo, I
finally figured out years later, that had me going—didnt really matter
whose picture was on it altho it was nice to've been Joe's because he
was about as great as you could get downsouth, post world war II as
the books say

Identified with Otis (think his name was) worked at grocery store in
Ocean Springs, came by, would sit & draw on pieces of brown
paperbag, drew in 1940s style of cartoons bordering on "serious"
sketching, i.e., in the manner of those sultan cartoons with the harem
gals by that black cartoonist Sims you see em all the time in old
Esquires & *Playboys.* Well, that's the way Otis could draw & he'd
show me in the make-do livingroom seated on do-fold how to do a
portrait of a chic perfect anglo-featured woman, say, in profile out of
his head built mostly from magazine & picture-show impressions, &
he could draw lots of world things, drew me for instance

Later Otis went up to Chicago, sadness, madness, wed, bled, dope,
hopeless, catapulted into the 20th century like the rest of us—rudely,
                                                    steeped in
homemade makeshift chemical bliss of/or flesh, waiting for nothing less
than The Real Thing

Pachuta Mississippi/A Memoir

> I too
> once lived
> in the country

> Incandescent
> fruits
> in moonlight
> whispered to me
> from trees
> of

1950
swishing
   in the green nights

                  wavelengths away
                           from
                  tongue-red meat
                           of melon

               wounded squash
yellow as old afternoons

                  chicken
                      in love
                          with calico

               hiss & click of flit gun

         juice music
                  you suck up
         lean stalks of field cane

                           Cool as sundown
                           I lived there too

For Poets

Stay beautiful
but dont stay down underground too long
Dont turn into a mole
or a worm
or a root
or a stone

Come on out into the sunlight
Breathe in trees
Knock out mountains
Commune with snakes
& be the very hero of birds

Dont forget to poke your head up
& blink
Think
Walk all around
Swim upstream

Dont forget to fly

Teaching

There's no such thing as a student,
only abiding faces unwilling
to change except with time,
the oldest force that still fools us

So you teach a feeling,
a notion learned the hard way,
a fact, some figures,
a tract, some rigors of childhood

The face out there
interacting with yours
knows how to grin & play with its pen
but misses the point so charmingly

A thousand moves later
that same shiny face
moving thru the world with
its eyes glazed or fully closed
reconnects with one of its own childhoods

Loosely we call this learning

Aunt

She talks too loud, her face
a blur of wrinkles & sunshine
where her hard hair shivers
from laughter like a pine tree
stiff with oil & hotcombing

O & her anger realer than gasoline
slung into fire or lighted mohair
She's a clothes lover from way back

but her body's too big to be chic
or on cue so she wear what she want
People just gotta stand back &
take it like they do Easter Sunday when
the rainbow she travels is dry-cleaned

She laughs more than ever in spring
stomping the downtowns, Saturday past
work, looking into JC Penney's checking
out Sears & bragging about how when she

feel like it she gon lose weight &
give up smokin one of these sorry days

Her eyes are diamonds of pure dark space
& the air flying out of them as you look
close is only the essence of living
to tell, a full-length woman, an aunt
brown & red with stalking the years

A Sunday Sonnet
for My Mother's Mother

for Mrs. Lillian Campbell

Consider her now, glowing, light-worn
arthritic, crippled in a city backroom
far from the farm where she was born
when King Cotton was still in bloom.

She is as Southern as meat brown pecans,
or fried green tomato, or moon pies.

Gathering now for eight decades, aeons
of volunteered slavery soften her sighs.

Talk about somebody who's been there,
this grand lady has seen, remembers it all
and can tell you about anyone anywhere
in voices as musical as any bird's call.

Loving her, it hurts to hear her say,
"My grandchildren, they just threw me away."

The Blues Don't Change

"Now I'll tell you about the
Blues. All Negroes like Blues.
Why? Because they was born with
the Blues. And now everybody
have the Blues. Sometimes they
don't know what it is."
                    —Leadbelly

And I was born with you, wasn't I, Blues?
Wombed with you, wounded, reared and forwarded
from address to address, stamped, stomped
and returned to sender by nobody else but you,
Blue Rider, writing me off every chance you

got, you mean old grudgeful-hearted, table-
turning demon, you, you sexy soul-sucking gem.

Blue diamond in the rough, you *are* forever.
You can't be outfoxed don't care how they cut
and smuggle and shine you on, you're like a
shadow, too dumb and stubborn and necessary
to let them turn you into what you ain't
with color or theory or powder or paint.

That's how you can stay in style without sticking
and not getting stuck. You know how to sting
where I can't scratch, and you move from frying
pan to skillet the same way you move people
to go to wiggling their bodies, juggling their
limbs, loosening that goose, upping their voices,
opening their pores, rolling their hips and lips.

They can shake their boodies but they can't shake *you*.

STARK YOUNG

Written at My Mother's Grave

It was in the early spring you fell asleep,
For I brought violets to your dear hands
Next day when they had laid you in the still
Dark room. And now from travelling many lands,
From many a stranger shore of level sands,
Made musical with waves, I come to fill
My weary eyes with my own native scene.
And now once more the spring brings everywhere
The warm southwind, these quiet trees are green,
And all along the ancient graveyard wall,
Amid the tangled sedge, the daisies bear
Their crowding stars. So all the memories
I have of you are green and fresh and pure,
Of that sweet childhood season when the flower
Blows fair, ere petals fall and the mature
Fresh-fruit of manhood ripening to its hour
Cumbers the plant. Listen! the dove's voice
In the distant brake sounding her sad pain,

Sadly I hear, and in her mournful note
I catch the measure of my sorrow's strain.

Had I but had you longer, mother, then
Haply my hours and deeds should miss you more,
But then my heart should have you always near,
Having your words and ways heaped up in store,
Sweet company for many a weary year.

Such as I have are but the clambering
Upon your patient knees to kiss your lips,
Or look long in your blue eyes wondering,
Or put the dark hair from your gentle brow,
Feeling a wondrous sweetness steal somehow
From out your hands through all my little frame.
Once I remember, when my terrier died,
Through all the long stretches of the night I cried,
And when at last I slept, they say I fell
Amoaning in my childish sleep, but you
Closed not your eyes, but held me always well
Pressed into your heart and kissed my face
As a mother can. And then the swift years flew,
Seating grim manhood in the innocent place,
And many-mouthed cares are knocking at the gate.
Yet though I have no comforter so strong,
I would not call you from your well-won peace,
From the sweet silence of rich death. The wrong
Men did upon your shoulders heavy sat,
Your summer of goodness had too full increase
And brought an early harvest of your life.

Would call? What mummery! Too well I know
That those we love and those we hate must go,
Down the dim avenues of death must pass
Out to the fields of the great forever—lo,
Are gone from us like shadows on the grass
To the dark region of their last abode.

The Mississippi hills are blue and faint,
The air grows stiller and the sounds more sweet,
The gray shades cluster round each marble saint,
And in the long box walks the shadows meet.
And on your grave, rich-ripe with golden days,
Nasturtium cups are lit with level rays
From the low-sunk sun. Still would I be a child,
And come with flowers here for your dear praise,

And with *Good morrow, Mother,* pause to tell
The marvels of the day—nay, nay, I know,
I only fancy, mother, ere I go
To say *Farewell forever,* and *farewell.*

AHMOS ZU-BOLTON II

the seeker

blackjack moses
returning from the war,
returned to seek the fugitive freedom
which hides in bright & open light,

talks
with tangents
tied to his tongue:

nothing is believable, the light
lies, at least in this reality,
for the same old songs
are sung.

blackjack hates
the fact that he cannot completely hate
& in this there is rage.

he cannot face
the night   the moon   the stars
seem to plot against him,
there are very few shadows
to hide in, & all the faces
frown.

but for blackjack
there is no fear here,
& sleep is possible.

the dawn approaches
& he prepares himself
as best he can:

he has no weapon
(he threw away his gun

when he threw away
his bible).

The Basketball Star

We define:
Livewire Davis. The one
with the million-dollar jump-shot.

Livewire as bebop star:
torn between his body's genius
for fast breaks
and a questionmark
called rage. Stumbling
thru a lifetime of all-star games
(he never hit the winning points
but was always a frontpager.

Livewire's days
were lawless theatre
(except for the 8 o'clock class,
except for the poetry of bullshitting
with the women,
except for the ritual of practice:
run   jump   "shoot their eyes out"
defense
defense
except for the terrible puzzle of books
he was free.

Sister Blues
with Livewire Davis

She couldnot make him over.
Or silence him.

She measured him
and he failed her so.
She couldnot kill the mirror
of her mother's eyes.

Her mother: the sad Negrolady
who could rule with a glance.
A properwoman of the blues.

He failed her mother
and didnot know his place:
much too loud in a prayerful
kingdom, too uncontrollable
in a world of controls.

This tore at her as if to cripple,
this loss of face.

So she made him babies
in the image of other men.
And spent her days in sturdy dream.
And spent her nights as
the darkmistress
of wounded love.

Struggle-Road Dance

*"when freedom comes
there'll be no more blues*

(repeat)

*but lawd lawd
it ain't here yet"*
—Adesanya Alakoye

This is the camping ground
the waterhole
the rest area

this is the tree
under which I will lay
this poem
plant it here
to see if there is growth:

Come to the campfire with me,
make peace with your brothers
love for the sisters,

we make this
a dance celebration:
circle the flames
warm yourself
and rest . . .

We only wait here
till it dawn on us:
what is the nature
of this distance

How hard was
that last mile . . .

Count our numbers
(we have never been all present
and accounted for:

> we lost Blackjack
> back at the creek
> bloodriver and some mean nigger
> shooting him down

> last we saw of him
> he was tiptoeing off into
> the white world

> at least we think
> that's where he
> was going . . .

But Livewire Davis
made it, and Sister Blues
survived—

this place
must be a workshop
for our people

make a home
and build a family

study
the growth
of our tribe

we know how far off
is morning

> *when freedom comes*
> *there'll be no more blues*

(this dance
will not be sung
when sweet freedom dawns on us
but

> *sing it now*
> *sing it now*
> *sing it now*

CONTRIBUTORS

JAMES A. AUTRY (1933) was born in Memphis, Tennessee, and grew up in Benton County, Mississippi, the son and grandson of Mississippi Baptist ministers. In 1955 he was graduated from the University of Mississippi with a B.A. in journalism. Autry is president of Meredith Corporation's Magazine Group which publishes *Better Homes and Gardens, Ladies' Home Journal,* and *Successful Farming* among others. His book of poetry, *Nights Under a Tin Roof: Recollections of a Southern Boyhood* (1983), was published by the Yoknapatawpha Press.

Autry writes: "I don't think one ever identifies intellectually the character-molding forces or influences of a time or place during those growing up years. We are usually too busy growing up. At least I was. It was only years later, after I had spent a lot of time and effort in trying to overcome the label of 'white southerner' (definition: racist), that I began to look toward the things which had contributed to making me the person I became. I saw a fading landscape, the homogenization of a culture, the death of family and loved ones. That's when the strong need to do what I could to preserve some of it found a way into my writing. The form became poetry.

"In examining that old life, I saw values still valuable, rituals which were more than chores, activities and events which not only punctuated time but which defined life itself. There seemed to me some of those old universal truths and universal experiences which writers bother themselves about a lot. But rather than take on the truths in all their glory—which only leads to self-conscious writing anyway—I decided to just write what it was and let the how it was speak for itself."

ANGELA BALL (1952) was born in Athens, Ohio. She received degrees from Ohio University, the University of Iowa, and the University of Denver. Since 1979 Ball has taught in the Center for Writers at the University of Southern Mississippi, where she is an editor for the *Mississippi Review.* She was a winner of the Sotheby's International Poetry Competition in 1982.

Of her collection of poems, *Kneeling Between Parked Cars,* to be published by Owl Creek Press, Bin Ramke says, "The seriousness of Angela Ball's writing is like the seriousness of a marriage, or of having children. It is fun, sometimes funny, but always there is an edge to get cut on, there is always the threat of loss which makes everything, Sunday baseball, the rhythm of what we are saying now, surgery, or even postcards, a little bit frightening. Or sometimes a lot."

RANDOLPH BATES (1945) was born in Meridian, Mississippi, and educated in Meridian public schools. He received a B.A. from the University of Missouri-Columbia and a Ph.D. from Tulane University. He now lives and writes in New Orleans and teaches in the English department at Tulane.

CHARLES GREENLEAF BELL (1916) was born in Greenville, Mississippi. After graduating in 1936 from the University of Virginia with a degree in physics, Bell went to Oxford University as a Rhodes Scholar. Since then he has had a varied career as a novelist, poet, educator, scientist, and humanist. Bell has been at work since the late 1930s on a synthesis of history, thought and the arts titled

381

"Symbolic History: A Drama of the Western Arts." He now teaches at St. John's College in Santa Fe, New Mexico.

In a 1963 essay, "The Symbolic Landscape," published in the *Delta Review* Bell writes, "To write about Greenville and the Delta—what else have I been doing all these years? . . Polarities are unavoidable. Unavoidable too is the mind's struggle to reconcile them. In my second book of poems, *Delta Return* (1956), and my first novel, *The Married Land* (1962), the Delta and its Queen City are always central, and the effort is to get them attuned to the world-field. All this about my writing would be inappropriate if I thought the problems only mine. But the Delta is what I call a symbolic landscape, and a symbolic landscape is shared." In addition to the two previously mentioned books, Bell has published two other books of poetry, *Songs for a New America* (1953) and *Five Chambered Heart* (1986), and a novel, *The Half Gods* (1968).

Of his childhood Bell says that his father was a "reforming idealist" who entered politics thinking he could clean up the state; his mother, from the hills, was "an idealist of a more mystical kind." His boyhood was spent, he says, "in trees and on the river, as far from books as I could manage. Then I got caught in the current, beginning with the more romantic things, astronomy and atomic physics."

KATHERINE BELLAMANN (1877–1956) was born in Carthage, Mississippi. In 1907 she married the writer Henry Bellamann and they began a literary partnership which continued throughout their thirty-eight years of marriage. Following her husband's death in 1944, Bellamann returned to Mississippi.

During her lifetime Bellamann published three novels and a book of poetry—*My Husband's Friends* (1931), *Parris Mitchell of Kings Row* (1948), *Hayvens of Demaret* (1951), and *Two Sides of a Poem* (1955).

Leslie Jean Campbell writes: "It is at once both sad and fitting that Katherine Bellamann is remembered primarily as the author of *Parris Mitchell of Kings Row*, a sequel to her husband's magestic *Kings Row* (1940). It is sad, because Katherine Bellamann was a woman whose many artistic accomplishments were generally overshadowed by those of her husband. However, it is fitting that she should be remembered for *Parris Mitchell of Kings Row* because the unique creative association that grew between the couple was a source of pride to her. In the foreword to *Parris Mitchell of Kings Row*, she describes vividly this professional closeness. The combined papers and manuscripts of Katherine and Henry Bellamann, located in the special collection at the University of Mississippi, testify to the fact that the work of the two writers is closely entwined: they often shared notebooks and sometimes even single pages. Because Henry Bellamann is the more famous artist, it is easy to lose sight of the fact that Katherine Bellamann published two novels in her own right, one seventeen years before *Parris Mitchell of Kings Row* and one several years later."

In Jackson, Mississippi, during the last years of her life, Bellamann devoted herself to poetry and several poetry societies. Her collection of poems, *A Poet Passed This Way*, was published posthumously in 1958.

LERONE BENNETT, JR., (1928) was born in Clarksdale, Mississippi. When he was young, his family moved to Jackson, Mississippi, where he received his education in the public schools. After high school, he went to Atlanta to attend Morehouse College, from which he was graduated in 1949. After further study at Atlanta University, Bennette became a journalist and worked for the *Atlanta Daily World* (1949-53). *Jet* magazine (1953), and *Ebony* magazine as an associate editor from 1954 to 1957. In 1958 he became the senior editor of Ebony, a position he holds today. Bennett is a historian, critic, poet, essayist, and writer of short stories. His *Before the Mayflower: A History of the Negro in America, 1619-1966* is considered by many the "bible of black history."

In an interview with Felicia Lee of *USA Today* Bennett says, "Black history studies saved my life. It's made it possible for me to have some sense of why black people are where they are; why black people are what they are. It's given me a sense of optimism." His love for black history was ignited, as he was growing up in Jackson, by the "extraordinary" teachers in the public schools, and grew stronger as he sought understanding of Jackson. "I developed the mad idea that if I mastered the written word I could figure out why Mississippi existed, why black people lived as they did. I *had* to know," he said. "It was a matter of life and death. It had nothing to do with academics, it had nothing to do with books. I had friends who were whipped, attacked. I was threatened. It was rare for a black person to reach adulthood without having that kind of an experience."

There were good times for Bennett too, of course—having his first newspaper editorial published when he was eleven; playing clarinet and saxophone in a jazz band; being the editor of his high school yearbook and newspaper; and editing the newspaper at Morehouse College.

Concluding the interview he said, "We have to go back to the beginning and create a common American history—one that takes into account that America is not a creation of white people alone. In too many presentations we pop up suddenly as slaves, and Lincoln 'frees' us. We came here before the Mayflower, and. . . we were essentially involved in creating the economic settlement of this country. It is my view that it's impossible for white people to understand themselves and this country without understanding black history."

In addition to *Before the Mayflower* (1962, revised 1969), Bennett is the author of *The Negro Mood and Other Essays* (1964), *What Manner of Man: A Biography of Martin Luther King, Jr.* (1964). *Confrontation: Black and White* (1965), *Black Power U.S.A.: The Human Side of Reconstruction, 1867-1877* (1967), and *Pioneers of Protest* (1968).

D.C. BERRY (1942) was born in Vicksburg, Mississippi, but grew up in Greenville, Mississippi. He received a B.S. degree from Delta State University and then served three years as a medical service officer in the United States Army. In Vietnam, Berry wrote his first collection of poems, *Saigon Cemetary* (1972). After his service was completed he returned to school and received a Ph.D. in English from the University of Tennessee in 1973. Berry teaches in the English department at the University of Southern Mississippi where he is poetry editor of *Mississippi Review* and widely published in magazines and anthologies.

About poetry Berry writes: "A poem is an X-ray saying. The sonnet, the villanelle, free verse, the surrealistic blur—each is a verbal jungle gym, each puts you in a different position RE splitting the wishbone with the Muse, and speaking of bones, any part of a poem should be as 'hot' as any part of a relic. A poem is the bare facts about the facts. The poems that I want to write are right now on the tip of the tongue of the human spirit. I want to use common things and common sounds to discover the uncommon insight. Plain but strange, that's what I want. It requires erasing: everybody writes, only writers erase. Writers are erasers. If art is water, work is the wave, erase it again. Technique and Inspiration—they're always apart but together like Clark Kent and Superman. And I don't want to subject the subject like Superman but to realize the subject like Clark Kent. The poet says, Oh, or Ugh, or Ouch, or Huh, then finds words to make the reader realize that same philosophical, intellectual, and emotional cackle. A poem is like a good marriage—chasing what you've caught. I want my poems to be as traditional, modern, and futuristic as a creek."

Growing up in Greenville, Berry says he started writing because of boredom, "those rainy Sunday afternoons in the delta when I couldn't go shoot snakes. I now write on pretty days, too, here in Hattiesburg, not out of boredom but to celebrate, to *realize*, to discover. No. That's what the poems do. I write because it makes me feel like a tuning fork struck, sometimes like the emptiness of a cathedral."

MAXWELL BODENHEIM (1892–1954) was born in Hermanville, Mississippi, and he lived there the first eight years of his life. In 1900 his family moved to Chicago, where his rebellious spirit and rejection of authority began to emerge. During the 1920s Bodenheim established a significant reputation as a poet and began to write fiction which "portrayed various kinds of disenchantment and conflict with the dominant culture in America." Bodenheim's private life was constantly touched by scandal, which overshadowed what might have become a respectable literary career. By 1935 he was forced to live on relief and by the 1950s, deep into alcoholism, Bodenheim sold his poems to strangers for drinks in seedy Greenwich Village bars. In 1954 Bodenheim was shot in the heart during a drinking bout.

Scholar Jack B. Moore writes: "Bodenheim's fiction has been generally ignored even by critics offering historical overviews of the period or genres (such as the city novel or the radical novel) in which he wrote. Unfortunately, far more attention has been paid to his notorious escapades, too many of which were real, but some of which were imagined either by him or by contemporaries and then rehashed by commentators who knew neither him nor his works. Critics of his own day were far kinder about his poetry, and through the early 1930s his succeeding volumes were reviewed usually sympathetically, especially by other poets such as Conrad Aiken. As late as 1939 he received the prestigious Oscar Blumenthal Prize from *Poetry* magazine. His poetry was noteworthy for its wit, its fancy (though lacking a deeper imaginativeness), its individuality, its humor, its use of jazz rhythms and idiom, and especially its incisive portrait of city life. His poetry was also deficient, however, in nuances of technique, and never displayed much philosophic or artistic growth. Bodenheim's fiction is most significant for its consistent opposition to various kinds of authority that, according to Bodenheim, dominate and stifle the private self in America. . . . In his emphasis upon the individual's need for private and sexual liberation, his attacks upon the impersonal bigness of a highly materialistic American society, and his insistence that even organized left-leaning battles against the state should be mounted from a personal rather than rigidly collectivized platform of action, he seems to anticipate much of the cultural dissent of the 1960s. His major problem as a writer was his major problem as a person—lack of control."

THEODORE BOZEMAN (1955) has spent all his life in Jackson, Mississippi, where he was born. He received a B.S. in art education from Jackson State University. His writing has been published in *American Poetry Anthology*, *Mississippi Earthworks*, *New Visions*, *Sunbelt*, *Reaction*, and *Jackson Advocate*.

CHARLIE R. BRAXTON (1961) was born in McComb, Mississippi, and received

most of his education through the public school system there. He was graduated from Jackson State University and has spent his entire life in Mississippi.
Of this Braxton says, "When I look back on my life in the Magnolia state, thus
far, I feel a strong sense of being. By that I mean, I feel that my soul is deeply
rooted in the soil of this state. Like the bittersweet gutbucket blues of Robert
Johnson, I belong here."

BESMILR BRIGHAM (1923), who is part Choctaw, was born Bess Miller Moore in
Pace, Mississippi. She received a bachelor of journalism degree from Mary
Hardin-Baylor University in Belton, Texas, and later studied at New School for
Social Research in New York City. Her poems and short stories have been
frequently anthologized from appearances in the *Southern Review, Atlantic
Monthly, Harper's Bazaar, North American Review, Open Places, Southwest
Review*, and other literary journals. Brigham received a National Endowment
for the Arts grant to complete her book of poetry, *Heaved from the Earth*
(1971).

Concerning her development as a writer, brigham says: "Journalism was not
my field. Very early i discovered i had to forget all i had learned, all the tricks,
and wrote without capitals or punctuation, except periods, to get at what i had
seen. Shortly after World War II i went to Europe, to France, on a French
freighter, reconverted from the war, the St. Malo—came in at Rotterdam, left
from Rouen. The short intensity of that time changed my life. I returned by way
of New York and my husband, Roy, and i began to live there, only in time of
work; when a little money was saved, within limited time, we'd go South. Lived
in Nicaragua, Honduras, Guatemala, Chiapas and other points in Mexico. This
was my father's world; he'd gone there young. I accumulated manuscripts. And
just as, at one time, i'd had to forget what i'd learned, at last. . .i began a study
of the Structure of Language. I've cleared the poetry, though i'm still writing
poems; and i feel the focus is changing, more intense. Working on a body of
fiction *Rainbow House*, three volumes, plus other long fiction studies, the
whole with its center on Central America. A House of Many Colors. A ritual,
like "Games for an Easter Child," study in poem of the Yaqui Pasqua. Recent
illness in the house, but Words are of the substance of bread.

"As for training, or a sense of Haven, appreciation is due to the New School
for Social Research, part of the studies done under scholarship: Dr. Charles I.
Glicksberg, Horace Gregory, and Sidney Alexander (author of "The Floren-
tine"). With Gregory (then on leave from Sarah Lawrence) I doubled: Poetry
and Fiction. 'I have never learned the difference!'"

VIRGIA BROCKS-SHEDD (1943) was born in Carpenter, Mississippi. After the
demise of the sawmill there, her family moved in 1948 to the community of the
now-extinct Bel Pine, near the Piney Woods Country Life School, twenty-four
miles south of Jackson, Mississippi. At the age of thirteen, she became a
boarding student at the Piney Woods School and lived there until 1961. Brocks-
Shedd discovered at a young age that she liked to read, beginning first by oil
lamplight late into the night in her shack home in the sawmill quarters and later
as a student who read hundreds of books in the children's library at Piney
Woods. There she was fortunate to discover the *The Negro Caravan* and later
the biographies of Ethel Water and Eartha Kitt to inspire her. When she was
sixteen she read *The Power of Positive Thinking* by Norman Vincent Peale and
she said that she realized then the potential within herself to pursue what she
wanted to be, a poet like Margaret Walker, who had read poetry to the students

at the Piney Woods School convocation. Brocks-Shedd decided that Margaret Walker was the one she wanted to emulate, and when she went to Jackson State University, she studied with Walker. Brocks-Shedd says, "Walker provided intrinsic and extrinsic values and attention to my life and my aim to do my best, my aim to be. I still marvel at how intellectual and competent she is in discussing any subject. I shall never stop trying to be like her. What I strive for now is to be a positive role model and influence for young people who might be experiencing insecurities and low self-esteem as I did before I heard and met Margaret Walker and read Peale's book. I heartily recommend these mighty forces from God and their works to everyone of all ages."

Brocks-Shedd received a B.S. degree from Jackson State in May 1964 and the M.S.L.S. from Atlanta University in August 1965. Now head librarian at Tougaloo College, Brocks-Shedd was working at Tougaloo as an assistant librarian in 1966 when she met writer-in-residence Audre Lorde, black feminist poet, who urged her to publish some of her poems in the Tougaloo College literary magazine, *Pound*. In 1970 she studied with Alice Walker. Mississippi poet Jerry Ward has also been an important mentor for Brocks-Shedd. During 1966 and 1971, she published many articles and poems in *Close-Up*, a Jackson-based magazine, through her affiliation as contributing writer and managing editor. Her work has also appeared in *Hoo-Doo II/III*, *Jackson Advocate*, *Northside Reporter*, and in chapbooks *Mississippi Woods* (1980), *Mississippi Earthworks* (1982) and the Farish Street Festival souvenir booklets.

JONATHAN HENDERSON BROOKS (1905–1945), minister and poet, was born in Lexington, Mississippi, the eldest child of sharecroppers. He was fortunate that his mother read aloud to him from the Bible and from the classics. Gaining insights from these exposures, it was arranged for him to attend high school in Missouri, and it was during this interim from Mississippi that he began an intensive study of poetry and began putting his thoughts into verse. Brooks continued his education at Tougaloo College with further study at Columbia University. After graduation from Tougaloo College, he was employed by the school for three years as assistant to the president. As a protégé of William T. Holmes, president of Tougaloo College, Brooks became an ordained minister and his rhetorical skills sharpened to such an extent that he frequently delivered commencement sermons and other addresses. In the last years of his life Brooks worked in the post office in Corinth, Mississippi. His posthumous collection, *The Resurrection and Other Poems*, was published in 1948. Many of his poems were inspired by his religious background and his study of the Bible. Some of Brooks's poems were anthologized in *Caroling Dusk* (1927) edited by Countee Cullen and *The Negro Caravan* (1941) edited by Sterling A. Brown, Arthur P. Davis, and Ulysses Lee.

ISABELLA M. BROWN (1917) was born in Natchez, Mississippi. As a young woman she saw the legendary Rhythm Nite Club Fire in Natchez (April 24, 1940) and has never forgotten the horror of it. After graduating from high school, Brown worked as a teacher in Chicago before returning to Mississippi. In addition to poetry, Brown composes the words and music of songs. Her poem "Prayer" was first anthologized by Langston Hughes in *New Negro Poets U.S.A.*; it was also included in *The Poetry of the Negro, 1746–1970*, edited by Hughes and Arna Bontemps.

WILLIAM BURT (1950) was born in Greenville, Mississippi and has composed free verse since his days in Greenville High School, where he and poet Brooks

Haxton spent World Literature class passing their latest works to each other for criticism. Burt was honored with the William Alexander Percy Poetry Award and the Hodding Carter Award for Creative Writing before moving to Cambridge, Massachussetts, to study film. His short subject "Rapport" was the second-place winner at the 1972 Wachussett Film Festival. Burt has continued writing while pursuing a career in broadcasting which has taken him to Utah, Wyoming, Montana, and Arkansas, and back to Mississippi, where he has won four Mississippi Broadcasters Association Awards for news and sports reporting. He has written over a hundred songs and several short stories. Burt says free verse remains his favored means of expression. "I hear poetry when I write it, and I want the reader to hear it, too," he comments. "Poetry was originally oral, and it included elements of rhythm and melody, as well as story line. The idea is to do all that and still keep it conversational."

JACK BUTLER (1944) was born in Alligator, Mississippi. He received a B.A. in English, a B.S. in mathematics, and an M.F.A. in writing from the University of Arkansas. Butler spent his early years in a house on a Delta cotton field. The son of a Baptist preacher, he claims the King James Bible and science fiction as his two major literary influences. He describes himself as a generalist who is fascinated by "words, voices, trees, tones, stars, friends, work, rivers, calculus, games, jokes, prayers, time, food, gravity, flesh, love, learning, and the miracle of the image."

Butler has made his home in Arkansas for most of the last nineteen years. His books include *West of Hollywood* (1980), *Hawk Gumbo and Other Stories* (1982), *The Kid Who Wanted to Be a Spaceman* (1984), and *Jujitsu for Christ* (1986). All were published by August House. *Jujitsu for Christ* has been released in trade paper by Penguin, and a new novel *Nightshade* will appear with Atlantic Monthly Press in the fall of 1988. He has also completed a new book of poems *The Circles*. He has also published frequently in *New Yorker* and many respected literary journals including *Atlantic, Poetry, New Orleans Review*, and *Texas Quarterly*. His works have won considerable attention and many awards.

Butler serves as chair of the Porter Fund, a non-profit literary award created in memory of Ben Kimpel. He lives in Little Rock, Arkansas, where he is a supervisor for capital recovery for the state Public Service Commission.

ROBERT CANZONERI (1925) was born in San Marcos, Texas, and grew up in Clinton, Mississippi, the son of a Sicilian turned Baptist minister. In 1943 he joined the United States Navy and upon discharge, attended Mississippi College, receiving a B.A. in 1948. An M.A. from the University of Mississippi followed in 1951. After teaching at several universities and colleges, Canzoneri received a Ph.D. from Stanford University. Since 1965 he has been at Ohio State University. His books include *"I Do So Politely": A Voice from the South* (1965), *Watch Us Pass* (1968), *Men with Little Hammers* (1969), *Barbed Wire and Other Stories* (1970), and *A Highly Ramified Tree* (1976), which won the Ohioana award for the best book of the year in the field of autobiography. His humorous essays and recipes, *Potboiler: An Amateurs Affair with La Cuisine,* will be published by North Point Press.

Canzoneri writes:

"I began writing poetry seriously (not necessarily serious poetry) after a Southern Literary Festival at Mississippi College in 1956, where John Ciardi reminded me that poetry is supposed to be fun. Ciardi taught me more about poetry over the years than anyone else except Yvor Winters, at Stanford. It was fascinating to watch those two driving so forcefully from opposite directions, but meeting, as I saw it, at the very core of things. Poetry that has influenced me ranges from Old English to modern American, and my subject matter ranges literally from Maine to California—but most of what I've written is right out of Mississippi, and all of it is from a Mississippian's perspective."

ANNE CARSLEY (1935) has spent most of her life in Jackson, Mississippi, where she was born. She received a B.A. from Millsaps College in 1957 and an M.A. from the University of Mississippi in 1959. For her essays she has received awards from Millsaps College, the Southern Literary Festival, the Mississippi Arts Festival, and the Mississippi Commission on the Arts. In 1970 she received third prize for a screenplay in a contest sponsored by the Mississippi Authority for Educational Television.

Since 1980 Carsley has published six romantic novels with historical settings—*This Ravished Rose* (1980), *The Winged Lion* (1981), *This Triumphant Fire* (1982), *Defiant Desire* (1983), *The Golden Savage* (1984), and *Tempest* (1985). Her interest in archaeology led her to set *The Winged Lion* in Sumer (now Iran) in 2350 B.C. and *The Golden Savage* in Crete in 1650 B.C.

"All that I write and will ever write," Carsley says, "grows out of this enduring Mississippi land, the sight, sound, and smell of it, the people, their lives, and passions. The pattern was set in youth and touches all I write. It all comes together for me and produces the reality—the power of words and the finished tale, the communication."

HODDING CARTER (1907–1972). Pulitzer Prize-winning journalist, was born in Hammond, Louisiana. He attended public schools in Hammond and received a B.A. in 1927 from Bowdoin College in Maine. He studied at the Pulitzer School of Journalism at Columbia University (1927–28), taught freshman English at Tulane University (1928–29), and entered newspaper work in 1929 a member of the staff of the New Orleans *Item-Tribune*. Night manager of the New Orleans bureau of the United Press in 1930, Carter began working for the Associated Press bureau in Jackson, Mississippi, in 1931. The next year he was dismissed from the Associated Press for "insubordination" and was told he would "never make a newspaperman."

In 1932 in the midst of the Depression, Carter returned to his hometown and with his life savings of $367 started the Hammond *Daily Courier*. Four years later, he sold the newspaper which had assets of $16,000. From 1932 to 1936 one of Carter's chief targets was Louisiana political boss and United States Senator Huey Long. In 1936 Carter was persuaded by William Alexander Percy and David Cohn to move to Greenville, Mississippi, to start a paper to compete with the Greenville *Democrat-Times*. Soon afterward, the *Democrat-Times* sold out to Carter and his backers, and the *Delta Democrat-Times* was born.

For the rest of his life he was actively involved in community affairs. Although his political and social views were often different from many natives, Carter remained intensely loyal to Greenville, following Percy's injunction that "our mission is to live as men of good will in Greenville, Mississippi, because it is the sum total of all the Greenvilles in our country that will make the kind of nation that we want or don't want."

Throughout his journalistic career Carter was a major advocate of racial justice and a fierce opponent of the system of state-supported racial segregation in Mississippi and in the South. But before becoming a prophet honored in his own country, there were years when Carter was one of the most hated white men in Mississippi. The Mississippi Legislature resolved in 1955 by a vote of 89 to 19 that he was a traitor for criticizing the white Citizens Council. At that time he was chairman of the Rotary Club's Ladies Night, a counselor to the Boy Scouts, a Cub Scout den father, a director of the Chamber of Commerce, a member of the Board of Visitors of Tulane University, president of the Mississippi Historical Society and a vestryman at St. James Episcopal Church. He was a frequent speaker to school and civic groups and served as master of ceremonies for horse shows, high school newspaper conventions, and debutante balls.

Except for brief periods—1940 as a Nieman Fellow at Harvard, a few years with the United States Army during World War II, and some time in New Orleans as a writer-in-residence at Tulane—Carter spent the years 1936 to 1972 in Greenville. In 1946 he was awarded a Pulitzer Prize for editorials in the *Delta Democrat-Times*.

During his lifetime Carter published numerous books including *Lower Mississippi* (1942), *The Winds of Fear* (1944), *Flood Crest* (1947), *Southern Legacy* (1950), *Where Main Street Meets the River* (1953), *The Angry Scar: The Story of Reconstruction* (1959), *First Person Rural* (1963), and *So the Heffners Left McComb* (1965).

TURNER CASSITY (1929) was born in Jackson, Mississippi. He received a B.A. from Millsaps College in 1951, an M.A. from Stanford University in 1952, and an M.S. from Columbia University in 1956. Among Cassity's books are *Watchboy, What of the Night?* (1966), *Steeplejacks in Babel* (1973) *Yellow for Peril, Black for Beautiful* (1975), *The Defense of the Sugar Islands* (1979), *Keys to Mayerling* (1983), and *Hurricane Lamp* (1985). In 1980 he was awarded a grant from the National Endowment for the Arts.

Of his experience in growing up in Mississippi, he writes, "In a sense I did not spend my childhood in Mississippi at all. I spent it in the orchestra pit—I grew up among musicians—and on the planet Mongo. The old cliché that music is a universal language is true, in that music is not a local language and has that in common with science fiction. My interests from the first, therefore, have been turned outward, and although I think I have an acute sense of place, it is not narrowly focused. Jackson used to be a small city, but it was a city, and I have had no experience—except in the African backveld—of the really rural."

CECILE BROWN CLEMENT (1932) was born in Jackson, Mississippi. She received a B.A. from Millsaps College in 1953. To students she writes, "Take joy in being nourished in a land where senators and bartenders alike speak in metaphors and similes in everyday discourse."

WILLIE COOK (1929) was born in Phenix City, Alabama, and has lived in Mississippi since 1949. While teaching at Jackson State University, he has completed his course requirements for a Ph.D. in English at the University of Southern Mississippi. He writes, "All of my work is Mississippi centered. Of all the places I have been, Mississippi probably has the richest resources for the writer. The constant gravity of time and folkways pulls against inevitable change, the foundation upon which Faulkner and Welty built their literary worlds."

CAROL COX (1946) was born in Washington, D.C.; less than a year later her parents, who were both Alabamians, returned to the South. She spent her childhood in Alabama and Tennessee and moved to Mississippi at the age of fourteen. After attending Millsaps College for two years, she left the state for some time, graduating from the University of North Carolina at Chapel Hill with honors in English and living in New York City (where as a special student at Columbia University she was co-recipient of the Woodberry Prize for best poems by a student) and in Wyoming, where she taught at a school for delinquent boys. In 1972 she returned with her husband to Mississippi, and since that time their home has been in the country just north of Jackson, near Tougaloo College. They make their living as woodworkers.

Her poems have appeared in magazines such as *Ploughshares* and *New Virginia Review* and been included in an anthology of women poets from The Crossing Press called *Mountain Moving Day*. Hanging Loose Press, located in Brooklyn, New York, has published two collections of her poems, *Woodworking and Places Near By* (1979) and *The Water in the Pearl* (1982). *Woodworking and Places Near By* was a Small Press Book Club selection and a finalist for the Elliston Book Award, and was included in Library Journal's "Small Press Best Titles of 1979."

Dave Smith wrote in the *New England Review*: "Carol Cox is a poet aware of the need to renew poetry's ability to render clear both the surfaces and the values of our lives. Often enough I feel she has said things importantly and nearly undeniably."

HUBERT CREEKMORE (1907–1966) was born in Water Valley, Mississippi. He began writing poetry in high school and continued writing at the University of Mississippi, where he graduated in 1927. At Yale University he studied playwriting under George Pierce Baker. In 1940 Creekmore received an M.A. from Columbia University and in that same year published his first volume of poetry, *Personal Sun*. His experience in the United States Navy during World War II furnished the material for his second volume of poems, *The Long Reprieve and Other Poems from New Caledonia* (1946). Between 1946 and 1953 Creekmore wrote four books—*The Fingers of Night* (1946), *Formula* (1947), *The Welcome* (1948), and *The Chain in the Heart* (1953). His last novel chronicles the injustices faced by a black family in Mississippi through three generations from Reconstruction days to the Great Depression.

Creekmore spent the last years of his life editing and translating. He died in New York City in 1966.

JOHN CREWS (1926) was born in Monroe, Michigan, but has lived in Mississippi since he was six months old. He received a B.A. from University of the South and a Ph.D. from the University of Virginia. A professor of English at the University of Mississippi, Crews writes poetry and plays. Of his poem "Caught Caught Caught" he says, "Its germ is in a game of chase I played as a child in Vicksburg; my earliest recollection of it is associated with the death of a friend." In addition to his poems here, Crews's poetry has appeared in *Cumberland Poetry Review*, *Christian Century*, and *Poetry Now*.

JACK CROCKER (1940) was born in Vance, Mississippi. He received a B.A. from Delta State University, an M.A. from Florida State University, and a Ph.D. from Texas Tech University. Currently Crocker is an administrator at St. Petersburg Junior College in St. Petersburg, Florida. His poems have appeared in *Mississippi Review*, *Southern Poetry Review*, *Texas Review* and *Studies in Poetry*; his short stories have been published in *Cimarron Review* and *Writer's Forum*.

HENRY DALTON (1909) was born in Rienzi, Mississippi, and has lived in Mississippi his entire life except for short periods in San Francisco and New York. His books include *Hill Born* (1954) and *Process of Becoming* (1977). Dalton says, "The two persons who had most to do with my beginnings as a poet were both Mississippians. George Marion O'Donnell, who had worked with the Nashville poets, used to help me by suggesting ways of improving my writing. The other was Jonathan Henderson Brooks, a Corinth resident like myself. Until I knew them I did not know that writing poems could be learned."

ROSALIE BURKES DANIELS (1944) of Choctaw and English ancestry, was born in Zama, Mississippi, and grew up in Neshoba County. She received a B.A. degree from Mississippi College and a Ph.D. from the University of Southern Mississippi. Daniels has published fiction, reviews, folklore, and poetry in a wide variety of newspapers and journals and currently teaches in the English department at Jackson State University.

JEAN DAVIDSON (1947) was born in Oak Park, Illinois. She received a B.S.E. in English, speech and drama from Northeast Missouri State University and taught high school literature and creative writing for several years before leaving Missouri in 1977 for New Orleans and the Mississippi Gulf Coast. She subsequently received an M.A. in creative writing from the University of Southern Mississippi Center for Writers and occasionally returns to the classroom to teach creative writing and literature. Her work has appeared in *Chariton Review, Mississippi Review,* and *Pushcart Prize, VIII,* among others.

Davidson sees writing poetry in particular, as a process of discovery. "The thing that keeps drawing me back to the typewriter," she writes, "is something Octavio Paz describes in his poem 'Objetos y Apariciones' which he dedicated to the artist Joseph Cornell—that rare and wonderful 'spark' during which I catch a glimpse of 'Fire buried in the mirror,/water sleeping in the agate.'"

L. C. DORSEY (1938) was born in Tribbett, Mississippi. Educated in Mississippi public schools, she attended Mary Holmes College and the State University of New York at Stony Brook, from which she received a Masters in Social Work in 1973. In addition, Dorsey studied for a year at the University of Mississippi Law School and at Workers' College in Tel Aviv, Israel. She has participated in two study tours of the Peoples Republic of China and recently completed work on a doctorate in social work at Howard University.

A civil rights activist, Dorsey has participated in numerous economic development activities in Mississippi and was one of fifteen people selected by President Jimmy Carter to serve on the National Advisory Council on Economic Opportunity. She was formerly the Administrative Director of the Mississippi Prisoners' Defense Committee and also the Director of Social Services of Washington County Opportunities, Inc. Dorsey also served as director, coordinator, and organizer of an agricultural cooperative serving 800 families in Bolivar County. Before going to Washington, Dorsey was the associate director of the Delta Ministry, a human rights group of the National Council of Churches. She was also state director of the Southern Coalition on Jails and Prisons, a nine state human rights organization devoted to prison reform, abolition of the death penalty, and a moratorium on prison construction.

Her publications include articles and editorials about prison life for the *Jackson Advocate,* a weekly newspaper, and for the *Southern Coalition Reports.* She is also the author of a column called "If Bars Could Talk," numerous social work articles and poetry for various periodicals, and two books, *Freedom Came to Mississippi* (1977) and *Cold Steel* (1983). Her essay "Harder Times Than These" was first published in *Southern Exposure*. Her unpublished work includes a study of an alternative economic system for displaced sharecroppers, the effect of chemicals used in agriculture, and a report of her China visit called "Serving the People."

"I would encourage students," Dorsey writes, "to look first for the rainbow's pot of gold at home. The experiences I have had in Mississippi, while viewed by some as harsh and oppressive, have been like the blacksmith's fire on steel. I'm stronger for the experiences. Without romanticizing the plantation, I learned how to survive there, and the knowledge gained there prepared me to understand the Washington, D.C. plantation and the United States-Russian plantations in the world community. Students should prepare themselves to make Mississippi a better community and not rush to escape its customs, tradition, racism, and poverty. For all of these things exist everywhere; only not always are they as obvious, or honest, as is our state."

SYBIL PITTMAN ESTESS (1942) was born in Hattiesburg, Mississippi and grew up in Hattiesburg and Poplarville. She holds a B.A. from Baylor University, an M.A. from the University of Kentucky, and a Ph.D. from Syracuse University. Her critical articles and poems have appeared in *Modern Poetry Studies, Southern Review, Southern Poetry Review* and *Shenandoah,* among others. She is co-editor of *Elizabeth Bishop and Her Art* and her collection of poems, *Seeing the Desert Green,* was published in 1987. Estess lives in Houston, Texas, and teaches creative writing at the University of St. Thomas.

WINIFRED HAMRICK FARRAR (1923) was born on her parents' farm three miles from Collinsville, Mississippi. She has spent most of her life since 1948 within Lauderdale County. Farrar received a B.A. from the University of Mississippi in 1945 and an M.S. from the University of Southern Mississippi in 1962.

An English teacher for thirty years in the Mississippi public schools, Farrar has taught on the secondary and the college level. She served in the Meridian public schools for twenty-four years as classroom teacher, publications advisor, and chairperson for both the English department of Meridian High School and Meridian Junior College. For eighteen years she taught creative writing to advanced students and sponsored a literary magazine.

Since 1965 Farrar has published several hundred poems in a variety of poetry magazines and anthologies. Among Farrar's books are *Cry Life* (1968) and *The Seeking Spirit* (1974). In 1978 Farrar was appointed Poet Laureate by Governor Cliff Finch. A past president of the Mississippi Poetry Society, Farrar is the Mississippi representative for Voices International, Inc.

About her writing she says, "I write primarily to find myself and to maintain a sense of balance. In trying for honest expression, my spirit is continually making and remaking itself in relationship to my total experience. What is happening within me and around me is infused into my poetry, the poetry taking on both the contours of my personality and the world at work upon me. I hope that the poems have life, particular and universal."

WILLIAM FAULKNER (1897–1962) was born in New Albany, Mississippi. When he was five years old his family moved to Oxford, where he lived most of his life except for brief periods spent in Hollywood and Charlottesville, Virginia. Faulkner's education was sporadic. Dropping out of high school in his senior year, he attended the University of Mississippi as a special student for only one year (1919–20). He was a voracious reader and, through his friend and earliest critic, Phil Stone, was introduced to modern writers, including the French Symbolist poets. Their influence, along with the influence of Hardy and Yeats, can be seen in Faulkner's first book, *The Marble Faun*.

Influenced by Sherwood Anderson, Faulkner wrote his first novel, *Soldiers' Pay*, which appeared in 1926. Its publication began an extraordinarily prolific career. The next decade produced eight novels, including many of the finest he would write: *The Sound and the Fury* (1929), *As I Lay Dying* (1930), *Light in August* (1932), and *Absalom, Absalom!* (1936). However, his creative output was not matched by financial returns, so, in 1932, Faulkner went to Hollywood as a screen writer, a position he kept, under financial duress, until 1948, when the commercial success of *Intruder in the Dust* and its subsequent sale to the movies enabled him to return to Mississippi. With the exception of tours for the State Department and time spent as a writer-in-residence at the University of Virginia, he remained in Oxford the rest of his life. Faulkner won numerous awards for his fiction, including the 1949 Nobel Prize and two Pulitzer Prizes, one for *A Fable* (1954) and another for *The Reivers* (1962). He is considered by many critics to be the finest writer America has produced and one of the finest writers in the English language.

Robert Penn Warren has said, "The study of Faulkner's writing is one of the most challenging tasks in our literature. It is also one of the most rewarding." Faulkner, who admitted that he had learned to write "from other writers," advised hopeful poets and novelists to "read all you can."

JACK FENWICK (1911) was born in Kosciusko, Mississippi. His father was a Scotch-Canadian builder who came south in 1892 to build gingerbread houses. Fenwick describes himself as a "retired builder who now divides his time between a small basement woodworking shop and a small but well-stocked library that is called the 'playroom' by grandchildren who frequently share it."

Fenwick explains his interest in poetry: "My family were always readers and quoters, with a weakness for argument. There were ten of us, in all, six boys between two girls who were oldest and youngest. Every evening, each of us had a corner in the light and a book for privacy. An incredible silence would last until one of us, such as I, the youngest boy, would disturb it with a sudden question. Then, everybody had to answer. Sometimes my mother would recite old ballads. I loved to listen to my oldest brother, Will, go through Scott's description of the battle of Flodden from Marmion. Poetry was to me what the brier patch was to Bre'r Rabbit. I have read and written it compulsively and privately all my life."

WILLIAM FERRIS (1942) was born and raised on a farm near Vicksburg, Mississippi. After attending a rural elementary school in Warren County and going to junior high in Vicksburg, he completed high school at Brooks School in North Andover, Massachusetts, and received a B.A. in English from Davidson College, an M.A. in English from Northwestern University, and M.A. and Ph.D. degrees in folklore from the University of Pennsylvania. While teaching at Jackson State University from 1970 to 1972 and at Yale University from 1972 to 1978, he spent summer vacations working in Memphis, Tennessee, at the Center for Southern Folklore, a nonprofit media center he helped found. In 1979 he returned to his native state as the first director of the Center for the Study of Southern Culture at the University of Mississippi.

As an undergraduate student Ferris began recording and photographing blues musicians and church services near his home in Vicksburg, and he studied Mississippi traditions and made films about them as part of his graduate work at the University of Pennsylvania. Since then he has produced many publications and films about southern life. He is the author of *Blues from the Delta* (1978; reprinted 1984), *Images of the South: Visits with Eudora Welty and Walker Evans* (1978), *Local Color: A Sense of Place in Folk Art* (1982), and numerous articles. In addition, he is editor of *Afro-African Folk Art and Crafts* (1983) and co-editor of *Folk Music and Modern Sound* (1982) and the *Encyclopedia of Southern Culture* (forthcoming). Among the films Ferris has produced are *Gravel Springs Fife and Drum, Ray Lum: Mule Trader, Fanny Bell Chapman: Gospel Singer, Give My Poor Heart Ease: Mississippi Delta Bluesmen, Two Black Churches, Four Women Artists,* and *Painting in the South: Artists and Regional Heritage*.

CHARLES HENRI FORD (1913) was born in Hazelhurst, Mississippi. His literary career began at age fourteen when the *New Yorker* published one of his poems. In 1929, at age sixteen, Ford started publishing *Blues: A Magazine of New Rhythms* (assisted by Parker Tyler and Kathleen Tankersley Young) in Columbus, Mississippi. In nine issues *Blues* published Gertrude Stein, Ezra Pound, and William Carlos Williams, among other well-established writers. In her *Autobiography of Alice B. Toklas* Stein wrote: "Of all the little magazines that died to make verse free, the youngest and the freshest was *Blues*." In the spring of 1931 Ford sailed for France, taking with him the typescript of a novel he had completed in collaboration with Parker Tyler. In Paris a publisher was found and *The Young and Evil* was published in 1933 with jacket encomiums by, among others, Djuna Barnes who said, "Never, to my knowledge, has a certain type of homosexual been so 'fixed' on paper. No one but a genius could have written it." Gertrude Stein wrote, "*The Young and Evil* creates this generation as *This Side of Paradise* by Fitzgerald created his generation. It is a good thing, whatever the generation is, to be the first to create it in a book."

From this impressive beginning Ford has continued to publish—*The Garden of Disorder and Other Poems* (1938), *The Overturned Lake* (1941), *Sleep in a Nest of Flames: Poems* (1949), *Spare Parts* (1966), *Flag of Ecstasy: Selected Poems* (1972), *Om Krishna I: Special Effects* (1979), *Om Krishna II: From the Sickroom of the Walking Eagles* (1981), and *Om Krishna III: Secret Haiku* (1982).

In 1952 Ford developed an interest in photography, painting, and drawing. His first photographs were exhibited in London's Institute of Contemporary Art in 1954, and his first exhibition of paintings and drawings took place in Paris in 1956 with a catalog foreword by Jean Cocteau.

In *Lives of Mississippi Authors, 1817–1967*, Eva B. Mills writes: "Ford is America's first surrealist poet. He has promoted and drawn public attention to many American and European avant-garde writers, and he deserves respectful recognition as an innovative, versatile, untiring, talented artist. In summary, one may say that this Mississippi native—world-traveler, surrealist poet and painter, photographer, pop artist, friend and companion of the well-known and not so well-known, editor of avant garde magazines, diarist, letter-writer, poster-poem artist and filmmaker—Charles Henri Ford will leave an indelible 'record of himself' in the annals of American and European literature.

Ford spends his time in Nepal, Crete, and New York City, where his sister, actress Ruth Ford, lives. He is working on a novel, tentatively entitled 'Mississippi,' and on other projects.

JOHN P. FREEMAN (1942) was born in Jackson, Mississippi. He received a B.A. from Millsaps College in 1964 and an M.A. from Mississippi College in 1967. In addition, he attended the Writers' Workshop at the University of Iowa and the University of Arkansas. Freeman teaches at Mississippi's Oakley Training School, a state reform school for male juvenile delinquents.

RICHARD FREIS (1939) was born in New York City. He received a B.A. from St. John's College in 1963 and an M.A. and Ph.D. in classics from the University of California in 1973 and 1975. Since 1975 he has been director of the Heritage Program at Millsaps College where he teaches in the classics department.

ELLEN GILCHRIST (1935) was born in Vicksburg, Mississippi. She received a B.A. in philosophy from Millsaps College and did graduate work at the University of Arkansas in creative writing. She has served as contributing editor of *Courier* in New Orleans. Gilchrist's works have appeared in such publications as *Atlantic Monthly, California Quarterly, Mademoiselle, New York Quarterly, Poetry Northwest, Prairie Schooner,* and *Southern Living*. Her books include two collections of poetry, *The Land Surveyor's Daughter* (1979) and *Riding Out the Tropical Depression* (1986), one novel, *The Annunciation* (1983), and three collections of short fiction, *In the Land of Dreamy Dreams* (1981), *Victory Over Japan* (1984), and *Drunk with Love* (1986). Some of her awards include the Craft in Poetry Award from *New York Quarterly* (1978), National Endowment for the Arts Fellowship Grant in Fiction (1979), fiction award from *Prairie Schooner* (1981), and the 1981 and 1984 Mississippi Institute of Arts and Letters Literature Award for *In the Land of Dreamy Dreams* and *Victory Over Japan*. In addition, Gilchrist received the American Book Award in 1984 for *Victory Over Japan*. Gilchrist has been a frequent commentator for National Public Radio's "Morning Edition." *Falling Through Space: The Journals of Ellen Gilchrist* was published in 1987. She lives in Arkansas and is writing a second novel.

Of the process of writing, Gilchrist says, "I no longer believe that I understand the creative process except for two or three things. I believe that it is some form of trusting yourself to know the truth and to be able to tell the truth past all the things which pass for facts. Truth is a beautiful and complex and very funny song. When I am lucky and trust myself I am able to sing it long enough to make a poem.

"The other thing that I believe is that a writer must be terribly healthy and very patient. It is hard work to be a writer. You have to make up the job as you go along. You have to keep on trying and believing in yourself when nothing seems to be happening and when what you are doing seems to be the most absurd activity in the world. But it is exciting work."

SID GRAVES (1946) was born in Memphis, Tennessee, but has lived in Mississippi since he was a year old. While a student at Millsaps College, Graves began publishing poetry in *Stylus*, the college's literary magazine. After graduating from Millsaps he received an M.A. from the University of Mississippi and an M.L.S. from Peabody College. Graves is director of the Carnegie Library in Clarksdale, Mississippi.

"I feel fortunate to have lived in Mississippi," Graves says, "the home of so many of this country's most creative and accomplished literary and musical artists. Their example and the fact that this state has been and continues to be the crucible for so many of the the most important challenges of our civilization offer great opportunities for meaningful motivations and actions for the artist and the individual."

DOUGLAS GRAY (1948) grew up in Laurel and Jackson, Mississippi, and began writing poetry while he was a student at the University of Mississippi. Between 1972 and 1974 he was deeply involved in the *Images* case, first as poetry editor and later as general editor of the University's literary magazine whose 1972 issue had been impounded by university officials for containing allegedly immoral material. This case ended when the courts affirmed the right of students to publish a literary journal without interference from their college administration. Gray now teaches English and Latin at the Pontifical College Josephinum in Columbus, Ohio. In addition to poetry, he has written criticism and has two unpublished comedy-horror novels set in north Mississippi. Gray says, "I've been away from the state for almost a decade now; but as soon as I pick up a pen, I feel that I'm back home. Whether my poems are ostensibly about the jungle or ancient Rome or the moon, they're really always about Mississippi. There is no other place that I know of where words are so real and so important as in Mississippi, or where people have such a sense of language as a moral act."

ROBERT HAMBLIN (1938) was born in Jericho, Mississippi, and spent much of his boyhood in neighboring Bethany (Brice's Cross Roads), where his parents owned and operated the general store. He attended schools in Jericho, Guntown, Baldwyn, and Booneville, and subsequently earned an A.A. from Northeast Mississippi Junior College, a B.S.E. from Delta State University, and an M.A. and a Ph.D. from the University of Mississippi. A member of the English faculty at Southeast Missouri State University since 1965, Hamblin previously taught English and coached baseball at Sparrows Point (Maryland) High School.

A Faulkner scholar, Hamblin has published critical articles in various books and journals, and he is coeditor, with Louis Daniel Brodsky, of *Faulkner: A Comprehensive Guide to the Brodsky Collection*, a multi-volume series published by the University Press of Mississippi. He has directed summer seminars on Faulkner for the National Endowment for the Humanities and lectured at the annual Faulkner and Yoknapatawpha Conference at the University of Mississippi.

Hamblin serves as poetry editor for *Arete: The Journal of Sport Literature* and as associate editor for *Cape Rock*, a little magazine of poetry. His own poems have appeared in a chapbook, *Perpendicular Rain*, issued in 1986 by Southeast Missouri State University, and in several periodicals and anthologies.

Hamblin says, "Every person, in growing up and seeking his own personal identity, goes through a period of rebellion against his 'father,' that is, against the traditions, the values, the institutions, the attitudes that have been handed down from the past. Those of us who are fortunate, however, are allowed to move beyond the period of rebellion to a new awareness of the positive aspects of our heritage, both personal and cultural. We learn that the ability and the willingness to admit the defects in our traditions do not require us to disallow the virtues of the past. We scorn imitation, but we cling to the good. 'Requital' derives from this kind of tension between the individual and his past, and the poem probably says as much about my relationship to my homeland (the South) and its traditions as it says of my relationship to my actual father."

RABIUL HASAN, the son of a police officer, was born in Dhaka, Bangladesh. Hasan was educated at the University of Dhaka and Alcorn State University in Lorman, Mississippi. He received an M.A. degree in political science from the University of Dhaka in 1975. He also received an M.S.Ed. degree in social science in 1978 and an M.S.Ed. degree in English in 1987 from Alcorn State

University. He has been staff writer for the Office of Public Relations at Alcorn State University since 1984 as well as teaching political science, history, and English. Hasan writes fiction and poetry and has translated the works of many British and American authors into Bengali. His publications are to be found in more than forty different periodicals and anthologies in the United States and Canada.

Hasan writes: "Although a bit confessional and personal—and often deceptively simple because of the association of free and elemental images—my poetry is distinctively 'country' and rooted in rural Mississippi. I was not born in Mississippi but it is my home now. I grow and sustain here."

BROOKS HAXTON (1950) was born in Greenville, Mississippi, and was graduated from Greenville High School in 1968, the fourth year of the token integration of the white school system. His childhood fascination with story-telling developed into an urge to write protest poetry when he and his friends became Bob Dylan fans in junior high school. He was graduated from Beloit College in 1972. After several years' writing on his own and working various jobs, he earned a Master's degree from the Syracuse University Graduate Writing Program where he held a fellowship from 1979 until 1981. Other fellowships, grants, and awards have been awarded him by the Academy of American Poets, the Wesleyan Writers Conference, the D.C. Commission on the Arts, the Ingram Merrill Foundation, and the National Endowment for the Arts. His poems have been appearing since the early seventies in magazines, including *Poetry, Southern Review, Sewanee, Kenyon,* and *American Poetry Reviews.* His first book, *The Lay of Eleanor and Irene,* published in 1985, is a narrative poem. His second, *Dominion,* published the following year by Knopf, is a collection of shorter poems.

Haxton lives in New York and teaches the writing of poetry to undergraduate and graduate students at Sarah Lawrence College.

KENNETH HOLDITCH (1933) was born in Ecru, Mississippi. He received a B.A. from Southwestern College at Memphis and an M.A. and the first Ph.D. in English from the University of Mississippi. Holditch is a professor of English at the University of New Orleans. He conducts literary tours of New Orleans; his book *In Old New Orleans* was published by the University Press of Mississippi in 1983. He has published numerous essays, poems, and short stories.

Holditch says of his Mississippi heritage: "I would simply say that most of the inspiration I have received to write fiction or poetry has come from my background, and that background is, of course, inextricably linked with Mississippi. It has been said so often that one does not need to say again that more writers have come from our state than from any other—more good writers. There is a reason for that. I don't know what that reason is. Part of it certainly involves the agrarian atmosphere which was so much a part of the state when I was growing up. I think of what Berry Morgan once said to me in describing the state from which both of us came and from which both of us have drawn great strength: Mississippi is 'a schizophrenic piece of heaven.' That says it better than I could say it in any other words."

JOYCE HOLLINGSWORTH-BARKLEY (1929) was born in Kosciusko, Mississippi. She was graduated from the University of Mississippi with a B.S. degree in English. Since graduation she has worked as a freelance writer and painter. In 1984 her collection of poetry, *Honeysuckle Child,* was published.

M. CARL HOLMAN (1919) was born in Minter City, Mississippi. He holds an A.B. degree from Lincoln University, an M.A. from the University of Chicago, and an M.B.A. from Yale University. A former English professor at Clark College in Atlanta, he has edited a weekly newspaper, the *Atlanta Inquirer.*

Hollman has served as Information Officer of the United States Commission on Civil Rights and is currently president of the National Urban Coalition in Washington, D.C.

Holman's prose and poetry have appeared in such periodicals as *Verse* and *Phylon,* and in such collections as *Poetry of the Negro,* edited by Langston Hughes and Arna Bontemps, and *Soon, One Morning: New Writing by American Negroes.* Holman received, as a University of Chicago graduate student, the John Billings Fiske Poetry Prize and has been the recipient of a Rosenwald Fellowship.

REBECCA HOOD-ADAMS (1949) was born in Grenada, Mississippi, and has lived in Mississippi most of her life. After graduating from Delta State University, Hood-Adams moved to Merigold, Mississippi, where she works as a reporter for the (Jackson) *Clarion-Ledger.* In addition to journalistic articles her writing has appeared in *Delta Scene* and *Best American Magazine Verse* (1979).

Hood-Adams notes, "Someone once asked me where I got all my stories. I come from a family of front porch rockers. Having laid-by the crops, my people passed the time swapping stories, embellishing local history, and trading lies. In this manner I inherited tales told by my father and grandfathers and their fathers before them. "Cotton Choppers" and "Diphtheria" are true stories, filtered by the process of time, perception, and memory. These particular poems were an experiment in combining verse with illustration. The old photograph of my father and his brothers leaning on their hoes in Webster County, Mississippi, spoke to me in almost audible tones. "Diphtheria" is a story recounted to me by an uncle. However, it was written to commensurate the recent death of my godchild. I hope my work echoes other voices silenced by time."

T. R. HUMMER (1950) was born in Macon, Mississippi. He received a B.A. and an M.A. from the Center for Writers at the University of Southern Mississippi and a Ph.D. in 1980 from the University of Utah. Hummer's books of poetry include *Translation of Light* (1976), *The Angelic Orders* (1982), and *The Passion of the Right-Angled Man* (1984). He is a member of the English faculty at Kenyon College and coeditor of *The Imagination as Glory: The Poetry of James Dickey.* During the 1986–1987 school year, Hummer taught English at the University of Exeter in England.

Hummer writes, "What can be said about the writer's experience in the South generally has probably already been said by others better than I can say it. I can't imagine a richer or more dangerous atmosphere for a writer to experience: rich and dangerous because of the overwhelming density of the material it provides. It's hard, I think, for a southern writer to find his own voice amid the multitude of voices already speaking. The most useful thing I have ever done, in coming to terms with southern material, is getting out of the South—moving to a place so alien (Utah, for example) that what I had lived in Mississippi came alive in my mind in a way it never could when I was there. I do not intend this as advice: only as a description of what I did. For me, it was a way to avoid being crushed by the weight of what a place, dearly loved and powerful, laid on me."

ANGELA JACKSON (1951) was born in Greenville, Mississippi, the fifth of nine children and the last in her family who was born in Mississippi. In an interview

Jackson said, "I just recently learned that the place where I was born, that section of town, was called Brown's Addition, and I like that a lot. In my mother's and father's children you can see two different personalities, and it comes from the sense of place. There's a difference between those of us who were born in Mississippi, and those of us who were born in Chicago, so I think that just being there, did seem to make a big difference in that I wasn't an absolute product of the city. Which is not to say that the city that I knew as a child was that much different than Greenville, in Brown's Addition."

Jackson is considered to be one of the most talented writers to emerge from Chicago's Organization of Black American Culture (OBAC) Writers Workshop during the 1970s. She has published her work in a wide number of magazines, anthologies, and periodicals. Her three books of poetry are *Voo Doo/Love Magic* (1974), *The Greenville Club* (1977), and *Solo in the Boxcar Third Floor E* (1985). Her writing has appeared in *Story Quarterly, Black Scholar, Chicago Review, Callaloo, Open Places*, and *TriQuarterly*, among others. Jackson is the winner of the Conrad Kent Rivers Memorial Award from *Black World* magazine, the Academy of American Poets Award, and the Edwin Schulman Fiction Prize. In 1977 Jackson was selected to represent the United States at the Second World Festival of Black and African Arts and Culture (FESTAC) in Lagos, Nigeria. In 1979 she received one of the two premier Illinois State Arts Council Creative Writing Fellowships. The following year she received a creative writing fellowship from the National Endowment for the Arts. *Ebony* magazine, in its August 1982 issue, included her among "Women to Watch in the 1980s." Jackson received the second Hoyt W. Fuller Award for Literary Excellence in 1983 and that same year was writer-in-residence at Stephens College. In 1986 Jackson returned to Chicago to complete revisions on her novel "Treemont Stone" and to plan the twentieth anniversary of OBAC.

AUROLYN CHARISE JACOBS (1957) was born in Chicago, Illinois. She received both a B.S. and M.A. degree from Jackson State University. Jacobs says, "I was born in Illinois, but after a few months was brought to Mississippi. I sometimes wonder, if the basics of my personality, my desire to write, would have been different, if I had not made that trip. Mississippi, among other things has made me a writer, for Mississippi is addictive and unique. Amid the cruelty of its history, is a gentle caring for its natives. Amid the fear and racial injustice, is a strong desire to embrace all who might choose to settle on its soil. The only other advantage, other than growing up in Mississippi, is being born here."

JOAN JOHNSON (1953–1986) was born in Laurel, Mississippi. She received an M.A. from the Center for Writers at the University of Southern Mississippi, and attended the Middlebury College School of English in Vermont while working toward an M. Litt. degree. She was a contributor at the Bread Loaf Writers conference in 1977 and was the John Atherton Scholar at the 1978 conference. In September 1986 Johnson was graduated from Brown University with a Master's degree. Johnson published both fiction and poetry, including a novella, *Kitchen Tales*, which appeared as a special issue of *Colorado Quarterly* in February, 1978.

About growing up in Mississippi, Johnson wrote, "People talked a lot where I grew up in Jones County, a lot of it lies or at least skewed versions of the truth. The style of talking and what was left out of it were just as important as the facts or beliefs that were explicitly stated. I was as quick as any child at manufacturing my own versions of events, persons, and objects: I suppose the liar's instincts are rooted in the same soil as the writer's. The point, for me, was never that I got the facts, the literal truth, right; rather, whether I told an interesting lie or a dull one.

"Too, in those woods there wasn't much to do if you didn't like to play with cousins or read. My grandmother taught me to read before I started school, and most afternoons we'd read to each other. Charles Dickens and Margaret Mitchell were read as if each was just as important as the other, and I have remained an indiscriminate reader. Although I have since learned the difference between Dickens and Mitchell, I still love the way the spoken word sounds.

"I'm not at all sure this sort of background is confined to Mississippi or to the South, but perhaps to rural areas anywhere. I don't consider myself a southern writer as that label is generally applied. My subjects, settings, themes, and characters are not limited to this locale. To steal a line out of context from Flannery O'Connor, I don't want my mule stalled on the tracks when the Dixie Limited comes through. I live and work in the modern world, wherever that might be, and write about it the best way I know how."

Before her death February 10, 1986 in a car accident, Johnson studied with Robert Coover, Michael S. Harper and John Hawks at Brown University. In July of 1985, Hawks wrote, "I have known Joan Johnson only during the past academic year when she was enrolled in my thesis workshop in the fall and in the spring worked independently with me on completing her thesis. But I know Joan well and like and admire her immensely. Joan suffers from multiple sclerosis, a fact I mention only because it was a final indication of Joan's great strength and detachment as person and writer. The steroids she was taking induced, as a side effect, a serious speech impediment, and yet Joan insisted on remaining in the workshop and contributed to it brilliantly, largely through her amazing scrawled notes which someone else read aloud for her. There was nothing sentimental about Joan's feelings about her illness or participation in the group discussions. She laughed at her problem and conveyed to us all thoughts, which were to the point, unusual, and always suggested the fine mind of a genuine writer. And Joan is that, a writer, not merely a graduate student (or former one) in a graduate program. Her imagination and prose are like no one else's, tough, serious, funny, horrifying in only the most significant fashion, the attributes of a person who has her own fictive voice and a masterful sense of form and where she wants her fiction to go. Joan writes about women generally, but is no mere women's writer; she writes about men and race with compassion and understanding. She creates her own worlds and is one of the handful of true fiction writers I've work with in Brown's graduate program. At Brown she earned her degree, with all the strength of the word, and accomplished much, much more. I'm proud to have been associated with her developing life as a writer and to know her."

LARRY JOHNSON (1945) was born in Natchez, Mississippi. He spent his first five years in Petal, Mississippi, then moved to Jackson, where he grew up, graduating from Mississippi College with a B.A. in 1967. He received an M.A. in English and an M.F.A. in creative writing from the University of Arkansas, taught at Alma College in Alma, Michigan, and lived nine years in Knoxville, Tennessee, where he attended the University of Tennessee, partially completing a doctorate. He has since lived in Hattiesburg where he was poetry editor of *Mississippi Arts & Letters* magazine, and at present teaches at the University of New Orleans.

"I'm almost always happy to be in Mississippi," Johnson writes. "Those of us who still live in the South can see it steadily and see it whole, as was said about a poet's perception, and we take beauty and irritation as they come, knowing that time changes everything."

Johnson feels "a line of poetry should be like a strong, lithe, sinuous snake— gleaming with the supple jewels of its iridescent scales, that is, the exact opposite of today's fashionable poetry of 'invisible words.'" Johnson continues to write poems and a novel. His intellectual passions, he says, are classical and rock music, science fiction, and Roman history and culture. His poems have appeared in *Transatlantic Review, New Orleans Review, National Forum, Iowa Review,* and *Texas Quarterly.*

EMORY JONES (1944) was born in Starkville, Mississippi, and has lived in Iuka, Mississippi, since he was seven years old. From the University of Mississippi he received a B.A.E. degree in 1965, an M.A. degree in English in 1966, and a Ph.D. in 1981. Jones has been teaching at Northeast Mississippi Community College since 1971. In 1978 he was instrumental in founding the Mississippi Junior College Creative Writing Association, an organization which promotes the development of creative writing among the students of Mississippi's junior colleges. In addition, he was influential in Northeast Mississippi Community College's establishing scholarships to high school winners in poetry, short story, and essay.

MARGARET KENT (1941) was born in Greenville, Mississippi. She received a B.A. from New York University, an M.A. from the University of North Carolina at Chapel Hill, and an M.F.A. from the University of North Carolina at Greensboro. Her writing has been published in *Poetry, Paris Review, Southern Poetry Review,* and a number of other literary periodicals. Her work has also been represented in *Pushcart Prize IV: Best of the Small Presses, Anthology of Magazine Verse,* and *Yearbook of American Poetry.*

ETHERIDGE KNIGHT (1931) was born in Corinth, Mississippi, and grew up in Mississippi and Paducah, Kentucky, with four sisters and two brothers. Quitting school after the eighth grade, Knight says of these years, "I didn't finish the white man's high school—ran away from home instead; later when I was seventeen years old, I joined the army disillusioned and got hooked. . . ." Knight served as a medical technician and saw active service in Korea where he received a "psyche/wound." Knight writes, "I died in Korea from a shrapnel wound, and narcotics resurrected me." This resurrection led to what Knight called "another death." He was convicted of a 1960 robbery committed in Indianapolis, Indiana, to support his drug habit. In prison he found poetry to resurrect him. "I died," he says "in 1960 from a prison sentence & poetry brought me back to life." In prison Knight says he found "a community and it was because of poetry—that's what brought me into communion with other people."

When his first poetry collection, *Poems from Prison,* was published in 1968 by Dudley Randall's Broadside Press, Knight was an inmate in the Indiana State Prison. Scholar Shirley Lumpkin writes: "His work was hailed by black writers and critics as another excellent example of the powerful truth of blackness in art that the black arts movement, then reaching its height of influence, was promoting. Gwendolyn Brooks wrote of the strong presence of blackness and maleness in Knight's poetry, and in her preface to his *Poems from Prison* she prophetically identified the enduring characteristic of Knight's poetry: 'Vital. Vital./This poetry is a major announcement.' When he was paroled Knight continued to write the poetry he had begun to write in prison in 1963. 'Poeting,' as he would call it, became a center for his life, and his work became important in Afro-American poetry and poetics and in the strain of Anglo-American poetry descended from Walt Whitman. Thus, a black poet whose work reflected the prison, the male experience, and the aesthetic of the 1960s continued to write into the 1980s, absorbing more and more of the Afro-American, Anglo-American, European, and African literary traditions into a body capable of forming a passionate, loving connection with black and white readers. A believer in the trinity of poet-poem-people, Knight seeks and often achieves a responsible and specific language true to his human experience. Using oral premises to govern his style, he consciously strives to create communion and communication with audiences through the words of his poetry as written and as spoken in his numerous readings of his work. Speaking of what is often ignored or left out of poetry, Knight succeeds in reaching his audiences and making them feel and see anew the meaning of experience."

A number of poets, Robert Bly, Gwendolyn Brooks, and Galway Kinnell, among others, consider Knight a major Afro-American poet because of his "human subject matter, his combination of traditional techniques with an expertise in using rhythmic and oral speech patterns, and his ability to feel and to project his feelings into a poetic structure that moves others." Robert Bly states that Knight is the best contemporary Afro-American poet and considers the poem "Ilu, the Talking Drum" one of the best poems in the last fifty years because of its original and intense use of rhythmical sounds. The poem came out of a summer Knight spent with Nigerian poet and playwright Wole Soyinka, who taught him how the African drum uses pulse beats and the tone of the human voice to communicate. Another of Knight's poems highly praised is "The Idea of Ancestry" which has been called one of "the best poems that has been written about the Afro-American conception of family history and human connection."

In addition to *Poems from Prison* Knight's books are *Belly Songs and Other Poems* (1973), *Born of a Woman* (1980), and *The Essential Etheridge Knight* (1986). Knight has been awarded fellowships by the Guggenheim Foundation and the National Endowment for the Arts and in 1985 was awarded the Shelley Memorial Award by the Poetry Society of America in recognition of distinguished achievement in poetry.

Of Mississippi Knight writes: "Growing/up/in Mississippi, one becomes extremely aware/of/the political, economical, and social systems that separate people from people (the religious system/is/included too). Yet, the language which/is/the cement that binds/all/the above systems (or institutions) together/ is the Souths 'saving grace.'"

SINCLAIR O. LEWIS (1930) was born in Greenville, Mississippi. He studied at Tougaloo College and Purdue University and was graduated with an Ed.D. from the University of Kentucky. Lewis has taught in the psychology department at Jackson State University and is past chair of their department of guidance and counseling. His poetry has been published in *Jackson State Review* and his collection of poems, *Discovery and Other Food for Thought*, was published in 1982. Lewis lives in Jackson, Mississippi, where he is dean of freshman studies at Paul Quinn College.

ROSEWELL GRAVES LOWREY (1895–1979) was born in Blue Mountain, Mississippi. He received a B.S. from Mississippi College in 1918 and an A.M. and

Ph. D. from Peabody College. After teaching at Amarillo Military Academy, Peabody College, and Blue Mountain College, where he served as dean of the college for nine years, he joined the faculty of the University of Southern Mississippi. From 1933 to 1960 he taught health, education, English and was dean of men and director of student welfare. In addition in two books of composition, *The English Sentence in Literature and in College Freshman Composition* (1928) and *Mechanics of English* (1939), he wrote a volume of poetry, *Stones and the Sea, and Other Poems* (1956) and coedited *Mississippi: A Historical Reader* (1937).

BIRTHALENE MILLER was born in Choctaw County, Mississippi, and has spent all her life in the state. Her stories have appeared in *Southern Exposure, Laurel Review, Moving Out,* and *Black Warrior Review.* "The Lonesomes Ain't No Spring Picnic" was her first published short story.

About her experiences in Mississippi, she writes: "Time never runs in a straight line, but like the twisting path of a rampant river, it twines around and into itself. Yesterday becomes today and today becomes tomorrow and yet they are all the same. Whatever affects us when we are young determines the person we are today and the person we will be tomorrow. It is this yesterday self still living in us that exerts the strongest force upon our writing. When I was a child, it infuriated me to hear people say a woman shouldn't speak in church. When I sat down to write "The Lonesomes Ain't No Spring Picnic,' I only knew I was going to write about a little girl and her grandmother. The story and the characters evolved out of my yesterday self. The characters wrote their own story."

Miller admits to "a lifelong rapacious appetite for written words." For her "the South of today is fast changing from the one it was when I was growing up in a sharecropper's shack. In many ways, though, it's still the same. Many of the same contradictions and the same conflicts remain largely unchanged. The sense of place is balanced by the sense of displacement."

WILLIAM MILLS (1935) was born in Hattiesburg, Mississippi. He holds a Ph. D. from Louisiana State University and a diploma from Goethe Institute, Blaubeuren, Germany. He is the author of three poetry collections, *Watch for the Fox* (1974), *Stained Glass* (1979), and *The Meaning of Coyotes* (1984). Among Mills's other books are *The Stillness in Moving Things: The World of Howard Nemerov* (1975), a collection of short stories, *I Know a Place* (1976), a novel, *Those Who Blink* (1986), and a nonfiction book with text and color photographs, *Bears and Men: A Gathering* (1986). Currently he travels and writes on nature and the environment.

KAREN L. MITCHELL (1955) was born in Columbus, Mississippi, and grew up in Holly Springs, Mississippi, where she graduated from high school in 1973. She was graduated from Stephens College in 1977. Mitchell has published poetry in *13th Moon, Essence, Obsidian, Open Places,* and *Southern Exposure* and has been a fellow at the MacDowell Colony. She says, "Mississippi—the South as a whole—is a land filled with history and a richness that is hardly matched in other parts of the country. I began writing by looking at my surroundings. 'The Eating Hill' is a look at the land and how our people become one."

CHARLES MOORMAN (1925) was born in Cincinnati, Ohio. He received a B.A. from Kenyon College and an M.A. and Ph. D. from Tulane University. Since 1954 Moorman has taught at the University of Southern Mississippi.

SANDRA NAPIER-DYESS (1954) was born in Hattiesburg, Mississippi, and has lived in Mississippi her entire life. She received a B.A. in French from Millsaps College and an M.A. in English from Mississippi College. Presently she lives in Jackson, Mississippi.

JOHN NIXON, JR. (1924) was born in Batesville, Mississippi. With the exception of a brief residence in North Carolina (non-military) during World War II, all of his early life was spent "next door to Yoknapatawpha" in the northwestern corner of his native province. Many of his poems represent specific Panola County locales. Toward the end of 1948, Nixon moved to Fluvanna County, Virginia, where he now resides. For sixteen years he coedited the venerable quarterly of poetry, *Lyric*. His own work has appeared in *New Yorker, Saturday Review, Commonweal, Mademoiselle, Arizona Quarterly*, and *Washingtonian*. Nixon has received, among other honors, the Bellamann Award.

LEWIS NORDAN (1939) was born in Jackson, Mississippi, and attended school in Itta Bena, Mississippi. He received a B.A. from Millsaps College, an M.A. from Mississippi State University, and a Ph.D. from Auburn University. Widely published in such publications as *Harper's, Redbook*, and the *Greensboro Review*, he won the John Gould Fletcher award for fiction in 1977. Nordan is now assistant professor at the University of Pittsburgh, where he teaches creative writing. His first collection of short stories, *Welcome to the Arrow-Catcher Fair*, was published by Louisiana State University Press in 1983. His second collection of short stories, *The All-Girl Football Team*, was published in 1986 and has received high critical praise.

Regarding the writer's relationship to his home state, he says, "A large body of Mississippi writers, white as well as black, do not live in Mississippi, and for their own reasons cannot. We are, in no romantic sense, expatriates. We will always be Mississippians—we will return to its swamps and cross its bridges and hear the stories, its rhythms will be our ritual, people will know us by them. And yet we could not write of our sweet home, or be proud of it, until we were gone from it and certain we would not return to live. We ache for Mississippi, but to its rich images and good people we are blinded by its light, we are smothered in its air. Still, we carry it in us, and it is a celebration so to do."

STEPHEN OWEN (1946) was born in Starkville, Mississippi and received the majority of his education in Clinton where he attended Mississippi College and earned a B.A. and an M.A. in English. While in college he was fortunate to have studied under J. Edgar Simmons, a teacher who has had a lasting influence upon his life and poetry. Owen has taken courses in creative writing and literature at the University of Mississippi, the University of West Florida, Vanderbilt University, and the Writer's Workshop at Long Island University, Southampton Campus. He lives in Meridian and teaches English at Meridian Community College. Publications by Owen include a book about Meridian's endurance flyers Fred and Al Key, entitled *The Flying Key Brothers and Their Flight to Remember*, and various prose and poetry published in magazines and journals such as *Mississippi* magazine, Writer's Digest, Piedmont Literary Review, and *Teaching English in the Two-Year College*.

PATSY CLARK PACE (1929) was born in Paden, Mississippi, and was graduated from Tishomingo High School in 1945. She received a B.A. from Blue Mountain College in 1949 where she studied creative writing and helped reorganize the Southern Literary Festival because it had become inactive during World War II. In 1950 Pace was graduated from the University of Mississippi with an M.A. in English. Since 1952 she has lived in Aberdeen, Mississippi, where she has taught English. She has been a member of the Mississippi Poetry Society since 1955 and in 1980 helped organize its North Branch. Pace has published poetry in *Connecticut Literary Review, Poetry Digest, Mississippi Poetry Journal* and in both the 1955 and 1982 anthologies *Lyric Mississippi*.

LINDA PEAVY (1943) was born in Hattiesburg, Mississippi. She received a B.A. in English from Mississippi College in 1964 and an M.A. in English from the University of North Carolina at Chapel Hill in 1970. After teaching English from 1964 to 1966 at Central High in Jackson, Mississippi, and from 1966 to 1969 at Glen Oaks Senior High in Baton Rouge, Louisiana, she became an instructor in English at Oklahoma Baptist University. Since 1974 Peavy has lived with her family in Bozeman, Montana, working as a writer, editor, and lecturer. Peavy's fiction, poetry, and essays have appeared in numerous periodicals, including *Southern Exposure, South Dakota Review, Texas Review, Cottonwood, Plainswoman, Crab Creek Review,* and *Memphis* magazine. In partnership with Ursula Smith, Peavy has co-authored *Women Who Changed Things* (1983), a collective biography of nine turn-of-the-century women of achievement, and *Dreams into Deeds: Nine Women Who Dared* (1985), a collective biography featuring women from the National Women's Hall of Fame. Peavy and Smith are currently writing *Women in Waiting: The Home Frontier in the Westward Movement* and have written the libretto for an opera.

Peavy notes, "When I was growing up in Mississippi, evolution was a forbidden word and creation was seen as an instantaneous affair. Salvation worked the same way. At some fortuitous moment you 'got saved' and that took care of matters forever. It took years for me to alter that mind-set and realize that what was really essential was process, not product—journey, not destination. All of nature speaks to this becoming, this slow evolution that takes one from beginnings toward some largely unknown destination. Because my beginnings were in Mississippi, my journey has been different from what it would otherwise have been. A part of my own personal evolution has been learning to accept, even cherish those beginnings, though raising the forbidden questions has meant that I can never return to them."

Of her poetry Peavy says, "'The Telling Tree,' written some thirty years after the childhood events that inspired it, confesses my lifelong compulsion to tell out all that I need to say to be free. Part of that telling concerns my memories of growing up as a white child in a segregrated South in which the black women I knew fit neatly into a hierarchical pattern I was too naive to recognize, but wise enough not to violate. A part of that telling out concerns my coming to terms with the unspoken realities surrounding the death of my baby sister, and a part of it has to do with the difficulties I face in returning home to a culture that has always equated churchgoing with salvation. The poems and stories I write are my way of finding out who I was in order to have a better understanding of who I am and might be."

WILLIAM ALEXANDER PERCY (1885-1942) was born in Greenville, Mississippi, where he grew up in a secure atmosphere that was rich with music and books. His early education took place at the Sisters of Mercy convent and was supplemented by tutoring from a judge, a local priest, and the superintendent of the public school system. At fifteen, Percy was enrolled in the preparatory school at

Sewanee. Disliking the uniforms that its students were required to wear, Percy took and passed the college entrance examination for the University of the South. He graduated with a B.A. in 1904 and spent the next year traveling across Europe and into Egypt.

Upon his return to the United States, Percy entered the Harvard School of Law, chiefly because he wanted to be near Boston. His interest in the law was marginal. He received his law degree in 1908 and returned to Greenville to enter practice with his father. It was during this period that Percy began to write poetry.

When World War I broke out, Percy spent two years in Europe in Herbert Hoover's Commission for Relief in Belgium. In 1916 Percy, after considerable effort, was accepted into officer's candidate school. He saw action on the front lines and returned to Greenville with the rank of captain and the Croix de Guerre.

His return to Greenville saw the advent of troubled years. In 1922 there was a resurgence of activity by the Ku Klux Klan, and Percy's stand against them, along with his father's, endangered both Percy and his family. In 1927 the Mississippi River overflowed its banks, creating the worst flood in recorded history. Because of his work in Belgium, Percy was appointed Chairman of the Flood Relief Committee and the Red Cross. He was responsible for soliciting and coordinating relief efforts within the state and from external sources. In 1929, both his parents died within a few weeks of each other. Percy was left with his father's law practice and possession of Trail Lake, 3,000 acres of some of the richest land in the South. In 1931 Percy adopted his three young cousins, Walker, LeRoy, and Phinizy Percy, after the death of their parents, and he turned his energies toward giving these orphaned boys the best opportunities he knew how to give them. Of his efforts, and of Will Percy, Walker Percy has said, "I will say no more than that he was the most extraordinary man I have ever known and that I owe him a debt which cannot be paid."

Percy's poetry was antiquated at the time of its writing. In the midst of one of history's greatest poetry revolutions, Percy persistently wrote in a Victorian vein. He was not unaware of this: "When you feel something intensely, you want to write it down—if anguish, to staunch the bleeding; if delight, to prolong the moment. When after years of pondering you feel you have discovered a new truth or an old one which suddenly for you has the excitement of a new one, you write a longish poem. To keep it free of irrelevant details and set it in some long-ago time, one, of course, you love and perhaps lived in."

Among Percy's books of poetry are *Sappho in Levkas and Other Poems* (1915). *In April Once* (1920). *Enzio's Kingdom, and Other Poems* (1924), *Selected Poems* (1930), *The Collected Poems of William Alexander Percy* (1943), and *Of Silence and Stars* (1953).

Of his 1941 memoirs, *Lantern on the Levee*, critic Herschel Brickell of the *New York Times Book Review* wrote that it was "a work of exceptional merit and importance. The high quality of the prose would entitle it to consideration for a permanent place in our literature, and it has numerous other virtues as well." It remains Percy's major work.

Brickell wondered why a man who was only fifty-five years old was writing his autobiography. He didn't know that Percy, always frail of health, had already had a debilitating stroke. In 1942, a year after the publication of *Lanterns on the Levee*, William Alexander Percy died.

ERIN CLAYTON PITNER (1921) was born in Tupelo, Mississippi. She attended

Mississippi State College for Women (now Mississippi University for Women) and Millsaps College before receiving degrees from the University of Mississippi. In addition, she has taken graduate courses in poetry and creative writing at Hartwick College in Oneonta, New York, and has been studied with D.C. Berry, Ellen Douglas, and Evans Harrington.

Of the process of becoming a poet Pitner writes, "Ten years ago I had the unique experience of being alone in my own house for several days. I was frightened and exhilarated at the thought of such a great block of time, and I decided to transfer to paper the verses and rhymes that had been chasing their tails in my head for months. I sat down in my favorite rocker and a vivid image began to emerge: I glimpsed mountains in the background, dark trees, a river and, in the far distance, a meadow, half-green, half-russet, diffused with sunlight. The whole picture was tinged by the hazy atmosphere of late summer, with its unresolved air of impermanence. I had recently reread *Lanterns on the Levee* by William Alexander Percy and the last chapter had become deeply pressed into my mind. He was in the throes of a fatal illness and he wrote of the dark woods before him and of his desire to linger in the sunny clearing longer. His description was heart-rending, and I walked the meadowlands with him. Did a masterpiece result from these grand visions? No, for I did not have the skill to portray the vivid images flashing through my mind. A very simple poem, in ballad form, did emerge and the imagery of that mid-summer afternoon lingers to this day."

STERLING D. PLUMPP (1940) was born in Clinton, Mississippi. In 1955 his family moved to Jackson, Mississippi, where he completed school. After being selected for a scholarship, Plumpp studied for two years at St. Benedict's College and in 1968 received a B.A. in psychology from Roosevelt University. He is currently associate professor in the Black Studies Program at the University of Illinois at Chicago.

Plumpp's writings include six books of poetry, prose, and essays. In 1972 Third World Press published *Black Rituals,* a book of black psychological essays; it is a probing analysis of the black man's way of coping in a technological, urbanized, and industrialized society. His books of poetry include *Portable Soul* (1969), *Half Black, Half Blacker* (1970), *Steps to Break the Circle* (1974), *Clinton* (1976) and *The Mojo Hands Call, I Must Go* (1982). The latter, published by Thunder's Mouth Press, won the 1983 Carl Sandburg Literary Award for Poetry. In 1982 Plumpp edited a collection titled *Somehow We Survive: An Anthology of South African Writing.*

Concerning his development as a writer, Plumpp says, "When I was thirty, I found my writing voice and the ability to master techniques to reflect my inner self. The more I wrote about the South, the more tranquil my voice was. By viewing my soul through Mississippi, I could maneuver into the reservoir of my being without first having to plod through attacks against whites; I could see the survival lines of my people concealed in the many ways they did things. Though there will be other places in my life none will be home, as close and as painfully or joyfully familiar as Mississippi."

NOEL POLK (1943) is a native of and grew up in Picayune, Mississippi. He holds B.A. and M.A. degrees from Mississippi College and the Ph.D. in English from the University of South Carolina. He has taught at the University of Texas at Arlington, the University of South Carolina, and since the day Elvis died he has been on the English faculty at the University of Southern Mississippi, as close to back home as he can get and still be at a University. He went to Mississipppi College to be a preacher and a writer, not necessarily in that order. He quickly found he had neither the wisdom not the patience nor the divine light for the one and, in Edgar Simmons's writing classes with Barry Hannah, he discovered he didn't have the talent for the other: "Barry once submitted a story which included a throwaway paragraph—that is, he did it prodigiously, with his left hand, as it were—in which he made it clear why when you eat fried catfish you drink beer instead of milk. I was beaten: if I can't write something like that, I might as well quit, and I did, for about twenty years. The paragraph was such a throwaway that Barry to this day claims he doesn't remember it, even though it devastated my own literary ambitions."

As a scholar, Polk has specialized in studies in Faulkner and Welty, and has lectured widely in this country and abroad. Among his books are *An Anthology of Mississippi Writers* (coedited with Jim Scafidel), *Faulkner's "Requiem for a Nun": A Critical Study* (1981), and *An Editorial Handbook for "The Sound and the Fury"*(1985). He is textual editor of the Faulkner Computer Concordance, and has edited, for Random House, three of Faulkner's novels: *Sanctuary: The Original Text* (1981), *The Sound and the Fury* (1984), and *Absalom, Absalom!* (1986). For the Library of America he will edit texts of all of Faulkner's fiction.

MARGARET PORTER (1949) was born and raised in rural Gloster, Mississippi, the fourteenth child in a family of fifteen. Of her childhood Porter says, "My mother had married my father when she was just thirteen. He died when I was five. Although we were not considered wealthy, we were a lot better off than many of our neighbors. After my father's death, life became tough for my mother, herself an only child with an eighth grade education. I have always admired greatly my mother's strength of character and generosity. She is by far one of the most gentle, loving people I've ever had the opportunity to meet. I've always wanted to make her proud.

"Growing up in Mississippi was a terrifying experience for me for the most part. In the quietness of that southern life lurked a sinister presence which took me years to defeat. In fact only in the last several years have I been able to appreciate the great beauty of my home state. When I was growing up there were always whisperings between my aunt, my mother, and her friends about someone having been hanged, tortured, murdered, mutilated, and other horror stories. We were constantly reminded about making sure we kept our place, and I always resented and despised this attitude. I was determined to escape this environment at the first opportunity. When I was eighteen, I moved to New York City determined to be an actress. Despite my feelings about having grown up in Mississippi, I found myself resentful of New Yorkers who always pretended they knew nothing of racism commonly associated with the South. I was amused every time a reference was made about how happy I must now be to be away from that place. To me growing up in Mississippi was like getting a doctorate in life as a black person in these United States.

"I began writing after I met my husband Quincy Troupe, who is a poet, journalist, editor and who has had a tremendous influence on my life. I've been published in *Sunbury 9, River Styx,* and *Confirmation: An Anthology of Third World Women.* I am the founder of a literary group called New Bones, which produces readings and jazz in New York City. I am especially proud that in spite of the history of Mississippi atrocities, that it is now leading the way in proclaiming a day to honor its writers and in publishing their works together, black and white."

SAMUEL PRESTRIDGE (1952) was born in Columbus, Mississippi. Because his family moved throughout the South, Prestridge grew up in a number of states—Mississippi, Texas, Alabama, Georgia. His family returned to Mississippi in 1969 and he was graduated from high school in Tupelo. Prestridge received a B.A. from Mississippi College in 1974 and an M.A. from the University of Southern Mississippi in 1977. For two years Prestridge was poet-in-the-schools for the Mississippi Arts Commission. During this time he worked toward a M.F.A. at Goddard College in Plainfield, Vermont, where he studied with Donald Hall and Thomas Lux and "though I didn't get to study with him, I hung around as much as possible" with Robert Hass. In 1980 Prestridge moved to south Louisiana where he worked in the oil fields. Since his return to Mississippi in 1981 he has supported himself as a para-legal, a credit manager, and a freelance writer. Presently he is employed by an advertising company in Jackson.

SUSAN PROSPERE (1946) was born in Oak Ridge, Tennessee, and has lived in many places, but considers Mississippi, where most of her family currently lives, as home. She earned degrees from Mississippi State University, Tulane Law School, and the University of Houston. Her honors include first place in poetry in the 1978 Mississippi Arts Festival, the P.E.N. Southwest Houston Discovery Award in 1983, the YMHA Discovery Award in 1984, and recently a fellowship from Ingram Merrill Foundation. Prospere's work has appeared in various magazines including *New Yorker, Poetry, Antaeus, Nation, Field*, and *American Scholar*. She lives in Houston, Texas, where she works in a law office.

LAVINE ROGERS (1929) was born in Alabama, but has lived in Jackson, Mississippi, since early childhood. She attended Jackson public schools and was graduated from Central High School. Under the school's diversified occupational program she worked for an insurance company during her senior year and has continued in the insurance industry since that time. Rogers returned to Jackson in 1969, where she now resides and operates her own insurance agency. She took a serious interest in writing when Berry Morgan selected her informal essay as first place winner in the Mississippi Arts Festival. Rogers writes of her latent writing interest, "Being the oldest of three children in a broken home during the depression and later, a wife and mother of four children, I was always so busy living life I never stopped long enough to understand life."

PAUL RUFFIN (1941) was born in Millport, Alabama, and grew up in Columbus, Mississippi. He received a Ph.D. in English from the Center for Writers at the University of Southern Mississippi and presently teaches creative writing, American literature, technical writing, and poetry at Sam Houston State University in Huntsville, Texas. Ruffin is director of their writing program and editor-in-chief of *Texas Review*.

Ruffin has published over 300 poems in such journals and anthologies as *Michigan Quarterly Review, Massachusetts Review, Georgia Review, New England Review, New Mexico Humanities Review, Kansas Quarterly, New Orleans Review, Mississippi Review, South Carolina Review, Southern Poetry Review, New Southern Poetry, Southwest Heritage*, and *Southern Humanities Review*. His books of poetry include *Lighting the Furnace Pilot* (1980), *Our Women* (1982), and *The Storm Cellar* (1985). In addition, he has edited three anthologies, *The Poets of Mississippi, The Texas Anthology*, and *Contemporary New England Poetry*. His poems have been anthologized in *Discoveries in Literature* (Scott-Foresman) and *Introduction to Poetry* (Little, Brown). His short stories have appeared in *Ploughshares: Southern Writers Edition, Florida Review, Southern Review, South Carolina Review,* and *Pembroke Magazine,* among others.

VELMA SANDERS (1912–1979) was born in Typlant, Mississippi. She finished high school in McAdams, Mississippi, and received training to become a registered nurse at Greenville Kings Daughters Hospital before spending three months at Johns Hopkins Hospital in prenatal care of infants. She was a member of the Mississippi Poetry Society and her poems appeared in *Progressive Farmer, New Anthenaeum, Kaleidograph, American Bard, Horizon, Beacon,* and *Writer's Almanac,* among others.

ROBERT SARGENT (1912) was born in New Orleans, Louisiana, but lived in Mississippi from the age of eight years old to the age of twenty-seven. In 1933 he received a B.S. degree from Mississippi State University. Sargent moved to Washington, D.C. as a naval officer in World War II and remained as a civil servant until his retirement. He began writing poetry in the 1950s and has been widely published in literary magazines including *Prairie Schooner, Antioch Review, California Quarterly, College English, Sou'Wester,* and many others. His books of poetry include *Now Is Always the Miraculous Time* (1977), *A Woman from Memphis* (1979), and *Aspects of a Southern Story* (1983).

Sargent notes, "I came to writing poetry relatively late, not in Mississippi, but certainly I have drawn more and more on my Mississippi background as time passed. I consider myself a Mississippian, and, although I have not lived in Mississippi for almost fifty years, I have returned for visits many times since. My poem "Aspects of a Southern Story" came straight out of my Mississippi background and I have many others that would not have been written without the growing up in Mississippi."

BRENDA E. SARTORIS (1940) was born in Kingstree, South Carolina, but grew up in Jackson, Mississippi, attending the public schools and receiving a B.A. in English from Millsaps College. She was graduated from Louisiana State University with an M.A. and Ph.D. in medieval literature. Since 1968, Sartoris has been a member of the faculty of the English department of Mississippi State University, where she teaches medieval and world literature, science fiction, and a poetry writing workshop. Her poetry has been published in *Texas Review, Southern Poetry Review, Plains Poetry Journal,* and *Cotton Boll/Atlanta Review.*

Of growing up in Mississippi, Sartoris says, "with a name like mine, I had been introduced to Faulkner by the time I was twelve, and reading and writing were such a part of my life by the time I graduated from high school that it would have been surprising had I not at some point tried creative writing. I write poetry, I think, because I love words, especially the possibilities for connotation and nuance, and poetry demands that these elements be stretched to their outermost limits."

JESSIE SCHELL (1941) was born in Greenville, Mississippi. She received a B.A. and an M.F.A. from the University of North Carolina at Greensboro. Her poetry and prose have been published in *Greensboro Reader, Greensboro Review, Vanderbilt Poetry Review, Virginia Quarterly Review, New Orleans Review, Georgia Review,* and *Atlantic.* Seven of her short stories have appeared in *McCalls,* and her stories "Alvira, Lettie, and Pip" and "Undeveloped Photographs" were selected for O. Henry Prize Awards (1975 and 1978 respectively). Her novel *Sudina*, published in 1967 under her maiden name of Jessie Rosenberg, was reprinted in 1978 by Avon under her married name. It is the story of a young southern girl's search for identity.

Schell says, "My growing-up years in the Mississippi Delta gave me a sense of the world which has served me well ever since, and will always be an endless source of delight, for which I'm grateful: a sense of the music of language, of joy in the landscape, of family and regional ties. Mississippi people taught me the lasting delight of story-telling, and in their daily lives, practiced its art instinctively. I treasure the time I spent there and find that I use that time, that place, and all the people I knew there constantly in everything that I try to write today."

JAMES SEAY (1939) was born in Panola County, Mississippi. He received a B.A. from the University of Mississippi in 1964 and an M.A. from the University of Virginia in 1966. He taught English at the Virginia Military Institute, the University of Alabama, and Vanderbilt University before joining the English department of the University of North Carolina at Chapel Hill, where he is now the director of the creative writing program. Seay is the author of two books of poems, *Let Not Your Hart* (1970) and *Water Tables* (1974), both published by Wesleyan University Press. Limited editions of his poems have been issued by Deerfield Press/Gallery Press of Ireland and Palaemon Press Limited. His poetry and critical writing have appeared in *American Review, Carolina Quarterly, Esquire, Nation, Southern Review,* and others. Among his honors are an Emily Clark Balch Prize and membership on the William Faulkner Fiction Award committee (currently PEN/Faulkner Award). In 1977 his work was selected for inclusion in an exhibit of poetry at the Centre Cultural Americain in Paris. More recently, in 1987 he was part of a delegation of Mississippi writers invited to visit the Soviet Union.

In his long poem "Said There Was Somebody Talking to Him through the Air Conditioner," Seay writes about his childhood and growing up in Mississippi. Seay agrees with his friend Vereen Bell who wrote in the forward to the reissue of his father's first novel, *Swamp Water:* "Men in the South generally relinquish their boyhood very unwillingly, and my father, I think, was no exception to that rule. Nor am I. To this day, when I am around my closest friends, all of whom are Southerners, though scattered now into various other regions, we behave together pretty much the way we would if we were twelve." Seay says, "So I guess it's still going on—my childhood in Mississippi, I mean."

EDGAR SIMMONS (1921–1979) was born and raised in Natchez, Mississippi. He received two degrees in English at Columbia University and studied at the Sorbonne in Paris. Simmons travelled widely, "touring the homes and haunts of poets in England and Ireland" and working as a columnist for the *Irish Press.* Upon returning to the States, Simmons worked as managing editor, city editor, and wire editor of the *Natchez Times* before beginning a career as a teacher and writer. Simmons has taught English and creative writing at De Pauw University, William and Mary, Southern Illinois University, Mississippi College, and the University of Texas at El Paso.

Simmons's poetry has appeared in over seventy journals, including *Chicago Review, Nation,* and *Poetry Northwest,* and in over a dozen anthologies, including *New Directions, Southern Writing in the Sixties,* and *An Anthology of Mississippi Writers.* He received the Bellamann Literary Award for Poetry in 1964 and the Texas Institute of Letters Vortman Poetry Award in 1968. In 1983, he was posthumously inducted as the first member of the Copiah-Lincoln Junior College Literary Hall of Fame.

Simmons's volumes of poetry are *Pocahontas and Other Poems* (1957), *Driving to Biloxi* (1968), and the posthumous *Oriris at the Roller Derby* (1983). Of Simmons's work, James Dickey has written, "The poetry of Edgar Simmons is wild, various, and almost unbelievably inventive and energetic. It would not surprise me if future notions of poetic form and what is possible within it are changed by what Simmons is doing."

JES SIMMONS (1954) was born in Farnborough, County Kent, England, and grew up in Natchez, Clinton, and Jackson, Mississippi, and in Carbondale, Illinois, and El Paso, Texas. Simmons received an M.A. and a Ph.D. in English from Texas A&M University, where he currently is an instructor in English.

Simmons's poems have appeared in *College English, River City Review, Mississippi Arts & Letters, New Poets Review, CEA Critic, Piddiddle,* and *Natchez Trace Literary Review.* He has had critical essays published in *Explicator* and in *Margaret Atwood: Reflections and Reality.*

Son of Mississippi poet Edgar Simmons, Simmons writes of his childhood: "Our family bathroom contained more books than towels, more pens and pencils than toothbrushes."

SUE C. SPIGNER (1939) was born in Alcorn County, Mississippi. She graduated from Tupelo (Mississippi) High School and attended Itawamba Junior College before receiving a B.S. degree from Memphis State University in 1961. Presently Spigner lives in Tupelo and works in vocational rehabilitation with the handicapped at Itawamba Junior College.

Of her experience in growing up in Mississippi, she writes, "The section of Mississippi where I grew up was the redlands area of the extreme northeastern part of the state. Hilly, heavily wooded, and more than a little secluded for many years, it produced a population with a unique view of life. Harsh realities, liberally salted with poverty, somehow did not manage to grind them under. On the contrary, they employed the most potent of weapons against adversity— laughter. I will always remember their vitality and their humor and be grateful I came from them. If they were sometimes petty, or even cruel, why, that simply reflected more sides of many-faceted human beings reacting to their circumstances.

"I grew up in Mississippi during those last years before we became industrialized and changed forever. I came from hill people who lacked great material wealth but were enormously rich in personal relationships, love, and humor. I write about them because I know them well and love them."

FRANK STANFORD (1949–1978) was born in a Mississippi orphanage and adopted shortly after birth. He spent his childhood in Greenville, Mississippi, Memphis, and in the levee camps along the rivers in Tennessee and Arkansas where his father directed levee construction and repair for the Corps of Engineers. Stanford's early connection with the black camp workers and their children imprinted deeply on his consciousness. This rich cache of experiences and images is at the core of much of his work. Already a serious and prolific poet, Stanford attended high school at a Benedictine academy in Subiaco, Arkansas. His writing frequently reflected the ritual and mystery of Catholicism and monastery life. He spent time studying at the University of Arkansas, Fayetteville, and, later travelling across the country filming and interviewing other writers. In his mid-twenties, Stanford began to earn his living as a land surveyor, walking the woods of the Ozarks. And, during all these years he was constantly, feverishly writing—poetry, fiction, translations, screenplays, essays. Stanford's strong sense of emotional isolation and psychic pain was another, darker current running through his life and surfacing in his work. This current finally overtook him at the age of twenty-nine when he ended his life in Fayetteville, Arkansas.

JOHN STONE (1936) was born in Jackson, Mississippi and grew up in Jackson and Palestine, Texas. He attended Central High School and Millsaps College in Jackson, Mississippi, and at both institutions edited the literary magazine and played in the band. Literature and music have continued to play important roles in his life. Stone received his M.D. degree from Washington University, completing postgraduate training in Internal Medicine and Cardiology at the University of Rochester and Emory University. Dr. Stone is now Professor of Medicine (Cardiology) and Community Health (Emergency Medicine) at Emory University School of Medicine, where he sees patients and teaches. Several times he has taught courses in the writing of poetry for the English department at Emory University, as well as two courses in literature and medicine taught at Oxford University, England. For five years, he has taught a course in literature and medicine for senior medical students at Emory University School of Medicine.

Stone has published three books of poetry, *The Smell of Matches* (1972), *In All This Rain* (1980), and *Renaming the Streets* (1985). The latter received the literature award from the Mississippi Institute of Arts and Letters. Stone's writing has also won several other awards, including citations from the Georgia Writers' Association. In 1987, he received the Theobald Smith Award from Albany Medical College of Union University for his "outstanding efforts to increase awareness in the public as well as the profession . . . of the essential humanness that is the ground-substance of clinical medicine." Stone has lectured and read from his work in well over half the fifty states and his poems have been widely anthologized.

For students Stone writes, "There are words growing all over Mississippi: Poems and novels and stories all along the roads, like perennials. Of course, these words are not yet in their best order: the writer has to have *something* to do. So much is being *said* all over Mississippi, though, that a person with good ears and a listening tongue simply has to ask one question, "How're you doing', and the rest of the verbal holiness follows as surely as an Amen. Well, not always, but often enough. The other thing, besides listening, that a writer who wants to be good has to do is *read:* there is simply no way to write well without first having read well. Fortunately, that's fun, too.

"I went one evening to Atlanta Stadium with some medical students to watch the Braves play. It was hot, we were on the third tier, and the Braves were losing. I began to jot down on some 3×5 cards a few disjointed lines which were to become part of the poem "Double-Header.' I'd had a recurrent dream of what it would be like to hide in a baseball stadium until the crowd had left, then come out. I had no idea, really, what such an experience would be like. But I learned when I wrote the poem. I think the whole poem is 'about' growing up. It's also 'about' what to do in the time remaining, which, it seems to me, is the only important question, whatever stage of growing up one is in."

WILLIAM SULLIVAN (1942) was born in Prentiss, Mississippi, the son of a Baptist preacher. He has lived in several different communities of Mississippi and was graduated from high school in Covington, Louisiana. After receiving a B.A. from Delta State University and an M.A. and Ph.D. from Louisiana State University, Sullivan taught at Louisiana State University and the University of Arkansas, Little Rock. Presently he is chair of the division of languages and literature at Delta State University. His poems have been published in *Cotton Boll/Atlanta Review*, *Delta Scene*, and *Journal of the Mississippi Council of Teachers of English*.

Of his Mississippi heritage, Sullivan says, "The most important influence on my poetry was my grandfather, Papa John Toney. His exotic stories of men and beasts set in the woods near his home, Magnolia, Mississippi, were long narrative poems like those being recited on hundreds of porches in rural Mississippi every day."

GLENN ROBERT SWETMAN (1936) was born in Biloxi, Mississippi, and attended the public schools there. He received a B.S. degree and an M.A. from the University of Southern Mississippi and a Ph.D. from Tulane University. Swetman has taught at the University of Southern Mississippi, Arkansas State University, McNeese University, Tulane University, Louisiana Tech University, and Nicholls State University where he now coordinates the creative writing program.

Swetman's poems, short stories, articles, and reviews have appeared in such diverse places as *Poetry Australia*, *Tributes* (Japan), *Mississippi Review*, *New Orleans Review*, *Prairie Schooner*, *Film Quarterly*, *New England Review*, *Agora* (Brazil), *Wisconsin Review*, *Accent* (England), *International Surgery Bulletin*, *Texas Quarterly*, *Greenwood Review*, *Gryphon*, and *Sea Frontiers*. He is the author of eleven books of poetry including *Concerning Carpenters and Childhood Saints*, for which he was nominated for the Pulitzer Prize, and *Poems of the Fantastic*, to be published in 1988.

Of his childhood and youth in Mississippi, Swetman writes, "Growing up there one feels a vast sense of history as well as a very stark sense of reality. There was an immense feeling of isolation as well as a grand intuition of our connection to all other places and times."

D. L. TARTT (1963) was born in Greenwood, Mississippi, and grew up in Grenada, Mississippi. Her first poems were published in *Mississippi Poetry Review* when she was thirteen. After one year at the University of Mississippi she went to Bennington College where she was graduated in 1986. Tartt worked as an editorial assistant at *Atlantic Monthly* in 1985. Currently she lives in Manhattan and is a student at the Parsons School of Design.

JULIUS E. THOMPSON (1946) was born in Vicksburg, Mississippi, and graduated from high school in Natchez, Mississippi. He received a B.S. degree from Alcorn State University and an M.A. and Ph.D. from Princeton University. His books include *Hopes Tied Up in Promise* (1970), *Blues Said: Walk On* (1977), and *Hiram R. Revels, 1827–1901: A Biography*. He is presently an assistant professor in the department of African and Afro-American Studies at State University of New York at Albany. His essays and poetry have appeared in *National Poetry Press*, *Negro Digest*, *Obsidian*, *Callaloo*, *Freedomways*, *Hoo Doo*, and *Jackson Advocate*, among others. His forthcoming books include *The Black Press in Mississipi, 1865–1985* and *The Anthology of Black Mississippi Poets*.

Thompson writes about his Mississippi experience, "I was born right after World War II. My first years were spent in Vicksburg and later my family ved to Detroit, Michigan, where I attended elementary school. In the late

1950s my mother, baby sister and I came back to Mississippi, and settled in Natchez. My life has always been in a south to north to south movement. Both regions have had an influence on my work as a poet, but Mississippi and the South stand out as the greater of the two. I often wonder if the themes of poverty and suffering (and the search for freedom) are the main contributions that Mississippi has made on my work. Probably. Yet, the great strength and sensitivity of many Blacks in the state have also influenced my directions as an interpreter of the human experience. I have also found encouragement and hope in the struggles of the past (against slavery, segregation, and fascism), the music of the blues, and the remembered things (written and unwritten) by the men, women, and children of long ago and today, who, in the worst of times, survived in spite of poverty and suffering—and went on to make a lasting contribution in the struggle for human justice and freedom.

HENRY TIM (CHAMBERS) (1903) was born in Mt. Park, Oklahoma territory, and moved to Mississippi in 1941. He attended the Oklahoma Institute of Technology where his English teacher was Mississippian Muna Lee, and later Henry Kendall College, now Tulsa University. He was first published in a local newspaper when he was four years old. In the late 1920s and early 1930s he contributed to *Atlantic Monthly* and had poems in *Harpers, New York Times,* and *Saturday Review of Literature.* In 1935 Henry Tim published his first book, *Young Man's Country,* and in 1981 he coauthored *Cotton Candy & Turnip Greens* with Jim Bateman of Hazelhurst, Mississippi. In 1982 Henry Tim and Bateman published *One!!* Tim lives with his family on 174 acres of wooded land ten miles from Jackson, Mississippi. Recently he has had poems published in *Green River, Kentucky Poetry, Mississippi Review* and *Negative Capability.*

GLENNRAY TUTOR (1950) was born in Kennett, Missouri, where his parents, both Mississippi natives, moved after buying a grocery store. From 1950 to 1973 Tutor's family shuttled from Mississippi to Missouri. Tutor says of this period, "The time I've spent in Mississippi equals about half of my life during those wonderful years of highways and woods and little towns and fields." In 1973 he transferred from Three Rivers College in Missouri to the University of Mississippi, graduating in 1974 with a B.A. In 1976 he completed an M.F.A. in painting with a minor in printmaking.

Although primarily a visual artist, Tutor has published stories and poems in a wide variety of publications including *Western Humanities Review, New Orleans Review, Voices International,* and *Cobblestone.*

A number of visual works by Tutor have been published in magazines and books, including the twelve charcoal illustrations in *Blooded on Arachne,* a collection of short stories by Michael Bishop. *Who Made Stevie Cry?,* also by Bishop, contains a full, wrap-a-round jacket painting by Tutor. Over one hundred of his drawings are in *Tales of the Quintana Roo* by James Tiptree Jr.

Regarding the breadth of his creative experience, Tutor says, "People should always be growing up until the moment they die. Mississippi has been a good and fertile place for me. Life supplies a thousand motivations every minute; the problem, if any, comes from trying to choose which motivation out of all of them to follow. The key to moving through this dilemma is letting feeling, above all else, lead you."

DOROTHY TWISS (1928) was born in Texarkana, Texas, and has lived in Mississippi for over thirty years. She holds a B.A. and an M.A. degree from Mississippi College and received a Ph.D. from the University of Southern Mississippi where she studied in the Center for Writers. Presently she is a professor of creative writing at Louisiana Tech University, but maintains her home in Morton, Mississippi. Twiss has published in *Mississippi Review, Poem, Poet, Cimarron Review,* among others.

Twiss says, ‟I feel fortunate to have lived and studied in Mississippi. Something in the mysterious atmosphere of climate, landscape, and social tension of Mississippi results in artistic production.”

OVID VICKERS (1930) was born in Gadsden, Alabama. He received a B.A., an M.A., and an ED.S. degree from George Peabody College. After serving in the military during the Korean conflict, he began teaching English at East Central Junior College in Decatur, Mississippi, where he is now chair of the division of humanities and fine arts. His short stories, articles, and poems have appeared in *Texas Review, Delta Scene, Southern Living, Mississippi, Teaching English in the Two-Year College,* and *Mississippi Folklore Journal.* In 1980 Vickers received an award of merit from the Mississippi Historical Society for his writing of over forty articles on the folklore of Mississippi.

MARGARET WALKER (1915) was born in Birmingham, Alabama, the daughter of a music teacher and a minister of the Methodist Church; she grew up in Alabama, Louisiana, and Mississippi. Walker received a B.A. from Northwestern University in 1935 and an M.A. and a Ph.D. from the University of Iowa. In 1942, after working for the WPA on its Federal Writers Project, Walker began teaching at West Virginia State College in the English department. In the same year *For My People,* her first book, was published as a volume in the Yale Series of Younger Poets. In 1949 Walker joined the faculty at Jackson State University as a professor of English and later became director of the Institute for the Study of History, Life, and Culture of Black People. Her novel *Jubilee,* published in 1966, won a Houghton Mifflin Literary Fellowship Award and became an international best seller. Her other books include *Prophets for a New Day* (1970), *How I Wrote Jubilee* (1972), *October Journey* (1973), *A Poetic Equation: Conversations Between Nikki Giovanni and Margaret Walker* (1974), and *The Daemonic Genius of Richard Wright* (1987).

Her novel *Jubilee* is an inspiring story for all people struggling for freedom and equality. In it Walker incorporated into the fictionalized life of her maternal great-grandmother actual historical events from slavery to Reconstruction.

Retired from teaching at Jackson State University, Walker is completing a collection of poems titled *This Is My Century: Black Synthesis of Time.* Her essays and public lectures are being collected by Maryemma Graham and will be published under the title *On Being Female, Black, and Free. Fields Watered with Blood,* a critical collection of essays on her writing, is currently being edited by Myriam Díaz-Diocaretz. The interviews of Margaret Walker are being edited and collected for publication by Dorothy Abbott.

JERRY W. WARD, JR. (1943) was born in Washington, D.C. When he was six his family moved to Mississippi. He received a B.S. from Tougaloo College (1964), an M.S. from the Illinois Institute of Technology (1966), and a Ph.D. from the University of Virginia (1978). Ward's poetry and essays have appeared in the *Southern Quarterly, Obsidian,* and *Mississippi Folklore Register,* among other professional journals, magazines, and newspapers. Former chair of the English department at Tougaloo College, Ward was on leave in 1985 to work in the Division of Fellowships and Seminars at the National Endowment for the

Humanities. He is currently researching the works of Lance Jeffers, Sterling D. Plumpp, and Ishmael Reed.

Ward grew up during the most turbulent period of twentieth century Mississippi history. Of that period, he says, "Growing up Black and male in Mississippi in the fifties and sixties was a less-than-pleasant experience, but the trauma of it all, including the psychic scars, armed me with peculiar strengths; Vietnam finished the oakening process. The thirty some years I've called Mississippi home have been inspiration and substance for my poetry. For young Mississippi writers I paraphrase the words of Sir Philip Sidney: Look into your hearts and histories and write. Mississippi is a culture of profoundest joys and pains. Its writers have a moral obligation to face naked truths squarely and articulate them for the future."

NAGUEYALTI WARREN (1947) was born in Atlanta, Georgia. She has received a B.A. from Fisk University, M.A. degrees from Boston University and Simmons College, and a Ph.D. from the University of Mississippi. Warren is currently chair of the English department at Fisk University. Her poetry has been anthologized in *Mississippi Earthworks, The American Poetry Anthology* (1982), and *Riders of the Rainbow* (1986). In 1985 Warren received the "golden poet award" sponsored by the World Poetry Association. She is presently at work on a collection of her poems entitled "Southern Talking Book."

Warren says, "Mississippi represents a land of startling contrasts for me—at once breath-takingly beautiful and grotesque. Mississippi's rivers, its lush green moss laden trees, its burning bright-red summer sun inspired the most productive period in my writing career. Mississippi's history of racial bigotry and hatred and its efforts to eradicate past injustices make for a place of colorful and poignant images, a few of which I have tried to capture—distill in what I call my Mississippi poems. When I lived in Jackson the Mississippi Writers and Actors Workshop was most helpful in providing the support I needed in order to write. Aside from their support and the land I was given additional inspiration from my son who came to life in Mississippi."

NAYO-BARBARA WATKINS (1940) was born in Atlanta, Georgia. She attended the University of Pittsburgh, Jackson State University, and the University of Mississippi. Watkins is past director of the Mississippi Cultural Arts Coalition and a founder of the Jackson Writers/Actors Workshop. Her poetry has been anthologized in *New Black Voices* (1970), *Black Culture* (1972), *Mississippi Earthworks* (1982), and will appear in *Black Southern Voices*, edited by John O. Killens. In addition to writing poetry Watkins co-wrote, with John O'Neal, the play "You Can't Judge a Book by Looking at its Cover: Sayings and Writings from the Life and Times of Junebug Jabbo Jones." The play premiered and ran for six weeks at Wisdom Bridge Theatre in Chicago and is included in touring presentations of Junebug Production.

Watkins toured extensively with BlackArtSouth, the writing workshop of Free Southern Theatre of New Orleans. From 1970 to 1987 she read and performed at numerous community, academic, and social events in Mississippi. In July of 1987 Watkins moved to Minneapolis, Minnesota, to become director of At the Foot of the Mountain theatre.

EUDORA WELTY (1909) was born in Jackson, Mississippi. Educated in Jackson's public schools, she began writing and drawing very early, publishing poems and sketches in *St. Nicholas* magazine as early as 1920. After attending Mississippi

State College for Women (now Mississippi University for Women) for two years, she transferred to the University of Wisconsin, graduating with a B.A. in 1929. In 1930 she attended Columbia University School of Business, but returned to Mississippi in 1931 when her father died. In Jackson, she worked in a variety of jobs before going to work for the WPA, traveling across the state taking photographs and writing copy for several small newspapers.

Two of her short stories "Death of a Traveling Salesman" and "Magic" were published in *Manuscript* magazine in 1936. Her first book, *A Curtain of Green*, appeared in 1941, and was a critical success. Her second volume, *The Robber Bridegroom*, appeared in 1942, and firmly established her reputation as a writer. Since the 1943 publication of *The Wide Net and Other Stories*, Welty has published *Delta Wedding* (1946), *The Golden Apples* (1949), *The Ponder Heart* (1954), *The Bride of the Innisfallen and Other Stories* (1955), *The Shoe Bird* (1964), *Losing Battles* (1970), *One Time, One Place* (1971), *The Optimist's Daughter* (1972), *The Eye of the Story* (1977), *The Collected Stories of Eudora Welty* (1980), and *One Writer's Beginnings* (1984) among others.

Welty has received great international attention and praise. Her many honors include the Pulitzer Prize, the American Book Award for fiction, the Gold Medal for the Novel by the National Institute of Arts and Letters, and the Howells Medal for Fiction by the American Academy of Arts and Letters. *One Writer's Beginnings*, a collection of 1983 lectures given at Harvard University, put her on the best-seller list. In 1984 the University Press of Mississippi published *Conversations with Eudora Welty*, interviews collected by Peggy Whitman Prenshaw.

In "Place in Fiction," she writes, "I think the sense of place is as essential to good and honest writing as a logical mind; surely they are somewhere related. It is by knowing where you stand that you grow able to judge where you are. Place absorbs our earliest notice and attention, it bestows on us our original awareness; and our critical powers spring up from the study of it and the growth of experience inside it. It perseveres in bringing us back to earth when we fly too high. It never really stops informing us, for it is forever astir, alive, changing, reflecting, like the mind of man itself. One place comprehended can make us understand other places better."

Novelist Reynolds Price says of Welty, "In all of American fiction, she stands for me with her only peers—Melville, James, Hemingway, and Faulkner—and among them, she is in some crucial respects the deepest, the most spacious, the most life-giving."

JOHN MILTON WESLEY (1948) was born in Ruleville, Mississippi. After graduating from Tougaloo College in 1970, he went to Yale University and Columbia University's graduate school of journalism. Before moving to Columbia, Maryland, Wesley worked as a news reporter for WLBT-TV. His poems have appeared in *Essence, Little Patuxent Review, Metropolitian, Close-Up,* and *Jackson Advocate.* Wesley was a consultant for the Baltimore television special "Negritude Poets from the Chesapeake Bay" and he is currently writing "The Soybean Field," a novel about his growing up in Mississippi. In addition to writing fiction and poetry, Wesley is an advertising/media consultant and lectures on "Higher Creativity in Business and at Play." In 1987 he appeared in the movie *The Tin Men.*

JAMES WHITEHEAD (1936) was born in St. Louis, Missouri, but grew up in Jackson, Mississippi. He earned a B.A. and an M.A. from Vanderbilt University and an M.F.A. in creative writing from the University of Iowa in 1965. He has taught at Millsaps College, at the University of Iowa, and is currently teaching in the creative writing program at the University of Arkansas. Whitehead was awarded the Robert Frost Fellowship of the Bread Loaf Writers' Conference in 1967 and a Guggenheim Fellowship in fiction in 1972. His poems have appeared in many reviews and journals including *Southern Review, Mississippi Review, New Orleans Review, Poetry Now, Vanderbilt Poetry Review,* and *Greensboro Review.*

Domains, his first book of poems, was published in 1966. *Joiner* (1971), his first novel, was given critical acclaim. George Garrett wrote, "*Joiner* would be a fine book in any season. In ours it is more than that. James Whitehead has undertaken and achieved a rare and wonderful thing—an original work of art." His second book of poems, *Local Men,* was published in 1979 and a chapbook, *Actual Size,* appeared in 1985 by Trilobite Press. In 1987 the University of Illinois Press published *Local Men and Domains.*

BENJAMIN WILLIAMS (1947) was born in Gulfport, Mississippi, where he now resides. He attended Alcorn A & M College and majored in voice. It was in college that his poems were first published. Williams served a tour of duty with the Marine Corps and after his discharge spent some time on the west coast before returning to Mississippi. His writing has appeared over the past twenty years in *Obsidian, Negro History Bulletin, Kitabu Cha Jua, Afro American Quarterly, Phylon, Callaloo,* and *Black Scholar.*

JOHN A. WILLIAMS (1925) was born in Hinds County near Jackson, Mississippi, but he grew up in Syracuse, New York, where his parents had met and married. However, following an old custom, they returned "down home" for the birth of their first child. When Williams was about one year old, his parents returned to Syracuse.

Before he finished high school, Williams joined the United States Navy (1943), serving as a hospital corpsman until his discharge in 1946. Returning to Syracuse, he completed high school, took a B.A. degree at Syracuse University, and did some graduate work. He has worked as European correspondent for *Ebony* and *Jet* magazines (1958-59) and as African correspondent for *Newsweek* (1964-65).

Williams books include *The Angry Ones* (1960), *Night Song* (1961), *Sissie* (1963), *Journey Out of Anger* (1965), *This Is My Country Too* (1965), *The Man Who Cried I Am* (1967), *Captain Blackman* (1972), *Flashbacks: A Twenty-Year Diary of Article Writing* (1973), *!Click Song* (1982), *The Berhama Account* (1985), and *Jacob's Ladder* (1987). *!Click Song* was reissued by Thunder's Mouth Press in 1987.

In *Lives of Mississippi Authors 1817-1967,* Professor Jerry W. Ward, Jr. writes: "The fact that Williams was born in the 1920s, when great numbers of black migrated northward in search of economic, social, and political advantages, has had a lasting impact on his work, for he is keenly aware of what it means to be the product of transplanted roots. Mississippi can claim him as one of her native sons by virtue of birth, but the enduring attitudes that give shape and substance to his writing are those formed in a northern milieu.

Williams has co-produced, written, and narrated several programs for National Educational Television. He received a grant from the National Endowment for the Arts for *!Click Song* and currently is a professor of English and journalism at Rutgers University. Additionally Williams is past chair of the board of directors for the Coordinating Council of Literary Magazine.

OTIS WILLIAMS (1939) was born in Grenada, Mississippi. In the seventh grade Williams started writing blues songs which later evolved into writing poetry. At the age of thirteen he started following local blues bands and eventually he sang with them around Grenada and into the Delta. He chopped cotton in summers and later shined shoes at the barber shop where his uncles Willie, Blain, and Tol worked. He credits a teacher Mrs. Ernestine Boclair and his aunt Arnada Purnell, also a teacher, with influencing his love for literature.

Williams attended Jackson State University before doing a five year tour in the United States Air Force. He received a B.A. degree from Morgan State College and an M.A. from the University of Maryland at College Park. Williams's publications include three volumes of poetry, *The Natural Truth, Hootchie Kootchie Man,* and *The Blues Is Darker Than Blue,* and three children's books, *Skeeter, Waldo the Monkey,* and *Bubba and Bobby (How Two Zebras Got Their Stripes).* Several of his songs have been recorded—the title song to the album "Sweet Bitter Blues" and "Hoo Doo Woman" by "Bowling Green" John Cephas & Phil Wiggins and the classic "Azanian Freedom Song" performed and recorded by Sweet Honey in the Rock. Williams appeared on the jazz album "Natchel Natchel" by Andy Goodrich.

Williams currently resides in Baltimore, Maryland where he is director of the Nyumburu Cultural Center at the University of Maryland's College Park Campus. In addition he teaches blues and jazz courses in the Afro-American studies program.

TENNESSEE WILLIAMS (1911-1983) was born in Columbus, Mississippi. After living his early years in various Mississippi towns, his family moved to St. Louis. This environment, and its effect on the young Williams, is described in his play *The Glass Menagerie* and his short story "Portrait of a Girl in Glass." Williams attended the University of Missouri from 1929 to 1931, when he was withdrawn by his father because of his failure to pass ROTC. He then worked for three years (1931-34) at the International Shoe Company in St. Louis and, as a way of escaping tedium, began to write more and more. Quitting his job, he attended Washington University, before receiving a B.A. degree from the University of Iowa in 1938.

Williams revised an earlier script called "The Gentleman Caller" into *The Glass Menagerie.* It opened in Chicago on December 26, 1944 and was his first professional success. In 1945 it moved to Broadway. With this impressive start, Williams began his career as one of the world's most popular playwrights. He won two Pulitzer Prizes, one for *A Streetcar Named Desire* and another for *Cat on a Hot Tin Roof,* and four New York Drama Circle Critics Awards for these two plays, as well as for *The Glass Menagerie* and *The Night of the Iguana.*

After changing his name to "Tennessee," the first work to bear his new name was "The Field of Blue Children, printed in *Story* in September 1939. About his name change Williams writes: "I was christened Thomas Lanier Williams. It is a nice enough name, perhaps a little too nice. It sounds like it might belong to the son of a writer who turns out sonnet sequences to Spring. As a matter of fact, my first literary award was $25.00 from a Woman's Club for doing exactly that, three sonnets dedicated to Spring. I hasten to add that I was still pretty young. Under that name I published a good deal of lyric poetry which was a bad imitation of Edna Millay. When I grew up I realized this poetry wasn't much good and I felt the name had been compromised so I changed it to Tennessee Williams, the justification being mainly that the Williamses had fought the Indians for Tennessee and I had already discovered that the life of a young writer was going to be something similar to the defense of a stockade against a band of savages."

AUSTIN WILSON (1943) was born in Waycross, Georgia. He received an A.B. from Valdosta State College, an M.A. from the University of Georgia, and a Ph.D. from the University of South Carolina. Since 1976 Wilson has taught in the English department at Millsaps College. He has published in *Mississippi Review* and *Apalachee Quarterly* and his poems have appeared in *Wind, Poem, Roanoke Review,* and *Hiram Poetry Review.*

RICHARD WRIGHT (1908-1960) was born near Natchez, Mississippi, the son of a country schoolteacher mother and an illiterate sharecropper father. Because of his mother's illness and his father's eventual abandonment, his childhood was one of poverty, frequent moves from relative to relative, and interrupted schooling. His story "The Voodoo of Hell's Half Acre" was, however, published in Jackson, Mississippi, in the local black newspaper when Wright was fifteen. In 1925 he graduated from the ninth grade at Smith-Robertson Public School in Jackson at the head of his class.

Wright was a voracious reader. While working in Memphis, Wright discovered the work of H. L. Mencken and began to read some of the works mentioned in Mencken's *Prefaces,* along with a wide variety of other works. In 1927 he moved to Chicago, where he would remain for ten years. In 1932 Wright joined the American Communist Party, believing that he had finally found a group interested in the plight of the American black. He had begun writing poetry and short stories earlier, and now, on behalf of the Party, his work began to appear in such publications as *New Masses, Left Front,* and *Partisan Review.*

In 1937 Wright moved to New York, where he was Harlem editor of the *Daily Worker.* His first book, *Uncle Tom's Children,* was published in 1938. This was followed by his two most famous works. *Native Son,* published in 1940, is the tragic tale of a Mississippi-born black in Chicago. Its success was phenomenal, and assured Wright a place in American literature. In 1945 *Black Boy,* an autobiographical work based on his traumatic childhood in Mississippi, was released.

By 1944 Wright had left the Communist Party and in 1946, unreconciled to the continuing racism in the United States, he and his family moved to Paris, France. There he was to remain until his death. After moving to France he was active in establishing such organizations as the Society of African Culture and worked with such African leaders as Leopold Senghor, later president of Senegal, and Aime Cesaire from Martinique. Among his nonfiction works of this time are *Black Power* (1954) and *Pagan Spain* (1957).

Wright's fiction includes *The Outsider* (1953) and *Savage Holiday* (1954). In addition, three works were published posthumously—*Eight Men* (1961), *Lawd Today* (1963), and *American Hunger* (1977).

GAYLE GRAHAM YATES (1940) was born in Wayne County, Mississippi. She teaches American studies at the University of Minnesota and chaired its women's studies program in its early years from 1976 to 1981. Yates is the author of *What Women Want: The Ideas of the Movement* (1975) and editor of *Harriet Mar-*

tineau on Women (1985). She is at work on a book that blends memoir and cultural history, tentatively titled, "Mississippi's Child, A Personal History."

AL YOUNG (1939) was born in Ocean Springs, Mississippi, and grew up in the South, the Midwest, and on the West Coast. Educated at the University of Michigan and the University of California at Berkeley as a Spanish teacher, he continues his life-long study of human speech and language. Along the way, he has been a professional musician, disk jockey, medical photographer, railroad man, warehouseman, laboratory aide, clerk-typist, job interviewer, janitor, editor, and screenwriter. Moreover, he has taught writing and literature at such institutions as Stanford, Foothill Community College, Colorado College, the University of Washington, and the University of California at both Santa Cruz and Berkeley.

Who Is Angelina? (1975), *Sitting Pretty* (1976), *Ask Me Now* (1980), and *Seduction by Light* (1988) are among his most recent novels. His books of poetry—*Dancing* (1969), *The Song Turning Back Into Itself* (1971), *Geography of the Near Past* (1976), *The Blues Don't Change* (1982), and his collected poems, *Heaven* (1988) have met with critical success. Film assignments have included scripts for Dick Gregory, Sidney Poitier, Bill Crosby, and Richard Pryor. With poet-novelist Ishmael Reed, Young edits *Quilt*, an international journal devoted to multicultural writing. His work has been translated into Norwegian, Swedish, Italian, Japanese, Spanish, Polish, Russian, French, and Chinese.

Young is the recipient of the Joseph Henry Jackson Award, National Arts Council Awards for editing and poetry, a Wallace Stegner Fellowship, a National Endowment for the Arts Fellowship, the Pushcart Prize, a Fulbright Fellowship, the Before Columbus Foundation American Book Award, and a Guggenheim Fellowship.

Bodies & Soul (1981), *Kinds of Blue* (1984), and *Things Ain't What They Used to Be* (1987) are all books of musical memoirs. The artists that inspired these essays include James Brown, Ravel, Billie Holiday, Thelonious Monk, Glenn Miller, Janis Joplin, Miles Davis, Bessie Smith, Charlie Parker, The Doors, Stevie Wonder, Rossini, Duke Ellington, John Coltrane, Sarah Vaughan, and many more.

Young writes, "I can still remember as clearly as if it were today the very first music that touched me: early songs that I sang, the first notes I ever sounded on a piano, spacious cricket concertos on summer nights, the tinkle of spoons against cups and water glasses, birdcalls, blues, spirituals, actual hollers in Mississippi fields where I picked my early share of cotton and corn and cut a little cane; my grandmother's voice and her constant humming as she went about her everyday tasks, the melodious rise and fall in the voices of Afro-Christian preachers in little tumble-down country churches, the rapid rat-a-tat of peckerwood percussion, country laments, heavy-duty juke joint fried fish and barbecue funk, jazz in all its endless guises and disguises, the swishing of leaves, the sounds of cities, the hush of streams and the roar of the ocean."

STARK YOUNG (1881-1963) was born in Como, Mississippi, and moved to Oxford, Mississippi, in 1895. He attended the University of Mississippi from which he received a B.A. with honors in 1901. In 1902 he earned an M.A. in English from Columbia University. Returning to Mississippi, he taught at Water Valley, then at the University of Mississippi. From 1907 to 1915, he taught at the University of Texas and from 1915 to 1921 at Amherst College, Amherst,

Massachusetts. In 1921 Young resigned from academic life and began writing and reviewing on a full-time basis in New York. He became drama critic for the *New Republic* and an editor of *Theatre Arts Magazine*.

In the next forty years, Young distinguished himself as a translator (his translations of Chekhov are still the most widely used), critic, poet, novelist, essayist, editor, painter, and playwright. He wrote thirty plays, many of which he directed. He is best remembered for his novel, *So Red the Rose* (1934), a story of the Civil War that preceeded *Gone with the Wind*, but never attained its popularity or commercial success. He died in New York on January 6, 1963.

AHMOS ZU-BOLTON II (1935) was born in Poplarville, Mississippi, the eldest of thirteen children. He grew up in the rural community of DeRidder, Louisiana, near the Texas border where he left high school in 1953 to help support his family. "I cut sugarcane and did farm work," he says, "and I bummed around a little bit, too." He traveled through the South from 1954 to 1957 as shortstop for the Shreveport Twins of the American Negro Baseball League. "I guess we were professional ballplayers," he says. "We got $25 a game and all expenses paid for the season. It supported me during the summer and, since we all knew about Jackie Robinson, it was a possible option of being so-called 'discovered' and getting into the major leagues. . .sort of how Columbus 'discovered' people who were already here."

In *Dictionary of Literary Biographies* poet Lorenzo Thomas writes: "Zu-Bolton returned to George Washington Carver High School in DeRidder in 1962 and when he graduated was among seventeen black students chosen to integrate Louisiana State University in 1965. He was sponsored by scholarships from the NAACP and the American Legion. After Louisiana State University, Zu-Bolton was drafted into the Army and served overseas as a medic in Germany and Vietnam. After his discharge from the Army, he attended Los Angeles City College and graduated with a bachelor's degree in English literature and journalism from California State Polytechnic University in 1971. He was one of many talented and socially committed black Vietnam veterans who sought to employ their skills and education for the beterment of their communities."

In 1972 Zu-Bolton began publishing *HooDoo* magazine. Later Zu-Bolton began producing a series of HooDoo festivals around the South featuring writers and musicians performing their works at colleges, churches, restaurants, and popular meeting places. The performances were taped for the radio broadcast. Zu-Bolton also expanded by directing a regional book distribution company and recently he opened a bookstore in New Orleans. He also co-edited, with Alan Austin and Etheridge Knight, *Blackbox*, a poetry magazine issued on tape-recorded cassettes. In addition to editing numerous anthologies, Zu-Bolton has published a book of his own poetry, *A Niggered Amen* (1975).